"What Works for Me"

16 CEOs Talk About Their Careers and Commitments

"What Works for Me"

16 CEOs Talk About Their Careers and Commitments

by

Thomas R. Horton
CEO, American Management Association

Random House Business Division / *NEW YORK*

Grateful acknowledgment is made to the American Management Association for permission to reprint the list of "competency descriptors" from the generic competency model of The Institute for Management Competency of the American Management Association.

First Edition

98765432

Library of Congress Cataloging-in-Publication Data
Horton, Thomas R.
  "What works for me."

  Bibliography: p.
  Includes index.
  1. Executives—United States—Interviews.
2. Directors of corporations—United States—
Interviews. I. Title.
HD38.35.U6H67   1986   658.4'09   86–6677
ISBN 0–394–55072–2

Manufactured in the United States of America

Book design by M.R.P. Design

Composition by Delphian Typographers, Inc.

Acknowledgments

I am deeply indebted to the CEOs interviewed for this book, all of whom gave generously of their time and candid thoughts in describing what works for them.

For encouraging me to write this book I am indebted to John P. R. Budlong, Patricia Haskell, and John Roach.

In addition, Patricia Haskell and her colleagues, Helen Louie-Sumser and Linda Goldfarb, provided superb editorial and production guidance, as did John Roach, who accompanied me on many of the interviews. Editorial assistance was provided by Peter C. Reid and Susan L. Polos. Technical guidance and assistance was provided by Stacy Zeifman, who patiently analyzed the manuscripts, identifying illustrations of management competencies, and Harry Evarts, who reviewed the research sections of this book.

To my assistant, Carol Becker, and to Carolyn Rapier fell the burden of converting the raw interview tapes into transcripts, the edited transcripts into chapters, and my writing into prose.

Finally I would like to express my profound gratitude to Marilou Horton, who both served as an effective sounding board and accommodated herself for many months to a houseful of tapes, papers, clippings, and notes.

To Marilou

Table of Contents

"What Works for Me"

16 CEOs Talk About Their Careers and Commitments

Leaders in Action

*W*hat works for chief executives? And what goes into the making of a successful CEO?

The job description of a chief executive officer is simplicity itself: to hold full responsibility for a company's success and reputation and to be accountable for overall results to its board of directors and shareholders. This simplicity gives wide latitude to how the task is performed, so chief executives do their jobs in an astonishing variety of ways. Through trial and error, over the course of a CEO's career, some approaches to management and to leadership are found to work well, others not to work at all. In this book 16 chief executives describe in their own words what has worked for them.

What makes a *"good* CEO?" Although someone has suggested that "first, you have to be good; and, second, you have to be CEO," more useful answers to this question have long been sought.

In one respect, becoming a CEO is like becoming a parent. There is no ultimate guidebook nor any training program quite adequate to prepare the man or woman taking on such responsibility, nothing to provide the final answers. CEOs must therefore find their own ways to fulfill the manifold responsibilities and multiple roles that are thrust upon them. Each person's approach becomes distinctive.

How good are today's business leaders? A specialist in management succession estimates that, based on their performance, one-third of current incumbent chief executives would not be selected again, while two-thirds would be considered effective.[1]

Who are these effective chief executives? Are they special people who reach the pinnacle to which they have aspired (or are reluctantly propelled) because of their unique leadership qualities? Or do they go through some magical metamorphosis once they are at the top? In truth, the CEO is just another manager who, like others, does not have all the answers. Still, he or she represents a rarity, a person selected from thousands of others—and in some cases hundreds of thousands—to take on the ultimate leadership responsibility.

Because of their position of power and prestige at the top of the organizational pyramid, chief executives hold a special fascination for observers of organizational behavior. First, it is clear from studies of working habits of top executives that they do not spend their time in an ivory tower serenely contemplating the future course of their enterprise. In reality, the chief's job is more like that of a juggler. The CEO must cope with constant interruptions, somehow finding time for the essential tasks of planning and direction-setting within the interstices of long, densely packed work days.[2] One unidentified wit described management as a series of interruptions interrupted by interruptions.

The CEO's job is further complicated by the increasing pressures of new constituencies, severe global competition, threat of hostile takeovers, changed values in the workplace, technological revolutions, emergence of third-world nations, unpredictable shifts in economic conditions, unpredictable human resources problems (e.g., AIDS and new kinds of controlled-substance abuse), terrorism—a list that could be indefinitely extended.

As the demands of the job have increased, so have the rewards. They have reached unprecedented levels of compensation and perquisites—limousines, club memberships, fleets of jet planes. Then there are the prospects of golden para-chutes should bail-out time arrive. Comedian Joe E. Lewis told of a man who had "everything": incredible riches, beautiful homes, wonderful cars, a yacht, a plane, gorgeous women—*everything*. "But do you think he's happy?" Lewis asked. "You're goddamned right he is!"

Many CEOs also seem to have "everything." But there is one thing they do not have: time. Some are workaholics who would devote the same excessive hours to lesser jobs, and in-deed have done so on their way up. (An associate who is a self-described workaholic suggests the need for a "Workaholics Anonymous" through which one member would call another at eight o'clock each night to suggest having a drink.) But even those chiefs who are not workaholics by nature are constantly pressed for time by the unrelenting demands of their jobs. Many of their perquisites help save scarce time and serve to lubricate the operating-on-all-cylinders engine that is the CEO.

But does all this work make them happy? Based on observa-tions of hundreds of chief executives, my answer would be yes, very happy indeed. In fact, the work makes them happier than the perqs.

But what makes them "leaders?" And just what constitutes "good" leadership? Though the ultimate answer to this ques-tion continues to elude us, the quest continues.

In 1940, Chester Barnard wrote, "Leadership has been the subject of an extraordinary amount of dogmatically stated nonsense."[3] Were he alive today, Barnard would still be justi-fied in that observation, though he would be pleased at least with the work of a few more recent scholars.

However, despite his reluctance to add to the dogma, Bar-nard did identify five "active qualities" of leaders, listing them in what he considered their order of importance: vitality and endurance, decisiveness, persuasiveness, responsibility (an emotional condition that "gives an individual a sense of acute dissatisfaction" when he does not take it), and, finally, intel-lectual capacity.[4]

Barnard intentionally relegated intelligence to last place. He emphasized that "intellectual competency is *not* a substi-tute, at least in an important degree, for the other essential qualities of leadership."[5] A familiar figure is the supremely brilliant person who is nonetheless ineffective—a "blithering genius," so to speak.

The sheer energy—physical, intellectual, and psychic—required to meet the demands of a CEO's job seem to justify Barnard's decision to place vitality and endurance at the top of his list.

In the near half-century since Barnard compiled his list, the CEO's job has become infinitely more complex and demanding. At the same time, we have made progress in defining the characteristics required for superior management and in understanding the important effects of organizational settings. Here are the results of some important studies:

To discover the managerial qualities required for what he called "the new CEO," George A. Steiner interviewed 25 chief executives, among others, and identified 14 characteristics:

- A thorough knowledge of the business.
- Administrative ability.
- Leadership capability.
- Sensitivity to external forces.
- Ability to balance interests of constituents.
- Willingness to take responsibility for effective advocacy.
- Ability to communicate effectively.
- Familiarity with public affairs.
- Strategic imagination.
- A global perspective.
- A broad-gauged intellect.
- High moral standards.
- Profit consciousness.
- Ability to maintain poise under a bewildering variety of conditions.[6]

After an in-depth study of six leading chief executive officers, Harry Levinson and Stuart Rosenthal defined leadership this way: "The leader: (1) is able to take charge; (2) has a strong self-image and a powerful ego ideal; (3) interacts with customers, employees, and other constituencies supportively; (4) provides permission to take risks; (5) is a thinker as well as a doer."[7]

Warren Bennis and Burt Nanus concluded that leaders share four areas of competency: the management of attention (each having a vision for the future); the management of meaning (each presenting his or her visions with great clarity); the management of trust (by demonstrating their reliability and tireless persistence); and the management of self (viewing themselves positively and inspiring positive feelings in others).[8]

In his five-year study of leadership, John W. Gardner says that the examination of the *tasks* performed by leaders helps distinguish among the many kinds of leaders. "Leaders," he says, "differ strikingly in how well they perform the various functions." Gardner deals with nine tasks: envisioning goals, affirming values, motivating, managing, achieving a workable level of unity, explaining, serving as a symbol, representing the group externally, and renewing. "This is not intended as a definitive list. These seem to me to be the most significant functions . . . ."[9]

In his Pulitzer Prize book *Leadership,* James MacGregor Burns identified two basic types of leaders: *transactional* and *transforming.* He described the transactional leader as behaving essentially in an "exchange" mode; for example, jobs are exchanged for votes, or reward is exchanged for effort. The *transforming* leader, in contrast, "recognizes and exploits an existing need or demand of a potential follower . . . (and) beyond that . . . looks for potential motives in followers, seeks to satisfy higher needs, and engages the full person of the follower." The result of transforming leadership, Burns says, is "a relationship of mutual stimulation and elevation that converts followers into leaders and may convert leaders into moral agents."[10] A further important result is organizational transformation or renewal.

The 16 chief executives interviewed for this book were selected because of their successful records as change agents: "movers and shakers." Their accomplishments, as revealed in these interviews, attest to their transformational capacity.

Transforming leaders can, of course, act in the transactional mode, and often do. But they go beyond this and create change as well. Look at the achievements of our interviewees:

- Jim Burke transformed Johnson & Johnson into a risk-taking company and inserted contention into its management system.

- Marisa Bellisario awakened a sleepy, failing, state-owned bureaucracy and turned it into a vital, profitable enterprise.

- Bill Marriott, Jr., transformed a first-generation family company into one of the largest, most successful, and fastest growing corporations in the service sector.

- Jim Guinan has used his dynamic brand of transforming leadership time and again to energize retailing companies and make them successful.

- Jim Martin injected modern financial controls and strategic planning into Massachusetts Mutual.

- Pete Scotese converted the family-dominated company that had been Springs Mills into the professionally managed major corporation known as Springs Industries.

- Ted Hesburgh greatly elevated the quality and reputation of the University of Notre Dame, while at the same time helping to create changes on the national and international landscape.

- Harold Burson extended the concept of the public relations function and created the world's largest public relations firm.

- Frank Cary transformed IBM into a technology-driven company while still retaining its customer-driven thrust.

- Charlotte Beers turned Tatham-Laird & Kudner around by being a "catalyst."
- Richard Zimmerman is developing Hershey into a fully diversified food manufacturer.
- William Kennedy III has helped to renew North Carolina Mutual by diversification and other means.
- Henry Schacht's team (he would insist it was not *his* team, but Cummins Engine Company's team) has expanded his company's vision for the future.
- Entrepreneur Portia Isaacson continues to create business enterprises from ideas (an entrepreneur, she says, is "an opportunity-seeking mechanism").
- Ichiro Hattori greatly diversified and internationalized Seiko.
- Tony O'Reilly improved profit margins for Heinz with his "fats and cats" strategies and his stress on the "Low Cost Operator."

All of these CEOs have left their mark. Yet while they all possess the power of transforming leadership, other similarities are few. Some were born to affluence, others to poverty; one was an orphan. Their educational backgrounds include physics, philosophy, English, and law. Some have spent their entire careers at one company, while others have made moves within and across industries, some across oceans. A few have practiced personal career planning; the others have simply concentrated on doing each job well. Some serve as directors of numerous corporations, while one has a policy of serving on no corporate boards other than his own. Some find refreshment in tennis or golf, others in intense commitment to entrepreneurial ventures or volunteer work. One has been married five times; another is a priest. Their self-described styles of management vary from semi-authoritarian to highly participative team management. In virtually every respect, these men and women are vastly different from one another. Yet, in selecting the representative chief executives to be interviewed, no effort was made to seek a wide variety of personalities and backgrounds.

Clearly, diversity is a marked characteristic of almost any group of CEOs. If one tried to identify the most impressive leaders one has known, chances are the list would comprise people who are unique and whose leadership styles are highly idiosyncratic. A similar exercise of identifying those corporations that one most respects is likely to produce a list of companies very different from one another. In its annual survey of America's most admired corporations, *Fortune* reported in 1986 that the top five were IBM, 3-M, Dow Jones, Coca-Cola, and Merck.[11] One would be hard pressed to find similarities among these firms, other than their commitment to high standards.

Because successful corporations and successful chief executives are unique, no claim is made as to the universality or completeness of the advice implicit in this book's interviews. What works well for one executive may work less well for another.

One recurrent theme, however, is "the willingness to pay the price." This phrase implies intense motivation, a need to achieve, an inner desire to pay that price. What does this price include? Not just long hours and longer days, but mental and physical stress, grinding travel schedules, a degree of responsibility for the economic well-being of employees, loss of privacy, putting one's reputation at risk, guilt for neglecting spouses and children—and at times even risk to their safety. The price is exceedingly high, but so is the willingness to pay it. Indeed, many compete for the privilege of doing so—they have a burning need to be the top manager.

Some insist that CEOs are leaders, not managers at all. A United Technologies advertisement entitled "Let's get rid of management" says, "You can *lead* your horse to water, but you can't *manage* him to drink."[12] (But then who says you can *lead* him to drink it, either?) Rear Adm. Grace Hopper of the U.S. Navy makes the distinction that things and projects are managed, while people are led. Yet CEOs do more than lead. Hands-on leaders manage; CEOs of small companies must manage as well as lead; often, acquisitions are personally managed by CEOs of even the largest firms. So the argument that leadership and management are at all times mutually exclusive activities does not seem to hold water—whether or not the horse can be persuaded, managed, or led to drink it.

Still, success as a CEO must require certain capabilities beyond managerial ones. Steiner, in identifying 14 qualities needed for "the new CEO," listed the quality of leadership as one.[13] This is an elusive talent which many have tried to dissect. Are the elements of a CEO's leadership capability those noted by the scholars quoted earlier in this chapter, such as Chester Barnard, who identified five "active qualities?" Or was he more on target when he described the writings on this subject as "dogmatically stated nonsense?" Peter Drucker has claimed that the best book on leadership was written three thousand years ago: The *Kyropaidaia* of Xenophon.[14]

Clearly, there is still no agreement on the ingredients of successful leadership. So this chapter ends as it began, with two questions:

"What goes into the making of a successful CEO?"

"What works for chief executives?"

Let's hear what some of them have to say.

What Works for CEOs: Interviews with 16 Chief Executives

The information presented on the biographical pages in this section was submitted by the chief executive officers.

James E. Burke

Chairman of the Board
Johnson & Johnson

*H*e is the rare CEO whose name has become a household word—unhappily because of the tragic poisonings by cyanide-laced Tylenol in 1982 and 1986. To the public, he is the man who handled both incidents forthrightly and with sensitive concern for consumers. Many editorials gave him top marks—with *Business Week* hailing his performance during the latest crisis as a "class act." But in the business world he is known also as a superb marketing executive who in nine years has led the giant family of 160 Johnson & Johnson companies from sales of $2.5 billion to over $6.4 billion. To produce these results, he has deliberately generated an atmosphere in which risk-taking and "constructive conflict" are encouraged. Johnson & Johnson executives may always seem to be arguing, he says, but from this contentious environment the best ideas and decisions are likely to emerge.

At J&J, he points out, corporate actions are based on strong beliefs in decentralization, managing for the long term, and the Credo of ethical principles written by the company's founder, General Robert Wood Johnson. It was the Credo—which gives high priority to public responsibility—that guided Burke and his people in dealing with both Tylenol crises.

13

Career Information:

1949   Joined Procter & Gamble as a brand manager

1953   Joined Johnson & Johnson as a product director

1955   Became director of new products

1957   Became director of merchandising for consumer products

1965   Named president of Johnson & Johnson Products, Inc.

1965   Elected a director and member of the executive committee

1966   Named chairman of Johnson & Johnson Products, Inc.

1971   Named vice chairman of the executive committee

1976   Named chairman and CEO of Johnson & Johnson

Other Affiliations (partial list):

- Member, President's Commission on Executive Exchange
- Member, Board of Directors, IBM Corporation
- Chairman, Employment Policy Task Force, Business Roundtable
- Chairman, Corporate Fund, Kennedy Center
- Chairman, Industries Advisory Committee, Advertising Council
- Member, Council on Foreign Relations
- Member and former chairman, Board of Directors, United Negro College Fund
- Vice Chairman, The Conference Board

Educational Information:

- Holy Cross College, B.A., 1947
- Harvard Business School, M.B.A., 1949

Personal Information:

- Born February 28, 1925, Rutland, Vermont
- Served as Navy ensign during World War II, commanding landing craft-tank in Pacific Theater

14

James E. Burke

"*A*ll of the strategic planning is done bottom-up. Our overall corporate plan is put together only after the individual companies have told us what their future goals are, and how they expect to attain them. Each of our managements knows that strategic planning is extraordinarily important to the business, and that in our decentralized environment it must begin at the company level.

"When I visit our companies around the world I try to discourage managers from telling me what business is like today. I'm really not interested. It's only natural for people to want to tell me how things are going at the moment, but I tell them to talk about the future. This is hard for them, but by my taking this attitude I am sending a signal that we are primarily interested in long-term growth, and we want to know how it is going to be achieved. This focus on the future forces our managers out of the rut of simply running the business as it is today. We must keep moving on to new things. If we are going to have a future, then we must concentrate on it.

"We have some very tough meetings, very open and often emotion filled. It is a style of management that I have always encouraged. By putting a lot of contention into our system we get better results. Certainly it makes us more honest with each other. I don't think it bruises people to argue and debate. You'd be surprised how easy some of our young people find it to politely say, 'You know, you're wrong . . . you don't have the facts . . . I do . . . and here's the evidence to prove it.' You then begin to get into the kind of debate that helps to make us all think better and helps us to reach a more satisfactory solution. This openness also makes people understand that we try hard to be fair. Anyone with the right answer, no matter who he or she is, is going to be respected. In recent years contention has become a part of our management culture, and as long as it remains constructive I encourage it. To suppress talented people from speaking their minds is to deny yourself your most important resource . . . ideas!''

> James Burke, who has led the Johnson & Johnson family of companies since 1976, believes that the best ideas often come through conflict and that progress comes only through risk taking. Because of these convictions he has done much to encourage both throughout his highly decentralized corporation.

"You have to take risks today. Business has become much more competitive on a world-wide basis. The answer to that challenge is no different than it's ever been: you've got to get better and better, and if you don't, you will be left behind. Young people perhaps understand this better than we do. The key is to get the very best people you can, and then provide them with an environment that encourages them to handle these challenges the way they see fit. There's no great magic to that. If you're not competitive—especially in Europe, Japan and the United States—and if you are not interconnected from a technological and marketing point of view, competing successfully is going to become increasingly difficult. You must create a system that will enable everyone to move freely and rapidly. There are important synergisms in a world business. Overlook them and over the long run you are out of business.

"We continue to have the old NIH (not invented here) syndrome internally as well as externally, and that is less affordable than ever before in our history. People must be conscious as to who is doing the best work and where, and how to move it from one place to another without suffering a sense of inadequacy. A decentralized organization calls for more voluntary cooperation. It is essential to the kind of competitive environment which exists today, and most of our people know that.''

> Burke joined Johnson & Johnson in 1953 as a product director, having spent three and a half years at Procter & Gamble just after graduating from Harvard Business School.

JAMES BURKE

"Plastic Band-Aid Adhesive Bandages were just beginning to come on the market and the product assigned to me was the old cloth version, along with first-aid kits. This was a declining business, though a relatively simple one, and a good assignment for someone just coming in. We had very few products

17

and a large market share, which we were losing rapidly. But nobody seemed to know this or even care about it, since domestic birth rates were climbing from 3 to 4 million per year and we were getting large volume increases just as a result of demographics. Johnson & Johnson was then a relatively unsophisticated consumer goods company, yet one with an extraordinary reputation that had never been fully utilized.

"In those days the consumer businesses we were in were small and limited in number—baby toiletries and adhesive bandages . . . and sanitary protection products. As the babies became older, they got cuts and scratches. Later, the female teenagers bought our sanitary protection products. That's about all the consumer business we had, and those markets were continuing to grow, even though we were losing share of market. It was deceptive. We used to buy Nielsen information in those days, but not many showed up for the meetings. It was the nature of both the times and that part of this business. Great dedication but not much marketing sophistication in the way the products were managed. I had come from the highly professional marketing environment of Procter & Gamble, and a lot of my early success here was just due to the luck of having come from a company where they taught the basics of consumer marketing in a way that hadn't yet been applied at Johnson & Johnson.

"There was little market or consumer research here; no one believed in it. On the other hand, the company believed strongly in decentralization, and in managing the business for the long term. We had learned that early and well. As a result, some of our decentralized companies today are bigger than the whole corporation was when I arrived. Today we have over 150 companies, and in terms of their relationship to the marketplace, they are really very independent, which is key to our system. By contrast, Procter & Gamble was a very centralized company when I was there. Though they decentralized by product management, the overall structure was highly centralized. I was astounded to find the degree of freedom that I found here.

"I really believe that individuals are capable of doing a lot more than they believe they can do. Given the right environment, you can get surprising results. General (Robert Wood)

Johnson, who built this corporation, understood this and, I felt, understood it better than Procter & Gamble did. Here we believe strongly in three things: decentralization, managing for the long term, and the ethical principles embodied in our Credo. The Credo is the sort of thing that inspires the best in people. I think that all of us have a basic moral imperative hidden somewhere in us. In some people it is more central to their being than in others, but it's always there. To tap that wellspring creates energy that you can't get elsewhere. This may sound a little pretentious . . . but I really believe it is true.''

The Johnson & Johnson Credo

During World War II, President Roosevelt made Robert W. Johnson a brigadier general and put him in charge of the Small War Plants Corporation in Washington. The SWPC's goal was to make small business a vital part of the war effort. When General Johnson returned to the company in the mid-1940s, he wrote the Johnson & Johnson Credo. It began:

We believe our first responsibility is to the doctors, nurses and patients, to mothers and all others who use our products and services. In meeting their needs, everything we do must be of high quality. We must constantly strive to reduce our costs in order to maintain reasonable prices. Customers' orders must be serviced promptly and accurately. Our suppliers and distributors must have an opportunity to make a fair profit.

The Credo went on to outline the company's other responsibilities, to employees, to communities in which they worked and lived, and finally to the stockholders. Johnson placed the stockholder last because he believed that if the other responsibilities were carried out properly, the stockholder would be well served. Burke believes strongly in the Credo's emphasis on Johnson & Johnson's mandate to serve the public in the deepest ethical sense. He was to be given the opportunity later to put that belief to the supreme test in the Tylenol crisis, and before that he had helped to solidify the Credo beliefs within the Johnson & Johnson organization at a time when they had begun to lag.

The Moral Imperative

In 1983 Burke was given the Advertising Council's Award for Public Service. In preparation for the occasion, he undertook an interesting study that was later widely reported in the news media. Working with the Business Roundtable's Task Force on Corporate Responsibility, and the Ethics Resource Center in Washington, Burke and his staff examined 26 companies that had a written codified set of principles stating that serving the public was central to their being. All of the companies had been in existence more than 30 years. Some were later dropped from the survey for various reasons, including not being publicly held.

"I believe strongly in the moral imperative of companies serving the public in the broadest possible sense. That's what intrigued me about doing this study. The results were eye-opening, though all along I suspected how it would come out. What we found was that those companies with a written commitment to be socially responsible recorded an average 10.7 percent growth in profits compounded over 30 years. This was 1.34 times better than the growth of the gross national product over the same period.

"The study included examples of how investments in these companies would have done over the 30-year period, and the results were striking.

"If any one of you had invested $30,000 in a composite of the Dow Jones 30 years ago, it would be worth $134,000 today. If you had invested the same $30,000—$2,000 in each of the companies remaining in the survey—your $30,000 would be worth over $1,000,000—*$1,021,861* to be exact! (If the Dow had grown at the same rate as these companies, it would be over 9,000—9,399 to be exact.)

"What this says is that companies that have a commitment, and know what they believe in, will over time outperform those which do not. While we get wrapped up in our own beliefs in the Johnson & Johnson Credo, the fact is that many other companies have developed their own set of principles and use them to guide their managements just as we have."

Early Entrepreneurial Ventures

"Like many young people, I went through a lot of confusion trying to decide what to do with my life. As a result of going to Harvard Business School, I realized that I probably would end up in marketing. Procter & Gamble had a great reputation as a marketing-based company, so I went there. After three and a half years I left, still not sure what I was going to do with my life. I was excited by the prospect of being an entrepreneur, and developed several opportunities along those lines.

"One of my products was called Moka, a mixture of coffee and chocolate which I produced through a packaging company in Newark. I thought Moka was a wonderful drink, and I had conducted some rather crude market research with some women's bridge clubs that supported my conviction. I decided to expand the test, packaged the product on a very muggy August day, and was looking toward some success. What I did not know was that the formula was highly hygroscopic, and by the time I got Moka into a few stores, it had turned solid as a rock. The little foil packets had become so hard that handling them was like handling a knife; people were cutting themselves on the package even before they could open it. In the case of the product that had been packed in a jar . . . it turned so solid you couldn't get it out. It was a total disaster.

"I was trying this venture in my spare time while working at Johnson & Johnson. I thought I had another great idea, a product I called Pink Cloud. It was a big effervescent tablet containing corn starch and a water-soluble lanolin. By dropping the tablet into the bathtub, a cloud of pink would form, providing women a luxurious bathing experience, after which their skin would feel soft and silky from the lanolin and corn starch. Well, that was a disaster, too. I never had enough money to get it off the ground. My orientation even in earlier years had been entrepreneurial, and I still clung to the dream of making it on my own.

"Luckily, about this time, Bob Johnson (the General's son) contacted me and said the company was interested in starting a new products division, and would like me to conduct a four-month feasibility study. Since the new products operation held a special fascination for me and I had come to appreciate the entrepreneurial opportunities in a decentralized company, I agreed to take on the assignment. This then led to my becoming head of new products, and working directly with Bob Johnson. He was a very creative marketing person and deeply committed to the company. Further, he wasn't afraid to take risks. That fit with my own views of how to achieve business success, so I now approached my job with a new outlook and renewed vitality. Together we tried to spread the new product concept throughout the company. We met with some successes, and some failures, but did raise the level of awareness and got people thinking in new directions. And, of course, the longer I stayed with Johnson & Johnson, the deeper my commitment became."

Career Confusion

Burke's earlier uncertainty about his career was somewhat more of a struggle than it is for most young people. But then he was more restless than most.

"While at Procter & Gamble I had been brand manager for a shampoo and for a home permanent, and I decided that was a rather frivolous way to spend one's life. It took me years to recognize this was a more egocentric attitude than I realized at the time.

"I had been offered the opportunity to run the Munich office of Radio Free Europe back in 1953, when I was only 28 years old. Through a number of lucky breaks, I had the chance to talk to several important people about this—the head of the Atomic Energy Commission, the editor of *Fortune,* the head of one of the large investment banks—and all of these great people said, 'Do it, terrific, wonderful idea, you'll just love it, it's a great adventure.' But something inside made me keep asking whether I should. So whenever possible I talked to people whose advice I respected.

"I happened to know Jim Weinberg, the son of Sidney Weinberg, who was called the 'Ivory Hunter of the Potomac' because he had helped to bring so many people to Washington. One day I had the chance to seek the advice of Mr. Weinberg.

"He asked me how much time I had, and I said, 'As much as you want, sir.' Then, for the next two and a half hours, he absolutely tore me apart, completely eviscerated me for even considering taking on the Radio Free Europe assignment. Among other things he said, 'One of the troubles with this world of ours is people like you having the pretensions that you are ready to take on an important public service job with no real background that qualifies you. The fact is that you graduated from Harvard Business School, have three and a half years of business experience, and that's all you've got. To take that job at Radio Free Europe would be a great disservice to this country.'

"I was somewhat shaken, but I knew immediately that he was right. I simply was not mature enough to think of anything other than the fun of being a big shot and making more money than I'd ever dreamt of making at that age. As I left his office, Sidney Weinberg put his arm on my shoulder and said, 'Son, stay in business until you have demonstrated what you are capable of doing. I'm sure that will be considerable . . . I can tell from having spent this time with you. When you have finally accomplished something important, then come back to me and I'll get you anything you want in Washington.' About seven and a half years later I was made president of Johnson & Johnson's operating company, and there was a little squib in the *New York Times* about that. Mr. Weinberg clipped the item from the paper and sent it to me with a note saying, 'Now what do you want?' I never again saw Mr. Weinberg, but I wrote him a letter of profound thanks for helping to change my life.

"I learned several things from that interview. One was about myself, for he gave me a sense of reality. But I also learned something about giving advice to young people. You need to tell them not what they want to hear, but what you really believe. Weinberg had been forthright enough to tell me the truth, and that meeting was an important turning point for me. Perhaps that is one reason why I make myself available to young people whenever I can.

"Through this and through my Moka and Pink Cloud failures, I learned how little I knew and how superficially I had approached life. I was beginning to learn what reality was all about . . . and I was enjoying it."

Organizing for New Products

When Burke was assigned to set up a new products division, which had been his own recommendation, he found that there weren't any other such organizational structures to model this after. He learned that two of his former B-school classmates were putting together an approach to studying new-product successes and failures, so he worked closely with them, developing statistics and an understanding of the new product process.

"The three of us spent a lot of time together, really as pathfinders in that field. We found that only three out of ten new products which reached the marketplace succeeded; this meant that I would have to get the company to be willing to try ten times for only three successes. I can remember people here saying, 'That's crazy! Why would we do that?' They wanted more assurance than I could offer. It was during that period that I began to understand the necessity for risk, and the realization that you can't grow without it. You simply have to create an environment that encourages risk taking. General Johnson was a great believer in encouraging risk, but he was very tough, perhaps not realizing that he sometimes frightened people away from the very things he wanted them to do.

"I remember once I came up with a new product, a children's chest rub, built around the concept of its being safer and easier to use. The chest rub was in the form of a stick, like the underarm deodorant sticks on the market today. It was one of three products, the chest rub, nose drops, and a cough medicine, all of which failed.

"One day the General's secretary called me. I went to his office and his desk seemed a mile and a half from the door. He asked me to sit down. He went on with his dictating as he always did, then he turned to me. I was certain that I was going to be fired. Still, I found this all pretty exciting. Here was a company where the chairman took the trouble to fire you personally. I decided I would defend myself, and was mentally preparing for a good fight. He said, 'I understand that your product failed.' I said, 'Yes, sir, that's true.' Picking up a piece of blue paper, he said, 'Furthermore, I understand it cost this corporation $865,000.' I said, 'Yes, sir, that's right.' He stood up, held out his hand and said, 'I just wanted to congratulate you. Nothing happens unless people are willing to make decisions, and you can't make decisions without making mistakes.'

"The first thing that flashed through my mind was that he was giving me a license to make mistakes. But he quickly added: 'If you make the same one again you're through, but that doesn't mean that you should stop making mistakes.'

"The General was smart enough to know that keeping the spirit of risk-taking alive was difficult. He had a great understanding of the basic human nature in any organization, and he was constantly doing things like that. On the otherhand, he could be very tough on people under certain conditions. He had fired people for doing much the same as he was now congratulating me for doing. He was not the most consistent person. We became good friends over the years, and from time to time we had some terrific battles. Once I thought he was going to have a stroke, but both of us survived that one, too. Even though he was completely committed to decentralization, he still could be very dominating. But he was shrewd.

"There is no way that a growth organization can make it if it doesn't encourage risk; it's human nature to play it safe. We've tried a lot of things institutionally. We have 'skunk works,' as others do. The General called this 'cottage research.' He would say, 'If a guy has a good idea, find him a small cottage someplace, ask him how much it will take to bring the idea into reality, and if he says it will take a half million dollars, give him a million. If he says it will take three years to do it, give him five. Then tell him that when the money is gone and the time is gone, he's gone.' This has long been a part of our culture. We now have an entrepreneurial bonus which we set up last year. We offer large chunks of money for entrepreneurial ideas. We've worked very hard at the business of encouraging risk. We hire around this idea and spend a lot of time at it."

Moving Up

When Bob Johnson had a falling out with his father and left the company, Burke became acting general manager of the operating company and later a member of the board of directors and of its executive committee. He describes this advance as having been regarded as premature in the minds of some in top management, and in his own mind as well. But it was the kind of opportunity intelligent and ambitious people don't turn down.

"I had learned a good deal in the years just before this move. I was 37 at the time and I knew that I was capable of managing this area of the business. But I was surprised that I was being given the chance. I ran the operating company in pretty much the same way I had handled earlier assignments. The responsibilities were far greater, of course, but my style of management didn't change.

"Even today, nearly 25 years later, we seem to function best in an atmosphere of constructive conflict. That doesn't suggest that we don't have a friendly relationship, because we do. We are more informal than many other companies, and all of our executives are on a first name basis—even the new, younger people. That helps communications and it breaks down the barriers that sometimes prevent getting at the truth. It also reduces tensions and adds to the fun. They kid me because I am always telling them to have fun on the job. We'll be in the midst of a raging argument and some wit will ask if we're really all having fun!

"But we know each other very well, and if you were to come into this office in the middle of a discussion of a difficult problem, you would probably find us in the middle of an argument. If you had come in here during the Tylenol crisis, you would have thought we were angry with each other. The truth is, we were all dealing with great anxiety and stress, and one of the best ways to relieve that is to get it out . . . It has a positive effect, so long as people understand that you're really not personalizing any of it. We have that kind of contentious environment, but it is not an ulcer-producing one. Most of us have a hell of a good time, and most of our people would probably say that they can tell me whatever they want to tell me, and they often do.

"I make it my business to reach down into the organizations periodically to challenge just about anything. We recently had a big meeting regarding a radical change in strategy on our baby shampoo which I thought was fundamentally wrong and bad for the brand as well as for the corporation. Johnson's baby products have a lot to do with how people view us as a corporation. After two relatively long meetings, the product manager won that one, hands down, and he was right. I was wrong.

"I've tried to make our meetings much more bottom-up. We have some major meetings every three years when we bring together our managers from all over the world. Just before I became chairman (in 1976) we had a meeting of this sort, and I found a great deal of disagreement and anger among a lot of our companies about how bureaucratic we'd become here at headquarters. Yet nobody here had been aware of it. I resolved at that time that we would have these meetings at least every three years, and that the meeting would belong to the participants and not just to what was on our minds here at headquarters. We've managed to do that successfully . . . and of course as a result we at headquarters get a lot more out of the process.

"About this same time I took a hard look at our view of the Credo, that unique document written by Robert Wood Johnson. At the top of the organization we believed in it fiercely. When Phil Hofmann was chairman, he called a series of ten Credo dinner meetings and attended every one of them to answer questions. Dick Sellars, who succeeded him as chairman, believed in the Credo—and practiced it—as faithfully as any person in the entire organization."

Challenging the Credo

"But about the time I became chairman I began to suspect that the Credo wasn't as meaningful to everyone in the company. While many had adopted it as our guideline for conducting the business, this wasn't universally true. The company had plants in some 50 or more countries, and the number of new employees had grown rapidly. I expressed these concerns to Dave

Clare, our president and chairman of the executive committee and my closest associate in the company. He agreed, so we decided to do something about it.

"So we began by bringing in about 25 of our managers and laying out to them what we called 'The Credo Challenge.' What we said, in effect, was this: If you do not really believe in the Credo, and you aren't urging your employees to abide by it, then it is an act of pretension. In that case, you should take it off the walls of your office and throw it away. Then we began the debate, or the challenge as we called it.

"We went through every section of the Credo, challenging each one. The assignment was to come out of the meeting either recommending that we get rid of it, change it, or commit to it as it is. And if we were going to change it, I said, 'I want you to tell us how.' By way of background, you should know that a number of people in the company questioned the wisdom of the challenge meetings. And my predecessor, Dick Sellars, was furious when he found out what we were doing. Only because he didn't feel the Credo should be challenged— he was a real believer in it as it stood. But the meetings became a turn-on, and for two days the debate continued. In the end, the overwhelming majority voted to retain the Credo philosophy but urged some word changes that brought the document more in keeping with the times. In substance, however, the Credo received reaffirmation. It proved my point that everyone has a value system. But by giving them the opportunity, through discussion and confrontation, to 'buy into' the Credo, it was now their philosophy as well, and not one foisted upon them by a previous generation.

"The dynamics of that meeting became so important to us, in terms of management involvement in this critical philosophical issue, that over the next three years Dave Clare and I met with all of the other managing directors. The same process ensued, and the results were the same as the first meeting. We then incorporated the recommended word changes into a revised Credo, and reissued it in 1979 at one of our world meetings. We continue the process by holding periodic Credo challenge meetings with new members of senior management soon after they join the company. Dave and I attend these meetings and issue the challenge. There can be no doubt in their minds as to the importance of this business philosophy to the corporation.

"It is well known that when the Tylenol crisis struck us in 1982, and we had to make some of the most critical decisions in the company's history, we turned to the Credo for guidance. Dozens of people had to make hundreds of decisions, etc., etc. Most of what people needed by way of direction was there. Not only that, but the entire organization had only recently reaffirmed its belief in it. Had we not made those decisions according to the Credo, we would have broken faith with our people. In the following few years we had a series of difficulties, including the withdrawal from the market of an important drug, Zomax[1]. In these situations the Credo again served us well, and in the process helped to further institutionalize our belief in it as a proper way to conduct a business."

Selecting People

"Everyone has a tendency to make judgments about people based upon their own experience, so I have certain views as to who should be selected for a top job, and Dave Clare has others. First, neither of us wants anyone in a position of authority who doesn't really buy into the Credo. It holds our group of 160 diverse companies together and keeps us moving in the same direction. Second, we look for the ability to lead others, and third we look for people who think as businesspersons. We are very bottom-line oriented and can be very demanding. Most of the people we lose, so far as we can tell, leave either because we've mismanaged them—and a decentralized environment may cause that to happen—or we're too tough and demanding of results. I don't think there's anything wrong with that. We want people who enjoy excelling and delivering superior results, high energy people, ambitious and competitive. You will notice that I have not mentioned the

[1] In early 1986, Johnson & Johnson also removed Tylenol capsules from the market, in response to another poisoning incident involving cyanide-laced Tylenol.

'smarts;' I suppose you have to be smart to be successful, but you don't have to be a genius.

"One hallmark that I find in almost every successful marketing person is an indiscriminate curiosity. I've never known anyone who is really successful who is not curious about everything; perhaps that is not an essential trait, but it's interesting to me that I've never met anyone really good without that trait.

"Then there is the matter of people skills. An important skill is to be able to help people to believe that they can accomplish much more than they think they can. I believe in the concept that all of us can do 10, 20, 30 times more than we might think. Of course if you assume, as I tend to, that every problem has a solution, then you're going to find yourself disappointed at times, particularly in the human area where there are some awesome, complex forces at work. That makes it very difficult for individuals to do as much as you think they can do, particularly if they are struggling with problems that you do not see or understand. So optimism can be a weakness as well as a strength.

"Yet, when we were recently debating about something, Dave Clare said to one of our top people, 'You know that Burke is an optimist, I know that Burke is an optimist, and Burke knows Burke is an optimist!' I think that most of us who succeed are just that. The world doesn't move except through optimists. Still, the key is to make sure that the organization protects you against yourself. One advantage of trying to keep an organization open is that most of the people who work for me know that is part of their responsibility. If I am about to lead them off the edge of a cliff, being so optimistic, somebody had better stop me. And they usually do.

"In addition, you have to be able to read people. If I find myself dealing with someone in the organization who I know is even more of an optimist than I am, I can play the other role, too. But I think the key to my management style is a sincere belief in people and a sensitivity to where they are and who they are and what they're trying to accomplish, so that I can anticipate some of their needs. As a communicator, I am pretty good, but probably better at communicating than at listening.

Yet, I've worked hard on this and usually listen fairly well even when a lot of people are expressing their views.

"During the Tylenol affair we counted heavily on the Credo, but another key was that I brought together the best people in the corporation, and we sat right in my office from beginning to end thrashing out the decisions. Just as important, I kept the windows open to ideas from everyone, in or outside the company. I called lots of people whom I knew in business for advice; others called or wrote to me. We used Burson-Marsteller for the strategy on the comeback, and one of their people came up with the idea, that some thought was pretty far out, for a satellite news conference to introduce the new safety-sealed Tylenol package. It was one of the best ideas we had. We also talked with consumers—and listened to them every day. Every night I took home video tapes of customers who were interviewed on camera all around the country. Ideas from the outside are extremely important, as we don't always look at ourselves too accurately. They are particularly valuable when they come from customers."

Burke's Management Style

"Although we practice participative management, I don't think you could call it consensus management. I could never be happy in a position where I could dictate decisions. I wouldn't do it very well, since I'm not that omniscient. I am most at home in the world of ideas. I love the advertising agency business and almost went into it; it's filled with very bright, thoughtful, sensitive, highly creative people. I put a very big premium on ideas of any kind and sometimes drive people nuts stimulating them. People have told me that J&J management will go laboriously about building the foundations for a decision, and then I keep looking at it and sometimes come in with a jackhammer and break the whole damn thing up, forcing people to start all over again. Well, that is a tendency, to keep looking at things in new and different ways. Sometimes that can be destructive, but I try to make it a positive creative force.

"I love to watch the mental process work, ideas floating up with disciplined challenges along the way, to see ideas become realities in the marketplace and then affect the bottom line. At meetings I tend to ask a lot of questions.

"When I meet the top-management people from one of our affiliate companies, I concentrate on the problems confronting their business. I challenge whatever they bring in, still hoping that they will be making the right decision by the time they leave, and hoping that I will not have to make that decision. Either they will have come in with the right decision or they'll leave with the right decision, but it has to be their choice, not ours. Now, if we have to override them, we will; but we don't do that very often, as the system doesn't work if you do. Not if your people don't really believe and know that they're running their own operations. If you don't encourage this kind of environment, then when you do get tough, your people will say, 'Well, that's the way they want me to do it, so I'll do it that way.' But if they know they have the right to fight back, you're much less apt to get into a position of dominating their decision, and that's the real key. If you do become too dominant, more than once or twice, your best people will go somewhere else.

"When I was running the operating company at Johnson & Johnson, I had more fun than I do now as chairman. I ran it differently—my own way—and I knew that I was going to make the final decisions. Now, although I'm responsible for the whole corporation, a lot of my time is spent with its companies. The only decisions I want to make now are the corporate decisions.

"The meeting we had earlier on the baby-shampoo strategy, when I was certain I was right but learned later that I was wrong, made me much happier than I expected to be. I had grown up with that brand, had helped to build it, had cut my teeth in that business, and thought I knew more about it than all the rest of the people in the room put together. After the first meeting, I went home somewhat depressed, knowing—or thinking—I was right and that my people weren't doing the right thing. But after the second meeting, I went home confident in knowing that they were right and I was wrong. That meant that the company was in good hands. Whole new dimensions in that business had completely escaped me. That's the way the contention system helped to enlighten me. . . and give renewed confidence to the brand group.''

Building an Outside Board

When Burke became Chairman, his board of directors was completely made up of insiders. It had in fact been one of General Johnson's strong commitments to maintain an all-inside board, never to let an outsider in.

"One of the first things I did was to bring in outsiders. This was an unpopular decision, and many of the former directors are still somewhat critical. I did it because I felt an all-inside board was wrong. While the Credo was a protection for the company . . . it also needed strong outside directors . . .particularly as it got bigger . . . it was after all the largest company in the world concerned with peoples' health.

"I also knew I couldn't make a fundamental cultural change like this overnight, so I've been at it steadily but gradually. We now have 11 insiders and 10 outsiders and in the near future will have a majority of 'non-employee' directors.

"I feel that a majority of outside directors gives the company added protection for the future. We have very strong people on the board. No one can challenge that. Still, it remains kind of a 'we' and 'they' situation. Our inside board members visualize their jobs as that of keeping the outside directors up to date. We're not yet where I want to be, for I'd like to get a more interactive contentious board itself, and this is beginning to happen, at least with small groups of directors.

"When I opened up the board, I said to our inside people, 'I know that none of you are going to like this. I can appreciate how you feel because I've grown up with all of you. But now that I'm chairman of the company I've got a responsibility, and this is what I think is best for the company.' I might add that new rules then being promulgated by the New York Stock Exchange for its member companies required an audit committee made up of a majority of outside board members. But I was determined to go further than that.''

Advice to Young People

"One of the things I would say to young people, as I have many times, is not to be too afraid or to worry too much about your own inner confusion. There is a myth which says that you ought to know when you get out of school who you are and what you are going to do with your life and how you are going to do it. I don't believe that. In fact I think a minority of young people have a clear view of the world and of themselves, and I'm not even sure that they are the ones who end up doing the best job. The confusion that we all go through in life is valuable; growth comes out of challenging that bewilderment.

"I number quite a few of the children of our friends as personal friends of mine in their own right, and I try to find as much of my time as I can for them. And while I give them all different advice, depending on their own interests, I do think business offers extraordinary career opportunities. I believe marketing is an especially good route, since every good company is in the long run built upon the principle of satisfying its customers. The closer you get to the customer, the more you know about 'who drives the bus.' But there are a lot of people who are not interested in marketing and would rather start in another direction. I try to help them think through why they want to go in a particular direction, and what they can do in that role to understand the totality of business.

"I try to talk philosophically about the simple totality of business, since young people have a tendency to think of it in a narrow sense rather than as a dynamic organism which tries to satisfy needs and to create wealth in the process. And I try to turn them towards a way that would get them to ask the things that are really bugging them. I find most young people don't always choose their first job very intelligently, or the second, or sometimes even the third. So they shouldn't be afraid to change jobs.

"I encourage them to follow their own 'gut instincts.' My son at the moment wants to be an actor, and we spend a lot of time talking about that; he's a wonderful young person, and watching him struggle with the rather heroic decision to try to be an actor is a wonderful experience. I watch him seeking and listening to advice, but it's the process that is fascinating. Perhaps the most important thing young people ought to understand is that one's life's work is most rewarding when you make it fun. Too often the word 'work' has a pejorative connotation. Nothing could be further from the truth. It is 'work' and 'love' that define us as human beings.

"To me business is as exciting as any other human endeavor, because it involves all facets of society . . . and it's hard to think of another profession where that is true. Where else do you have to be intimately aware of the needs of the consumer? Deeply involved in providing rewarding work for others? Involved in the communities that are impacted by your activities . . . local, state, and federal . . . and finally the financial institutions that provide the capital that makes it all work? I know of no other human activity that provides the opportunity for a more fulfilling and rewarding life than business. So if young people look at business in that sense, particularly in a free society like ours, they will find a way to do their own thing and be rewarded in the process."

Marisa Bellisario

Managing Director and Chief Executive Officer
Italtel Società Italiana Telecomunicazioni

She is Italy's most talked-about executive—
and not only because she sometimes wears
jeans to the office. With a blend of enthusiasm, energy, and tough-mindedness she
took on an enormous challenge: rescuing a
giant state-owned telecommunications
manufacturer in Italy that was losing over
$200 million a year. What she had to work
with was a top-heavy, slow-moving bureaucracy weighted down by a swollen payroll.
After she became CEO in 1981, it took her
only three years to turn this lumbering corporate dinosaur into a lean, up-to-date
organization that started to make profits.
Most observers agree that it's been a
remarkable performance.

Her basic belief is that people are more
important than organization. "As long as
you can operate with smart people and with
efficient people—with people who have a
sense of humor—you can deal with almost
any problem." She thinks work should be
fun and she makes bets with her people. "If,
for example, someone is responsible for a
very complex project, that we must install
and put into service at a particular time, I
will say, 'By November, if it works, I will
pay for dinner; otherwise you will pay.'" So
far, she has always had to pay for the dinner
—the projects have all been on schedule.

Career Information:

1960 Joined Olivetti, where she headed a group of engineers working on a pioneer computing project

1965 Joined General Electric Systems Italia, as head of Product and Operations Planning

1969 Joined Honeywell Information Systems Italia, with responsibility for product planning and business planning

1972 Rejoined Olivetti as Director of Corporate Planning; later became Director of the Distributed Data Processing Group

1979 Became president and chief executive officer of Olivetti Corporation of America

1980 Joined Italtel as deputy general manager and member of the executive committee

1981 Became managing director and chief executive officer

Other Affiliations:

• Member, Commission for Equality Between Men and Women

Educational Information:

• University of Torino, Economics, 1960

Personal Information:

• Born in Ceva, Italy
• Married

Marisa Bellisario

*"I*n these difficult business times—
and with our rapidly changing technology—you have to rely more on people
and less on organization. . . . Choosing the right people is essential. If you
don't have smart, professional people,
you can have the best organization in
the world, but it will not work."

What does work, according to Marisa Bellisario, is getting the
best top-level people to help manage the company—"It's the first
thing I try to do when I take on a new job." And it was the first
thing she did in mid-1981 after she was named CEO of Italtel, Italy's
leading telecommunications manufacturer. A troubled, state-
owned giant, Italtel was burdened with a noncompetitive product
line, a rigid culture and an excessively layered corporate bureaucracy. It had just reported a 12-month loss of $188 million on an-
nual sales of $255 million, and its operating deficit was growing.

Bellisario's capabilities as a turnaround specialist had had one
previous major test—a 14-month stint as president of Olivetti
U.S.A. This had not been a completely satisfying experience, and
beyond a few key directors of Italtel, not many besides Bellisario
herself were betting on the ability of this energetic young individ-
ualist to overcome the monolithic character of the organization
and transform it into a successful modern industrial enterprise.
Looking back, she recalls that "most would have given me no
more than a 10 to 15 percent chance to make it."

But the doubters failed to take into consideration several
facets of the Bellisario managerial personality. First is her
supremely confident readiness to take on responsibility.

"Always in some way I tend to take on more . . . I never
refuse it—maybe I am counting too much on myself—but when-

ever I have taken a job, I have never thought that I couldn't make it."

Then there is her enthusiasm for new ideas and situations.

"I like to take risks."

Taking on the Italtel Challenge

Bellisario combined both of these strengths at Italtel. Granted full responsibility to organize her own top management team, she immediately initiated a restructuring of the Italtel organization and its outdated product line. Her operating and marketing strategy called for a turnaround from an operating loss in 1981 to break-even status by 1984. In fact, under her leadership, the company earned a modest profit one full year ahead of schedule and more than doubled that performance in 1984, earning $13 million on total revenues of $609 million.

This turnaround is all the more remarkable because of the monolithic character of the Italtel organization, part of the IRI-Stet Group (Istituto per la Ricostruzione Industriale, the state holding group controlling Italy's largest conglomerate; and Società Finanziaria Telefonica, or Stet, the holding organization for state-owned telecommunications and electronics companies). Italtel, itself then a sleepy, overblown bureaucracy, was thus enmeshed as one of many state-owned companies in a still larger web of governmental bureaucracy.

Bellisario had spent her early career in exciting high-technology companies—the Computer Division of Olivetti, General Electric Information Systems Italia, and Honeywell Information Systems Italia. It was with this background that she had become President and Chief Executive Officer of Olivetti Corporation of America.

"That Olivetti experience was very important to me. For the first time, I was responsible for an entire company, and a company that was losing a lot of money. I would later face this same problem at Italtel; I would need to reduce staff, to increase revenue, to review the organization, to create a new executive team, and so on. But at Olivetti I was very unlucky also from a pricing point of view, because at that time the dollar was

Photo: M. Saglio

MARISA BELLISARIO

very low, only about 800 lira, so Olivetti's prices were much too high for the States. This was only one of the problems. And although we managed to reduce significantly the loss, we continued to lose money. We needed more time for managing the turnaround.''

In 1980, Bellisario relinquished her post as CEO of Olivetti U.S.A., apparently in mutual agreement with Olivetti.

''Quite frankly, I had some disagreement with my boss. We had a different view as to what should be done for the U.S. market. I needed more time to make the recovery work. Looking back, six months later, it was clear that one of the problems of the loss would have been automatically solved, as the dollar went up to 1200 lira. But obviously this was not known at the time.''

> No longer CEO, she returned to Italy and spent another few months with the parent corporation before joining Italtel. Bellisario was recruited by Italtel not as CEO, but as Deputy General Manager and a member of the Executive Committee, reporting to its chief executive. Hence she lacked the full authority needed to restructure and renew a failing company. This situation was all too familiar to her; she had been in precisely the same position at Olivetti's American subsidiary.

"At Olivetti I learned basically that one should not take a turnaround job without having full responsibility and agreement about the time which is necessary to achieve it. I don't complain about my time at Olivetti, because for me it was a very important experience—an essential experience—which I took into account when I later proposed a plan for Italtel to IRI and Stet, the holding company, asking quite clearly to be given sufficient authority and time to make a turnaround. Consistent actions, at least over a three-year time span, are required for turning around a company; at Olivetti, this had not been understood."

> Until she joined Italtel, Bellisario's whole work life had been spent in the private sector and most of this in the fast-growing computer industry. Arriving at this state-owned company, she found herself in a totally different environment.

"I can tell you of some very strange things. For example, when I arrived, managers at Italtel were making reports of all meetings, spending more time doing these reports and agreeing on them than they had spent in the meetings themselves. After a meeting among, say, ten people, two or three of them would take days and days just doing the minutes and getting them agreed upon. Everyone had formally to agree. I told them either they would not do the minutes—we would get along without them—or if we had to have minutes, then one person could write them up, and we would rely on these. If someone disagreed later, we would handle that. What was important was to eliminate these unproductive steps."

This corporate mentality of a company employing almost 30,000 people is just one example of the many problems Bellisario had to face in trying to rescue Italtel from itself. Another major challenge was to find a way to sharply reduce the size of the staff in this highly unionized company. Moreover, the product line needed both pruning and modernization.

After several months as Italtel's Deputy General Manager, she called fully on her Olivetti experience. Shortly after she described to Italtel's holding company (Stet) and the Board of Directors a strategic plan to turn the company around, and the backing she would need, Bellisario was made CEO.

"The telecommunications business is becoming similar to the computer business, and this has been true for the last five or ten years. Yet Italtel had stayed with the same telecommunications product for 30 or 40 years, and for many of them it was almost impossible to change. But it was obvious that many changes needed to be made. Microelectronics has shortened the life cycle of telecommunications products, which require continuous investments in R&D and innovation to be competitive."

Workforce Reduction and Management Recruiting

Armed with confidence, she attacked her task on several fronts with great rapidity.

One of her first moves was to design a program of early retirement and severance incentives. Putting such a plan into operation was not easy, because the package had to be sold to the unions as well as to management. In doing so, she acted in her characteristic style of soft-spoken but persuasive directness, warning both the unions and her directors that unless her proposed reductions were agreed upon even more cutbacks would be required later. This program, combined with normal attrition (there were no outright dismissals) and transfers to other Stet companies, cut the staff from about 29,000 employees in 1981 to 19,000 in 1985, an astonishing feat for any organization but especially so for a European state-owned company. Throughout the downsizing and reorganization, Bellisario focused particularly on the talent at the top.

"Therefore, the first thing that I look for when I take on a new job and the first thing I did at Italtel was to try to get the best top-level people I could to help manage the company. I chose a team of highly professional managers both from outside the company and from within. Working with this new team, we defined a new organization, because the company had been a huge one with a very traditional organization—organized like separate companies, by division, by product, and so on. But even with the right organization, without the right people it would not work.

"The most important part of the solution is to find the right executives. You can make changes from the top, but it is quite impossible to make them at the bottom without the right leadership. Normally, when a company is slow, when a company is very conservative, the pace is coming from the top, not from the bottom. And there is no question that when I arrived at the company, the people at the middle levels and the blue-collar employees understood the company's problems better than the top executives."

Although she was reducing the staff at all levels, she aggressively recruited capable executives, managers, and professionals from other companies. About two-thirds of upper management was replaced by new managers either hired outside or promoted from inside the company.

Bellisario's Managerial Growth

Then there was the matter of organization. To restructure Italtel, Bellisario relied on her instincts and lessons she had learned over her career in the computer industry. Her work life had begun as a computer programmer in 1960 at Olivetti Divisione Elettronica, the company's Computer Division, which became part of General Electric's Information Systems Italia in 1965.

"Because the computer business was at its beginning and growing quite fast—and also partly because of my particular personality—within three months, while I was still programming, I became mainly a supervisor. In that job I had extensive direct marketing contact with customers. For the next three or four years I worked as a young manager in marketing support, helping customers to implement their applications on computers. So I had a taste of management from the very first part of my career.

"Later, when General Electric acquired the Olivetti Computer Division, it became evident that product planning was needed, and I was appointed as a product planning manager with responsibility for interfacing with GE's people in America, France, and other countries. This was a very technical job, for we needed to make our systems compatible. While product planning and other planning activities were already quite well established functions in the United States at that time, this was not true in Italy. I had to help create the product planning function—and in some ways invent it. At the same time, it was also very important for each plant to establish its own mission, for each research and development activity to define its own mission, and so on.

"During that time one product which became very successful for General Electric's Italian company was the G115 computer. In some ways this product became quite a little son for me, as it was planned and designed with our own research and development, and we succeeded in having the whole organization sell it, so it was a big success from an international point of view."

In 1969, the General Electric unit was acquired by Honeywell Information Systems Italia, and Bellisario began to broaden her responsibilities from product planning to business planning.

She regards the highlights of her early career as key guideposts to what came later.

"The first turning point had come quickly, quite soon after I first started to work, when I was given team responsibility for programmers. I immediately liked being a manager."

Cultural Differences in Management

"The second big step came when I was appointed product planning manager. Together with this, it was very valuable to have the opportunity to work for several years with American companies, General Electric and Honeywell. This really broadened my mind. I was so lucky to be the product planning manager who had the most to do with the American and French parts of the organization. I was really quite young at that time, and by spending time in France as well as in the States, I learned different ways of doing things, different ways to lead. I learned about methods and mechanisms such as planning, control, and organization, all procedures that were quite new to Italy at the time.

"There are differences in management and especially differences in atmosphere between all countries. Italy is very different from France, France is different from Germany. The main difference between Italy and the United States is that American companies rely on much more detailed organizational schemes and much more specific techniques than do Italian firms. In some ways the American system works according to a standard. And while you may rely on this, at the same time you cannot always ask something different from the standard, for if you ask something too different, you just create a complication.

"This is true not only in management; rather, it represents a sort of national atmosphere. For example, if you go to a restaurant in the United States, you will get salad. I don't happen to like salad, but as many times as I have tried to tell the waiter, 'I don't care for salad, please,' the way of the system is such that whoever orders a meal will get salad. I have tried many times, but now I just give up.

"Similarly, when I visit an American company, I notice that their people are expected to do certain things and to do them in a certain way. They have standards, procedures. In some ways you might say that these procedures are rigid, but in other ways they are comfortable, because you know exactly how the system works.

"In Italy, we have quite fewer standards, fewer procedures, and therefore you cannot rely on the system. You need to check to see if it works. At the same time, without procedures you have an advantage of more flexibility. I have been impressed with the small high-tech companies which give more room to the individual. When you find a highly organized, systematic company in Italy, its procedures may become blocks. This is especially true in the government and public administration and also in public companies. In such cases you have all the bad of the organization and nothing of the good that you have in the United States."

In 1972, Bellisario rejoined the Olivetti Corporation as Director of Corporate Planning and in 1978 became Director of the Distributed Data Processing Group.

"This was a very interesting management experience, because up to that time I had mainly learned from and contributed to important projects, for example, General Electric's G100 line, which they lived on for years. When I went back to Olivetti, I had a corporate responsibility in a company that was approaching the problem of changing from electromechanical technology to electronic. They had a very old-style organization and no real planning procedure. What I did was to apply to Olivetti everything I had learned at General Electric and at Honeywell. It was a very good environment, as the technical and management people at Olivetti were very good, very smart, but in some respects they were quite naive, particularly in their lack of knowledge about planning and control. Though they had many technical capabilities, they could not, for example, organize the way they should control their research and development work. Managing R&D takes a very special skill. There are some very specific things you have to do in motivating technical people and in controlling the result. In particular, you must let them know that you really care about the progress of their efforts. Italian firms in the '60s and '70s tended to treat R&D as an end in itself: researchers were insulated from the rest of the corporate activities and worked in a sort of ivory tower, irrespective of their concrete contribution to corporate goals. My experience with American multinationals operating in high-tech sectors taught me that R&D, too,

47

can and should be managed by objectives. The latter can be defined in various ways—for example, according to topics, schedules, etc. Obviously, since R&D requires creativity and imagination, managers should be careful not to impair these fundamental resources by excessive bureaucracy and regulation."

Counting on People

Bellisario, now Italtel's CEO, began restructuring the Italian telecommunications monolith.

"I reorganized on a functional basis and eliminated many management layers. Between the general manager and the engineer responsible for a specific project there had been four or five levels of management. I made the organization much less formal. For example, today the project engineer talks with all the key people, talks directly with the general manager and sometimes with me as well. Ten years ago you could count on a good organization even with a medium quality of people. But with today's ever more technological and competitive market, the financial pressures around the world, the changing work scenario—the changes also in political situations—it is much better to have smart and flexible people rather than to count so much on the organization, even a good one.

"I believe that organizational change should be carefully evaluated. One must be consistent, because you cannot assign a responsibility to one manager and six months later change it, and six months later change it again. So long as there is no major change in the environment, you should be consistent and give people the time to reach their objectives. Otherwise, they will lose their motivation.

"Responsibilities should be as clear as possible, but what is really very important is that both key people and lower-level people know well what they are supposed to do for the company and why. If they know these objectives, and the reasons for them, you can solve most problems.

"Italtel's top management understands very well what our key programs are. We have a management-by-objectives structure in which more than half of our three hundred executives have an important part of their salary based upon incentives which are related to reaching certain objectives. So they know our plans very well. But all people should know this, and we try really to communicate to all our people what the company is trying to do. For example, every two months a company newspaper is sent to all of our workers' homes. Through this we are continuously telling our people our financial results, our objectives, everything. All our people are aware of what is happening. They even receive a summary of our five-year plan.

"This is not a common practice in European countries. Some managers are stupid enough to believe that information is equal to power, and they don't exchange it, but keep it to themselves. On the contrary, I believe that as long as people are informed and involved, they can work better. So far as I know, Italtel is the only large Italian company which provides and explains the five-year plan to the unions—not only to our employees, but to the unions.

"This idea came from my experience. While working at General Electric and Honeywell, I began to put plans together, to explain them to my colleagues. I saw that they became much more aware and much more motivated. I did this later in Olivetti as well. I had observed this need also in myself, during my early career; I remember feeling quite frustrated whenever I was not informed about what really was happening in the company, even when I was at the middle management level. So since you rely more on people than on organization, you should motivate the people, and the first way to motivate them is to let them know what you are trying to do.

"Whenever I look for good people, obviously I look for professionalism, the person who is smart, who is flexible, who has the capability to motivate and to communicate. Communication in management is more and more important, because in this changing world either you are capable of interrelating with that world or you are killed.

"Much of my job is communicating, and the message must be conveyed through our management. Because of changes I have made, perhaps 160 of our 300 executives are new, half having been hired from the outside. While the fact that the company is being renewed in this way is a positive factor, it also creates problems. And communications must be based on reality. Sometimes I get complaints from people to the effect that what we are saying is different from what they see in the factory or in their own departments. Management must pay attention to this kind of feedback.

"We are in a very competitive business, but for me this has forever been normal, since I grew up in the computer business, which has always been very competitive. The first thing I look for is the competitiveness of a company's technology. You can also look to see whether your company is efficient, at least as efficient or more efficient than other companies operating in the same market. To me this is the most natural way to deal with a problem—simply first of all to ask whether others are doing better than what we did, or how we compare with the others. This was not the way Italtel people thought when I arrived, since they had been dealing with the same product for many years. And they were not accustomed to the informal use of organization.

"Getting our people to understand the nature of competition and to trust the organization is essential. We have a one-week basic training program for all blue-collar workers, to tell them what is happening in the company, why electronics is needed, what telecommunications in the world are like today. This is very important, particularly in view of the reduction of about 10,000 people, most of whom were blue-collar or low-level white collar workers. So when the people look around and see that one person out of every three has left the company, obviously they have a big concern for themselves. But we must explain that if we cannot stay competitive, we would have jobs for no one. The employment level would be zero.

"I believe that we have partially succeeded in this, for recently we commissioned some research by a noted sociology professor at the University of Bocconi. We asked him to make a study to see what the 10,000 people who left the company are thinking about, what they are doing, whether they have a job. Of course, we fired no one, but we strongly motivated them to leave.

"Commissioning this study was a risky thing to do, because

we had no control over the outcome of the research. The results show that there are few bad feelings, and around 60 or 65 percent of the people understood that Italtel had to reduce its staff because of technological change.

"It is important to get as much participation as I can from all the people and to communicate as much as I can throughout the company. Whenever I can, I visit our executive course. When I cannot, my general manager or other top management attends.

"I like to make sure that people know their responsibilities. I contact directly those who report to my general manager to ask them certain details or at times to give them some direction, or I call someone to visit with me, or we can have a meeting. I believe it is very important to have as many informal contacts as you can. But in the meantime, one should be careful not to reduce the responsibility of those who have it. I believe that my general manager or the general manager of one of our subsidiaries, for example, should be responsible for giving direction and control over its own operations, and therefore I do not change any decision which they have made, because this would be wrong. Whenever I talk with employees, I never make decisions. I say, for example, you should talk with Mr. Randi, the general manager, about this, and he should decide. This same applies to other people referring to other managers. Sometimes he sends people to talk with me. I believe in dealing this way; it is a matter of personality and also of being smart.

Bellisario's Management Style

"We have a very good team of top management, and we work very well together. I may meet, together with a man who reports to my general manager, to talk with an official of another company who wants to know more about Italtel. Such an activity has nothing to do with who reports to whom. While my general manager is taking care of one thing, I'm taking care of another thing, and we keep each other informed."

Marisa Bellisario runs Italtel much as she would a private company.

"There is no difference. We have a Board of Directors, and the only difference is that the Board's appointments are made by our holding company and by IRI, the public entity responsible for all state-owned firms. But the relationship with the Board is exactly the same. In many instances its members are executives of our holding company or of IRI, and there are external executives as well. Being part of a big entity like IRI, we have a certain number of procedures to be followed, but we have flexibility in making normal operational kinds of decisions.

"The character of an organization depends upon the personality of the CEO. Italtel today is very action-oriented, as I am. There are a few exceptions regarding our Board's power of decision. For example, if we wanted to acquire a company, in this case it would not be enough to have approval just from the Board of Directors. We would need also to get a special approval from IRI, and IRI would need to advise the Minister, and so on. This could take some time, but it is up to me to make sure it works. In normal activities we operate really like a private company, at least I operate that way. We submit our long-range plans to the Board of Directors, and in this case we need to submit them also to Stet, our holding company, and to IRI. But this is not so much different from big corporations where there is an additional corporate level that must receive and approve plans.

"I said earlier that people are more important than organization, and smart people are very important. It is really the most frustrating thing to have to deal with boring and stupid people. As long as you can operate with smart people and with efficient people—with people who have a sense of humor—even if things are difficult, you can deal with almost any problem. I need a counterpart—someone who will react and counterreact—and I like to have smart people around. I know some managers who don't like to have people who are too smart, but I really like the smart people. They may require some of your time, but they will never be boring. I believe that stupid people are something that no company can afford, for they simply cannot contribute. So therefore I try first of all to extend myself to make sure that I am not misjudging someone, for I can also make a mistake. But if I am not, stupid people do not stay with me long—either they change their job or we ask them to go away. I am too busy to work with such people.

"My schedule changes very fast day by day, period by period. I try to be systematic, but that is difficult, for I cannot remember every little thing. Therefore, one habit which I have is to do the little things very quickly. For example, if someone calls to ask for information, I get it right away. If a customer calls with a complaint, I do what I should do right then, for otherwise I risk forgetting it. I am action-oriented. In some ways by reacting rapidly, I create time, making me appear more efficient than I really am. Yet half the reason that I do this is that I know if I don't do things right away, I may forget them.

"But I especially try to remember things that are important to other people. I ask my secretary, for example, to remind me if there is some specific objective or specific thing which should happen in a technical program so that I can check out what has happened. If the schedule has been met, I call the person with a compliment. It is important to good technical people that their managers focus on and praise good technical results.

"There is not so much difference between technical people and other people, but the best technical people are perhaps more sensitive to their specific job, more motivated by the technical results of their specific job. If they are good, they are in love with their job. One of my top technical men, one who really loves his work, talks about his product as he would speak about a beautiful girl or even a lover. The relationship between good technical people and their work is generally quite an emotional one, and I like this.

"I also think that work should be fun. Very often I make bets with my people. If, for example, someone is responsible for a very complex project, that we must install and put it into service at a particular time, I will say, 'By November, if it works, I will pay for dinner; otherwise you will pay.' One of my people has recently bet with me that by the end of June a certain number of new systems will have been produced, and produced within budget. His is a very tough budget, and if he produces the specified quantity within that budget, I will pay; otherwise he will. Up to now I have always had to pay for the dinners; the projects have all been on schedule. I also like my colleagues to share in this fun, so I encourage a technical manager to make a bet with the marketing manager; if the technical manager makes his schedule within budget, then the marketing man has to pay. And all of these bets are on my calendar.

"Like other executives, I have a very complicated schedule, in the same day perhaps eight important meetings or appointments. Quite frequently I am late, simply because I commit to doing too many things, and there are always the telephone calls. I delegate to my secretaries in Milan and in Rome the job of watching my schedule. Someday we will have electronic calendars, but for now I count heavily on my secretaries; we review the schedule to see whether the things have happened which were supposed to have happened.

"I am very busy, and I confess that I certainly am impatient. Sometimes I become impatient if people do not understand quickly enough. Sometimes I become impatient with my secretary for no real reason, but I try later to tell her I am sorry. Sometimes my personality makes me a bit too aggressive, and if I ever threaten anyone or say the wrong thing, I try to call back and say, 'Well, I am sorry for what I said yesterday.' But people who know me know that if there is some little misunderstanding, in ten minutes I will have forgotten about it.

"A sense of humor also helps, and many of the best technical people have this. Some of us recently had dinner together and were joking about a meeting we just had and a number of other things. Sometimes they joke about the fact that I am a lady CEO. Yesterday they joked about the fact that one of the persons recommended to us as a consultant was also a lady. 'Not *another* lady!' Just a little joke. They also joke about my reputation for being impatient for results. Whenever I say, 'You can take your time,' they smile; they say, 'Well, she means tonight!'

"I have tried to decentralize the organization. I believe that I delegate, but many people tend to believe that I do not delegate as much as I think I do, for in some ways I stay very close to many problems. I try never to take decisions with people who do not report directly to me, but sometimes people feel I am giving them direction. When I am in the office, I try to see each person who reports to me at least two or three times a week, and when I am out, I am in constant touch by telephone."

Marisa Bellisario is out of the office considerably these days. In addition to accelerating internal research and development activities, she has actively been pursuing partners to expand Italtel's communications technology with companies in Italy, France, Germany, Britain, and the United States. She is also in great demand as a speaker and issues bold challenges to her fellow high-tech executives. As chairperson of an international conference held by American Management Association's Management Centre Europe with the cooperation of *The Economist,* she said:

"In this scenario of profound change, the very concept of Europe is at stake: have we to work toward a splendid future or continue to talk about the marvelous past? Will Europe be diluted into a larger economic agglomeration, whose center will lie elsewhere? Will European companies be at the wrong end of the stick when they make agreements with companies of the rest of the industrialized world? Today the rationale underlying most corporate alliances or joint ventures between European companies is to barter the European market in exchange for American or Japanese technology. . . . It has become apparent to European governments and to bureaucrats in Brussels that Europe cannot go on lavishing its money on cows while denying resources to computers. It has also become evident that, if redundant workers in antiquated sectors are not pensioned off, the whole continent risks being pensioned off by history."

Marisa Bellisario has been referred to as the "manager in jeans" because of her informal and youthful style. But another nickname is "Italy's Iron Lady." Neither sobriquet quite captures her unique blend of enthusiasm, energy, and tough-mindedness. She says of her management team, "We have a good professional relationship and a friendship, too."

At times of little victories, when one of her technical managers has won a bet, when a project has been achieved on time and within budget, she celebrates with a little *spumante* party in her office, or with a special dinner.

"I like to amuse myself, and perhaps I amuse others as well. I like to have nice relationships with people, as it is much more easy to work with people who are not only colleagues but friends.

"And I believe in taking risks. I never recommend to young people that they plan their careers. I never planned mine. When the objective is to run a company successfully or to make a turnaround or to put into production a certain product on time, then if I am successful, the next step of my career will follow."

J. Willard Marriott, Jr.

Chairman of the Board and President
Marriott Corporation

*H*e's the hands-on CEO of the nation's most aggressive and innovative hotel empire and its third largest restaurant business. He travels 200,000 miles a year to visit Marriott hotels and restaurants—and takes pride in being able to tell almost immediately whether one is being well managed. He attributes this ability to what he calls an essential factor in Marriott's success: Knowing the business. Says he, "I've been hanging around restaurants ever since I was old enough to walk and talk." He believes in strictly controlled procedures for every part of the business—for example, there are 66 prescribed steps for making up a room. An open, informal man, he says he is basically action-oriented and optimistic.

He is also a man in a hurry—with plans to commit $3 billion to develop four new major markets: luxury hotels; moderate-priced Courtyard hotels; time-sharing condominiums; and "lifecare" communities for older people. The company has already invested more than $4 billion in hotel development since 1970—and its earnings have grown at a compound annual rate of almost 25 percent since 1980. In 1955, Marriott had just one hotel.

Career Information:

1956   Joined Marriott and took over the company's fledgling hotel business

1959   Elected vice president of Hot Shoppes, Inc.

1964   Elected executive vice president and member of the board of directors

1964   Became president of Marriott-Hot Shoppes, Inc.

1972   Became chief executive officer of Marriott Corporation

1985   Elected chairman of the board

Other Affiliations (partial list):

- Director, United States Chamber of Commerce
- Director, Polynesian Cultural Center
- Director, Business-Industry Political Action Committee
- Chairman, Citizen's Choice
- Member, national executive board of the Boy Scouts of America
- Member, The Conference Board
- Member, United States Trade Representative Services Policy Advisory Committee
- Member, President's Council for International Youth Exchange

Educational Information:

- University of Utah, Banking and Finance, 1954

Personal Information:

- Born 1932, Washington, D.C.
- Spent 18 months as ship's service supply officer on aircraft carrier USS Randolph
- Married, has four children

J. Willard Marriott, Jr.

"*O*ur competitive edge? Number one, we know the business, and we are committed to it. Our family has been in the food business for 58 years; we have been in the lodging business for 30 years. It is the only business we know. We don't claim to be in the gambling business or even the real estate business as such. However, we have developed some expertise in designing and building hotels at a reasonable cost. We are not really interested in the real estate play; we are in real estate to make money through managing and running hotels and restaurants. As such, I think we understand the dynamics of the business. We also understand the importance of taking care of people who work for us. We understand the importance of a good work environment and fair treatment of our people, and we believe that if we do a good job of motivating our people, then they in turn will treat our customers well. If we treat our customers well, they will come back. It all boils down to service.

"When have I felt most stretched in my career? Always. I have been in this business for almost 30 years, president of it since I was 32. I've been very stretched and still am. We have a lot going on, and we've been growing 20 percent a year for 20 years. The next 20 percent gets harder. So I'm pretty stretched out."

Bill Marriott, Jr. began his career as a young boy in his father's restaurants, where he learned the importance of service. Later, as a young man just out of the Navy, he dramatically demonstrated that Marriott could succeed in hotels, laying a foundation to expand the hotel business to equal all of the company's other business. Then as President, through a combination of shrewd financing and a total commitment to service, he transformed this once small family business into one of the most successful growth companies in the service sector, with revenues exceeding $4 billion. Still in his early fifties, Bill has the capacity and the commitment to make the company even more preeminent than it is today, employing his personal style of intensive hands-on management to a business he understands from top to bottom.

For the past five years, Marriott's earnings have grown at a compounded annual rate of almost 25 percent, despite the highly competitive nature of the food and lodging business.

"Every business is becoming more and more competitive. One of the main reasons that this is true in the hotel business was the tax bill of 1981, which not only gave the investment tax credit but speeded up depreciation, so that a lot of buildings were built for tax shelter purposes, instead of for good economics. Today there is much more market segmentation and more sophistication, with better hotels being built today than ever before, including many very expensive hotels. There is the peak of the pyramid with $200-a-day rooms, all the way down to budget hotels at $20 a day. You've got all-suite hotels, long-stay hotels; you've got mega-convention hotels, airport hotels, and suburban hotels; you've got the old Ma and Pa hotels, budget motels, inner-city commercial hotels—of which not very many are being built—as well as a variety of resort hotels—resort convention hotels, small resort hotels, and big resort hotels. A lot of convention business is now going to resorts, which was somewhat true in the past, but not nearly to the extent that it is now."

Marriott's Market Niches

The Marriott organization carefully identifies and tests niches in the lodging market. In 1984 it entered the large, moderate-priced segment with its Courtyard units, first probing the market with five test units in Georgia and later announcing plans to develop this format into a national chain of over 50,000 rooms by the early 1990's.

"We are also looking at the life-care business. We have been serving hospitals through our food service management

J. WILLARD MARRIOTT, JR.

division for over 30 years, and we are beginning to build a life-care unit, providing nursing facilities as well as lodging and food."

Although the Marriott Corporation is noted for its hotel management capability and its aggressive expansion program—more than $4 billion has been invested in hotel development since 1970 —about half its earnings come from food service and related businesses. With its Hot Shoppe, Roy Rogers, Host, and Big Boy chains, Marriott is the nation's third largest restaurateur. In addition to size, Marriott delivers quality; its hotels have received more top awards from Mobil and the American Automobile Association than any other chain. It is also the world leader in airline catering, through which it serves meals on over 150 airlines.

"Airline catering is a very competitive business. The airlines tend to be price buyers—they want a lot for their money, and they're tough. My father started that business in 1937, catering airlines out of Washington—providing meals for DC-3's. In the early years, all the caterers began just like my dad did. He had a restaurant at an airport, and the airlines would come to him and say, 'We've got to have 30 box lunches, fix them.' Later they'd get up to 300 box lunches and then 500 box lunches, and then a little kitchen would be built on the back of the restaurant just to cater the airlines. When the jets started coming in, this got to be a really big business, and a lot of these small entrepreneurs had to make a decision as to whether or not they were going to stay in it and build a big kitchen just to cater the airlines or whether they were going to get out. At that point we started moving into many different markets. We are now at 70 airports. When I started out in the business, we were at only six.

"Our food business soon expanded tremendously into other areas as well, such as the terminal restaurants. We are now the largest feeder in the U.S. at airport terminals. That's a very different business—in addition to dealing with the people whom you are serving, you also deal with the airport management authorities, who are your landlords and who have a lot to say about the kinds of restaurants they want, prices, service, numbers of seats, what space you can have, and so on.

"Then there is the turnpike business, which is still different, because a traveler can leave a turnpike at any exit and grab a sandwich; but when you are at an airport, you don't have as much choice. Yet there is one similarity—with the turnpike business you have to negotiate with the turnpike authorities and keep them happy. In that kind of business, you need to sign up for a 10- or 15-year contract, and you try to work it out so that your property depreciates over that period of time. You try to zero out at the end of the contract, so that if you have to move out, you have no investment. There are a lot of niches in the restaurant business, and you really have to understand what you are doing.

"I have been in the restaurant business all of my life. Actually, I have been hanging around restaurants ever since I was old enough to walk and talk. I used to follow my father around when I was seven, eight, nine, ten years old, and I think all of this was invaluable. Today I can walk into a hotel or a restaurant and within a few minutes know pretty well whether or not it is being well managed and well run, because I know what to look for, what's good and what's bad. It is second nature to me, like riding a bicycle, and it is just part of the Marriott culture.

"What do I look for? I look to see how the service is going, that's the most obvious thing. You can tell by walking through the dining room whether people have food on their plates or whether they are just sitting there waiting to have their water glass filled or are waiting for the check or to have their orders taken; if so, they have a look of concern about them, and they are looking around the room trying to find the waiter or waitress. You can tell whether the hostess is on the ball—whether she is just standing at the door holding menus, or whether she is out working the floor. The quality of service is a thing that you can pick up on right away.

"The next thing to do is to go into the kitchen and see whether the food is being prepared the way it should be; whether the waiters and waitresses are picking the food up from the kitchen as fast as they should, whether a lot of orders are backed up, or if the waitresses are just standing around waiting for their orders."

Entering the Hotel Business

By the mid-50s, the Marriott Corporation had launched its first hotel, and Bill, Jr., who by then knew every facet of his father's restaurant business, volunteered for a new challenge. He had grown up in the Hot Shoppe restaurant chain, working at every level, and had returned for still another year following a two-year hitch in the Navy.

"We had one hotel, and since no one in the company seemed to want to manage it, I asked my father if he'd let me try to manage that one hotel. That was in 1956. Later we built a second one, and our hotel business went on from there. I was put in charge of the hotel division in 1957.

"Whenever you get into a new job, the first thing you have to do is to find out where the problems are. When our first hotel opened—it was the Twin Bridges Hotel in Virginia, very near Washington, D.C.—we didn't have any real base of business. In the summer we did great, but when winter came, there was no business at all. So I asked, 'What are we going to do to get winter business?' The only answer seemed to be to add convention facilities and start doing group business, but we were too far from downtown, and back in those days people never even considered having a meeting or convention anywhere except in downtown Washington. So I went to Richmond and visited the Virginia state associations, which were always looking for different places to meet in Virginia. There were few ballrooms or meeting rooms in Virginia at that time —just a few hotels in Roanoke and Richmond, Virginia Beach, Norfolk and Williamsburg. The associations wanted to come to northern Virginia, because they could then visit Washington. So we made a big dent with the Virginia associations, and that was really our first breakthrough in the convention market.

"You have to go out for the business, and we have always taken the position, with the exception of a few selected resort hotels, that we wanted all three legs of the hotel business stool: the commercial traveler, the convention business, and the pleasure business. So we built swimming pools, health clubs, game rooms. Now almost every hotel has movies in its rooms, but we were one of the first to have them. We put in a lot of landscaping, provided free parking, and made certain that our places were easy to get to, safe, and secure. This helped with the pleasure business. We put in enough meeting rooms and ballrooms to do convention business; then we'd do enough development and promotion to get the transient commercial travelers.

"Of course there are places like Palm Springs where there is no commercial business, all pleasure and conventions; but you have to have at least two of those three legs of the stool at every hotel, or you can't be very successful. Resort hotels today, unless they are very, very small, simply have to do group meeting business.

"Before I took over the hotel business, I had really learned the restaurant side by having worked every station in restaurants. Although I had held some management positions, I had never been the general manager of a restaurant. Even so, I had learned something about management by spending some time on the staff. I had worked on service procedures, in the test kitchen, and in numerous other staff functions. In this way I learned how the staff worked and how it interrelated with the restaurants. However, my first real line job was as manager of our first hotel."

Over the years, there were many occasions when Bill Marriott, Jr. and his late father had different points of view. This was particularly true in the case of the hotel business.

"Dad was a lot more conservative than I, as he had gone through two depressions, one in 1918 and one in 1929, and hence was very loath to borrow money. He was very concerned about the risk involved in building hotels, since every hotel he knew had gone broke in the 1930's. And while he liked the restaurant business in the early days, he recognized that it had become complex, very competitive, and very difficult to run. It was a real challenge to put out an outstanding product in restaurants such as those he had built, which had by then 250 different items on the menu. Putting all of that out for lunch and dinner every day was a real chore. The only way it could be done right was with a tremendous amount of supervision, particularly supervision on his part, including a lot of hard work and tough hours."

Yet despite the increasing demands of the restaurant side of the business and the risks he saw in the hotels, Bill Marriott, Sr. had the courage to enter the hotel business.

"Our first hotel, the Twin Bridges, became tremendously successful. It continued to be our most successful hotel for the first ten years we were in the hotel business simply because of its unique location—three minutes from the airport, two minutes from the Pentagon, five minutes from downtown Washington and on Interstate 95. It had good highway visibility. And once we put in convention facilities, it had everything."

Maintaining a Successful Operation

Marriott ran the company's hotel division for eight years, from 1956 to 1964, before moving up to Executive Vice President and then President of the Marriott Corporation. This hands-on experience and on-the-scene involvement in every aspect of hotel operations—coupled with his long apprenticeship in Marriott restaurants —have solidified his views on what makes an enterprise successful.

"I don't think anyone can run any business today unless he really understands it in detail. That has been shown in the studies of why many mergers don't work—when companies buy other companies that they are not familiar with and when executives with no experience in the acquired businesses try to run them. They don't know *how* to run them, because they don't understand the business—they don't understand what makes it work.

"You also need to know your competition. At Marriott we emphasize it, talk about it a lot, and have our people shop the competition, to see what they are doing differently—what they are doing that we're not doing. I stay at competitive hotels three or four times a year to learn about the new things they are doing, plus see what they could do better and to think about things that we could do better.

"When my father founded the company, he spent at least half of his time out of the office and in operations. I try to do the same thing.

"How do my managers handle it when I bounce in on them and talk with their chambermaids and chefs? Well, I don't imagine it's very comfortable for them, but they know it is going to happen, so they just have to deal with the inevitable. When I visit a unit, I go into every area: kitchens, dining rooms, employee locker rooms, laundry, housekeeping, guest rooms, grounds, service areas. I just walk the whole hotel and shake hands and talk with the people.

"I usually have a meeting with the management, the eight or ten top people, to find out how they are doing, what they think they can do better and how they can do it. I want to know how business is going and want them to know what we are doing in headquarters that helps them and what we are doing that offends them, gets them upset. I try to link up the communications between the home office and the field to learn what their problems are. The personal insight I get in this way helps me learn what's going on in the business and what has to happen to keep us successful.

"I have also studied management. When I was first promoted to Executive Vice President, I enrolled in an American Management Association Presidents Course. When I came back, I had Keith Louden, one of AMA's speakers, come down to put on a similar course for all our senior management. We talked about standards of performance and performance appraisals.

"Our company does a lot with performance appraisals and management by objectives. All of our senior managers have to submit their objectives to me every year, and we compensate them on whether or not they have achieved those objectives. For every manager at any level in the company, there are bonus points based on meeting their objectives or not meeting their objectives. They must meet financial objectives as well as individual goals. Twice a year, we check up to see how they are doing.

"I am a believer in training. We spend between 20 and 30 million dollars a year on training. We have a very detailed and defined system for every job to be done."

For example, Marriott's hotels have a checklist of 66 steps to make sure that a room is made up in precisely the right way.

"If each maid made up her room differently, you would just have a hodgepodge. Consistency in the service business, particularly in the food and lodging business, is vital, and training is essential to achieve this consistency.

"In management training we have a general course on how to manage, how to motivate, how to teach, how to plan. We also teach a little about finance and accounting, through much the same kind of classes that are given by AMA.

"We have a permanent training staff and offer many food courses which teach our people how to cook and how to follow our recipes. There is one school in California and one here in Maryland. Then for all new employees, we have a major orientation course, given once a month. Every manager who comes to work here spends a full week going through personnel policies, management philosophy, something of the company's heritage and values, and basic issues of management. I usually give these new people a short speech at the opening sessions. This orientation is important, for our people must understand our culture and what we expect from them."

It has been said that Bill Marriott, Sr. would read every customer complaint.

"Well, I'm not sure. Perhaps he did at one time, but now we get over a thousand letters a day, plus cards and forms which we leave in rooms. These are analyzed and tabulated, and I respond to the ones which report the most serious problems and those which convey the nicest compliments. The manager in each hotel sees these, but the people at headquarters see them as well. These are summarized by computer, for every single hotel, and whenever I visit a hotel I take these reports with me and discuss them. If the rooms are not as clean as they should be, if the attitude at the front desk or service is not what our guests think it should be, then this is something that we all work on. Our senior executives visit these hotels regularly with the primary purpose of doing what we can to smooth out the system, to make sure we give better guest service. But the emphasis on this all starts right here. All our people know that I take guests' comments very seriously and want these reports followed up. Visiting our hotels is very important to me, so they do it, too.

"Whenever I visit an out-of-town hotel, our people know that I am coming, but in the hotels near our headquarters, they don't know this. Three or four times each week I'll go for dinner and check the kitchen and the restaurants. During each visit, I give feedback to the manager. If the results are good, I tell him; and if they are bad, I tell him this also.

"At times I have been pretty shook up, but I have never released a manager right on the spot. I make a few notes and go back home and later talk with the senior manager who is responsible."

Dealing with People

"I spend a lot of time with our people, not only our line management of hotel and restaurant activities, but headquarters people as well. And today, because our business has become so complex and sophisticated, we have a number of highly technical people and some very creative people on our staffs. Some say that you should be more sensitive when you are dealing with creative people, but I think you have to be sensitive when you deal with anybody. Sensitivity on the part of management to people is very important.

"When I look for someone to take on a major job, the most important thing to me is integrity. I also look for drive—a high energy level and a high level of commitment. Intelligence is extremely important, as is knowledge of the business. Does he or she understand the job? If he or she is a finance person, what has been their specific financial experience? If they are general managers, have they been in operations, how much do they know about operations? What have they learned about our business?

"And of course everyone makes mistakes. The easiest mistake to make is in judging people. When I have made such a mistake, I try to work with the person to get him to see how he can improve and do better. The toughest thing to help a manager correct is people problems. When a manager doesn't know how to get along with people, doesn't know how to lead a team, or tends to go in and bust up all the china, that's a hard problem to fix.

"Another difficult problem occurs when the manager simply doesn't have enough drive. If they are lazy and want to work only six or seven hours a day, you have to try to motivate them, get them turned on about what they are doing, get them excited about the business.

"Perhaps it's because I have such drive and such commitment that I tend to be impatient. But I think I do a fair job of controlling that. For example, when I write a sharp letter, I'll put it in the bottom drawer, then wait for a week before I send it or rip it up. If I am unhappy with somebody, I'll wait. A cooling-off period is probably the most important thing of all. If you get upset, you shouldn't pick up the phone and start ranting and raving and carrying on. Learning not to do this comes with maturity, and it comes with being on the job and learning how to deal with problems.

"I work hard, and I expect the other people around here to keep up. This is a very demanding business, and it just requires a lot of hard work, so if I find a guy who doesn't want to keep up—doesn't want to work hard—and there is no way that I can get him to work hard, then we've got a problem. Maybe he needs another job, and maybe not in this company. People like this usually get the message—they find that they're not comfortable in the culture of the company and its work ethic, and they go do something else.

"Because it's a demanding business, I am always pressed for time. I have my own problems, my own agenda and my own things to do, and I do things the best I can. Studies show that seven minutes is the average time an executive spends on any one particular subject, but sometimes you spend seven hours and sometimes you spend only a minute and a half. While this may average out to seven minutes, there are a lot of different activities, which is what makes it fun. Doing the same thing day in and day out could drive you crazy.

"I have had to learn a lot on this job, particularly from our finance people. Finance today has become far more sophisticated, far more of a science than it used to be. Our chief financial officer for many years was basically a controller. Then we put in a chief financial officer who had the different skills of a modern CFO and hence became involved in improving the profitability of the company, finding ways to improve the return on our equity, and managing the assets of the company better through more in-depth, sophisticated analyses of new financial projects.

"I have also learned a lot in the people area and in the management development area, but the people I've learned the most from are members of my own family and others who are close to us. My wife has always been a good sounding board, and a couple of our directors have been very helpful. I have always been close to my mother, who understands this business very well. There is always a lot of business talk among our family, though not as much now as there used to be. Of course, as my dad and mother grew older, they were not able to stay as close to the business as they once did. But growing up in the business and being around the house was a constant learning experience—family gatherings were always full of all kinds of discussions about how the business should be run and not run, who's doing what, who should be doing what. I have to say that this ruined many a vacation!"

Decision Making

"I really don't have any theories on how decisions are made, but I think that most are made in small pieces. When you make a decision on an acquisition, then that's a big decision. When we decided to acquire Big Boy restaurants, back in 1967, I'd only been in the CEO job for three years, and that was a major decision for us at the time. We've had to make a lot of hard decisions on individual hotels, such as whether to buy the Essex House in New York, for example, in 1968. We had never operated in New York City—they wanted a lot of money for the hotel—so that was a tough one. Acquiring our first resort hotel, Camelback—that same year—was also a big decision. But most decisions are made gradually."

A major factor in the success of Marriott's aggressive hotel expansion program has been its creative use of financial techniques. This development did not occur overnight.

"We began this particular expansion strategy by selling hotels to insurance companies, taking back management contracts. Then we worked through developers, who would come to us with a piece of property, saying that they would construct a building and give us a management contract. Then we asked ourselves why we really needed developers; we could do what they did ourselves. So we went out and bought property, built the buildings ourselves, sold them off and took back management contracts. First we sold them off to insurance companies, and when the insurance companies began running low on money for real estate, we started bank financing. We were never really interested in owning a lot of property, so we obtained financing and then sold the equity off to individual investors. We were not the first to do this. Hilton International started the management contract business back in the 50s, and Hyatt was doing it before we started. But no one I am aware of was doing tax syndications in the hotel business until we started doing it. Since then we have done close to a billion dollars worth, and it has really paid off for us, as it has allowed us to use our money in other ways."

What Marriott refers to as "tax syndications" are limited partnership agreements. These allow hotel properties to be purchased by the partnership, with Marriott Hotels, Inc., a wholly-owned subsidiary of Marriott, responsible for the management of the hotels. This arrangement provides to the limited partner an investment and tax shelter opportunity, and to Marriott, a source of cash. As a result of such aggressive and creative financial strategies, Marriott currently owns only about one-fourth of its hotels. This approach, which makes its business much less capital intensive, has enabled Marriott to expand far faster than other hotel chains.

"We are a very transaction-oriented business. Our Board of Directors is small: my mother and until his death, my father, my brother, myself, and four outside directors. I look for people who are willing to put in the time, people who can bring something to the Board.

"The financial side is very important to us, as we are always involved in buying something or selling something or making deals. We are a very deal-oriented company. At most companies our size, maybe three or four big issues go to the Board each year, but we may have four or five big items at each meeting: buying one hotel, selling another, building a flight kitchen, buying a restaurant chain. There is just lot a going on. So we need people on the Board who understand financial transactions, people who can say, 'I don't think that's a good deal,' or 'I think that's a *great* deal.'

"It would be difficult to put anyone on our Board who really knew anything about the restaurant and hotel business who would not have a conflict of interest. So our family brings the know-how of our own business to the Board, and the outside directors bring their financial expertise."

> The pace of Marriott's transaction-oriented way of doing business is rapid. For example, in 1984 the company sold and financed nearly $1 billion worth of hotels and decided to sell its theme parks, dinner houses, and Mexican restaurants "for a total consideration of more than $310 million."

"Not all of our decisions have been perfect. We've had to sell some companies we bought. For example, after acquiring Farrells, an ice-cream parlor company, we expanded it faster than we should have, not realizing that the demand for ice cream at a sit-down parlor was infrequent. It just never worked very well. We had a guy who thought he knew the ice-cream business, but he delegated it all out and didn't really run it, so we finally had to get rid of it. It was simply a business that we didn't know anything about.

"Farrells is a restaurant which features various concoctions of ice cream; some of the units did well, some of them continue to do well, but many did not. After we sold Farrells, the people who bought it couldn't make it work either, so now we have it back, but with fewer units. We are trying to fix it and make it work the best we can.

"We also bought a security alarm system company, again something we never should have done. In both of these cases, we were like a lot of other companies who don't stick to their knitting and don't know anything about the business they're buying. Still, these didn't kill our company, and we made money on the sales of these businesses.

"We've never really lost a lot of money. We've had a bad hotel every now and then, and perhaps one out of every twenty flight kitchens doesn't work out. But by and large, most of what we have done has worked pretty well.

"You really have to measure what you are doing. Again, you need to understand your business. In the restaurant business, for example, the chief indicator is sales per investment. Annual sales should run one and one-half times the investment. If you invest a million dollars, you should do a million and one-half a year or better, and you should do it fast. If a restaurant does not start out well, it usually is not going to be very good, for when a new restaurant opens, everyone wants to try it. If the customers don't come the first month, you've got a problem.

"Hotels are different. It takes a hotel three years to get up to speed, as you're building your customer base from all over the United States. With restaurants, however, you're usually building your customer base from within a two-mile radius. People drive by it, see it, want to try it. Others will tell them they've been there, and they all go. If they don't, you've got a problem.

"One of the really major transactions we've made in recent years was to go into New York City in a big way. We've been there with the Essex House, which was recently sold to Japan Airlines. But we simply felt that New York City needed a major convention hotel. There hasn't been a new one there for over 20 years.

"New York is the number one convention city in America, the number one visitation city in America. More people come to New York than to any other city, and they come for lots of different reasons, which makes the market even stronger. People come to do business in the financial community, in advertising, in media, and in lots of other businesses. They come for Broadway, they come for shopping, they come for restaurants, and for the arts. Every international visitor wants to visit New York. We weren't planning to sell the Essex House, but simply got a very fine offer from JAL which we decided to take. So now we're concentrating on our new hotel there, the Marriott Marquis. John Portman developed the Times Square site, got the land, and designed the building. He spent about ten years on this. We took over the financing, having put most of the money in, and of course we're managing it."

Some months before the October, 1985 opening date of the New York Marriott Marquis, the *Wall Street Journal* reported that Marriott "has already accepted one million reservations for the new hotel it plans to open in Manhattan." Besides the New York Marquis, Marriott will open four other "mega-convention" hotels around the country within a four-year period and is actively developing high quality hotels in selected cities overseas.

Marriott's Leadership Style

Bill Marriott, Jr. is a man in a hurry. Regarding his management style, he says:

"I guess that I am reasonably participative. Our finance committee, about eight of us, sit around and discuss all the major investments, and each member gives me his views. They're not afraid to give them to me; they're very vocal, they let me know what they think, and that's good. It's not going to do me any good to have them around if they've got opinions which they don't express. I think that your people simply have to tell you what they think. If your people quit talking to you, you've lost your most valuable asset. We look for feedback from every level of the organization. Some of it doesn't filter up here, but all the senior officers in this company, everyone in the line operations and many from the staff, are out in the field a lot, looking for feedback.

"I have a lot of outside activities. My involvement with the Church of the Latter Day Saints of Jesus Christ takes 10 to 20 hours a week. The other major activity is my involvement with the U.S. Chamber of Commerce, an opportunity to try to help business. I am also on the National Executive Committee of the Boy Scouts. My father was active with the National Restaurant Association—at one time he was president of it—and was chairman of two presidential inaugurals, and my mother was a Republican committeewoman. Though I am involved in perhaps 20 outside organizations, most of them do not take an inordinate amount of time. I have not been involved in politics, and I serve on no outside boards. I was on a Florida bank board for about eight years and learned a lot about the banking business and something about other businesses. If I were to join two or three outside boards, I'd be spending a third of my time outside this business. And if I did that, everyone else would want to do it, and no one would be tending the store. There is plenty to do here."

Opportunities in the Industry

"If I were talking to young people about this industry, I'd say that there will continue to be growth—a lot of it. It will continue to be concentrated with the chains, which have the sophisticated marketing, management, and financing capabilities that individuals simply don't have.

"In the future you'll still find individual hotel entrepreneurs who have one unit, but by and large, the majority of the hotels will be built by chains.

"I would say to young people that whatever they decide to do, they simply have to learn the business. One of the biggest problems we have today is young men and women who are in too big a hurry to get to the top without taking the time to learn the business. If they will take that time, they will develop a foundation for learning, a foundation for work, a work ethic, an ability to deal with people, and a willingness to train them and to teach them. This is the foundation for success. I think that young people today have a stronger work ethic than those back in the '60s and early '70s. The Vietnam War was hard on this country and hard on our young people, and I think that young men and women today are more serious about their careers and life. They want to do well. There are a lot of conflicting reports about some of them still wanting to do their own thing. Certainly some want to be entrepreneurs, which is good, but you don't see as many going up into log cabins and eating berries as you used to see.

"The hotel and restaurant businesses offer great career opportunities. But they require a lot of sacrifices that many people just don't want to make. There is considerable night work, weekend work, and travel—but it pays well. It doesn't pay well starting out, but down the road it does. It's an interesting and challenging business, one with many different facets.

"A general manager of a big hotel in a major city, for example, the general manager of our Times Square hotel, has a real management job. He has 2,000 employees and all kinds of things going on. He's got a show to put on every day. He can't close on the weekends or Christmas. He's open 365 days each year and has perhaps 10,000 contacts a day between his people and his guests. There are lots of opportunities to do a good job, lots of opportunities *not* to do a good job. So he has got to be sure his people are well trained and highly motivated. . . . It is a fascinating business, a good business, a tough business. It's hard work.

"It's also a good career for women. Four women are general managers of Marriott hotels, and they are all doing well; they are responsive, and they enjoy it. There are even more women managers in the restaurant business than on the hotel side.

"In choosing a job, young people should look very hard at the industry they are going into to make sure that it is the industry they want to be involved in, one where there is growth and potential and opportunity to get ahead. Once they are at work, it is important to remember in dealing with one's boss that he *is* the boss. So try to do what he wants you to do. If you disagree with him, you really ought to let him know, but do so in a way that doesn't offend him. If you decide that you are in the right industry but you are not getting ahead, there can be only one of two reasons: either no one has noticed you or you are not capable. If nobody's noticed you, then you've got to figure out something to do about that—and there are lots of ways to get visibility. If you're not capable, then you need to improve your skills or to decide whether the reason is because you don't like what you're doing. Some people believe in career planning and some believe that you should just get out there and work your tail off until you get recognized. I believe that you should do some of both.

"There is a lot of challenge in *this* business, almost more than I can handle right here. We are looking hard at the future, trying new things, discarding things that don't work if they really can't be fixed. Over the past five years we've had the fastest growing hotel business in America, and remember, hotels represent only 50 percent of our business. As I say, we are a highly transaction-oriented, deal-oriented company. We are willing to move, to do whatever makes good business sense, and we plan to continue to do so."

James M. Guinan

Chairman and Chief Executive Officer
Caldor

W hen he was 10 years old, he worked in a Brooklyn candy store, and his first task was cleaning out the cellar. The owner said he'd done the best job anyone had done. Now he heads up a $1.5 billion mass merchandising operation—but he says that what motivates him most is no different from what it was then: to do a good job.

He began his career as a writer and still uses his writing skills to clarify his thoughts before conveying them to his people. One of his greatest strengths is the ability to suggest creative solutions even in areas in which he is not expert—such as computerization.

He took charge at the Caldor division of Associated Dry Goods when the store chain "seemed to be doing many things wrong." He applied his signature approach with which he had successfully turned other troubled operations around: Focus on building a winning team. His model was Vince Lombardi, famed Green Bay Packers football coach, whom he says was "a superb management person."

Now Caldor is expanding strongly, with 110 stores ranging from New Hampshire to Virginia. He has achieved this by pushing for results rather than demanding rigid conformity to procedures and methods. "We run a very relaxed place, we don't wear coats, the President and I play platform tennis with a rotating group of management—it all goes back to no ego, no pomp, no circumstance."

Career Information:

1958   Started retailing career with Bamberger's stores, in various personnel and operations posts

1966   Joined Boston Milwaukee division of Federated Department Stores

1977   Became president of Boston Milwaukee division

1979   Became president of Gold Circle, Federated's northern mass merchandising division

1982   Became chairman and CEO of Gold Circle

1984   Became president of Bloomingdale's, Federated's largest division

1984   Became CEO of Caldor division of Associated Dry Goods

Other Affiliations:

- Vice chairman, Retail Council of New York
- Member, Executive Committee of Board, National Society to Prevent Blindness

Educational Information:

- Brooklyn College (N.Y.), B.S., Psychology

Personal Information:

- Born April 1, 1932, Long Island, N.Y.
- Married, has three children
- Outside interests are tennis, sailing, and history

James M. Guinan

"*I* tend to be a verbal person. Coming from journalism, through speech writing, I learned to conceptualize what I wanted to write. I still think as a writer does, and when I see something on the written page, I can understand it better. Even though working in retail is much different from the journalistic discipline (gathering the who, what, where, when, why and how), to this day if I want to have a 'watershed' communication with one or all of my vice presidents, I tend to write down the salient points. Although I am still essentially a writer, my people don't see what I've written. I talk to them, but by having written the key points first I know I'm going to cover them. 'How do I want to say it? This is going to be sensitive to these people, so I must say it in a careful way.' I write it down, then I rehearse it in my mind.

"When you're in the retailing business, the customer tells you loud and clear what you're doing wrong. You have to respond to lots of isolated incidents, and that's where much of your time goes. At every level retail managers are kept hopping by the customer. In most other industries management is once removed from this pressure; people are not coming right at you. In contrast, all retailers have one experience in common: you're at a cocktail party, and a woman says, 'Oh, you're the President of Boston Store? You're the President of Bloomingdale's? Let me tell you about my china.' It's never the good news, always the bad news. If you mind hearing this sort of thing, then you're in the wrong business."

James Guinan is a man who knows retailing. Introduced to it at Bamberger's, where he spent eight years, he later became President of Federated's Boston Store division, President and then CEO of Gold Circle and briefly President of Bloomingdale's before joining Caldor as CEO in 1984.

"In a few words, Caldor is a high-quality mass merchandiser. We don't sell dinner jackets or cocktail dresses, since we're not Lord & Taylor; we're Caldor. But we do sell the same high quality. If you buy a $110 Wilson tennis racket from us, we should be able to persuade you to buy a $90 brand-name warm-up suit. We're trying to get into common-sense fashion soft goods. Caldor never really was a K-Mart or even a Gold Circle; it caters to a distinctly more upscale customer, in terms of both income and education.

"Our products cover a wide range. For example, you can probably buy a junior tennis racket for around $30. Our strength over the years is that whatever we have in stock tends to be good for the price, and if it breaks, we will take it back. We don't want them back. A good gut tennis racket at today's prices may be down to $50 or $60, a real tennis racket which won't break or warp too quickly. Then if you become a better tennis player, you'll want to go for a $100 racket.

"We'll sell you a Canon AE-1 at as a low a price as you'll find anywhere, telephoto lenses, accessories, and the whole works for home developing, all at a very good price."

To keep the focus on the satisfied customer—tens of thousands of them—a mass merchandiser must develop a strong management team and a comprehensive, responsive information system.

Priorities in Mass Merchandising

"We have built a management team as good as any around. There are some heavy hitters here, a team which not only can run the present Caldor but is truly expandable. And we're concentrating on managing information. Whatever you do manually tends to get you into diseconomies of scale, which was beginning to happen before I arrived. If a buyer has to keep track of socks in 106 stores, he has to be able to call the item up

JAMES M. GUINAN

on the tube. We've spent over $15 million this year on computerization and we'll spend that much again next year. Distribution is a second major priority. We are retrofitting a $23 million distribution center that had only opened in July of 1984 but which we've already outgrown. We're making it a modern high-speed distribution system. We have decided to handle big bulk items—storage sheds, canoes and other items that can't be handled on conveyor lines—in a new bulk facility by next year. Soon after that, we'll be opening a $35 million distribution center. We're putting an enormous amount of money into distribution and computerization.

"When I arrived here, I found that expense management was highly centralized. No one but the president and the executive vice president knew what the real budgets were. Even the senior vice president of stores, responsible for a $110 million budget, never saw the real budgets. There was no real analysis of expenses. In my view, a major policy decision has to do with the way you let people spend or not spend money.

"Because of the pace of this business, unless you want to die early—and I don't—you have to employ hands-off management. This means that you need some fairly formal indicators: a daily sales report by store and a weekly sales report by store and type of merchandise. You ask, 'Why has knock-down furniture stopped selling?' 'Are we sure we have enough goods?' If I see an area like distribution starting to run awry, either much too low or much too high, then I'll get into the detail. In every functional area there are a number of other indicators. Right now there are 16 stores in some state of construction, 47 potential sites for other stores, so I have a monthly real estate meeting with the proper heads, a very bang-bang meeting: 'How's it going?' 'This one's falling two weeks behind, what can we do about it?' I don't get into the minutiae, but I do what I call 'reality tests.' For example, I flew out to some Philadelphia stores the other day, compared what I saw to what I had been told a few days before through a computer printout. In the area of distribution, you have expense on one side, but you also want qualitative evaluations. If you phone today for a truck reservation, when will you get that truck unloaded? How many trucks are in the yard? In receiving operations, how off-standard are you? We have a 72-hour standard; if gloves arrived 3 days ago, they should be moving on the selling floor now. In finance, how backed up are we on the processing of paper? I get periodic reports on expense and service quality, and I spend time on the highs and lows of that when necessary.

"We have 109 stores now open, 13 legally committed to open next year—not counting acquisitions, and a couple of those are cooking along too. We haven't closed any stores since I've been at Caldor, but there are obviously a couple of candidates for that, and we have to avoid any emotional vesting. We break our profit performance by store into two bites: first, we look at it as a four-wall business—that is, looking at the store as though it were an entity by itself, without apportioned overhead; if the store can't cover its own expenses, then closing it would be a net positive, especially if it starts losing a quarter million or more annually. Our stores tend to be relatively high volume operations, the average store running at $13 million per year. Good stores make a million and the real bad ones lose, maybe, $300,000 or $400,000. If we can't turn these around, they'll be closed.

"But we simply have to delegate budgeting and expense control. We give our managers an efficiency factor, an inflator factor, dollars and people, then we look hard at the expense impact of capital projects. For example, we say, 'You told us that if we gave you electronic markdown capability, you could save this specific amount of money! We block that in and watch it. Each store manager gets a P & L statement each month.

"We now go directly to foreign markets to buy. Previously, Caldor bought only through domestic importers, which meant that someone else in this country was going to foreign markets, bringing back products, pocketing perhaps 13 percent, and then selling them to Caldor. This fall we are receiving $80 million worth of direct imports into stock. Last fall this was zero. Thirteen points of gross margin 'ain't chopped chicken liver,' and it enables us to spread the money between new programs, greater value for the customer, and profit."

Building a Team

Guinan's key focus in keeping Caldor—or any other organization—at a keen competitive edge is on team building and team operation.

"The first thing I do when I get into any new job is to try to get a winning team together. When I went to Wisconsin to join Federated, it was at the very height of the Vince Lombardi-Green Bay Packer glory years. I was privileged—a word I don't use very often—to hear Vince speak several times. He was not just a football coach, but a superb management person, and that hit me from the very first time I heard him. The Packers never were a collection of superstars. Bart Starr was a 13th-round draft choice, Jimmy Taylor couldn't cut worth a damn, and Paul Hornung spent more time in motels than on the playing field. What Lombardi understood was the team. It was the best *team* ever put together, and when Lombardi left, the Packers fell from grace very fast without superstars. Starr couldn't throw downfield worth a damn. Taylor, the fifth all-time runner, was fast in the open field—but what makes a superior halfback is quickness, making that little cut around the blocking tackle, and he couldn't do that worth a damn. He was like a diesel once he got going, so Lombardi's whole running strategy was to find a way to break him loose and get him going. He'd have someone like a tight end come off the line unexpectedly to knock down a safety, for example, just to get Taylor free. It was the minutiae of that strategy—Lombardi's knowledge of the strengths and weaknesses of each player—that made that team. As I listened to Lombardi and watched the Packers, my management style became coherent. I realized that I was not the chief ingredient, my players were. I finally realized that I'd think the same of myself if I were running a tugboat in New York Harbor. How successful you are or what you do doesn't have anything to do with who you really are. As a result of having recognized this, I don't go through a lot of ego dances."

> When Guinan approaches a turnaround situation, as he did at Gold Circle, or a situation with immense potential such as he found at Caldor, he begins by recruiting top talent for his team.

"I identify all the things that need to be done, hire myself the best direct-report senior vice president I can get, give the team some conceptual direction, get agreement on objectives, and agree on touchback points. I need to know how to monitor the players without being all over them. For example, there must be touchback points for the Vice President of Information Systems. If a system is coming on stream in December, I don't want any surprises. I require a lot of touchback points on MIS right now, for that's an important activity, but I stay off the guy's back. Still I do some reality testing. If computers are supposed to come up live in the Bedford Hills store on the first of November, I might check on that during a store visit. If I find that the people at that store don't even know about the computer yet, we're going to have a tough few minutes. I try to do just enough reality testing to make sure I'm not being snowed.

"It's the team that has to perform. During the annual visit from my Corporate Office, I probably will not speak for more than five minutes. My people will make their presentations and take full credit for their accomplishments, and I might chime in enough to make sure that they even get some extra credit. What a good executive has to add is the 'Lombardi ingredient' —my people know I'll stay off their backs, but they have to produce.

"I will never hold back anyone. I took great pride at Gold Circle, producing as many senior executives for corporate in as short a time span as any division ever. I even got to the point that I thought Federated should reimburse my division for all of those leaders I was producing. People who work directly for me will say, 'My God, I've never been this free in my life,' but they know that I'll hold their noses to the grindstone on budgets and results. Budgeting is a process I find very important. When you tell a manager that he's going to have $1.7 million—not $1.8 million—for the next half year, you're helping him shape policy, for then you need to talk out what this change will do, what is the lowest priority, what will not get done, what will be the negative impact. If it all sounds too negative, then you'll need to talk about it some more. How can the negative impact be ameliorated? The two budget sessions each year really become policy sessions for me. It takes a full week to go through this process, and at the end I'm wringing wet, and so is everyone else.

"I also have objectives sessions twice a year, but these are usually after the fact. Obviously, if you don't give the manager enough money and help for his new distribution center or the right to buy trucks, he's not going to get the job done. The better he is, the more likely he'll get it done even within the limitations you placed on him, but he still has finite limitations. I tolerate mistakes, but if my quarterback throws downfield 7 times in a row—if he's 0 for 7—I'm going to find someone else to throw the ball. He can make colossal mistakes as long as his averages are good. We all occasionally make real whoppers: 'My God, I forgot to budget,' or 'I knew they were supposed to be delivered, but I never figured freight.' We make mistakes, but about the third time that I find I'm doing someone else's job, I get rid of them. I do this with humanity, with dignity and no ego involvement. At Gold Circle I had to fire a very senior executive, and for the next three Sunday mornings he and I played tennis. When I do let someone go, the person understands the why of it by the time it gets to that point.

"Anyone who works for me knows that if he or she is performing in any idiosyncratic way, they won't get killed provided their averages are good. We run a very relaxed place, we don't wear coats, the President and I play platform tennis with a rotating group of management—it all goes back to no ego, no pomp, no circumstance.

"When I was at Federated, all the store principals were sent to an assessment center, where our heads were shrunk a little bit, to help us become better team players. Before going there, the two lines of management below an executive assessed that person on a whole lot of management factors. I was marked down on the basis of 'formal meetings held;' I wasn't sure this was bad, but I had to think about it. And, looking at my own style, I know that that was an accurate assessment. When I first arrive at any new job—the Boston Store, Gold Circle, then Bloomie's, now here—I try to develop a clear picture of what strengths and skills are needed. For example, if I were managing the Packers right now, I'd probably conclude that they desperately need several interior offensive linemen to hold off everybody who's going to come after poor Lynn Dickey, who can't run; that's a specific need. First I start building the team, and then as the strengths and weaknesses of the early acquisitions and their departments become apparent, I adjust the way I approach my responsibilities. For example, if I had an MIS department that was running routinely, I'd want a senior statesman who would keep it up-to-date, understand the future changes of the state of the art. But if I found an MIS wasteland, three guys with a bookkeeping machine, then I'd need someone who could run very fast, a scrambler, perhaps someone who is less than perfect on detail. This happens to describe the guy I have, who is bringing up some of the biggest retailing systems on the shortest time frame ever, and if he drops some loose ends, I'll pick them up for him. He is good at what he does and does not need to be super strong on budgets or communications. This man understands the state of the art in MIS in retailing from a technical point of view, and knows what the merchant and the store needs. He has surrounded himself with bright young people who are thrilled to work for him, and together they are doing some marvelous things on a very short deadline. I watch him closely, and if we find ourselves off and running with a system that we, for instance, forgot to tell a certain accounting department about, and learn that as a result there are three forms which they needed to be changed, we'll deal with those loose ends. But boy, can he move!''

When one takes on a new key responsibility, Guinan believes it important to ask just what is needed for the particular jobs. Is the need for a disciplinarian? A conceptual person? A statesman? A soother and a healer?

"Once this is known, one can start recruiting the first few people. After they're in place, you need to think not only in terms of what is needed for the remaining jobs, but how the new people will fit in with the existing teams. You need to find people who are not immediately intolerant of other people, for example, those who happen not to be good with numbers. There may be a job which you want to fill with a conservator. And, if you bring in a fire eater and ask him to be conservator, he will be very unhappy. Racehorses don't plow very well and shouldn't be asked to do so.

"The penalty you get for allowing people to run as freely as I do is that the third time I have to do your job, I will have to replace you. The first two levels of Caldor—with the exception of perhaps a half dozen out of the top 30—are new faces, new since my arrival. When I was in the Navy I was taught in Damage Control to get the hole filled and then worry about whether you've put in the couch, three life preservers, and two balks of timber. But when you just ram a lot of new people in, you are likely to have a failure or two, and we've just had our first, a general merchandise manager (that is, a senior-most vice president for merchandising), a man who was very intelligent, but had no gut feel for the business.

"At the opposite end from a team builder is the one-man band, who tends to develop superb gofers; if you operate that way, you can't blame anyone but yourself for results, good or bad. When I arrived at Caldor, I found I was expected to approve a change in the shade of beige on a cardboard blanket box. My predecessor used to approve that sort of thing and signed all payroll increases right down to assistant store manager, of which we have about 400. Decisions need to be pushed down, not up. The top team really has to move."

| The retailing business, Guinan says, is unforgiving.

"If you have three general merchandise managers, each week the printout tells how each of their subsections of the business is doing. If one area is marching relentlessly behind the rest of the company, that computer printout says a lot about the quality of that management."

General Management as a Skill

"I suppose I could go into some other business totally unrelated to retail and develop a sense of that, but it would take considerable time. You need to develop a gut feeling about the business you're in. Still, there's an awful lot about this business that I know nothing about. The closer you get to general management, the more *that* becomes a pure skill. I give speeches on distribution and MIS, but if you listen to my speeches, you'll hear only conceptual and managerial kinds of things. I can't even start a 65-foot tractor-trailer and don't think I should ever want to. I can barely turn on a computer terminal, but I can read what it says. Pure management skill becomes much more important than specific skills. What you need to ask yourself is what you need to know to manage a business, and what are the gut issues. When you get into mass merchandising, you find that it is subtly—yet vastly—different from department stores. It is a business of velocity, a matter of how fast goods move, tonnage, how much of everything is moved, and distance, how far your stores are. Department stores face none of that on our scale. Then you have to add to that, timing —because tonnage, velocity, and distance are always timing problems. I can have wonderful delivery of chairs to my stores, but if they arrive the day after the ad, all I've got is chairs, no business. So what do you need for that? You need a highly developed computer system that tells you what you have where. Lots of communication. I even use a terminal for electronic mail, I'm on line to everyone who reports to me."

Listening to Customers

The skill or art of general management, Guinan believes, depends heavily on one's ability to ask the right questions at the right time, and to insist on answers that make sense. And while much of general management cuts across industries, some principles are specific to retailing. One pertains to management's attitude toward customers. The customer is always right, Guinan insists. Yet he feels that the ability to listen to customers has been lost by some of America's largest corporations.

"For example, I recently bought a rather expensive American car which turned out to be a lemon. I wrote to the president of the company and about eight weeks later I finally got a reply, a prototypical form letter with a customer representative's signature printed on it. I had concluded that the reason that their repair response time is so slow is that the company doesn't keep parts in stock. If it takes six weeks to get a car repaired, it's because it takes that long to get the part. The form letter explained that the reason for this was that the dealers are independent, and 'we can't make them carry parts.' My God, if I headed up that company, this would be a very important gut issue. It's like saying that we can't have a running game because we don't have a good halfback. But what does that tell you? I had mentioned in my letter that my previous car—I had bought one from another company about every two years—could get repaired very quickly. Parts were available, even the most exotic ones, within 72 hours.

"When you get a form letter, especially a form letter which tells you why the company can't do something, you know that the company isn't listening, and that's a real weakness. I read every single letter sent to the Chairman or the President, and I either respond personally or decide who it's to be routed to. This year we'll do about one billion, six hundred million dollars worth of business, and if we don't listen to our customers, we've got a problem.

"What we do beyond reading letters is to have an outside firm do a major marketing survey. Focus groups are set up in about 20 carefully selected markets, from Baltimore to Boston. You sit in a room and look through a one-way glass at a bunch of housewives and some male customers—though men usually don't understand shopping as well as women. A very subtle, skillful moderator gets them to talk about discount stores, and he weaves in names like Caldor or Gold Circle in order to get their opinions. If in a given area the customers say that you have a lousy health & beauty aids department and you never carry the right sizes of Crest, the computer printout which says that Crest is always in stock is meaningless. If 12 housewives in Baltimore say it, and you hear it again in Hartford, and then again in Boston, perception is absolute reality. Whatever the customer thinks is *in fact* reality. It takes a while to accept this, particularly if you are hit with a criticism about something you thought was wonderful. You want to go rushing into the room and hit somebody because you do have pride! Still, they are right. Maybe you have Crest located in the wrong part of the store. Maybe your signs aren't right, maybe your recovery time on Sunday—after the big Saturday shopping volume—is too slow. You can't know what it is just from listening to these focus groups, but you need to find out and find out fast.

"When we finished all of those one-way mirror focus groups, our outside consultant also conducted 2,000 interviews, with questions which zeroed in on weaknesses which surfaced in the focus groups. So by now we know very well what the customers like about us, what they don't like, right down to 'by department.' We learned some things that didn't make us too happy as well as some pleasant things. But we now know what the customer thinks of Caldor as of May, 1985. By God, we'd better respond to it, and we are doing just that.''

Communications with Management

The assessment center's observation that Guinan does not have many formal meetings was quite accurate.

"Most of the time I'll have a lot of quick one-on-one meetings, and when I do, I just appear at the guy's doorway. If a meeting lasts more than a half hour, it's probably because we're making some major conceptual change. As important as information systems are to Caldor, I wouldn't dream of sitting down with the vice president and saying, 'I've noticed that you have only 17 people on your design team.' Maybe I remember at Gold Circle or in some other way know that that kind of system should take 22 people, not 17, but that's his business. And I can't care. Since I'm never into much detail, my meetings tend to be short. We have an Executive Committee, the pyramid heads who report either to me or the President, which meets once a month. We go over the profit-and-loss statement, high and low points, disasters, tragedies and triumphs. Everyone knows in advance that the meeting is going to be held—we try to run the calendar out six months in advance —so there's almost no excuse not to be there, unless you're in the Far East. Everyone sees the agenda beforehand, anyone who wants to can add something to it, so nobody gets sandbagged. There's also an executive dining room here, which was my predecessor's private dining room, and a kitchen, and any member of the Executive Committee who wants to have lunch here any day can do so. Just let the cook know in time. We have a rule that no confrontational topics can come up in the lunchroom, but we try to keep each other informed partly through these lunches. If there is a need for any sort of 'watershed' meeting—for example, right now some big systems are about to come alive—we'd better get together too. There may be some last minute problems between the Finance Department and MIS, so I'd better get two or three people in one room to make sure that they've talked. But I'm certainly not going to tinker with the minutiae of their operations. Then there are always certain decisions that I cannot ask vice presidents to make, the kinds of decisions which might cause dissension with other VPs, so I'll make those decisions. And when I do, it's important that I communicate them adequately.''

Caldor's culture is just evolving. Prior to Guinan's arrival, it had been a very autocratic, one-man-directed culture.

"There was a high premium on being gofers as opposed to being thinkers and challengers. We're trying to reverse this. So four or five times a year all the store managers come in, and I exhort them to let us know what's going on. For instance, we recently had two problems: we were beginning to see some customer service problems having to do with slow response time on checkouts, yet our study had reported that we were the best in the business in May. So what was happening? Second, the stores were beginning to pile up stock, we were becoming much more aggressive, and we were in a culture that couldn't handle this. I sent out a letter suggesting several things that might help and setting guidelines just to make sure we were understood. But I emphasized, 'we'd like to hear from you,' directing them to the two vice presidents of stores, with a copy to me. I said, 'You are on the firing line and know what's really going on, so let us know what we can do to help.' I was surprised, getting 16 replies, each of which was very helpful.

Reality Testing

"I also like to reality test by wandering around stores. Out of our 109 stores, I've probably visited 85 and hope to visit the rest. I try to listen to anybody and am very careful never to chew out anybody, and I pass back what I hear without making judgments about it: 'Hey, I don't know what the real story is, but South Wopsit tells me they haven't had a truck there in five days, and our minimum standard is twice a week.' If I hear enough of this, I may begin to worry or to suspect, but I try not to make any judgments, just pass on what I'm told, as long as I trust the pyramid head. The stores seldom know I'm coming. In our kind of business, if they know I'm coming, I may not see the real store. Having been in this business a while, I know all the tricks: you can rent old klunker trailers and hide all the the goods someplace so the stock rooms can be cleaned up; maybe the manager and the assistants are personally running buffing machines until four in the morning, just to make the floor in Receiving look pretty. If they knew I were coming, this could hurt the customer sooner or later by diverting human assets. We don't need four days of hysteria to get ready for me. I explain to the store managers that when I walk in and find the store operationally untidy, I expect that; but it can't be three-days-old dirt, it can't be a blouse that's been lying on the floor covered with dust. But 'Can you have three rolling racks on the floor because you're busily putting things out?' Of course you can, because that's 'operational untidiness.' If it's ten in the morning and there are some departments that haven't totally recovered from the previous day, is someone working on it? I'm careful to remind them that I spent eight years in Bamberger branches and understand that you can't look like you're ready for company all the time. If the President and I get on a plane, we may hit two markets, him to Brockton and me to Springfield. There is simply no way that stores can be portrayed artificially. A little bit perhaps, but not much, and we'll be seeing five stores in five hours, mostly 'the way they are.''

Guinan's Early Years

A very bright person, Guinan began college when he was 15½, spent four years in the Navy, then finished his last college year. His career began not in retailing but in the newspaper business, first as a stringer for *The New York Times* and *Brooklyn Daily*, then night editor of the *Palisadian* in Cliffside Park, N.J. Shortly after this, in 1956, he became editor of a weekly newspaper—the oldest newspaper in Delaware.

"A fun little weekly in Laurel, which is way down in the swamps. I was sort of a boy editor—maybe 24 by then—and after two years of running that under absentee ownership, I answered a blind ad in *The New York Times* for a ghost writer. Knowing that I'd never make money in publishing, unless I owned a newspaper, I decided to make a career change but wanted to continue my writing. The ad turned out to be for Bamberger's. I was attached to the Training Department and also helped do some speech writing for Dave Yunich, then CEO of Bamberger's. I was called Director of Internal Publicity, ran the company newspaper, and handled internal press releases, sort of in-house journalist.

"Then one day, Wade Bennett (King Wade Bennett, later President of Macy's, New York) called me in to see him. Then Senior Vice President of Personnel at Bamberger's, Bennett offered me a choice, either to go into a Personnel job or to join the Publicity Department. I chose Personnel, which was fortunate, for in those days Bamberger's provided lots of experiences. You'd go in and out of large branches, back to downtown, in and out of Operations, in and out of Personnel—they cross-ruffed you all the time. Wade was a firm believer in the principle that many retailing jobs are interchangeable and that the worst thing in the world would be a senior Personnel person who had always been in Personnel. He thought that that was just awful. So I went back and forth, in and out of Operations, assistant to a manager, and so on, learning all sorts of things about logistics, distribution, budgets, the physical plant, labor relations, the whole works. This began in 1958. I then became Employee Relations Manager for Bamberger's, which was and is unorganized, non-union except for Newark. At various times I was either the Personnel Manager of a very large branch such as Paramus, or the Assistant Manager for Operations. I opened the Cherry Hill store, was in Plainfield, and Paramus twice—the second time as assistant manager—and I learned a great deal at Bamberger's.

"I was then recruited from Bambergers by Federated Stores to go to their Boston Store in Milwaukee, where I became Vice President/Personnel & Selling Services. This combination is not strange in retailing. I had all the selling budgets, the biggest budget in retailing, therefore a strong operational tinge—responsible for mail, phone, switchboard, customer service, gift wrap, Personnel. I became Vice President of Operations and Personnel, then finally Executive Vice President for everything except Merchandising in 1975.

"Pete Scotese was there as CEO. You'd have to understand the workings of Bamberger's at the time to realize that I had a more senior responsibility than my title implied, but still I was attracted by the possibility of becoming a Vice President. I was around 32 at the time, was interviewed by everybody and spent the weekend in Milwaukee, since the Executive Committee would be meeting on Monday. I learned later that Pete Scotese had decided on another person. I had been the second finalist. I heard that Pete came in and said, 'We've decided on (the other guy).' The President of the Boston Store said, 'Yeah, I think you're better off; he has the track record, is solid and dependable; and besides, that kid' (referring to me) 'would be after your job in a year.' Pete said, 'Oh?' And they reconsidered the whole thing and hired me instead. I have heard that story from a lot of people, so I am sure it's true. I became involved in a lot of strategic things at the Boston Store, which is a division of Federated, and learned a great deal from Scotese. It's a high quality merchandise store, higher than a Macy's or Gimbel's, and is about as sophisticated an operation as you can get in the Midwest. Later, for several years as EVP, I was the only person reporting to Ed Watson, the then about-to-retire Board Chairman, so everyone knew that I was a 'Dauphin'—and very much at the policy-making level.

"Shortly after I joined the Boston Store as Vice President/Personnel & Selling Services, I developed a coherent, ongoing college relations program, with three executive training squads a year. Within a short period of time, although believing that you should hire from 5 percent to 10 percent from the outside in order to avoid organizational incest, I had this group of young college graduates going through executive training, becoming assistant buyers to branch store sales managers, to buyers, and the equivalent in all the sales-supporting divisions, so we became totally self-sustaining, and it is this way to this day. In fact some of the people here at Caldor came from these training squads of the late '60s. The last year I was at the Boston Store it had its best year ever, then I left to join Gold Circle as President in late 1979, becoming Chairman in 1982.

"When I got to Gold Circle, I did the same sort of things: looking for the holes, recruiting a team, building it. And the third year I was at Gold Circle they had their best year ever, too. They've been in something of a slough since that time."

Guinan speaks of one problem of team management in the retail industry.

"First of all, there's a tremendous mobility in retail. And because of my management style, letting them do what they want to do, they get fairly high profiles. They get asked to speak here and there, and the next thing you know they're on national programs at the NRMI (National Mass Retailing Institute), people get to know them, and suddenly they start getting phone calls. Second, I suppose in a sense they get spoiled with my loose reins and irreverent ways: 'If I have to fire you, I'll do so with love, otherwise I'll push you and reward you like crazy.' So in a sense perhaps, having enjoyed that environment, they might have trouble working for someone else. All the way back to my time at Bamberger's, no one who reported to me directly ever quit. I've fired a lot of people, but not a single person who worked for me has ever quit."

This raises an interesting question: What effect has Guinan had on the organizations that he has headed up and passed through? On the bright side, he has developed hundreds of people within the industry, helping them and the industry to grow. But the darker side may be that as he has passed through these organizations and has helped his people to become visible, his very management style may have increased attrition in the top management level of the companies which he has left.

"That may be true. There are different management styles. Too much breezy irreverence after a while could become a pain, I suppose. Then there's another problem: I noted in the management assessment operation back at Federated, that people seemed to enjoy my management style but even those who reported to me had very different styles from mine. I said to them, 'You guys are the ones who said you liked this management style. If you like it, why don't you treat your people the way you've told me you want to be treated?' That may have been one of my failures; I did not see the change in the personnel which I expected to. Perhaps my style is not contagious.

"Because of my idiosyncratic ways, perhaps I need to spend more time thinking about succession. I have known somewhat incoherently in the back of my head that my style may create a volatile situation. A man who took my place not too many jobs ago pulled all the controls back in and insisted on knowing in painful detail what everyone was going to do tomorrow. The kind of team I built there can't handle that. They all went away; some of them came here.

"In any career there is the matter of what you might call 'comfort level.' Some people are more comfortable in a loose environment, others in a tight environment. I've gotten to know myself fairly well, but much more so only recently."

Line-Item Retailing

In March, 1984, Guinan left as Chairman and CEO of Gold Circle to become President of Bloomingdale's in New York City. Only seven months later, he left Bloomingdale's to join Caldor.

"At Bloomingdale's I was not the Chief Executive Officer. There, in the Federated environment, the Chief Operating Officer reports directly to the Corporate Office, as does the CEO. In fact I wrote a 'white paper' about two or three years ago to the effect that the position of CEO should be abolished because it simply doesn't exist in Federated. Of course you need someone to sign legal papers, attest to financial results each month, and so on. The parallel reporting structure is just the way things are done within Federated. For example, when I was CEO of Gold Circle, the President did not report to me, but to the Corporate Office, as I did. Here at Caldor it's quite different.

"At Bloomingdale's and at Gold Circle there were always lots of interfaces. For example, at Bloomie's my partner might want a new department built for Junior Sportswear, and I am in charge of the construction he needs; we might have to discuss the quality of the pickled walnut he wants or whether we really need new carpets. What's the time frame? How much money are we willing to spend? Those are interface issues. Since we both had about the same level of authority, this created many interfaces.''

Item Selling Versus Mass Merchandising

"In some ways Bloomingdale's is a peculiar organization, certainly a unique one. It is probably the closest to an item business left in the department store field, at least in the U.S. While there is a basic business there, there's a great premium on selecting 30 Ming vases at several thousand dollars each; as a result, you can get away with a lot more in the way of idiosyncratic personalities. In fact this may even be necessary, lots of emotion, lots of show biz. Yet I'm not at all sure how expandable that merchandising model is. With 14 Bloomingdale stores now in operation, you still have to ask whether all the ready-to-wear will arrive in time at any one store. For example, I opened one store in The Falls, a mall in South Miami, and 65% of ready-to-wear was flown in by air freight at the last minute. You have to wonder if there's any profit left in such a situation. In the item business there's lots of talent, lots of hysteria, and I'm not sure how much of this can be handled, once you get up to 20 stores. Lots of talent, lots of creativity, not much discipline (in fact, an incredible lack of it) can be handled in an item business, if it's managed well. But Bamberger's couldn't handle this, for it's basically a commodity business. Neiman-Marcus could get away with this when they were still in Texas, but as far flung as they are now, I suspect that this mode of operation could cost you at least five points off your profit.''

Guinan's method of operation—systematizing a business, building a structured team, pushing for results—works better at Caldor than at Bloomingdale's.

"I'm not sure why I made the decision to come to Caldor, but I think I would have had a lot less impact in an item business like Bloomingdale's than I can have here. And I'm not sure that if one could ever get that yeasty I'm-gonna-have-a-nervous-breakdown atmosphere at a store like Bloomingdale's totally under control, whether it would really be Bloomingdale's anymore. If I were running the Federated stores, I doubt that I would have made the decision to greatly expand Bloomingdale's. In a sense, it's like trying to train racehorses to pull fire engines.

"When I was approached to come to Caldor, I recognized that the top people at ADG (who own Caldor) were people with whom I had real empathy, real vibes: they understood what I wanted to do and thought it was marvelous. And the challenge of Caldor—a company that even in its darker days of 1983 and 1984 was making more pre-tax dollars than Bloomingdale's—was just too tempting to turn down. Caldor seemed to be doing many things wrong for a business that had even 50 stores, and it had many more than that.

"I can't overstate the difference between an item business and a commodity business. Other than Bloomingdale's, probably no other department store really operates that way; even Lord & Taylor is probably more of a commodity business. By the way, the term 'commodity' has nothing to do with price necessarily: if Lord & Taylor can blow out 500 blouses at $120 each, that's still a commodity business, which needs controls. But if you're in the item business, you don't need a lot of electronic rates of sale, and you don't deal with velocity and tonnage. Still, you have to deal with distance, and that could eat an item retailer alive. For example, if you were running an ad all over Bloomingdale's featuring $120 blouses, but you did not have them in Texas, that could cost you a fortune. But that isn't the way Bloomie's runs its business. Its advertising is localized, and if a buyer forgot to buy the $120 blouses, you'd have something else, some other pretty blouses."

Analytical Skills

Guinan possesses a curious mind and an intelligent way of looking at problems from many different angles. He obviously enjoys the challenge of a complex problem, and his particular skill is in sorting out the principles or issues of a problem, even one whose details he does not fully understand.

"Perhaps a strength of mine is the ability to stand aside from a problem and dissect it even in areas I am unfamiliar with. I've been effective, for instance, in computerization, the most exotic field I have delved into lately—and not too deeply at that. But this is true also in distribution, labor relations, and whatever. I try to say, 'I don't really understand your specialty, Mr. Specialist, but as an outsider looking in, isn't there a way to do such and such?' The specialists look at each other and start to whisper and say, 'Well, you really could do that, because if you did this and then did that, this would result.' So I've had the experience of getting these specialists off and running conceptually. I'm not sure that I really understand this mental process, but it works. It's not just a matter of drawing people out by asking uninformed questions, it's more of a synergistic skill; often I can see a solution even though I don't know how to get to it. I'm not sure why I see solutions as quickly as I do, but I've always been able to do this. For example, several of us were sitting around trying to determine how to combine the massive computer systems of Richway and Gold Circle. One of the hang-ups was that they had both evolved separate, giant computerized systems. We were talking about how many man-years would be required to rebuild one system into the other. I said, 'Gee, it would seem to me if (and I guess you can't really do this) you put all the Richway material in here and translated it . . .' They suddenly started talking about blue boxes and transliteration tables and other things I didn't understand, and it turned out to be possible to do exactly what I suggested, even though I didn't really know much about what I was talking about. Another example: we had a big breakthrough in the use of a private fleet of trucks, using these trucks to deliver for other people, making about $1.8 million net by doing this in my last year at Gold Circle. Before this, for instance, we had had trucks at loose ends up in Rochester which had delivered goods to our stores, so I suggested that they take a load of film from Eastman Kodak to A & S, then pick up a load of dresses for Rich's in Atlanta, swing over to another place in Georgia to pick up a load of dinner plates for Gold Circle, and so on. The trucks were never to be empty. The whole concept of the 'round robin' for Gold Circle just dawned on me one day when we were talking about all the empty trucks we were having to support. The first step, of course, was how we could use the trucks more efficiently for Gold Circle; then, how we could use them more efficiently for Federated stores outside of Gold Circle. Then somehow I got to the third step which caused me to ask, 'What's wrong if we go outside of Federated?' So we started delivering for Huffy Bike, Rubbermaid, Ashland Chemical, and Hamms Beer, and we made money doing this. There's nothing profound about this.

"Sometimes suggestions you make just don't work out, but I always try to keep control. When you get about a third of the way down the face of a mountain and realize you can't get down from there, you have to be able to go back up. One example of this was at Gold Circle, where we changed the people who ran the departments in the stores from essentially being one-year college dropouts to college graduates. I had thought there would be some positive effect, but there was no effect at all. I guess I was guilty of laying on an old department store concept, which is that the more people you have thinking, the more it's going to help profitability. That's no doubt true in a department store, because there's so much creative activity going on. But when you think of it, a Gold Circle store is more like a cookie cutter. The premium is on doing things the way the central office tells you to do them. The Crest tubes are all lined up—in fact, you give them a picture of the Crest layout. College graduates go crazy in that atmosphere. So at Caldor I backed off from this. Out of 15 department managers I wanted only about three of them to be college graduates, in order to have an adequate stream of promotables."

Management Style

Guinan gives great credit to Pete Scotese, now Chairman of the Executive Committee of Springs Industries, during the time that Scotese was Chairman of the Boston Store.

"I liked the way I was treated by Scotese. He was a fun guy. He'd chew the hell out of you when you were wrong, then he'd let you run and suddenly on Thursday he'd be standing in my doorway with his sneakers on saying, 'Come on, let's go sailing.' I've learned to do that myself quite a bit; if you treat a person in a certain way, let him stumble, help pick him up, be demanding, yet understanding and fun, he'll work better and he'll like to work for me. I'm not sure when this became totally coherent to me, but probably as I reached the Executive Vice President level and really had to think about management. Then there was Ed Watson, who succeeded Scotese at the Boston Store as Chairman. He was not the mover and shaker that Pete was, but he was a statesman. When he drew me up short, it would be because I was doing an ego dance. He'd say, 'That shouldn't be important to you, let the other guy think it was his idea to move the china department, we're getting it moved aren't we?'

"From Pete I learned to surround myself with bright people, yet to remember that it is my responsibility to set important concepts in motion. He was a gutsy guy, never hesitating to get his feet wet. I also learned that your subordinates should never get hit by lightning from anyone but you. My people know that the only lightning that will hit them will come from me, no side bolts coming in from anywhere else. Then from Ed Watson I learned to take that next step backwards, learned to wash out a little more of my ego. I don't need to take the credit. I'll get some of it anyway. I do need to take the blame since I am the captain of the ship. I guess the thing which motivates me the most is to do a good job. When I was 10 years old, I worked in a Brooklyn candy store, and my first task was to clean out the cellar, get rid of all the old Coke bottles, candy, and rats. The owner said I had done the best job anyone had done. I don't know why it makes me happier than it does many people just to do a good job. Then the next thing that is important is to do another good job. It's not important to me to learn to play golf. Maybe I'll do that at age 60 or 62. I don't have any great urge to be Chairman of the Board of ADG or Federated or anything else, I really don't, I just enjoy being *really* good at what I do.

"I enjoy very much speaking publicly. One reason I like it is the empathy I receive from the audience, possibly a stroking thing. But it also is a form of discipline that requires me to stand up and talk in a way that I can capture the essence of my philosophy on management, organizational style, distribution, computerization, merchandising. If I can't do this in 20 minutes, I probably have not thought it out well enough.''

Advice to Students

"If I were talking with a group of students who might be interested in retail, I would describe the traits which seem to make a successful retailer. The most important of these is self-confidence. Considerably down the scale is intelligence. I have seen retailers who were self-confident but not brilliant who have been great successes, but I've never seen a successful retailer who was bright but not self-confident.

"Then I'd try to debunk some myths. When I started here, everybody worked on Saturdays. We did away with this; the building is dark on Saturdays. Do some work at home, some reading, some thinking. I would say that retailing is not long hours necessarily, and I'd tick off three or four firms—Dayton Hudson, for example—where long hours are not a premium. And I would say that in retailing the customer tells you loud and clear what you're doing wrong and what you're doing right.

"Now in your first job, if you're not talented I can't help you. But if you are, then you should establish a bottom-line relationship with your first boss that says, 'Leave me alone, let me do this, and I'll do it well, and then you'll leave me alone some more.' If after a while your manager does not recognize that for every success you have, he can give you a little longer leash, or if he wants you to play politics, you should get away and work for someone else. If you're lucky, you'll get someone who continually expands your responsibility and authority, and you should demand this—but only when you've earned it. Don't demand what you haven't earned. Don't ask, 'If I do this, this and this, will I get a shot at that job?' First, just do it. Then say, 'I want that job; I've done these things.' Your demands must be based on the credentials of what you've done.

"At any level in the retail business, know your competition. Identify it. Your competitors may be tiny or big, and when you get into the level of management where you can make a strategic difference, don't let *everybody* be your competition; you'll go crazy. Identify who they are, keep track of what they're doing that's different, go see their stores regularly, understand their strengths and their weaknesses. Ask your customers about them, so that you understand where they're better than you are. Don't ever pooh-pooh what they're doing that's different; they may be right. If the customer says they found an absolutely spiffy live plant department at Bradlee's, you'd better go take a second look."

Guinan's Strengths

One reason for his business success is his ability to build, maintain, and retain unusually effective teams.

"But then there's strategic planning. At the CEO level, you just can't get away from it, and I've run the whole gamut in the way of thinking about this. For the Corporate Office, you really have to commit to a five-year fiscal plan, but clearly you can't put numbers on a piece of paper and commit to them until you understand at least somewhat how to get there, your limitations, what can and can't be done. So you take some broad-brush strokes to ask what needs to be done to expand the company. Maybe the answer is to make the environment more computerized, to develop an overseas import program, to emphasize soft goods. Whatever your strategy is, it doesn't mean that when you get to year three you'll find that you needn't change. Chances are you'll have to—you should! But you need to know what you're changing from. And certainly you change *tactics* all the time.

"It's absolutely vital to stay in touch with the outside world. The whole world is impinging upon us. There are so many things that are going on. If you don't understand what's happened in the world since 1960, then you can't understand your own work force. You'd better understand their value systems. How do you motivate a first-line assistant buyer today with what he's gotten out of college, if you don't know *what* he's gotten out of college? He was alive during the '60s, was a college student in the '70s, saw the clay feet of Nixon—if he's old enough to have really observed that at the time! Our new hires have totally different value systems than we did in the '50s. If I didn't keep up with the world, you'd identify me as an old fashioned hick without any real leadership capability.

"Curiosity. That's very important."

James R. Martin

Chairman
Massachusetts Mutual Life Insurance Company

*H*e used management techniques learned
as a World War II lieutenant colonel to lead
Massachusetts Mutual successfully through a
period of turbulent change in the once
placid insurance business. His self-styled
management approach is "a combination of
authoritarianism and impatience." But he
believes strongly in the importance of
honest feedback from his people—so strongly
that he persuaded his senior executives to
meet twice a year to critique his performance and report the results directly to
him. He is deeply dedicated to long-range
planning, calling it the core concept of successful corporate management. He has no
sympathy for chief executive officers who
complain that they don't have time to do
long-range planning and other important
parts of their jobs. According to him, that
time can be created by delegating details to
capable executive assistants—the "unsung
heroes" of the corporate world.

As CEO for 12 years, he gives the credit
for his success to Mass Mutual's "high
quality, professional sales force." Others
would say that his no-nonsense management
style and ability to meet the challenge of
change had something to do with transforming Mass Mutual from a conventional
organization to one of the leading companies in its industry.

Career Information:

1940 Entered life insurance business as salesman

1946 Joined Home Life of New York in Peoria, Ill.

1950 Became agency manager in Rochester, N.Y.

1951 Joined Massachusetts Mutual as assistant superintendent of agencies

1962 Elected vice president and head of Agency Division

1965 Elected to Massachusetts Mutual board of directors and to executive committee

1968 Named president and chief executive officer

1974 Elected chairman

Other Affiliations:

- Director, Textron, Inc.
- Director, Hasbro, Inc.
- Director, Stanhome, Inc.
- Chairman, Board of Trustees, American Management Association
- Vice Chairman, Board of Trustees, National YMCA Retirement Fund
- Chairman, Board of Trustees, Business Council for the United Nations

Educational Information:

- University of Illinois, Business Administration, 1940

Personal Information:

- Native of Peoria, Ill.
- Served as Army Air Corps officer during World War II, reaching rank of lieutenant colonel

James R. Martin

"One of my key characteristics is impatience. Sometimes that is a plus, but more often it is something that I have had to cope with. I am very conscious of this—for one thing, my wife reminds me of it with great regularity. Recognizing fully that I have this tendency, I have had to develop techniques to keep me out of trouble, ways to make my style yield results."

The life insurance business, when Martin entered it in the 1940s, was probably the most stable, predictable, and unchanging business in America.

"We had only three things to worry about—interest, mortality, and expenses."

The first two could be forecast with great accuracy, and expense was of minor consequence in those pre-inflationary times. In fact, even in 1968, the year Martin became Mass Mutual's CEO, the company still had no formal budgeting system, despite its annual sales of approximately $2 billion.

"The prevailing attitude in the 1960s was epitomized by the comments of the newly-elected president of a large life insurance company, who said upon his inauguration, 'In my considered opinion, it would take two successive, totally incompetent managements to do any material harm to a large mutual life insurance company; and, even then, they would have to be doing so deliberately.' Sad to relate, that new CEO disproved his own theory within the next few years."

The life insurance industry today bears little resemblance to that industry in 1968.

"First came inflation, making the control of expenses a vital element of management for the first time, and then came higher interest rates, which turned an antiquated federal income tax law that applied only to life insurance companies into a nightmare. Under that law, the progressive tax rate moved in accordance with the rate of return rather than with the amount of income. Had it been permitted to continue, Mass Mutual's marginal tax rate would have exceeded 100 percent within a very few years. Then came deregulation, which encouraged everyone—banks, investment companies, stockbrokers, and life insurance companies—all to get into each other's businesses. And finally, there was the introduction of new products, some of which made many salesmen more like investment advisors than traditional life insurance salesmen.

"Because of these changes, we have had to become much greater risk takers. We have had to become interest-sensitive to everything we do. Some might say that the insurance industry, like other industries, simply should be expected to take major risks. Still, you have to remember that insurance is the longest-term business that exists. When you are planning for a contract that is fixed in its terms, one that is going to be in force for 50 or more years, you had better be pretty conservative. People have been educated over many generations to believe that no matter what happens, their insurance policy will be there to pay off when they need it."

Assuring that this stability can be delivered, despite decades of revolutionary change and economically turbulent times, is the job of the life insurance CEO.

Martin's Management Style

In coping with all these changes, Martin used a management style that he describes as "a combination of authoritarianism and impatience." Whatever style he used, it certainly worked. During his 12-year tenure as Chief Executive Officer of the Massachusetts

JAMES R. MARTIN

Mutual Life Insurance Company, its assets rose from $3.7 billion to $8.5 billion, and the annual amount paid back to policyholders in dividends rose from $350 million to more than $1 billion. Any company that can achieve such results must have something unique about it, and, in Mass Mutual's case, Martin is quick to claim its sales force as its unique attribute.

"Only Mass Mutual and perhaps one or two other companies have built a high quality, professional sales force, something achieved over a long period of years; and Mass Mutual was one of the first to recognize the value of this asset by in-

111

cluding representatives of the sales force as an important part of the company's decision-making process."

The single largest influence in shaping his management style, Martin says, was four years in the Army Air Corps during World War II.

"At a very young age, I was thrust into positions of responsibility and authority which might not otherwise have come my way for 10 to 20 years, if ever. Many of the management techniques that I used and saw others using in the military proved to be directly transferable to business life. Further, this experience provided a test for the satisfactions and rewards of leadership, and it whetted my appetite for more of the same."

That appetite is still keen; in addition to being Chairman of his company, Martin served a number of years as Chairman of the Board of Regents of Massachusetts Public Higher Education and is the current Chairman of the American Management Association and the Business Council for the United Nations.

Over the years, Martin modified his early authoritarian management style, which no doubt derived from his military experience, to include some elements of participative management. Foremost among these, he feels, is the need to encourage effective upward communication.

"It's a lead-pipe cinch for the person at the top of any organization to communicate to subordinates, whether they number 100, 1,000, or 10,000. The difficult, but equally important, job is to get accurate communication and feedback going in the other direction. Very few companies have solved this problem."

Approaches to Improve Communications

Martin took on the challenges of upward communication as he encountered them, and initiated action to solve them. For example, one of his big problems was how to encourage open communications among the top executive team.

"Many people are reluctant to be completely open with top management. Of course, there are some people, some jewels, who are willing to give you the bad news—some of them even seem to enjoy it! One such officer would come into my office and warn me that things were getting ready to go to hell in a handbasket, and he seemed to get a real inner satisfaction in doing this. But what he might have lacked in interpersonal relations he made up for in guts and integrity, and that moved him right along in his career. But most people are not that way, so in a not too subtle fashion I would challenge people as to whether they were really telling me everything I needed to know—and if I found out that I had not been given the bad news soon enough, I'd let them know about it. Sometimes this directness scares people away, but eventually people got to know me well enough that they knew I wanted to get the bad news early, at least in enough time to do something about it."

But Martin still needed a positive way to encourage upward, open communications among his top people, particularly the six most senior officers at Mass Mutual, who reported directly to him. These executives formed the "Executive Council," and it was upon them he relied most heavily to carry out his plans.

Recognizing that his authoritarian style apparently inhibited these otherwise strong executives from giving him the accurate and sometimes negative feedback that was required, he tried an experiment. He persuaded members of the Council to go off by themselves twice a year for a one- or two-day meeting at a location conducive to informal discussion. He would assign certain problems on which he wanted the group's views but, more important, he proposed these sessions as a risk-free opportunity for members of the group to criticize him and the way he worked. Following each meeting, one group member would meet with Martin to tell him of changes the group felt that he should make in his management style or actions. These post-meeting sessions, always confidential, inevitably began with the group representative saying, "Of course, Jim, these don't necessarily represent my views, but the group feels that you should. . . ." Martin said he often got more criticism than he bargained for, but the meetings evolved into an accurate and effective way of getting important feedback from his top associates, who, he says, "never ran out of things to tell me!"

"Another communication challenge common to every large organization is how to cope with the rumor mill. Rumors among employees can and usually do travel faster than the speed of light. And rumors have two things in common—they are always exaggerated and are almost always wrong. As a result, they can do great damage. They create morale problems and unrest among employees. To handle this, Mass Mutual established a rumor hot line, a telephone number that any employee could call anonymously to inquire whether a rumor was factual. If the person handling the rumor hot line did not know, an authoritative answer was promised by the following day. The system, installed in the early 1970s, is still in place, and it works.''

Still another communications challenge concerned the detailed feedback required to develop important changes that had to be made. For example, as part of its health care cost containment efforts, the company planned to restructure many segments of its Group Health Plan for employees. To assure the best approach, Mass Mutual formed a ''Sounding Board,'' a group consisting of some 50 employees selected at random from all levels in the company. These employees were asked which parts of the Health Plan were most important to them and which potential improvements would be more desirable than others. They were also asked to consider costs and other factors. Later, when a Group Dental Plan was to be introduced, another ''Sounding Board'' was created to advise management how employees felt about various options that could be made available.

Martin also relied on strong internal communications techniques to tap the often hidden creativity of employees whose routine responsibilities tend to limit their opportunities for more visible innovative activity. Because of this communications gap, many companies tend to go outside for new ideas without realizing they have a wealth of internal resources just waiting to be tapped for improvement of bottom-line performance.

''Like most corporations, we seem to hire consultants by the ton, and often they are very helpful, bringing to a problem the all-important advantage of complete objectivity. They are not inhibited by the experiences of the past or by the emotional feelings for the impact of their recommendations on the people who will be involved. However, if you want good, usable ideas about your company, look to the employees who are doing the work, particularly those at the lower level. They have, locked up in their minds, hundreds of ideas that will save real money and represent better ways of doing things that otherwise never come to the surface. The corporate structure seems to stifle the bringing of ideas forward. The attitude of 'don't rock the boat' is a real inhibitor. Yes, we have a company suggestion system, as do most others, and it is of value. But unfortunately all suggestion systems are very slow to react, and the necessity for three or four committees of fellow employees to review every idea submitted causes many to hesitate.

"One thing that has worked for us to help bring forth these ideas and also to reward exceptional work is a 'spot bonus system.' At the time that we budget for salaries in the next succeeding year we normally allow an additional one-half percent of the payroll increase of each division to be used at the sole discretion of the division vice president for these spot bonuses. These are rewarded, as the name implies, on the spot, in amounts from $200 to as much as $2,000 for a person who has done an exceptionally fine job or who has come forth with a quick, usable idea. We don't need to publicize these rewards or to put them in the company newspapers. You can be sure the rumor mill takes care of that—within 24 hours everyone in the building knows when someone has received a spot bonus. It's a good idea, and I recommend it."

Yet another management tool for upward communication at Mass Mutual has been its "Open Door." Each division vice president announces, in the weekly company newspaper, at least one two-hour period in the forthcoming week when he will be available to see employees on any matter they choose, so long as it concerns company business. The ground rule is that the employee must first discuss that problem with his or her supervisor. If satisfaction is not obtained in this way or through other normal channels, the employee is entitled to see the most senior person in the division on a confidential basis. The Chief Executive Officer makes himself available on a similar basis. "How many employees take advantage of this opportunity? Not many. I would guess that no more than 10 employees (out of 4,000) in the entire company use the open door during any given week, but the fact that it's available is important."

"A final upward communication technique we use at Mass Mutual is the McCormick Management Issues Board, a group of 10 to 12 young managers to whom the Chief Executive Officer assigns corporate problems for a recommended solution. The group is afforded research resources and, in addition to presenting recommendations on specified problems, members often initiate projects and ideas of their own. Of course, a decided plus to this is the opportunity of working from an overall corporate standpoint."

Problem Solving

Throughout Martin's tenure as CEO, he leaned quite heavily on task forces. These consisted of one topnotch person from each major department involved in the particular issue addressed by the task force—for example, a second-ranking or third-ranking actuary, an underwriter, and a sales manager. Relieving the members of the task force of all or most of their normal responsibilities, Martin would set specific deadlines for reaching a solution of the assigned problem—"not an actuarial solution or an underwriting solution, but a corporate solution." He would insist from the start that they tell him of the resources they would need to get the job done.

In most cases, the task force approach worked quite well. Sometimes it failed.

"It was because the wrong people—usually those of insufficiently high level—had been appointed. You need people who are close enough to the vice presidents in charge of the departments to be able to speak with their authority to make a decision, yet also close enough to the troops to get a real understanding of the problem. My direction to the members of a task force has always been to keep in touch with the top people of their departments as they go along. I sure don't want the department managers to disassociate themselves from the recommendations, once the task force has done its job."

Long-Range Planning

"I mentioned earlier that the most significant influence on my management style and technique was my experience in the Army

Air Corps. I'd like to add to that my attendance, just before becoming CEO, at AMA's Management Course for Presidents. What I learned—partly from the other students, most of whom were chief executives, was clearly on a par with my Army experience. This five-day course contained by far the most practical, usable management ideas to which I had ever been exposed. In addition, the value of spending several uninterrupted days with 25 to 30 others who were responsible for managing their companies, both large and small, was in itself worthwhile, the exchange of ideas after hours being almost as valuable as the course itself.

"During this course, for the first time I was exposed to the concept of long-range planning as a system of management. I didn't just accept the idea, I swallowed it lock, stock, and barrel. We installed it at Mass Mutual during the next two to three years and, with considerable variations, it is now used by my successor as the core concept of corporate management. It has been successful for us, and one of the keys to that is that the Chief Executive Officer has always been deeply and personally involved.

"Not long after the long-range planning concept had been installed as a system of management, we sent the top echelon, those reporting to the CEO, to another course which covered the same material I'd been exposed to, but on a somewhat condensed basis. The great advantage in doing this was that the credibility and the professional experience of the outside staff helped to sell these management concepts to my immediate associates, and this enabled all of us to learn to speak the same language. Perhaps a year or two after that (in my judgment, we waited too long), we took the final step of having an in-house briefing for the top hundred members of our staff. Again, the key was that it enabled all of us to speak the same language and to understand the same concepts. Of course, we faced the same problem that every company would in that our corporate training staff would have preferred to handle this project themselves. Let's grant that they have equal capability; what they lack, however, is the credibility of an established management development organization such as AMA or others and the ability to get their ideas adopted that comes from using a professional staff. I strongly recommend this concept."

Board Effectiveness

"One of my company's foremost assets is its Board of Directors, and it has been interesting to look back on how it has evolved over the years. I had the unique advantage of helping the Board's Nominating Committee select two-thirds of its outside members during my first six years as Chief Executive Officer. This came about because my predecessor had wisely instituted a mandatory retirement age for board members. One thing that our 18 outside directors have in common is a proven track record of success in their chosen fields. They have over the years steadily become increasingly involved with our company, but at no time have I felt there was any intent to overstep that mythical line between the responsibilities of management and the Board. Today they are very heavily involved in our strategic planning process and, as will happen again shortly, when they go away with our top officers for the annual three-day strategic planning session, their influence is positive and strong. I foresee this trend as continuing.

"An entirely separate reason that I favor a strong outside Board of Directors is the necessity in any large organization of having a qualified and responsible group to check on the power and the actions of the Chief Executive Officer. Most of our companies have a very distinct impact upon the public, and there must be some outside body to monitor our performance—to make certain we are held accountable.

"It's vital to recognize that each board member is a unique individual with his or her own way of being helpful. They certainly do not all want to be treated the same. Some make outstanding contributions during the Board meetings. And others can make very valuable contributions between meetings. During the meetings, those with the loudest voices, like mine, may have an edge. But some of the more soft-spoken ones who meet with you afterwards or give you a call on the telephone can make remarkable contributions. The first job of the CEO and that of the directors as well is to let one another know what is expected of them and how they want the working relationship to develop. Of course, the first secret is to have a good, capable board."

An Executive Support System:
The Executive Secretary

"In my view, the unsung heroes of successful corporate life are executive secretaries—a more apt description for them is executive assistants. I have been blessed with the best and am certain beyond all doubt that my career would not have gone nearly as well as it has for me or my company had it not been for the very effective people I have had carrying out this important role. Every executive will find his or her best way of working with an assistant. For me, it has always been to share everything I do with them—to make them confidants and direct participants in everything I do. Some functions they can carry out better than I can. Foremost among these is maintaining the daily calendar—deciding who must be seen and when —screening telephone calls and anticipating the needs for appointments in the future. Of course, this same screening goes on with the mail. I wouldn't think of making a business appointment on my own, and people have over time come to recognize that once my assistant makes a commitment, I will back it up. She develops a keen sense of my priorities; for example, she knows I want to be at all long-term planning sessions, so she simply assures that I am there.

"An important part of the art of administration is attention to detail, and a well-trained assistant can relieve you of that— freeing your mind for other matters. I have been fortunate in having assistants who have done that and much more. When I'm not sure what past corporate policy has been on a matter, I have always felt free to ask them to find out for me, and to give me the history, the why's, and so on. Our top staff members have learned to deal with my assistant in routine matters and, again, to recognize that when that assistant makes a commitment for me, I will consider it just as binding as though I had made it myself. Maybe more so. I have little patience for today's executive who complains about not having enough time to do the important parts of his job. That only tells me that he isn't delegating enough to a capable assistant."

Paying the Price

"In judging people, all of us have to rely to a large degree on our experience and intuition. The two characteristics I look for first are self-discipline and a willingness to pay the price. The person who will not discipline himself in personal matters as well as in business is too often undependable when the going gets rough. Similarly, while I have rarely met a businessperson who didn't proclaim to have an inner drive and a great desire for progress, there are only a few who demonstrate the willingness to pay the price that is necessary for success at the top in today's world."

Corporate Responsibility

Relatively early in his tenure as chief executive officer, Martin began to accept what he describes as the "responsibility" of major organizations and their CEOs to a variety of constituencies beyond their stockholders.

"The old concept, which is still advanced by some, that a corporation is responsible only to its stockholders, as long as it is not breaking the law, is as outmoded and dead as the dodo bird. Today's corporation must accept that in addition to its responsibility to stockholders, it has an equal responsibility to its employees, to its customers, to its suppliers, and to those who live in the communities where it operates. Quite often these constituencies have conflicting interests, and it is the chief executive officer's job to balance these interests and see to it that all are treated as fairly as possible. This is not a 'dogoodnik' concept, but one that is essential for long-term success in today's social environment."

Along with these areas of concern, as Martin sees it, a CEO must also remain constantly alert to all aspects of the environment in which today's corporations operate, not the least of which is government.

"I have had to modify my Midwestern free enterprise upbringing, at least enough to recognize that when your business is as much in the public interest as ours (the insurance industry) is, you need to have some regulation. But you will get the kind you deserve. So you had better pay attention and work with the government. Any CEO today, no matter what business he is in, who does not recognize that his company is in partnership with the federal government and the state governments as well, is flirting with disaster. So he had better get to know his partner well and learn how to work with him. For example, there is now a new insurance company federal income tax bill—and like all new tax bills, we still do not know how it will work. It was passed more than a year ago but is still being rewritten, the regulations are being modified, the so-called technical amendments are being put in—and one technical amendment can be more significant than a month of debate in the House of Representatives. To work effectively with the government, you have to do your homework."

> CEO homework also includes keeping current with your industry, which Martin does through membership in groups of life insurance company CEOs. Among these are a group of 12 mutual companies and a group consciously designed to represent a mix of companies—large companies, small companies, stock companies, mutual companies, and companies from diverse geographical areas.

"One hears a lot of baloney about its being lonely at the top, but these groups always encourage you to speak openly about any problem you are having. It is always a relief to learn that the rest of the group are similarly afflicted in dealing with the community or their boards or the government or whatever. And one can learn a lot just from watching outstanding people operate. Don McNaughton, who led the Pru, for example, was always interesting to observe and to listen to. Although the Met at one time was much larger than Prudential, now the Pru is head and shoulders above them. Don is the person who made this happen, and I think he did it by getting others to make it happen. He is a lawyer by background, but he has the great capacity to make everyone about him want to do their very best. He retired at age 60, having told the Board in advance that he was going to do that, and he became head of the Hospital Corporation of America, making something very substantial of that as well. Another CEO whom I greatly admire is Ed Bates, who heads Connecticut Mutual. These and a handful of other leaders were extraordinarily successful in managing in a well balanced way, in a way which would satisfy the needs of all of their companies' constituencies.

"There is a great deal of outstanding leadership in this country. And in the long run, people are what it is all about. The fun of building a company and managing it successfully comes from the accumulated contribution of the people whom you have the opportunity to work with over the years.

"Somehow my semi-authoritarian style (I guess I have improved a little bit—I *had* to) and my impatience were continually tempered by the people with whom I worked. Impatience may not be a virtue, but sometimes it has helped me; it has helped to get things done, and I still believe that an important part of the CEO's job is to rock the boat from time to time, not just to steer it."

Peter G. Scotese

Chairman, Executive Committee
Springs Industries, Inc.

*H*e appreciates parachutes that work, having parachuted behind enemy lines during World War II. But he doesn't like today's "golden parachutes" that provide rich rewards for CEOs who are no longer contributing to the business. In his direct way, he calls them "an abomination"—because they violate what he considers the underlying requirement for a successful business life: integrity. He also believes that top executives should have interests outside their jobs. He practices what he preaches, with strong interests in the arts, fine food, tennis, and more. Intellectual curiosity is one of the qualities he looks for in a potential executive recruit.

From his orphaned childhood, he rose to become the first nonfamily president of Springs Industries since it was organized as Springs Mills in 1887. During his 12-year tenure as president and CEO, he transformed the company into a professionally managed public corporation—now a large manufacturer of finished fabrics and home furnishing products with more than 16,000 employees in 31 states and Mexico. Under his leadership, Springs' sales tripled; earnings from continuing operations more than quadrupled; the company was divisionalized; product lines were expanded; and formal long-range strategic planning was established. With a self-made management style that depends on no formulas, he is truly a transforming manager.

Career Information:

1947 Joined Nashua Manufacturing Company (later acquired by Indian Head Mills), serving as territory salesman, eastern regional sales manager, and general sales manager

1954 Named corporate vice president and general manager of Finished Goods Division, Indian Head Mills

1963 Named chairman of the board of the Milwaukee Boston Store Division of Federated Department Stores

1964 Named vice president of Federated Department Stores

1969 Joined Springs Industries as president and member of board of directors

1975 Elected vice chairman

1976 Elected chief executive officer

1981 Named chairman of executive committee

1985 Retired

Other Affiliations:

- Director, Bell & Howell Company
- Director, Armstrong Rubber Company
- Director, National Distillers & Chemical Corporation
- Director, Dollar Dry Dock Savings Bank
- Director, Duty Free Shoppers, Ltd.
- Fellow, National Association of Corporate Directors
- Vice-Chairman, Business Committee of Metropolitan Museum of Art, New York
- Member, Photographic Committee of Museum of Modern Art, N.Y.
- Chairman, Board of Trustees, Fashion Institute of Technology
- Member, Board of Trustees, Boys Clubs of America
- Chairman, Board of Directors, Harvard Business School Club of New York

Educational Information:

- Wharton School of Business of the University of Pennsylvania, 1942
- Harvard University Advanced Management Program, 1960

Personal Information:

- Born March 13, 1920, Philadelphia, Penn.
- Served during World War II as officer in anti-aircraft artillery and parachute infantry. Won Bronze Star medal and Purple Heart with Oak Leaf Cluster
- Is married, has daughter and son
- Outside interests: Collecting original art, sailing, tennis, golf, fine food

Peter G. Scotese

"*D*irectness. That's what works for me. I am very direct," said Pete Scotese. "Maybe to some people that's a defect, but that's the way I am. I generally don't sugarcoat the way I feel, and I am *constantly* in situations where I am very blunt and direct."

Donald Frey, Chairman of the Bell & Howell Company, on whose Board Scotese serves, comments: "I am not sure I'd use the word direct as much as I would the word realistic. Pete is both realistic and instinctive; he is very intuitive. He will listen to the most obtuse technical presentation, and at the end he'll say, 'OK, but what does the customer want?' I remember once when he had finished listening to a very gloomy economist reporting that the market was going to hell, he said, 'Well, my sense is that the market is OK, and despite what you say, we are going to have a Christmas anyway.' That's a response I particularly remember. He has the rare ability to cut through things, no matter how complex they are.

"Pete will also at times act as an interceder on behalf of someone, usually against the tide, saying, for example, 'Don, I think that guy's underpaid.' When you are around Pete, you have to deal with the realism which he presents. In observing an executive whose performance may not be up to par, he will say, 'I have been hearing a lot about this guy for a long time, and I am tired of hearing about it,' the implication being that we had better do something about it."

"For me," said Pete Scotese, "there is no middle ground; I simply have to be very straightforward, and that's my style. I don't for a moment think that it is the ideal style; I'm not sure there is such a thing. I'm not sure that I recommend this to others, but there it is. It works for me. I tell you, I go to bed at night, and I sleep. I've done my job."

Peter G. Scotese in 1969 became the first nonfamily President in the history of what was then Springs Mills. He had the task of transforming that company into a professionally managed public corporation that has become Springs Industries, Inc., one of the nation's larger manufacturers of finished fabrics and home furnishings products. During his 12-year tenure as President or Chief Executive Officer, Springs' sales tripled, earnings more than quadrupled, product lines were substantially expanded, and a formal long-range strategic plan was put into effect. Directness, taken to an extreme, had been a tradition at Springs Mills. Its owner, the fabled Colonel Elliott White Springs, had been a genius, but also a martinet.

"A sales manager named Charles O. Wood, who used to be my boss, worked for Springs. The Colonel knew his name was Wood, but he called him Woods. He didn't want him to think that they were familiar, even though there was no possibility of that. On the day of Christmas Eve, the Colonel called the sales manager, saying 'Woods, you have 50 cases of sheets left in the warehouse and the year's almost over.' Wood replied, 'Yes sir, Colonel, we have plans to get rid of those very soon.' 'Well, when do you plan to get rid of them?' 'Oh, we'll get rid of them before the year end,' meaning the following week. The Colonel said coldly, 'That's not good enough, Woods. Get rid of them by tonight and call me back when it's done.' Boom! Wood spent most of Christmas Eve trying to find out the home telephone numbers of Broadway jobbers to whom he could give away the sheets at close-out prices. At about 11 o'clock, he got another call from the Colonel: 'Did you sell the sheets, Woods?' 'Yes sir, Colonel!' The Colonel hung up the phone with no thank you or any other comment.

"Another story: When the Colonel learned that he had probable terminal cancer, he called his Board together, saying, 'My son-in-law is going to be running this business, and I am going into the hospital. I have cancer. The doctors do not think I will recover. You, you, and you are no longer on the Board. I want to correct my Board mistakes before my son-in-law takes over. Goodbye, gentlemen.' He left and never came back."

Transforming a company with such a climate into a modern corporation that practices participative management was no mean

PETER G. SCOTESE

task. Scotese, as usual, moved directly, yet he did not characterize his job as difficult.

Building a Board of Directors

"Difficult? No, but it was different. Taking a family-oriented business and making it a publicly-oriented company could be very difficult. But I was fortunate due to the fact that I was able to bring in a largely outside Board of Directors. That single act probably gave the transition more impetus than any other thing I could have done. It exposed the family to a group of executives who were almost entirely from outside of the industry. People from many different disciplines who were bright,

127

smart, sharp, and who shared the same kind of responsibilities as I did. I think that had to impress them. And wherever we had differences of opinion between the family members and myself, the Board was able to resolve them with little or no difficulty.

"The support of the Board made it all possible. I had felt that if anything happened to me, what this family needed most was direction from the outside, so that stronger-willed family members growing up and getting involved in the business, if they chose to do it, would not be too disruptive or too dissuasive. I simply felt that this would be a good survival strategy which would stand the company in good stead for a long period of time, even without Pete Scotese.

"As I think back about the Board members, my objective was to find people of specific characteristics and experience. I recruited a lawyer (something which I might not do today) who was in a law firm which represented the family's interests, was a trustee of the family's trusts and foundations, a post to which he had been appointed by the Colonel, Springs' predecessor owner and operator. Having known him, I felt that he would be objective in terms of the course of the business and would not let the family interests kill the goose that laid the golden egg. The lawyer was an obvious choice to bridge the relationship between the family and me.

"The next thing I needed were chief executive officers from non-textile companies. But I also wanted someone who could oversee a strong internal audit function. The internal audit area was getting a lot of attention within Boards at that time, and I believe strongly that this is essential in order to assure the financial integrity of an organization. I recruited the ex-head of Arthur Andersen & Co.'s Atlanta office, a man who had retired and had become a professional Board member. He had been involved extensively in community activities as well, a person who could give us a power base on the board in terms of internal audit.

"Then I knew I needed CEOs who had similar problems to mine, people who would be sympathetic to the vicissitudes of the business, people with other experience. At that time I was serving on the Board of Bell & Howell, and I was most impressed with the then and now CEO, Don Frey, who is certainly one of the most brilliant personalities to which I have ever been exposed. I went shopping for chief executive officers, got Don Frey and got the son of a former Board member who lived in the South who ran a family-operated business, Sonoco Products. Charles Coker, Jr. came on our Board, representing another family-owned business and also representing South Carolina, where we were one of the state's largest employers. So each spot was filled with a specific mission in mind, a specific objective. I would identify what the company needed and then go out and find the person who met those needs. I wasn't then and am not now inspired by the idea of having some widely publicized chief executive officer of some major corporation on the Board, just for the sake of a name and visibility.

"Again, I would say that my approach was that of directness. I needed to start at the top and advised the family that we needed an outside Board. I hope that my direct action has continued to be a strength of the company ever since that time."

Assessing People

Those who know Scotese consider him to be an outstanding judge of people.

"The first and basic tenet is integrity. That has not changed and never will. If there is the least bit of a lack of integrity, or a shading of it, it simply isn't there. It is not a 95 percent thing, it is 100 percent, and if you don't have it, you don't have it. The lack of integrity is easily detectable.

"A second tenet is that a good manager has to be intelligent, and I do not necessarily rank intelligence with book learning. What's needed is extraordinary common sense with judgment. A strong manager must have steel intestines and sticktoitiveness. That is also something that has not changed. But underneath it all is integrity."

Whenever Pete Scotese goes into a new job, he spends a generous amount of time getting to know his people, and he recommends this investment of time to others.

129

"The people I know in both the profit and not-for-profit sectors *rarely* have the opportunity to talk to the boss on an uninhibited open basis. I cannot think of any device that will attract someone to a new person more quickly than just sitting down and saying, 'I'm new here; I don't know very much and maybe not a damn thing about the company; you have an important role here, so would you please help me; tell me about *yourself*; tell me about the strengths and the weaknesses in the organization as *you* perceive them. I may or may not do something about it, and I may even see it differently, but I have got to have as much knowledge about the operation from where you sit as I can get.' For someone just coming into the situation, this is essential. I have never found the act itself to be anything but a tremendous blessing. Secondly, you generally do get an extremely valuable input on a broad range of subject matter, and once you finish with the key people, you can put together a jigsaw that gives you a fairly good impression going in of what the company or the organization is all about. I think that this is an invaluable tool.

"You can have a very good batting average on judging people if you spend enough time with them. This is where I part company with testing, which is certainly an important adjunct. But in many cases I think that testing has become to many executives a substitute for hours and days and weeks of interviewing. I think it is impossible to get to know a key executive on the basis of one or two interviews, and it is wrong to make any judgment so quickly. I think it is absolutely essential to spend as much time on several separate occasions with an individual if you really want to draw out his strengths and weaknesses. If you are willing to pay the price of that amount of time and effort, you will rarely go wrong.

"I would suggest that good executive recruiting is really no more than what I have just described. The best recruiters get paid enormous fees. And yet if you take a look at an outfit like Nordeman Grimm, you will find that 95 percent of the CEOs they place stick. And if you look further at what they do essentially, you will see that they simply spend hours, days, and weeks interviewing and finding out as much as they can about the individual. I don't believe that there is any substitute for that. You certainly can't do it with tests. There are cases, and we all know them, where we get fooled. There are unusual situations where it is impossible to predict the outcome. Still, you can have a very successful batting average about people if you follow this practice. The past, after all, is a hell of a good indication about the future, unless there has been some major interruption, some major change. If you spend enough time, you'll find out about that change as well.''

Pete Scotese likes to test people in subtle ways. He is alert to certain indications that may set off an alarm in his mind about a person's capability or character.

"A lack of consideration is, I think, a basic defect. Being political, where it becomes obvious that someone is trying to politicize a situation, is detectable. Shading the truth, noting just a shade of larceny in an individual who may think that cutting corners represents being smart. I am talking about things that are not on the record. Things which I try to smoke out by observation. I look for little things. To me, it is a defect if a person cannot spell properly. That bothers the hell out of me! I can't tell you why, and maybe it's unfair. But it bothers me when someone is careless enough to spell my name wrong or to write Spring Mills instead of Springs Mills. Such things represent a lack of attention. More than that, this shows a lack of intellectual curiosity. Whether someone is curious about items I mention is easy to smoke out. I make it a practice to send little notes or items I come across which I think will be helpful to people who work for me or to CEOs of boards on which I sit. I stand back to see whether this will trigger any response or any curiosity. I am simply not impressed with people in higher levels who are not intellectually curious.''

At one time there was a very attractive piece of sculpture on Scotese's office desk, large enough so that no one could fail to see it. Yet Pete remarked that a number of people had come into his office without mentioning it. This lack of response made him wonder about their level of curiosity.

131

"I think that intellectual curiosity is particularly vital today. There is so damn much going on. Staying narrow and deeply burrowed in your work is great for a specialized situation. But if you are going to advance, to move ahead to the top, you constantly have to have your antennas out there, asking yourself what the hell is going on, because the higher up you go, the less specialized you are going to be and the more you are going to be looking out at the world and looking further into the future and watching the telltales to see what is going on. What is the next thing on the horizon? Look at the suddenness with which teenage movies hit Home Box Office and Showtime. Somebody in Hollywood woke up and said, 'Hell, all the movies we are making are for audiences of people 40 and over; but the people who watch movies, those who have the time to watch movies, are ages 14 to 17. They are the television and movie audience.' Now every damn time you put on Showtime, you get these junk teenage movies with girls undressing, and suddenly this fare has gone from zero percent to 70 percent or 80 percent of the fare. Whether this is good or not, somebody recognized an opportunity in terms of market. And it was so damn obvious, that I have to wonder why it took so long for somebody to finally recognize it. There has *got* to be an element of curiosity in a successful manager."

Art and Business

Scotese's curiosity extends deeply into the world of art. He is both a collector and supporter of the arts.

"I think a CEO has the responsibility to help bring some piece of the outside world, whether it be art or public affairs, into the life of his people. After all, the CEO has more opportunity than most, and he should take advantage of that, not just selfishly but for the sake of his organization. But quite apart from that, art simply enriches, whether it be the opera or the symphony or anything else. I don't think anyone necessarily has to be interested in art, but a person should be alive, should be interested in something. In my case, I found art to be important, because I think that art is the great interpreter of what is happening and what will happen. I think that it is also a great interpreter of the temperature of the people. You remember the violent anti-Vietnam protest art in the early stages of the Vietnamese War; that was telling us something. It was saying, 'Hey, don't believe what you read in the media or what the President is telling you, here is what is happening, and this is the feeling about it.' I was in Sweden once during the middle or later period of the Vietnamese War, visiting Brud Holland, then U.S. Ambassador to Sweden. The art that I saw in a Stockholm museum was *pungent*, not just provocative, but *lethally* outrageous when it came to what it said about President Kennedy and his wife, what it said about Lyndon Johnson. It was vulgar. I was appalled, astounded, astonished—it was bizarre. It was venting against all the institutions and the people of the U.S. for creating this kind of violence. I talked to Ambassador Brud Holland about it, who had not yet seen it. He saw it later and was just as shocked as I.

"Art interprets, whether it is the performing arts or the static arts. People at the top have to have an interest in something, maybe bird watching. They should have some dimensions outside their specific jobs. This is useful, indeed essential. I do not say that a CEO cannot be successful without this; but without outside interests, one has a limited life. People who don't have these outside interests, these needs to satisfy their intellectual curiosity, are the ones you can't get out of their jobs when the time comes for them to quit. It is impossible for them to move, since they have nowhere to go. I was just reading about a recently retired executive of a major bank who seems to be searching for something to do. I was surprised to learn this. It is very important that people at the top or near the top develop a much broader perspective than just their own business. A person must develop his or her own dimensions. To me the arts represent a dimension that is useful and interesting and will become even more so as time goes on.

"Occasionally such an interest will spill over into business. For example, because of my interest in art, I encouraged working with the Metropolitan Museum of Art to get an exclusive to access essentially everything in the Museum, and we brought out a Metropolitan collection of sheets by Springmaid. Springs has paid the Met over $3 million in royalties, but we have sold over $100 million of bedsheets at a much higher profit. And we have enhanced people's outlook as a result.

"A second example is the way we have supported photography at the Museum of Modern Art and elsewhere to the tune of $1.5 million plus. Photography is a great art form, and it is not as expensive to support a photography exhibit as it is a major "blockbuster" exhibit of paintings. Yet I feel that Springs has helped to bring outstanding photography to a lot of people, and of course the company gets credit for that. But it started with my interest in art, my curiosity—not a narrow interest in business."

Decision Making

"I did not try to impose this idea on people; instead, I talked about it, we talked it through. There are rare occasions where I would impose a decision upon people. Generally, decisions are made by talking them through within a group. Almost all of my decisions are based upon how well they can help move the ball ahead. At Springs, all of the division heads have monthly meetings—on manufacturing, marketing, merchandising—and of course they have their own divisional management committees as well. These meet so that the whole group is exposed to how the division manager operates. The corporate management committee is exposed to how the chief executive officer operates. So you have a potential training ground within that group, as they see the process work week after week, month after month, year after year; and eventually someone will say, 'Hell, I could do that, I could probably run a company, or I can run a division.' It is very participative. Our new management cross-fertilizes between divisions. If there is an opening in one division, they will look within all divisions to see who can fill the job the best. The committee structure, let's say the committee on asset utilization, might consist of people from the internal audit department and a sales manager from a consumer products division who knows absolutely nothing about asset management. And the head of the international division and another division's marketing guy. I mean they just put them in jobs whether they have had experience in it or not. Throw people into a committee. Give them an agenda, make sure someone smart is there to lead them, and everyone learns.

"As to job changes, Springs might move someone from manufacturing management to personnel director, from the legal department to the head of human resources, or from the legal department to head of purchasing. We just do not accept —certainly I don't—that you cannot move between disciplines and run something. The management I have been involved in is very participative. Anybody can go anywhere and be anything he wants, if he has the capability to do it. This process is not just for the top level, either. Within the salaried group, which totals about 2,000 people, this goes right down the line. We also have training at all levels—from first-line supervisor and up. All of our middle managers at Springs attended the General Management Course at the American Management Association or similar training elsewhere. There is plenty of participation for those who want it, and sometimes there is a lot whether they want it or not."

Scotese's Early Career

Pete began his career as an accountant, but his time in the Army during World War II changed his perspective about what he wanted to do. When he came out of the Army, he decided that he did not want to be in an "office-type sedentary position" and concluded that the way to success, at least then, was through marketing. He decided to be a salesman. He left a very secure accounting job for a highly insecure, low-paid sales trainee job in a textile company, the old Nashua Manufacturing Company, later acquired by Indian Head Mills.

"I bloodied my nose three or four years, getting promoted into a regional manager's spot. I think if I was starting out today I'd have the same proclivity toward marketing. I think that route is still a good one and still maybe the best, maybe even bigger and better than it used to be.

"I remember covering eastern Pennsylvania with boxes and packages, and trunks and suitcases full of blankets and sheets and bedspreads and stuff—not having a car. I used public transportation, but the excitement of traveling and calling on new customers overcame the inconvenience of getting into those trucks and trains and streetcars and buses and what not, sleeping in railway stations, and so forth. So I really have to say that on balance, the novelty and the excitement of this early part of my career overcame the negatives, and I very quickly got to the point where they gave me a fleet car, so I was a little more mobile. I complained so much about the way they were running the business at headquarters that they brought me to New York to shut me up—made me a regional sales manager. As one guy said, 'Pete was complaining so much so we brought him up here to get rid of the complaints and to cure all of the diseases that we had.' Sure, I guess I was a little cocky, but I thought the suggestions I was making were good ones, and I guess others eventually thought so too.

"I was very happy to be in sales. When I had been one year out of the Army, I was sick and tired of being in the accounting arena. I made a major decision, for I agreed to make about half of what I had been making and go into a totally new field. I had read a newspaper ad which said that if I wanted to work very hard in a textile company as a trainee, with very few benefits initially and very low pay, but with very good future prospects, then I should answer the ad. I was reading it at dinner one night at home, and I said to my wife that I had to get the hell out of here and go up and see the man that placed that ad. Deciding to make that move from accounting was one turning point of my career. I got to know the textile industry pretty well. The next turning point—a major one—was blasting myself loose from the textile industry to go into retailing with Federated Stores. I had been approached through a headhunter and had gone through a very soul searching, wrenching experience when I decided to give up 16 years with a wonderful mentor, Charles O. Wood. His son is Charles Osgood, a newscaster on radio and television. My other mentor was Jim Robison, who founded Indian Head. I had become slightly rich, but very rich indeed in terms of observing leadership qualities and personal qualities and moral qualities. The Federated job was a very significant change for me, for it was out of the supplier area and into the retail end. That had a very profound effect on me in the sense that it was a very different kind of business, a new culture, totally consumer oriented, with great opportunities to make an impact on the community, as well as business.''

Community Leadership

Pete became Board Chairman of the Milwaukee Boston Store Division of Federated Department Stores in 1963. While in Milwaukee he was named a Vice President of Federated, a position in which he became a real community leader.

When he left Federated for Springs in 1969, a *Milwaukee Sentinel* editorial said: "Scotese and his firm have been in the forefront of efforts to promote equal opportunity and fair employment, both in word and in deed. He has also shown an aggressive interest in the community's economic and cultural development. In the process, he has molded something of a model for involvement of the business sector in civic and governmental affairs."

"At Federated I could contribute to the betterment of the city and county and yet serve the business at the same time. I also learned the business from the consumer point of view backward to merchandise. Then later I went back to the supplier side. There is an enormous difference between the retailing business and the manufacturing business. There are no bricks and mortar in retailing. If something isn't selling, you mark it down, get something else in its place pretty fast, if you are going to succeed.

"I was six years in retailing and at 43 the youngest chief executive officer of any major department store in the Federated or AMC group, and the only nonretailer up to that point who was ever brought in to run a store by Federated or any AMC store. I think that not having been a retailer gave me a hell of a plus in that particular situation, where they needed a totally different strategy to survive and prosper. And again, when I went back into manufacturing, that point of view was very helpful to have as well.

"There is probably no exactly comparable situation today. Today a young man or woman entering a large corporation would probably be placed as a trainee, exposed to many different areas of the business—personnel, marketing, financial, research and development, and what not—in the course of the training process, and then the young person would drift toward some particular area or be shifted around until the company and you had a good idea of what you might be best suited for. That probably cuts short the need for the kind of experience I had, which was to experiment on my own from one type of business to another, from stenographer to accountant, from accountant to sales trainee and changing from one industry to another. There is a little more structure in today's opportunities, in affording incoming trainees an opportunity to get exposure to a lot of different segments of the business. Things are much more structured today. I recently talked to a young man about to graduate from Lafayette and who has written three different kinds of resumes—one oriented to marketing, one oriented to financial services, and one to another area. He has spread these resumes out among a range of companies to see whether this bait will work to attract some people at least to interview him. That is one way of going about it in today's environment."

Sensitivity to People

> Pete Scotese rose to his position from very modest beginnings. He graduated from Girard College High School, a school for fatherless orphans, so when he talks about making it on one's own, as one who has been given the Horatio Alger Award, he knows whereof he speaks. Moreover, his early experience, he says, makes him constantly conscious of the inherent worth of people. He is as comfortable in conversing with elevator starters and "the group in the mailroom" as he is with fellow corporate directors.

"I have never forgotten my roots. I've been there. I know what others go through, and I am very sympathetic. That's why I'm active in the Boys Clubs and other organizations. I don't do it for show, I do it because I've been there. I know how heartbreaking it is for people who don't have parents or must struggle to get ahead. Someone can come into my office and say, 'My God, what a lucky guy he is—just look at all this!'

But it took 40-plus years to get here. So I am very sympathetic, and I think that is important. I think I am honest. I don't believe I've ever exuded an Ivy League, narrow-lapel kind of attitude or that I've been supercilious toward anyone.

"I am flattered that the Springs family never asked me what my religion was. There were not many Catholics among our employees in South Carolina when I went there, just 18,000 Baptists and me. They never asked me about my nationality or my religion, and I have known people in the past on my way up who would shudder at the thought of hiring someone of Italian descent who was a Catholic. To them it would have been reprehensible to have someone running the firm with that kind of background.

"I had an amusing experience when I joined Springs. I had been giving a talk about personal philosophy, and when I was finished, one man sneaked up to me—the room loaded with plant executives—and quietly asked, 'Are you Catholic?' And I said that I was. He said, 'There are four of us! Come here, I want you to meet the other three—Pat Mullineaux and a lawyer and someone else.' Frank Keene and the others—now there are *five* of us. Frank ran the cafeteria, and Springs fed more people hot meals than any other manufacturer in the country except- ing possibly Ford Motor Company—three shifts, five days a week then, seven days in some of our plants, hot food every time—a big plus in keeping employee morale up. This guy ran it, ran it with a plant that was ten times the size of this room, feeding 22,000 people then—three times a day—and he was a Catholic. So I guess some of us Catholics worked out. The point is that no one asked me. They simply took it as a given that I was an individual, with perhaps some potential. No one cared about my religious persuasion or my nationality.

"I think that it is important when you deal with different people that you treat them the same way. Today a lot of techni- cal people are coming into the business, men and women with degrees in economics, computer science. I would not treat any of this new breed today any differently than I would treat any- one else. It would be wrong to say that I am one kind of person to you because you are technically oriented, and another kind of person to someone else.

"I also believe that it is important to get to know various kinds of people. I have had considerable cross-fertilization with academic people. In Milwaukee, I started discussion sessions between businessmen and professors and deans at the University of Wisconsin, a very liberal institution. Some of the faculty were socialistic as hell, but I found that when we could sit down over a table and talk directly, even bluntly to each other; even when we disagreed, we understood each other. We knew where we were coming from.

"My experience on the Board of Trustees at the Fashion Institute of Technology, even though that is a specialized kind of school, has led me to believe that I can get along with the deans and professors and that they can get along with me, even when we don't agree with each other.

"Don Frey, Chairman and CEO of Bell & Howell, is remarkable in being able to get along with both technical and non-technical people. He has a double Ph.D. in technical fields, yet he is probably one of the best marketers I have ever met. He used to confuse the hell out of me because he would change his mind between meetings—change his mind about people, about products, about anything. At first that would drive me crazy. It took me about two years to realize that this was not only *not* a defect in him; it was a hell of an asset. His mind is like a computer. Every time he talks to somebody or reads something, the information goes into his computer brain and a different product comes out. You talk about intellectual curiosity. He is incredible."

The Importance of Integrity

"I talk about the five I's—integrity, intelligence, intestines, imagination and 'inthusiasm.' But notice that the first of these is integrity. I am easy to understand. Everything is in the open, it is written on my sleeve, and if you cross me, you're dead. I expect you to have the other four, but integrity is absolutely basic.

"People ask me about directors and officers liability policies. 'What do you think about the way premium rates are going up,' they ask. I'll tell you what I think about it. You can take all the directors and officers liability policies and throw them in the East River or the Hudson, because if the guy at the top isn't honest, forget it. If he is honest, you don't need any insurance policies, because an organization reflects the integrity of the man at the top. If he is honest, you can go to sleep at night as a director. If he is dishonest, no amount of insurance or checking or reading what he is saying or anything else can make your net worth safe. If there is integrity at the top, the organization will sense it. And they will be careful. You may still make a mistake, but it won't be on purpose. If there is no integrity, they sense that too. If you've got a top guy who's devious, there is no damn way a director can find out what the hell he is doing. You see it every day with the banks, federal savings and loans, and other businesses unraveling, with very smart directors, sometimes. Look at Continental Illinois, which had stellar directors. But they didn't know what the hell was wrong. They were served up stuff, they read it, and they figured what the hell—he's running the company, he knows what he is doing. A strong internal audit function in any company helps build financial integrity in a corporation, but the place to start building it is at the top. And if it isn't there, then it isn't anywhere.

"I have written and spoken about 'golden parachutes,' and you know that I don't believe in them. I believe strongly that a chief executive officer should be very well paid. He takes a lot of risks and carries a lot of responsibility. Golden parachutes may have done more to discredit CEOs among the public than all the various instances of white-collar crime and fraud. When executives seek to multiply their just rewards and guarantee that they keep getting rewards at a time when they are no longer contributing to running their business, this is outrageous. It is an abomination and a violation of integrity—my first 'i.'"

The Global View

"I mentioned five I's, but today there is another one, international. Looking toward the future, you have to make assumptions, and one would be that you will have to get global in your perspective. That will be vital. Perhaps people in the future won't have the same degree of loyalty or sticktoitiveness that we had in the past, and there may be more movement among executives than in the past, and that's an environmental assumption. But the internationalization of business, the globalization, is fundamental. The Swiss, the Swedes, and the Japanese are not only willing to put in more hours and display more loyalty and sticktoitiveness, but, more importantly, they work much smarter. They expose their young executives to world travel and world work more than we do in this country. Let me give you an example. Springs deals with a large trading company, C. Itoh and Company, and Toray Industries, which is kind of the DuPont of Japan, for we import a significant amount of Ultrasuede® brand fabric and other products. The young Japanese men that we see in America who might be on their first overseas assignment are generally in their '20s. We may track them for 10 to 14 years and find that they will have lived and worked in as many as seven or eight countries. By the time that they are in their mid-'30s, they have infinitely more sense of different cultures, languages, and customs than our chief executive officers have gained in a lifetime of international managing. That's an enormous plus. American companies are going to have to learn from this and to do the same thing. I don't think there is any way you can compete in the global environment without having a sense of the culture of at least one other country. If there is a single deficiency in this country—not just politically in our State Department and in our Presidents, but in our companies as well—it lies in our not being able to understand other cultures and how they work. The fact is that such flexibility is mandatory. The British have it. The Swiss have it. The Japanese certainly have that sense of understanding of how vital it is for them to be flexible in other cultures. In contrast, we feel that we have to democratize everything or make it like the United States. There will be infinitely more cross-fertilization between countries and among executives who have lived and served overseas.

"Looking toward a future that will be full of international trade, I don't believe that any red-blooded U.S. businessman favors a slowing down of free trade in any way. Whether in the auto industry or the steel industry or the textile industry, I don't believe that any businessman with his head screwed on right believes down deep that anything but free trade is the best idea for this country or any country. On the other hand, I also believe that some constraints will be imposed—some have been imposed—to force those countries that are not playing fair to play more fairly. I am not saying we will get them to play all our way. There are many countries where political pricing and the cooperation of the government, the banks, and the corporations are making it impossible for us to compete effectively. You can't eliminate all of this, but I think there will be negotiation and eventual moderation. But it has just got to be a free trade world, since it is a global world and becoming more so. The whole damn environment is just moving, rushing toward it. It is inevitable. Yet everything is not so gloomy. There are many areas which are overlooked by the press and not mentioned, where there are no restraints. The service businesses are one example. McDonald's is being promoted overseas, as well as temporary employment agencies; and advertising agencies are sprouting out in new branches all over the world. There are few constraints in the service business in foreign countries, and it is growing dramatically. U.S. industry is co-franchising and doing other things. But I believe the textile industry view is probably about where everybody else stands. There ought to be a way to moderate imports to the extent that the domestic industry can reshuffle its asset base into areas that are less competitive or noncompetitive with imports, and I think that that's what we are pleading for more than anything else. In other words, can the rate of growth of imports be controlled a little bit better? And where growth of imports is totally the function of a political process to gain market share without regard to cost or anything else, as the Japanese have done in many areas, then it needs to be treated and controlled pretty harshly. But I don't think we are going to have any serious efforts on the part of our government to have import restrictions or tariffs that are unbearable to the exporting countries. I just don't think that will or should happen.

"If I were talking to a young man or woman today, I would try to get them to understand the need to branch out globally. In fact, I just recommended to a young man who is planning to get an M.B.A. that he go to work abroad for a couple of years before he does his graduate work. He needs to live overseas, learn some languages, live in another culture for a couple of years if he can. If there is one regret in my life, it is that I have not lived in another culture for even a couple of years, and I recommend that strongly. You simply have to live in another culture—and it can be any culture—to understand how other people think and work. I don't give a damn if it's South Africa or England. I think it can even be an English-speaking culture, but it certainly is preferable to have had a couple of years living somewhere else in order to understand other people who live and think differently than we do. This experience helps us to recognize the need for flexibility in our own thinking. We have to understand the Palestinians. We have to understand the Turks—and their enemies, the Armenians. And we have to understand how the Japanese economy works, with its distribution systems that make it virtually impossible for them to open a market without shattering the ranks of the unemployed.

"We have to understand that in Italy they don't have monolithic farming organizations with 20 or 30 harvesters going in. There they farm in their back yards or on one or two acres. We need to understand that maybe their cottage industries are their strength—versus the industrial combine in the U.S. We just have no perception of this.

"Understanding another culture helps us to understand our own. Understanding how they look at our markets helps us better to understand our own markets, not to mention theirs."

On-the-Job Learning

"Another thing I would recommend to young people is to find a mentor. I have had wonderful ones. In my first job, my mentor encouraged me to go to school at night at Wharton. He was a vice president and treasurer of a large real estate operation in Philadelphia. I had good mentors also in Charles Wood and Jim Robison. Jim went on to found Indian Head. (Roy Little was his mentor.) Later I had good mentors in Ralph Lazarus of Federated, and particularly in Fred, Jr., his father, who taught me a great deal and gave me a lot of encouragement. Then there was

Paul Sticht, who was CEO of Reynolds Industries until recently. I learned a lot from all of these mentors, a lot about integrity. Robison, I'd say, had the most impact on my life because he had an enormous sense of integrity and was very articulate.

"By the way, another thing which disturbs me about some people in business is their inability to state their thoughts well in writing or orally. This simply is a defect for a top management job. It is vital that people be able to express themselves articulately in short speeches and in writing. I founded six Toastmasters Clubs—two in New York, two at Springs (one of which was a Toastmistress Club), and two in Milwaukee. One, still going on, is the Sales Executive Club of New York, which is called Roughriders. By the way, Smith Richardson of Richardson Vicks and Rawle Deland of Thorndike Deland were members of these clubs.

"I believe a lot in self-improvement, too. The American Management Association has had a profound influence on me over the years—going to AMA seminars, workshops, Council meetings, and getting a cross-fertilization that contact with people in similar jobs in other industries provides.

"If I were just getting out of Harvard or some other school with an M.B.A., I wouldn't give a damn about current salary and perks if I could empty wastebaskets for somebody who is really good. Again, I'd probably go into sales. As Red Motley, who used to run *Parade* magazine, said, 'Nothing happens until somebody sells something.' I think that that is still true, a basic which is not going to change.

"Other basic things? Well most things in management are basic. I don't think they have changed one iota. I think that *One Minute Manager* and *In Search of Excellence* are all very fine reading, and I applaud them, and I think we ought to get the message out as much as we can. But when it comes down to practical matters, everything is coming full circle. All the things we did a hundred or two hundred years ago are now beginning to emerge as something new. We are going all over the world for old Chinese cures or remedies that your mother used to use. And just as the old remedies are coming back in vogue, natural foods are coming back. So is natural management. Management *cannot* be any different than it has been forever.

If you have honesty and intelligence at the top, directing itself in whichever way is most comfortable and sincerely projecting itself, I don't think that *style* of management is critical at all. What *is* critical is the honesty and sincerity of management in whatever it does.

"I do believe in management by objectives. It's a nice name for something that has been going on for centuries—and that is sitting down with people and letting them share the responsibility and know how you feel about it. Concepts like the *One Minute Manager* and management by walking around and all that—and now there is a new name for entrepreneurship: 'intrapreneurship'—seem to get people all excited. An MIT professor who is a director wrote a letter saying 'God, you guys really ought to try intrapreneurship,' and I am amused by this. I realize it sells a lot of books and gives people a reason to run out and say 'Hey, you know we got something new: intrapreneurship.' But I'm old-fashioned that way, and I'm not saying that there is anything wrong with talking about these things. What is importantly new is the fact that as employees we are more sensitive as to whether there is integrity at the top, whereas we used to say, 'Oh hell, they're all crooks anyway, the hell with it.' At one time the unions would go out on strike, and there would be bitterness and bloodbaths and everything else. Now we expect integrity and we insist upon it. If you can project integrity sincerely to people, then style is not critical.

"At Springs I suspect that *every* division manager has a different style, and if you looked at all the CEOs of the Fortune 500, you would probably find many very different styles there. You can formalize style, you can put it in books and distribute it, you can publish organization charts and all that sort of thing—by the way, I once tried to get an organization chart from Sears and they didn't have any, but they seem pretty successful—but the truth is you get ahead by getting ahead. You just seize opportunities, and someone recognizes your potential and says, 'Let's promote him.' You know there are all kinds of different styles. One can be rigid, one can be loose. But I have not seen anything startlingly new in 25 years, though I do see different styles. However, maybe it is desirable to have different styles. You can talk about hands-on management versus delegation; someone who loves to have meetings and believes strongly in setting up committees versus someone who hates them; there are lots of ways of going about things. Some people want to bring in 20 new M.B.A.s and keep only 10. But to me, styles have to do with a particular person's area of interest and the focus he or she gives to it. All good managers, it seems to me, have to have a sense of the strategic, particularly at the divisional level, an ability to look out. That's critical. Again, there is integrity. If your managers do not have an honest way of thinking strategically about the future, then that's dangerous. And the style cannot be *too* wild. It should not outrage others, but should encourage communication. But hell, I haven't said anything. Times have changed, but the basics haven't. In the days when all you made in the bedsheet business were white bedsheets in four widths—63, 72, 81, and 90 inch—or when cars were only black, you didn't need a strategic thinker. All you did was to take one year's budget and project it out for five years. But what we are seeing today is that different characteristics of a good leader are becoming more important than they used to be, some perhaps less important, but the ability to strategize in business is far more important and necessary than it was twenty years ago, ten years ago or even five.

"One way to develop these traits in managers is to encourage management education, something I have always believed in. One of the great things that happened to me was an early contact with the American Management Association and other managers who were attending AMA's programs. I think I got a lot of my strategic planning ideas from exposure to people who, like myself, were exposed to your planning process. We always have a couple of our executives at the Harvard Business School or the University of Virginia or somewhere. Year round we send people out to get away from the business to get into a management education program, not just to learn about the techniques or tools or devices, but, more importantly, to find out what their counterparts in other industries are doing. And they may come back having verified that what they are doing is good or with a feeling that there is a need for change, some new ideas on this or that, some new tool, or some reorientation.

You can come away from a human resources meeting as our human resources man did, saying, 'Gee, I have got to rethink my whole benefits program,' or 'We need to change our thinking on this,' and the people you meet there are important. This guy may come back and say, 'Gee, we have a problem,' so he calls up Joe Blow at General Foods and asks how the 401(k) plan was communicated to the employees there, because we are about to do it here. There are enormous pluses to that kind of cross-fertilization.

"Integrity is not a short-term thing. I remember when I was in sales, years ago, I was calling on my prospect and customer list intensively. I called on a wholesale dry goods jobber in Philadelphia by the name of Al Weintraub and overheard him talking to his father in the back of the room. He said, 'That guy has got to be one of the most uninformed salesmen we have ever had, but he's trying so hard, Pop, we have got to give him an order.' And he did give me a pretty good order. In later years he said to me that I was so sincere and trying so hard (and he knew that this call was among my first calls), that he told his father that they just had to buy something from me. Interestingly, 23 years later, this man called me, when I was president of Springs. He said, 'I didn't think I'd ever want to do this, but you have a sales manager working for one of your divisions who is harder to see than President Nixon. And he is trying to take my line away from me. You know, Pete, I have been doing business with Springs for 23 years, and I hate like hell to do this to you, but I just thought you ought to know about it.' I said, 'Just stay where you are, don't go away.' I called the president of the division and said, 'You come up here with the sales manager.' He did, and I asked Al to repeat that story. He said, 'You have a sales manager who is harder to see than the President. I think I could get an interview with President Nixon within about three months, but this guy is telling me that he'll see me six weeks away or a month away, and here's my story.' The sales manager was on his way to Philadelphia the next morning. Before he left, I told him the old story about Al's giving me that order. I said, 'I want to tell you that that guy can have anything he wants from Springs. Did you hear me? Anything he wants, he can have. Because I know he won't take advantage of us, I can say that.' I knew him, had known him for many years, and I knew he had integrity. It was up to us to show ours as well.

"I believe also in delegation. I used to attend division manager meetings but decided that they were affecting me too much. I would think, 'If I were running this meeting, I would do it a different way.' So I just stopped going, because I did not want to tempt myself to second-guess the division president. I believe in letting people have lots of freedom in their operations. But at some point I have a tendency to come down pretty hard and sometimes irrevocably. That goes back to my trait of directness.

"I also try to give people the benefit of the doubt. I try to be patient and tolerant, but I keep a little record in my mind. I just wrote a letter to a fellow with whom I have an investment in a venture capital field. 'I'm going off your Advisory Board,' I said. 'The decision is not negotiable. I'll remain an investor— an interested investor—but here are the four things you have to do: one, two, three, four, sincerely.' I had been patient with this guy for about a year and a quarter. I had given him all the rope he needed to hang himself, and he did it. I tried to help him as often as I could, without success. But when I finally come to the point where I have had it, whether it is with a CEO or a subordinate, then I have to be direct. I do believe genuinely in decentralization, and I'll give anybody his head. I don't give a damn what a person's management style is as long as it doesn't lack integrity. If he is getting results, I'll leave him alone. If he isn't, I may have to find a new person. But in the meantime, I won't listen to anybody or anything that detracts from that person or his style. I will support him. Now because of that, someone can take advantage of me, up to a point, but then when I come down, I come down *hard*. And usually, when I do so, I have made a decision which is irrevocable.

"Once in a while I will—just as any CEO should—make a specific decision myself which I will force on others. I don't do this in isolation, but on *rare occasions* I may force a decision because I feel very strongly in my head and in my stomach that it is the right thing to do, for example, setting a particular blend level in sheets. It must be something very basic, where I smell it out. Maybe I'm a bit removed and have a point of view which others might not have. Let's say, for example, if bed-sheets were 65 percent polyester and 35 percent cotton, I might wake up one morning and say 'Let's go to 50 percent cotton, 50 percent polyester.' And then I expect people to carry out that decision. But until I've reached that decision, I will listen to others very carefully.

"I believe that my directness is constructive, but whether it is or not, it works for me, and I simply can't be any other way."

Theodore M. Hesburgh, C.S.C.

President
University of Notre Dame

*H*e may be the only university president in the *Guinness Book of World Records*, for receiving the most honorary degrees: 106. He's been president of Notre Dame since 1952, the longest tenure of any current U.S. university chief. During those years, he guided Notre Dame brilliantly through a turbulent period of change and growth. But he is known equally well for his public service career. Fourteen Presidential appointments have involved him in major social issues: civil rights, atomic energy, campus unrest, Vietnam amnesty, Third World development, immigration reform, and more.

Two hallmarks of his leadership approach are his total accessibility and his talent for concentrating on one problem at a time despite his many responsibilities. He is also an outstanding delegator who "never does anyone else's job," yet applies hands-on management when it is needed.

Under his leadership, Notre Dame has undergone remarkable growth and change. Numbers tell part of the story: Enrollment up from 4,979 to 9,500 . . . faculty from 389 to 913 . . . operating budget from $9.7 million to $162.6 million . . . endowment from $9 million to $286 million. Overall, he has transformed Notre Dame, raised its standards, and elevated its reputation—and he has done it with a combination of compassion, commitment, and strong leadership that have made him a superb CEO.

Career Information:

1934 Entered the Order of the Congregation of Holy Cross, Notre Dame, Indiana

1943 Ordained to the priesthood

1943 Became chaplain for the National Training School for Boys, Washington, D.C.

1945 Became chaplain to veterans, University of Notre Dame

1945 Became assistant professor of religion, Notre Dame

1948 Became head, Department of Religion, Notre Dame

1949 Became executive vice president, Notre Dame

1952 Became president, Notre Dame

Other Affiliations (partial list):

- Member, Board of Trustees, Overseas Development Council
- Member, National Academy of Science Panel on Advanced Technology Competition and Industrialized Allies
- Member, Board of Directors, Freedom Foundation at Valley Forge
- Member, Board of Trustees, United Negro College Fund, Inc.
- Member, Board of Directors and Chairman, Membership Committee, Council on Foreign Relations
- Member, Chief Executives Organization
- Member, American Academy of Arts and Science
- Member, National Science Board, 1954–66
- Member, U.S. Commission on Civil Rights, 1957–72; Chairman, 1969–72
- Member, Presidential Clemency Board, 1974–75
- Member, President's General Advisory Committee on Foreign Assistance Programs

Educational Information:

- University of Notre Dame, 1937
- Gregorian University, Ph.B., 1940
- Holy Cross College, S.T.L., 1943
- Catholic University of America, S.T.D., 1945

Personal Information:

- Born May 25, 1917, Syracuse, N.Y.

Theodore M. Hesburgh, C.S.C.

"When I have done something, it is over. I don't worry about what I said or how I said it. I do the best I can while I am doing it, and so be it. There are a zillion things in between, so paying real attention to each thing as it comes along is important. It is just as important to learn to wipe out what just happened. Let what's coming next be your focus of attention.

"I also try not to carry stuff with me and certainly never to bed at night. I doubt if I've been kept awake a half dozen nights in 40 years worrying about anything, even though there were a few things to worry about. I simply put these worries aside, say my prayers, and go to bed."

Building a University

The job of chief executive of a major university is both similar to and different from that of a CEO of a for-profit corporation. At the core of a university is its independent-minded faculty, which, to them, *is* the university; the administration is seen to be primarily responsible for fund-raising and support. The students generally have an even fuzzier perception of what the administration does. Yet the president is subject to unremitting, conflicting pressures from these two groups as well as the University's trustees, alumni, donors, parents, townspeople, and others. Hence, running a university requires participative management to an extreme.

Adding to this challenge is the fact that a university is a complicated organization.

"We have police and fire departments, restaurants—which serve 6 million meals a year—and 26 residence halls. We main-

153

tain libraries and special collections of precious manuscripts and works of art. We spend a lot just to keep the place green and looking beautiful. If you put youngsters in gracious surroundings, they will respond in a positive way. We have enormous facilities for recreation—a golf course, lakes for sailing and swimming. Over 500 outside lecturers present topics each year, so we have a half dozen auditoriums. We have a major student health center. Of course the most important endeavors are teaching and learning. Yet it is hard to think of any kind of human activity that is not going on here.''

When Father Hesburgh became President of the University of Notre Dame at 35, he resolved to concentrate on excellence, ''to point it to the top.''

''I wanted Notre Dame to be a great university and also to be a great Catholic university. The first is easier to do than the second, for there are many great universities; but there has not been, since the Middle Ages, a great Catholic university. So we were working in an unknown field, creating something new. In the university world, we need to compete with the best, and it is pretty obvious how you go about trying to do this. A great university is fairly simple at its core: it must have a great faculty, a great student body, and a great facility. This requires, in turn, a great endowment. Over and above all of this, a great university must have a great spirit, one which is cohesive, not just a lot of separate parts which operate around a central heating plant.

''Take something simple, such as faculty salaries. You can't get the best faculty if you are paying much less than the best schools are paying. We have come from the bottom of that pile to the top, and now that we are in the number one category, we have a good chance of attracting the best faculty member of the world in any field.''

To achieve this, Notre Dame had to excel in fund raising. When Hesburgh began, there were no endowed professorships at Notre Dame. Now there are 60, each endowed for $1 million.

''I expect to see 100 endowed professorships before I leave.

THEODORE M. HESBURGH, C.S.C.

"One must also concentrate on quality and diversity of students. Today every state and 66 foreign countries are represented, and we are very ecumenical. About 70 percent of our students come from the top 10 percent of their high school classes.

"Looking at our facilities, we knew we simply needed to virtually double them over the past 30 years. To replace what we have done even over the last 20 years could cost over a billion dollars today. But the new facilities are built and paid for and cost closer to $200 million. We moved from a small library packed with a quarter of a million books into a large one that will hold three million, now only half full; to fill the other half will take resources as well. The last computer plan I saw requested a campus network costing about $25 million.

"If our endowment is managed well, you get to a certain critical mass and then see it move quickly upward. It took 14 years to go from $1 million to $5 million, then only seven to go from five to ten. During the last ten years, we have gone from $68 million to $286 million. I hope to get that endowment up to half a billion dollars before I leave.

"There is also a great spirit here. About one-fourth of our student body are engaged in some kind of service to the less fortunate. Over 800 students do tutoring in town. Others visit the elderly, or deal with migrant workers, street people, or battered women. That spirit is also reflected in the fact that of our graduating class last year, about 10 percent volunteered to give one or two years of their lives here or overseas for the less fortunate."

Accessibility

"I found some years ago that students who wanted to talk with the administration would go right through the vice president to me, on the first bounce. It would have been better to have someone else talk with them first, help them get their thoughts organized so that I could get at it later. For when I say something, that's the final word, apart from the Board of Trustees, many of whom are located distantly. So I organized the university to have only two people reporting directly to me, the Executive Vice President and the Provost. The Provost handles all academic and student affairs. The Executive Vice President has responsibility for finances, buildings and grounds, university relations, athletics, and everything else. I call together those two plus all the other vice presidents and their key associates about once a month. Anyone can put anything they want on the agenda. In this way I am not constantly having a stream of vice presidents running in and out. I see the Provost and the Executive Vice President almost every day, and the other vice presidents are free to see me any time; but they know that they'd better not be coming to me about something they haven't talked over with their own VP first.

"I have a general policy that anybody can come in at any time—student, faculty member, anyone. You might think that this would be ruinous, but it really doesn't turn out to be this way. In fact, if it were difficult, they would probably be fighting to get in. But since all they have to do is to make an appointment to see me, there really aren't that many who do so.

"I find that people do not abuse my accessibility. When I am on campus, the lights may be on until two or three in the morning. A student might stand outside and yell, 'Father Ted,' and I'll go to the window and say, 'What's up?' If the place is buttoned up at night, I'll run down to the front porch to chat with them. It's certainly better that they want to see you than that they not want to see you.

"Then there are our 80,000 living alumni. Suddenly we find we have 800 CEOs and senior vice presidents around the country, astronauts, admirals, generals, bishops, lots of people in high places. This all adds up to an enormous financial and spiritual resource, and I am always grateful to talk with any of them.

"I find that I actually save time by having adopted this policy of being totally accessible.

"The big thing you learn is that you don't want to be isolated or insulated. That's why I encourage just anybody to walk in here."

Dealing with Multiple Responsibilities

On the Notre Dame campus, there is a statue of Jesus Christ with his arms outstretched vertically, as if signalling a touchdown. It is irreverently called "Touchdown Jesus." Some wag suggested that there be a statue of Father Hesburgh, striding and carrying a suitcase, symbolizing his frequent comings and goings.

"I am probably gone a third of the time. But the fact is that when I am here, I work in double shifts, so they get their money's worth out of me. If I am in New York City or Washington for the day, I return that day, getting back at around eleven o'clock and putting in two or three hours on my return. I haven't seen a Broadway play in 15 years, yet I have been in New York practically every week for the last 15 years. I have to say that I do put in long hours.

"I've never held just one job but rather about five concurrently. But I pay attention only to what I am doing right now. I manage to be able to focus only on what I am doing, and then when that is over, I'll take up the next thing.

"There have been many years that I have concurrently been on the National Science Board, the Civil Rights Commission and some other government job outside of that, plus being on the Rockefeller Foundation Board, the Institute of International Education, and a whole variety of private endeavors. I recently made a list and found that I have spent 45 years (albeit part-time) working for the federal government since I have been President of Notre Dame. In 34 years, I've spent 45 years (these years overlapping) working part-time on commissions and major task forces, and I have put in more than that number of years on private organizations—ten years as Chairman of the Overseas Development Council, 21 years on the Rockefeller Foundation Board and six years as its Chairman, seven years on the Chase Manhattan Bank Board, with a meeting every month. Concurrently I was Chairman of the Immigration and Refugee Select Commission, a very tough assignment, an exercise undertaken only twice. This required ten hearings all over the country, not just a casual meeting once a year.

"When you have this degree of multiple calls on your attention, you simply have to learn how to do what you're doing now and then leave enough time for the next thing later. This means reading the minutes of the last meeting, in preparation for the next one, on the airplane, carrying in my briefcase (more of a Gladstone bag) four or five fairly thick folders. When I read this material just before a meeting, I am freshly briefed on it. And it is quite refreshing to me to be able to turn from one thing to another. If you have been wrestling with a refugee problem all day long, it might even be fun to deal with the troubles of a bank.

"You get wonderful experiences, of course, in all these things, and you bring everything home in some way or another. I would say an awful lot of the things I've been able to do around here grew out of the experiences of all these other jobs. Some people would say that I've squandered myself by spending so much time on outside jobs, but I'd say that I've enriched myself and Notre Dame as well. I've been able to approach this job with a lot more savvy because of what I've learned in all these other jobs."

Crisis Management

Students today are protesting about South Africa and other social issues. But the level of protest does not compare with that of the 1960s.

"The most critical internal affair during those years was the student revolution. It looked to me as though the whole establishment was going up in smoke. And at that point, I decided I just had to do something, not just improvise every time there was a crisis and wonder what the next one would be. You would get up in those days with a knot in your stomach, as every university president did, saying, 'What's going to happen today, and what am I going to do about it?' I remember talking with Ed Levi, who was then President of the University of Chicago (and later was U.S. Attorney General). After 12 days of being locked out of his office, with students in there tearing things up, he finally got back in without calling the police. After things simmered down for a while, I called him up and asked, 'How did you do it?' He said, 'Well, I got up every morning and asked myself what is the worst thing I could do today—like calling the cops to go in and bust heads or throw the students out the window—and I didn't do it.' He said his advice was not very profound, but it was just to avoid the worst.

"At that point, I decided to call the shot ahead of the students and say, 'This is the way it's going to be, and there's no fiddle-dee-dee about it. I'll give you time to escape out the side door for each step you take, but at the end, if you're stepping on other people's rights and harming the ongoing work of the University, you're certainly not going to be here.' So, I wrote a letter to the students with essentially that message.

"Even the people who I thought were very wise and good friends of mine just looked at me like I was crazy and said, 'Wait till the other shoe drops.' They just didn't think it was going to work. I said, 'They are going to try me out, and I'm going to have to do what I said I was going to do, and then that's going to be the end of that.' You can't be a toothless tiger; some wanted to be tigers but didn't want to get bit by the other tiger. They didn't understand the principle that nonviolent revolution permits you to resist the law, but you have to pay a penalty for resisting the law. They did try me, and I did have to toss out a dozen students, and that was the end of it.

"Before writing this letter, I just sat here at the desk late at night, solitarily thinking it through.

"My conviction had been growing, growing; and of course, I had been meeting with other presidents all that time. During that period the Carnegie Commission on the Future of Higher Education had been meeting—very good people, half of them university presidents, half of them public. That experience helped to settle my mind. Across the land everybody was pretty much giving in. At many schools the curriculum was corrupted by putting in lots of foolish special studies that were labeled 'relevant.' What was judged 'relevant' often became the most irrelevant thing of all. All kinds of unwarranted freedoms were given to students, students were put on boards of trustees, made advisors to presidents, and all this kind of nonsense. That trend kept growing, so I finally sat down and wrote that letter, late at night, right out of my guts. I ran it by the people here, who were not very anxious to sign on. Still, I didn't soften any of it. I was on a national television program the following week with King Brewster of Yale, Jim Perkins of Cornell, and Mac Bundy, who had been the dean of Harvard. They said, 'We couldn't do that, and we don't even think that you will get away with it.' There were a lot of people cheering, but the practitioners really wondered if it would work. When it did work, the corner began to be turned."

Hesburgh had sent the letter to the students when they were home on break, as he had wanted their parents to see it as well. The next day it appeared in full in *The New York Times* and *The Wall Street Journal*. Other newspapers also ran it. Soon he received a four-page telegram from President Nixon, saying that Hesburgh had said exactly what was needed and telling him—since Nixon was about to go to Europe—that he had asked Vice President Agnew to assemble the governors to decide what national action should be taken regarding student unrest.

"Nixon had seen all the wrong things in that letter, and Agnew wanted to call up the National Guard for campuses in trouble. That was the last thing I wanted to be associated with—we've never had any police or militia on this campus.

To call on force is a profession of failure unless you're up against a physical force you can't control, and this was mostly a moral force, though there was some physical violence on some campuses.

"I wrote an explanatory reply to Nixon and Agnew from Colombia, South America. I finally got the letter delivered to Washington through Sol Linowitz, a special Ambassador to South America at that time, whom I caught just as he was running to the airport. The governors had already voted something like 44 to 6 in favor of using the National Guard in their states, and then Pat Moynihan came busting in with my reply —he had made copies of it—and the vote turned exactly around the other way: 44 to 6 *not* to call in the National Guard. It was that close. Had the Guard been called up—had my reply not been delivered—there would have been even greater chaos, even more violence, perhaps more deaths."

Delegation

Because of Hesburgh's remarkable schedule of outside responsibilities and his special management style, he has developed strong ideas about how to delegate and about what should (and should not) be delegated.

"I really think that you're an idiot if you think you can run a place this size and this complicated by yourself. What you have to do is sort it out into its component parts, which I try to do with the vice presidents, the deans, the department chairmen, and the directors of big functions on the nonacademic side. Then you try to find the very best people you can for these many assignments. But I don't think that's my job. What I tell each vice president is this: 'I want you to find the very best people you can find, but you're going to have to choose and appoint them, since you are going to work with the people you select. If they're successful, you're going to get the credit for the success of that operation, and if you pick the wrong people, who are unsuccessful, you're going to take the blame for it. I'm not going to take credit from you, and I'm not going to take the blame for you.

"They have to pick the very best people they can find, then give them their heads. Even if you're running the lawn mower department, if the lawns don't get kept properly, by golly, it's your problem. It's not my problem; it's not somebody else's problem.

"I would say half the people who call this office should be calling someone else. But many do the easy thing: they call the President's office. Someone wants to know why the snow isn't being shoveled, or what time mass is in the morning. In those cases, I just say, 'You're calling the wrong person; call so and so.'

"It's my rule never, never to do anyone else's job. If I hear of something startling, then I may put a little note on it, but I never make the decision for them. If someone writes a really nasty letter about someone who works for me—says he's cheating on his wife, abusing his kids, and has three Swiss bank accounts or is knocking off the university—the first guy to see that letter is going to be the person who is criticized. I always put a little note on such a letter, saying that my practice is that whoever is criticized gets the first crack at responding to it.

"This really gets you the loyalty of your people. Sometimes there may be a little truth in it, but 90 percent of the time you find that it is a biased story. And the accused gets a chance to be the first one to rebut it. Because of this, people don't have to go around worrying about what I know or what I don't know. Also, people who are getting full credit for the good things they're doing will give you a lot of loyalty, too.

"I try to delegate everything that should be delegated, right down through the organization. I swear I could leave this place today without notice and be gone for two weeks, and the place would be running like a top on my return. Everybody is doing his own job."

Selecting People and Working with Them

"When I select people for jobs, I want intelligent people. The worst combination a person can have is power and stupidity; that's what's wrong with a lot of sergeants. So I look first for intelligence; and in administrators I look for flexibility, people who won't just hammer others down. I look for someone who has some imagination and creativity about how to do the job, and for a person who really wants the job and has ideas about how to do it well. I try to get the most competent person I can, but I never take all that seriously the multiple screening and selection committees that universities go through today. I have almost never gotten the right guy from a search committee or that kind of thing.

"I'll give you two examples. The number two job here is Provost. The man who now holds that job was chairman of the search committee, which finally came in with three names, after going through all the right motions. They weren't the right names, but it wasn't their fault; they had done everything they were supposed to do, had a stack of letters two feet tall, had searched the country, advertised, and came up with three names.

"The man heading the search committee was fine; its members were all fine—I couldn't have picked five better people in the University. But they had searched the country, done all this work, wound up with 86 serious candidates, sifted them down, finally narrowed it down to three, had me interview these three—and I said I would not appoint any of them; these were not guys that were going to turn this place around.

"Then I said to Tim O'Mara, the committee's chairman, 'Tim, do me a favor and call your wife to tell her you won't be home for supper tonight.' I took him to the best restaurant in town, up on the roof, and said, 'Did it ever occur to you, Tim, that you're better than all three of the names you brought in? Every time we have a committee elected by the top body of the academic council, you're on it. And then when these committees elect chairmen, you wind up being the chairman. That says something to me. You must have the confidence of our faculty. And you have done a good job in administering the math department, which is a pretty tough group of prima donnas. I'm sure that if we look around, we can find another candidate or two, but I think *you* ought to get in the running for this job. Let's take a second run at it with some other people—mostly internal this time.

"We did this, and he got the job. He's been a splendid provost for seven years now and has made an enormous change in the place.

"We had the same experience in looking for the vice president of development, Bill Sexton. We got an outside search group to help us find someone to head up our development and fund raising. A big head-hunter company spent six months and came up with three people. I interviewed them all and then said to Ned Joyce, our executive vice president—since this function is under his jurisdiction—'I don't really think any of those guys can do it.' (Incidentally, Ned and I are quite different from each other. We've been working together for 34 years, but he is a Southerner, I'm a Yankee; he's conservative, I'm liberal; he's an accountant, I'm more at home with ideas than numbers; and he's very practical, I'm sometimes not. But we've worked together for all these years and never had a fight, never had an argument, even though we disagree rather fundamentally on a lot of things. I always listen to him, he listens to me, and we generally come down the middle pretty well.) In the search for a development head, Ned said a very wise thing: 'This whole fund-raising business isn't just ballyhoo and technique. You have to begin with dedication to a place and to what you're trying to make that place become; you can learn the techniques, but you can't learn that kind of dedication; either you have it or you don't, and it's not easy to get; and it takes quite a few years.' I said, 'If you're saying that we ought to get somebody from inside, do you have someone in mind?' He recommended Bill Sexton, a bright guy, a good professor of management. Bill didn't need another job and he was doing very well where he was. But if we could get him to take on this task, there was no question about his dedication and total devotion to this place. So I took Bill and his wife out to dinner—since this would very much involve her, too. They were very surprised at first, but he took it on. As early as his second year, he outdid the best guy in the field I had ever known. It was fantastic! Last year he raised more money than we've ever raised before.

"He brought a new kind of management, the development operation is running like mad, and he's got ten guys, each one magnifying his energy, each helping to build a greater Notre Dame.

"If you can get the right person, your problems are over. Still, you have to treat your people well. You've got to listen to your people. If you think they are the best, then they've got something to say, and you'd better darn well listen to them. If I'm overriding one of my people more than 5 percent of the time, something is wrong with him or me, one or the other. Generally, I don't have to."

Hands-on Management—When it's Essential

Hesburgh's management style involves crisp, deep delegation. But he also applies hands-on management where it counts the most. For example, chairmen of academic departments and the Provost, to whom they report, go through all of the homework involving recommendations for faculty promotions and recommendations of faculty members for tenure. Hesburgh describes the stack of folders, four feet high.

"I read them all, for this is my job. I know before I start reading them, and I hate to read them—it's really not exactly light reading—that I can believe in the contents of the folders, records of what faculty members have published and what they've accomplished. You have to make a careful, honest judgment on each one recommended for promotion or tenure. The Provost has already had his committee go over them, and he's cast his vote. The deans have been in on it; the department committees have been in on it. Thirteen people have passed on those recommendations before I see them.

"Still, I have to scrutinize every blessed page, since I have the last say, and if I say okay, then the faculty member is promoted or tenured or both. It's a miserable task. I read myself blind until nine o'clock three or four nights. But I have to do it, because I'm dealing with people's lives. If the answer comes out no, the man or woman is finished here in another year. If it comes out yes and he's 35 years old, we'll have him for the next 35 years.

"You have to know when to do hands-on, and obviously it's hands-on when people's lives are involved.

"I also read all the departmental reports because I have got to know what goes on around here. Even as President, I don't have much influence on what's going on academically. The

Provost has some influence, up to a point. And if I say no on something, he isn't at all backward about coming up the next day and saying, 'I'd like to reopen that; I think you made a mistake saying no.' And I say, 'Fine. Let's do.'''

New Ventures

"We have just started a new organizational entity at the University, an Institute for Peace Studies. There is quite frequently a lot of pressure to start something new here. I am personally interested in peace; that's the one thing I'm spending most of my time on now, nuclear peace. We have an excellent man helping us, a former Governor of Ohio, former Congressman, former head of AID, and Woodrow Wilson Fellow. We're very lucky to have him. A university needs to have a few people around who are public persons. Technically he is my assistant for public affairs. He wrote two or three memos which persuaded us that this Institute is a good idea. We once tried to set up a Peace Institute in Jerusalem, but it didn't really work, as it was just too far away. It became obvious that to do it right, we had to have the Center here.

"The proposer of a major idea like this will give me some very strong reasons for doing it, and I just ship these down to the Provost and ask him to react. Half of my mail goes out with a pink slip on it, to get somebody else in the act, because you need involvement to get a good decision. When we decide to launch a new venture, invariably we don't have the money for it. So then I have to nose around and find the money. Maybe I can get some start-up funds and say, 'I'll launch you and help you for two years, but by the third year, if your tub isn't standing on its own bottom, your program has a two-year life.' So now he's started. Whether it survives or not depends on whether he's able to finance it. We'll know in two years.

"Of course, there are always many great ideas in a University like this. For example, we were just asked to go in with a group in Ecuador—to set up a university for vocational and business training, which they very much need. I consulted with the two or three people who know that situation best, and they concluded that since we are already working with

Chile and with China and since we've got the Institute in Jerusalem, one more would probably overextend us; we're doing about as much as we can handle in the way of overseas collaboration at the moment, given our manpower and money. We just had to decide we can't do it.

"I suspect that this kind of decision process is very similar to what you'd find in for-profit corporations. For the implementation of new ventures, we need the same things that corporations need: a champion who is competent and committed, and money."

Advice to Young People

"If I were talking to young people today, youngsters just going into the job market, I'd first tell them to find something they will enjoy doing. Don't just start down a road of drudgery. I worry about kids who get too narrow an education. There's nothing wrong, for example, with being an accountant, but I tell our students that they probably won't want to do that all their lives; they may wind up managing accountants—that's a different kind of work. But, I say, broaden yourself all the time, even around here. Get into something you enjoy doing, get satisfaction; otherwise, you won't do it very well. I tell them not to resign from the human race; wherever they are working, people are going to need their voluntary services, and they'd better start that now and be generous about it— because that will give them another whole dimension of satisfaction.

"Then I tell them that there's no knowing where they are ultimately going to end up, so they shouldn't expect their first job to have them niched for life. I say, 'Keep your options open; do the job well, but don't be afraid to take a chance on doing some other things.' For example, after an overseas experience, they'll never be the same. I tell them to develop flexibility and broader interests. Then I tell them never to quit reading.

"I read very widely—science, theology, weapons systems, philosophy, current affairs, whodunits as well. On top of that, I read perhaps 15 periodicals a week. I can't read them all carefully, but I have to know what's going on in the world at large.

167

Major newspapers are clipped for me, so I've always got a pile of clippings on 30 subjects I'm interested in, whether it's immigration or Russia, Africa, or Nicaragua. So I would say to students to keep their curiosity alive; stay interested in a lot of things.''

Taking on a New Job

"When you step into a new job, you should first scout the terrain, to get some idea of what the possibilities are and whether the people who are there can deliver. In most of the jobs I've had, I've had to build the staff from scratch.

"There's great value in a liberal education. I had the most impractical education in the world, majoring in philosophy as an undergraduate, then taking six or seven years of theology on top of that. You might say that prepares you for just about nothing. The theology training didn't even tell me how to baptize a child or how to marry people; that wasn't a part of the routine; it was all academic and philosophical.

"The list I made of all the completely different jobs I've held shows that it is possible—if one has an open mind and can read and wants to learn—for you to go into a job for which you're totally unprepared and do it successfully. If tomorrow morning, they asked you (as they did me) to chair the Select Commission on Immigration and Refugee Policy, which means that for the second time in the history of the country you're going to try to redo the whole law—and it's probably the second worst law in the country (the worst being the tax law), involving 36 reasons why you can't come into the United States (goofy things like being a wanton woman)—you really have to start from scratch and get on top of your challenge. In such a role, you would be heading a commission of outstanding, very important people. The Secretary of State isn't going to be pushed around, nor is the Attorney General. I found not only outstanding fellow commissioners, but also a very good staff director, a marvelous guy, one who knew a lot about ethnic differences and the laws and mores of immigration, a person who worked his heart out, surrounding himself with young people who worked their hearts out, too. We were getting literally 80 hours a week out of these people toward the end, when we just had to get the reports out on a deadline, before the Administration changed. One youngster worked 72 hours without leaving the office. I told those kids, 'Not one of you is going to be up the creek without a job. If I have to go out and personally push somebody, I'm going to to see that all of you get jobs once this thing is over.' It was a two-year task, a tough one.

"Yet I'd say that starting from scratch, knowing nothing, I wound up knowing more about immigration and refugees than probably 99 percent of the people in the country. Obviously, I didn't know more than the people who have spent their whole lives in the field, but I read what seemed like a million pages and spent days on end in hearings. So if you've got curiosity and if you read widely, you can take on almost any tough job—pick it up, get on top of it, and be able to go in and talk in the Senate and the House, hold press conferences and even argue with the President—but you've got to really work hard at it."

Hesburgh's Life-Style

"But if you want to live this kind of life, it means that you just don't have time to play golf, or to sit and play bridge for three or four hours; you don't have time for a lot of chitchat. You have to grab every free moment there is. Now some people will take on one of those tough assignments, but if you have three or four of them going at once (or ten), then that requires a certain amount of discipline to make every minute count. Time is the greatest of all commodities."

Hesburgh's remarkable track record of handling multiple major responsibilities, all while still running and building a major university, has led to reports that he requires little sleep.

"No, that isn't correct. I sleep as much as I can. I don't believe in sacrificing rest. It's something you need. My secret, if there is one, is that I pack my time very full. Most people who tell me they get along on four hours of sleep a night end up nodding all day long. You find them sleeping at board meetings, when they're supposed to be listening. Eleanor Roosevelt said she needed very little sleep, but you'd get in a cab with her and she'd fall asleep—bang!''

Boards of Directors and Trustees

> Father Hesburgh has been on dozens of boards, mostly of not-for-profit organizations, such as the Rockefeller Foundation, and also served as a director of the Chase Bank for several years. He describes the similarities and differences between the two types of organizations.

"Most not-for-profit organizations have an idealistic purpose, and everybody's committed to that. Still, they have to make enough money to fulfill that purpose. So there are some similarities. I certainly was concerned about profit when I was on the Chase Manhattan Board. But concerned also about integrity and trust. It was very funny how I got on that Board, because I had taken as a rule of thumb that I would not go on any commercial board. Years ago I turned down several such invitations. Tom Gates had wanted me to go on the Morgan Guaranty Bank's Board, and I laughed. Then one day David Rockefeller asked me to join the Chase Board, and I laughed at this, too. He said, 'What's so funny?' I said, 'Well, I think it's funny. The Chase Manhattan Bank, the number three bank in the country and one of the very top in the world, wants me on its Board, and I have never even had a bank account, much less a course in economics or money and banking.' He said, 'We don't want you on the Board to teach us about banking—we know about that—but we have a lot of moral, ethical problems in banking today, and to put it bluntly, I would like you to represent the conscience of the Board. We have some very tough moral problems to face—we operate in many countries. We're doing about $43 billion worth of business a year, so maybe there's some good to be done in that, as well as some evil to be avoided.' I said I'd try it for a year, and if at the end of the year I was just a drag on the Board, I'd get off. The directors of the Chase Board were heads of the big corporations, all splendid people, some of whom I had known before. Most business people think educators are dreamers, and most educators think that heads of industry are swashbuckling, unethical entrepreneurs. We found out quickly that both of those were myths. The second thing I found was that David was entirely serious about what he had said. When we confronted a moral problem, which we did about every second or third meeting—we were talking about problems in the millions of dollars—he would let it roll around the Board for probably ten minutes, and almost always there'd be an A position for doing something and a B position for doing something else; the Board would be split down the middle, and David would say, 'We've got somebody here who does this for a living, so let's see what Father Ted has to say about it.' I would start by saying that moral principles aren't worth a hoot unless you understand the facts to which you are applying them. So I would see if I could get the facts straight. I would say, 'Is this the problem?' I would lay it out in a factual way, and everyone would say, 'Yes, that's the problem, all right.' Then I would try to define the principle that applied to that kind of problem—and lay out that principle. Most people would agree on general principles, and moralities were fairly clear. And I'd say, 'Now here's where we get to the short strokes. This is the way that principle applies in these matters,' and I'd lay it out one, two, three. I didn't claim any infallibility, but in my judgment, this is what we ought to do. David would bang the gavel, and say, 'That's that, let's go on to the next item.' Almost inevitably, following those principles would cost a lot of money, but that's the way the Board went.

"That experience initially was a mine field for me. I was neither an expert in their business nor infallible in mine. But I wanted them to know I understood what they were talking about.

"You can't begin to make moral judgments in any field unless you know what your facts are. I wanted to make sure that we were all talking about the same problem. Secondly, I wanted to make sure that there was no serious disagreement about whether the moral principle I outlined was indeed a principle that had bearing on the problem. The next step was the tough one, exercising what's called prudential judgment.

Applying a principle can yield a recommendation for action—which can be very costly or even dangerous. It can backfire on you.

"My basic principle is that you don't make decisions because they are easy, you don't make them because they're cheap, you don't make them because they're popular; you make them because they are right. Not distinguishing between rightness and wrongness is where administrations get into trouble. The Watergate guys said they did what would work. They were very good plumbers or practitioners, but they never asked themselves whether it was the right thing to do. Just the result was what they wanted, the end justifying the means. A lot of people do things to be popular—politicians get votes that way. A lot of people do things because they want to make money. Obviously in business, it's better to make money than to lose money. In the long run you make it or go out of business. But if you do it just to make money, without consideration of other factors, you can pollute a beautiful river, wind up closing a factory, or even kill people."

> Those who have served widely on both for-profit and not-for-profit boards see some similarity but often notice that board members of not-for-profits do not take their responsibilities nearly as seriously as they do when they serve on for-profit boards.

"I think the reason for this is that on corporate boards, they see themselves making a difference by what they decide, whereas on the not-for-profit boards, they feel they may be frosting on the cake. They're not as involved, and they're given cut-and-dried stuff to say amen to. What I try to do with the Notre Dame Board is first of all to get them involved. If we have a faculty problem, they may have to sit down and talk to the faculty about it. If we have a student problem, they've got to talk with student leaders about it. When they emerge from their committee work, the chairman may have to sell the Board on a policy."

Some Hesburgh Principles

"I have learned a lot from many people. One was my predecessor, Father Cavanaugh, who gave me three years of a very tough apprenticeship. He emphasized the importance of deciding what is right—I've found that the most useful principle of all. Then, to be human is terribly important, because otherwise you're just playing a game. Another principle is not to take yourself too seriously. That's a terrible thing to do. You have to avoid pomposity and self-importance and being easily hurt.

"I'll give you a classic example. During the student revolution, our former provost—a tough young guy—and I were meeting. My secretary called in and said, 'There are a bunch of revolutionaries out here who want to see you.' I said, 'Come on, Jim, you might as well come out and meet them, too. These were students who were unkempt, unshaven, and in a very ugly mood. They had wanted to come into my office to demand something. But we went out, instead. I reached out my hand, but the student just looked at it, wouldn't shake hands. We did our business in as civilized a way as you can with uncivilized people, and then they left. After they were gone, the provost said to me, 'You should have kicked that guy right in the guts and thrown him out of the building.' I said, 'Let me tell you something: when you're in this office, being easily hurt or standing too much on your rights is a luxury you just can't afford. If I'd kicked him in the guts or thrown him out, we wouldn't have had the discussion we had.

"You can wound my dignity and injure my sensibility, you can hurt me deeply, but I'll survive that. There are certainly some things I won't put up with, but if a guy simply won't shake my hand, I can live through that."

Success and Luck

"I'll have to admit that I've been very fortunate. Success—real success—almost always has at least a minor ingredient of luck. There's nothing quite like being in the right place at the right time when nobody else is there. It's as though you're standing outside and it starts raining dollars from a mail sack that fell out of an airplane. You can't take credit for that kind of thing. I was a very young guy, just turning 35 when I was made president. The man who was on the job was sick, and he had to go out at the end of his six years. I was coming in for only a six-year term, but then they decided to change the rules that had been in effect for the previous 40 years, allowing only one six-year term.

"Second was the experience of having met a lot of wonderful people in a wide variety of roles, which came from my willingness to do outside work. There was no reason in the world I should be appointed to the National Science Board—I was a philosopher and a theologian. When they called me from the White House, I told them that, and they said that President Eisenhower wanted a theological point of view on the Science Board. This may sound incredible, but I learned a lot of science that way, and this got me into a whole lot of other things. But mostly there were people, a whole list of people. The curious thing is that most of the people who are my best friends and from whom I've learned the most, almost none of them are Catholic, just outstanding people I met almost by chance on these different jobs. I was almost always the only Catholic and certainly the only priest.

"I was so fortunate to be on the Carnegie Commission on the Future of Education, for example—to watch the quality of people I worked with for six years, three days a month, during a time of great crisis, an enormously important thing. And I was just very fortunate in having great people around here. We've gone through five of every kind of vice president, except for (Father) Ned Joyce, who has been Executive Vice President all my time here. We've had a variety of interesting, good, dedicated people filling jobs in which they tend to burn out after a while; and I never could have done the job without them, the kind of people who make you look good.

"The real leaders of this world all have a very deep sense of dedication—they're willing to give time to something. They don't say, 'I can't do it because I've got to play golf.'

"Top, successful executives are willing to pay the price. They give up a lot of personal things that they would love to do but don't have time to do. Second, most of them have a pretty good vision of the world they'd like to see. They help make it a little more just, a little more caring, a little more equitable, and they're willing to put in the time to do that. You don't find them doing the more frivolous things—nor are they interested just in making money. I've got nothing against that;

this place is kept going by people who have made money and given it to us. But at the same time, if that were the only thing that one would do in life, it would be rather empty, a lot less satisfying than that of a person who could say there are youngsters getting schooled or getting vaccinations today because I helped to get a certain law passed. There are people who have jobs today who wouldn't otherwise have them, or houses, or decent neighborhoods—the whole quality of life in America may be changed by people who have earned the power and use their influence beneficially. It may take 20 years, but it begins to happen.

"I would love to think that because of those two years I spent on the Select Commission, anywhere from three to six million people living in the shadows as illegals may become legalized because we were able to effectively close the border, and that's the price of being able to legalize those who have been here living good lives. If you can really affect the lives and opportunity of hundreds or thousands or millions of people, that's a great thing. If you can help an underdeveloped country to become more developed, that's something you can leave behind you.

"I've often felt that you can really tell the quality of people by the things to which they give their precious time. If they give it totally to frivolous things, I don't find them very interesting as people. Perhaps I am an anomaly in some ways, but so are some of these other people we're talking about, in that they give very little time to matters of personal satisfaction— apart from eating and sleeping, and doing the things they need to do, just to keep going. Fellows like Cy Vance and David Rockefeller—people who could do almost anything they want to do—spend a lot of their time doing things *pro bono*. They start the Asia Society; they're concerned about the Council on Foreign Relations or Latin American affairs. Sol Linowitz, for example, spends an extraordinary amount of time doing great things going all over the world, trying to achieve to help others—some efforts are successful, some are unsuccessful.

"As for myself, I would never have been able to do the variety and number of things I've done if I had had a family. You could have a lot of arguments about celibacy, but celibacy has freed me. But one could use celibacy to be selfish. You're not interrupted by having to spend time with kids, you don't have to worry about fixing their teeth, and so on. But if you can use celibacy to be open with everybody and to give a lot more time to people, it makes a lot of sense for the kingdom of God, if you will.

"Now the fact is that I've had some youngsters who were just given to me by their parents, because they were coming here to study and then never went home again. I've had them until I got them married off. That's been a wonderful experience, but luckily they were here, so I didn't have the full responsibility which other parents have.

"The only way you can accomplish a lot is to concentrate on the one task you have at hand at the moment. Otherwise you'll go nutty. Yesterday I was down in New Orleans. I had everything cleaned up before I left on Sunday, except the unfinished reading on the window sill, and that's always going to be there. I took everything I could pack into my bag, and read an awful lot of stuff along the way. Then I came back and the stack was two feet high. And lots of phone calls to return. But eventually you catch up; you just have to remember that.

"I was reading the Bishops' Statement on the airplane, pretty significant stuff. Then, arriving home, I had people coming in who I just had to see—the head of the alumni board on a problem with black alumni and how to get more black kids into school, a couple of company officials coming in to give us a check; you've got to spend a little time with them and talk about their project and how it is going. And it's interesting. In the midst of all this, I was absolutely shaggy, so I said, 'Whatever happens, get me to the barber!'' At five o'clock I ran to the barber and must have gotten stopped four or five times enroute by the kids, but that's just fun. They wanted to ask me something nutty, so I gave them some nutty answers, and we laughed about it. I got the haircut, ran back—I'd been gone for three days—was up at six o'clock yesterday in New Orleans to catch the plane back here in time to say mass at 11:30, which I did—I say mass every day I'm here or anywhere else—and then after a lot of other activity I had to break a long-standing appointment in order to have dinner with some top Chinese students whom I had first met in China. I had promised we'd get together, but I was still mindful of that two-foot stack of mail on my desk. I had to find out what was in it and after glancing at it, I had to consult with some people, and I remembered that I had a bad week coming up as I've got to go again to New York to help to select a new president of the Council on Foreign Relations and knew I had to go through that stack of candidates, every sheet.

"But instead of doing anything else, I went out and had a four-hour Chinese dinner with these guys, because you can't do a Chinese dinner right in less time than that. I thoroughly enjoyed the dinner and the company of the students, who talked about a wide variety of things. Four hours later I came back here, finished reading the stack of candidates and got to the bottom of that mail pile, and those letters that had to get out right away—and they were here to sign when I returned this morning. When I had quit at 2:30 this morning, the out-box was piled pretty high.

"But the whole point is that the world doesn't stop, you have to roll with it and not get excited about it.

"Let me correct that. The world doesn't stop, and you *should* get excited about it."

Harold Burson

Chairman
Burson-Marsteller

Since its birth in 1953, he has been CEO of what is now the world's largest public relations firm. Far from the stereotyped image of the "p.r. man," he is soft-spoken and understated, analytical and reflective. He lets his people work in their own way—and sometimes wonders if he's considered too much of a "pussycat." But he does demand that they adhere to the vision and values he has conceived for his firm. And he makes it clear that working at Burson-Marsteller requires high energy, hard work, and a high threshold of pain. He believes strongly in delegation but stays close to his clients, because, as he puts it: "We exist solely to serve our clients."

He emphasizes the importance of long-range strategic planning. Burson-Marsteller's phenomenal growth is no accident, he says. It is based on a long-range plan drawn up in 1960—a plan that accurately describes the firm as it exists today. The overall vision saw Burson-Marsteller as a worldwide organization working with a strong client base of large multinational financial and industrial organizations. In realizing this vision, he and his people opened up new frontiers for the public relations function, including investor relations, legislative relations, sales meetings, public issues, and crisis management. He stresses the need to take advantage of opportunities, but the record shows that he went beyond that—he created the opportunities.

Career Information:

1938 Became director of Ole Miss News Bureau

1940 Became reporter for *Memphis Commercial Appeal*

1941 Became assistant to president and public relations director for The H.K. Ferguson Company

1946 Started own public relations firm

1953 Became chief executive officer of Burson-Marsteller

Other Affiliations:

- Executive vice president, director, member of Executive Committee, Young & Rubicam, Inc.
- Member, Executive Committee, Young Astronauts Council (presidential appointment)
- Member, Executive Committee and chairman, Committee on Public Information, Joint Council on Economic Education
- Trustee and member, Executive Committee, Foundation for Public Relations Research Education
- Director, Catalyst, Inc.
- Member, Public Relations Advisory Committee, U.S. Information Agency
- Member, Public Relations Society of America
- Member, International Public Relations Association
- Member, Overseas Press Club
- Member, New York Society of Security Analysts
- Associate Member, New York Academy of Medicine

Educational Information:

- University of Mississippi, 1940

Personal Information:

- Served in Europe during World War II with combat engineers and as news correspondent for American Forces Network

Harold Burson

"*If* you hold the senior job in a public relations firm, you have to be sensitive to your major clients. They want to know that they are getting the best talent, and for some reason they think the person with the CEO title represents that best talent. That is doubly demanding when the senior person's name is on the door. My associates would probably tell you that my biggest problem is that I am too accessible."

Burson-Marsteller, today the world's largest public relations firm, began in 1953 as a partnership owned by Harold Burson and Marsteller Advertising.

"Bill Marsteller was one of the few advertising people of his time who recognized the difference between public relations and advertising. We've been the only organization that has grown to the extent we have side by side with an advertising agency, yet maintaining a professional position of respect within the public relations community. And without Marsteller's financial support, we could not have expanded into Europe so early nor could we have developed so many domestic locations."

Both Burson-Marsteller and Marsteller Advertising were sold to Young & Rubicam in 1979.

"Again, without Young & Rubicam's backing, we would not have expanded as rapidly as we have. Our revenues were less than $30 million then and over $100 million now. That may not be a large figure in comparison with the revenue of many of our clients, but it represents a lot of public relations fees. And we've roughly tripled our number of offices since 1979."

> Harold Burson, a soft-spoken Tennessean who graduated from the University of Mississippi, believes that he has principally helped his firm to become the leading public relations counsellor by selecting and recruiting unusually talented people and providing an environment that encourages them to do their jobs. The firm has also grown, he says, because it helped to expand significantly the traditional definition of the public relations function.

The Extension of Public Relations

"When we first started, public relations was very narrowly defined. There were some people who performed a broad counseling role, but they were the exceptions. Press relations was regarded as the heart of the function, as much as 75 percent of the effort, and much of the press today still thinks that's what public relations is all about. You might publish the company magazine for a few companies, but many thought of that as an industrial relations function. After a few years came the recognition that public relations must help companies to effectively reach the financial community. So we started investor relations. During the 1950s, we hardly thought at all about public affairs, since business was enjoying an unusually good climate. It had won the war and was creating a lot of prosperity, so business was a hero back then. But in the '60s, beginning with the civil rights movement, consumerism, the environmental movement—which perhaps began in the Kennedy years but really developed during the Johnson administration—there was a lot of legislation with which companies had to cope. At Burson-Marsteller, we recognize that this should not be left to the lawyers but should become an integral part of the public relations function.

"In the early days in the marketing area, we concentrated primarily on product publicity. Since that time, we have taken a substantial role in broadening that function, because before a product can reach the consumer, it must be moved through its various channels of distribution. Now we assist companies in

HAROLD BURSON

helping to motivate the people who sell the products to the retailer and in helping to motivate the retailers who deal directly with the customer. For example, we produce major sales meetings, write newsletters about products and services, help develop sales incentive programs, and are involved deeply in educational activities. Because of this expansion of our activity, we must know much more about the way a client's business operates than we ever had to know when public relations was narrowly defined.''

According to Burson, this change is strongly reflected in the kinds of people who need to be recruited for the firm. For many years, he says, perhaps 80 percent were "press people." Today probably fewer than 20 percent come from the media, the other four-fifths representing men and women with experience in marketing, those with financial backgrounds, former Congressional assistants, attorneys who can simplify complex language, and research specialists with advanced degrees.

"While we still buy a lot of research, we have our own specialists who can thoroughly analyze data, know what questions to ask, test the validity of samples, and all of that. We do this both for our clients and to test our own effectiveness. We are very involved today in sales meetings, something we would never have engaged in a few years ago. For example, we regularly put on meetings across the country for Metropolitan Life for perhaps 1,500 or 2,000 people in six locations, handling all of the logistics and all of the programming. Today that is a business for us. I think that perhaps we have been more alert to opportunity in looking at these new businesses than some of our competitors have been. We provide language simplification capability to banks and insurance companies and for warranties and employee benefit booklets. We're working, too, on a lot of public issues requiring advertising support, in order to get across our clients' positions. Some would leave that business to advertising agencies, but we see it as a natural part of our business.''

In an address to the Tenth World Congress of the International Public Relations Association, held in Amsterdam in 1985, Burson said:

"In my view, the definition of public relations is very simple —even if the implementation is not. Public relations is any effort to influence opinion—to influence the attitudes of people. You can do three things to public opinion. You can try to change it, if it suits your purpose to do so; you can try to create new opinion, where none exists; or you can reinforce an existing opinion. *This*, I submit, is what public relations today is all about; a growing recognition by leaders of institutions of all descriptions that their legitimacy—the legitimacy of the institutions they head, whether it be a corporation, a city government, a hospital, or a hotel—depends, in the ultimate, on those eight words crafted in Philadelphia by Thomas Jefferson during the steamy summer of 1776: 'A decent respect to the opinions of mankind.'''

Burson's broad-based concept of public relations has been carried out through virtually all types of media.

"Television has had a tremendous impact. We have people who create and produce 90-second newsclips which we send across the country. In effect, we have created a syndicate, a network which knows that the kind of material we turn out is credible and reliable and produced to the highest professional standards. When we produce a newsclip for a client, we generally assure that we can get it shown on 60 or 70 of the top 100 markets in the United States. A clip can be based on the introduction of a new product—for example, it can show how to get your car ready for winter, if we have a client who has a useful product for this. But the newsclip has to represent a legitimate news angle. We did not invent this technique, for there were independents who were turning out such newsclips before we did, but I think we were the first public relations firm to do it, and certainly the first to pre-test the clips."

Through expanding its services and its client base, Burson-Marsteller has steadily grown. In 1970, the firm was selected as public relations counsel for General Motors. Burson regards this as a major milestone, since GM's endorsement represented a "Good Housekeeping Seal of Approval" for a public relations consultancy. Another milestone was passed through their working with Johnson & Johnson in 1982, when Tylenol capsules were poisoned. This represented a national crisis and demanded careful and thoughtful information management. Since that time, crisis-management public relations has been an important part of the agency's business.

Crisis-Information Management

"That's a field which today is almost synonymous with Burson-Marsteller. We are easily the point of first reference. Several of us had been doing this kind of work throughout our careers, but we attained prominence in this field when we had the good fortune to be working with Johnson & Johnson when its crisis occurred. Because of the genius of its Chairman, Jim Burke, who made some remarkably sound decisions, and to whom we were providing input, we got identified with the constructive handling of the Tylenol crisis. Jim and others at Johnson & Johnson have been very generous in recognizing that we were a part of the process. We have developed a team of people headed by Al Tortorella, who might be called 'Mr. Crisis Manager.' From the time of the Tylenol crisis, hardly a two- or three-week period has gone by that members of our crisis team have not been called upon. Many of these problems start locally, and if you handle them well, they don't become national in scope. The work of this team is not widely known, simply because they are very effective in getting problems tamped down at the very beginning. I don't mean that you ever plaster over it; you simply have to get to the bottom of it and correct a fundamental problem. We always try to get management to take a realistic approach toward finding a solution, for you simply can't start working with the press successfully until management recognizes the problem and does something about it. Our goal, of course, is to be relatively invisible. Still, there are a number of such crises that have helped to build a reputation for us in this field. One was the crisis with Girl Scout cookies, involving razor blades. That really killed the sale of Girl Scout cookies for that particular year. The financing of the Girl Scout organization is highly dependent on the sale of those cookies, with perhaps a third of their annual income coming from those sales.

"In more recent times, we have been working with Union Carbide's overwhelming tragedy at Bhopal. The head of our crisis team has been to India, and the team has been working very closely with Carbide on many aspects of that tragedy. In such cases, there are enormous legal implications; in effect, you are betting the company. Sometimes legal considerations have to prevail over public relations considerations, but some accommodation must be reached.

"Very few people remember that until Bhopal, the greatest industrial tragedy involving an American company was the explosion of a ship containing ammonium nitrate off the coast of Texas. Over 400 Americans were killed, at a time when we didn't have broad television news coverage, in 1947. In those days, there were crises, defective products, people being killed in accidents, but you didn't see the blazes in your living room. Today bad news is transmitted very fast. We were called in when Jewel Foods in Chicago had their salmonella problem. More recently, there was the tragedy of Jalisco Cheese of Mexico, very serious, reportedly resulting in 40 or 50 deaths. The lawsuit is going on and will go on for years. So the whole field of crisis management is one in which we are very active."

Integrity and Humility

Burson recognizes that "p.r." has long suffered a reputation for exaggeration. Although he does not choose to discuss such cases, he is known to have resigned accounts by refusing to release information which he considered to be less than candid. He believes, in fact, that fulfilling the role of a corporate conscience is a part of the job description of the chief public relations officer of any company.

Some public relations crises that are not of life-and-death consequence are still of significant importance to clients. A prime example was Coca-Cola's decision in 1985 to change its 99-year-old formula. Because Coke was a Burson client, he was in the thick of the worldwide furor that forced the company to reconsider its marketing decision and reintroduce the original formula.

"The changing of the formula had had a tremendous amount of market research behind it, and of course we all knew there would be some opposition, but no one anticipated its intensity or extent. In retrospect, you might ask why we weren't able to anticipate the reaction of the public. One reason is that the change had to be made with no security leak. Since this was the ground rule, it was impossible to ask people

—the 200 thousand involved in the taste tests—'How would you feel if Coca-Cola withdrew its product?' Security inhibitions hamstrung the research findings. Once major resistance to the change erupted and was recognized, it became a matter of how to react to the adverse publicity. And then finally, when Coca-Cola's management made its decision to bring back its 'Classic' product, what would be the best way to present this to the public, what posture should be taken by the company in making the announcement? The early evidence is that it was well handled and graciously received by the public. If Coca-Cola had been less humble, the reintroduction might not have been so well received. The corporation was quick to say, "We'll give you what you want; we made a mistake in taking it away from you; and we did not know you cared so much.' I can't name another product where the intensity of feeling is so great. And it was a front page story in Tokyo, just as it was here."

This combination of honesty and candor, a Burson trademark, was evident to insiders in the public relations field.

Planning

Burson-Marsteller's success is due not only to its integrity and its highly intelligent people, but also to Burson's commitment to basics, especially strategic planning.

"It may be difficult for some people to believe, but in 1960 we wrote a long-range plan for this business that pretty well describes the business as it is today. We wanted to work for large multinational corporations; that was our prime client target. And we wanted to be internationally based. We wanted to go to Europe first, which we did, and then to Asia. Going there was opportune on our part. In 1980, we went into Australia. I said, 'Let's get started down here, right now.' I didn't really talk this particular move over with anyone else. We really had a vision for a long-term strategy, we plugged in the pieces as we went and changed it as we had to.

"We try to be a no-nonsense, emphasis-on-production kind of company. We charge the market what we should, but we try to give the client an advantage. That's been my ethic, and I think it has permeated the organization. Even when the company first began, I had a kind of vision for it: it should be a worldwide organization with a very broad spectrum of activity. Over the years, the communications process, by whatever name you want to call it—public affairs, public relations—has become recognized by the chief executive officer as a function which is absolutely critical to the accomplishment of his mission. An effective CEO realizes that if he is going to accomplish his objectives, he must communicate with a lot of different people, different publics. Because of this, our business has expanded. During the 1980s, we've grown by about 24 percent annually. Even during the last recession in 1981 and '82, the deepest since World War II, our business grew. That's proof of the importance of professional communications, both to companies and to not-for-profit organizations."

| Succession planning is a part of strategic planning.

"One of the biggest problems in businesses of our kind is the transition from the first generation of management to a second generation. About three years ago, Jim Dowling was made chief operating officer worldwide, and he has helped move the company into a lot of new areas—many beyond our original charter."

In a recent issue of *Public Relations Journal*, Dowling, himself a product of the Burson-Marsteller culture, says "Harold Burson created an environment for people to grow. He was an unusual sort of entrepreneur. Harold was always willing to share; he was receptive to ideas and let people execute them. He created an institution and I am simply part of it," adding that "in 1990, Harold Burson will still be Chairman, and I will be a legend in waiting."

Visions and Values

Burson-Marsteller believes deeply in the importance of a company's culture. To help its client organizations sharply define and communicate their values and beliefs to employees at all levels, the company established a new business unit called "SynerGenics."

"In institutionalizing cultures, we have worked with companies such as Manufacturers Hanover, DuPont, General Foods, and now we are doing the same thing for ourselves. We are communicating with our people, and we are doing it strategically."

The basic missions, goals, and beliefs of the agency have been articulated in a document called, "Our Vision, Our Values." Burson-Marsteller has held meetings on this topic at its branches all over the world at a cost of more than $1 million. Through this program all staff members are told that "high energy, hard work, even a high threshold of pain are constants at Burson-Marsteller," and that the qualities of achievement, team work, commitment, curiosity, sharing, and risk are encouraged. Says the document: "As the world changes, we will change with it. The only constant is our dedication to excellence in thought and deed." The document emphasizes that "We exist solely to serve our clients."

Even without this effort to institutionalize the firm's culture, that unique culture would be clearly evident; and its "vision and values," now sharply articulated, unarguably represent the vision and values of Harold Burson and his senior associates.

One evidence of this is that although Burson sees himself as essentially a hands-off manager, he stays very close to the chief executives of important client companies.

Staying Close to Clients

"I think I am fairly good at giving people an assignment and saying, 'It's yours.' I have done that all my life. Of course we have to have good controls and must be very conscious of profitability, where we put our assets, and so on, but spending time just looking at computer reports is not my idea of a good life. I guess I was more comfortable when I could visit every office each year and know almost everyone by first name. I can't do that now, but while we were growing, I always had a pretty good sense of priorities, and even though 'Account A' in Chicago was being handled by the Chicago office, if it were one of our top five or ten clients, I maintained a very close relationship with the senior people in that client organization.

"Clients have always felt comfortable calling me, and I've enjoyed interacting with them. And incidentally, we have had absolutely minimal defection of people who have taken clients with them. As we have grown larger, maintaining that close relationship has become increasingly difficult. There are layers of management that we never had before. When a client calls and says he'd love to talk with me, I often realize that there is someone else who knows so much more about that client's program than I do, but I owe it to him to listen and perhaps even to visit. But I always take along the person who is the expert. In the case of the older clients, I've tended to have a personal relationship with the top people, but now there is the problem of my time. I tend to overschedule myself, and if our manager in Houston calls and urges me to visit an important client, I'll say, 'O.K., when do you want to do it?' If he reaches out far enough in advance, where there is a blank on my calendar, I'll fill it in. Probably 90 percent of the things I get involved in with our employees today have to do with client matters, and I think my over-accessibility tends to encourage others around here to be accessible too. Everyone around here knows that I get to the office, whenever I am in town, by 7:25, and if anyone really wants to see me, all they have to do is stand at the doorway.

"But you still have to make time for strategy. Within the communications business, which is sort of a simple catch word, there is the strategic and there is the executional. You can have some kind of communications without the strategic factor, but the strategic factor is really the most difficult, yet most important, part of it. In working with a client, the strategic factor requires that you work with the top people. If a client describes a problem, the first thing we say is 'Well, is that really the problem?' Then we try to determine exactly what the problem is. We want to avoid the right answer to the wrong problem. We try to seek out the root cause, and there aren't many people capable of doing this, but we have our share. Many of our people fly 150,000 miles a year, just so our resources can be where the need is."

People and Principles

> Despite the somewhat intangible nature of public relations and the vicissitudes of its clients, the company has experienced virtually no real crises, nor has Harold Burson himself over the course of his career.

"Unlike a lot of entrepreneurs who had to remortgage the homestead or didn't know where.the rent check was coming from, I've never had that experience. Our problems have been decisions of opportunity. The toughest 'problem' decisions I have ever had to face were dealing with people who were not adequate to take the next step, and to tell them so or to separate them from the organization. Over the past 25 years maybe half a dozen such situations have caused me sleepless nights before I did it, and sleepless nights afterwards. But from a business standpoint, each year has been better than before.

"Decisions have never been very hard for me. In any real important decision, I generally knew what the answer was going in. Sometimes, but not frequently, I've been persuaded to change my mind. Through the years I've followed the practice of making a decision and announcing it up front, for fear that I might not get the decision I wanted if it were debated too much, or if I had to overrule someone, there might be too much rancor. I have always tried to avoid strife, so if there would be any large discussion about something, I would line up my votes before the decision.

"No one around here has been very humble in my presence, and I think that's good. I doubt that there is anyone who is afraid of me. The problem may be the other way around; perhaps I'm considered too much of a pussycat. What I have tried to do is to encourage people to act as though they're running their own businesses, but they have to conform to a general set of principles in order that the integrity of the whole can be preserved.

"In the final analysis, people are the chief ingredient of our success. Almost all of the people who have made it to senior positions have been around for a long time, and they share a common characteristic of being pretty smart. Beyond that, to succeed, one certainly has to have the ability to work with other people internally. You may find someone who is great with clients, but if he is not accepted by his peer group, it won't do anything for you as an organization. 'Getting along' assumes emotional stability, a minimization of ego, an appreciation of the whole, and a respect for one another. I think we have that, even an affection. We have been able to advance people very rapidly, and that helps.

"The cornerstone of any successful career in this business is the ability to communicate, and to me, that means the ability to write. One of the great tragedies today is that there are so many people who have grown up looking at the television tube and getting all their information from it, that they don't read and don't know how to write. I suppose the ideal career preparation would be to start out by working on a newspaper for a couple of years. Everyone around here knows that I began as a teen-age copyboy on the Memphis *Commercial Appeal*, so maybe I'm prejudiced. If you want to work in government affairs, you should work for a Congressman. You can prepare for marketing public relations by working for a corporation in marketing. But I feel that a broad-based, liberal arts education with a heavy emphasis on writing is the best preparation; then applying that in some disciplined job is next. After that, if you have enough 'brights,' you can learn this business very fast. Then you have to keep learning—never stop learning—on the job. For example, I've learned a great deal from heads of client corporations. I would mention especially George Spatta, who was chairman of Clark Equipment Company; today I am learning a lot from Coca-Cola's chief executive, Roberto Goizueta. And I've learned a hell of a lot from our own, very bright people."

> The public relations practitioner, Burson says, must earn credibility and acceptance if he or she is ever to participate in strategic leadership. This requires a deep and comprehensive understanding of the business or institution with which the practitioner is working and its relation to society.

"Leverage comes from understanding—and being *recognized* for understanding—the goals and priorities of your peers, your superiors, and your constituents. That much is required *at a minimum* if one is to earn the opportunity to participate in strategic leadership. And I don't suggest that there is a quick or easy way to earn it. This is the first piece of advice I would give to young public relations people who want to get ahead in our craft."

Even to begin, a mastery of the English language is a *sine qua non*, says Burson. To succeed, at least at Burson-Marsteller, requires the talent and high energies of an over-achiever and the ability to work as an effective team member. As the agency's Vision and Values statement puts it, "We prize the individual, but celebrate the team."

Frank T. Cary

Chairman of the Executive Committee
International Business Machines Corporation

*H*e was CEO from 1973 to 1981—eight crucial years during which he guided his company skillfully through a barrage of litigation, helped to triple IBM's revenues, built a strong, professional management team, and directed IBM's energetic technological drive toward computer breakthroughs. Throughout this period of risk, pressure, and crisis he seldom veered from his calm, unflappable manner. His basically cerebral management approach is to ask questions, questions, questions—until he thoroughly understands what is behind a problem or what assumptions underlie a proposal. He uses words economically, but he is willing to explain his decisions rather than simply announce them.

Many have praised him for anticipating IBM's manufacturing needs and investing billions to meet them. But he would rather talk about the billions that IBM risked on R&D to make significant breakthroughs on the frontiers of technology. Without those breakthroughs, he says, there would have been no need for more manufacturing facilities. He helped to transform IBM into a company that is technologically aggressive while still retaining its traditional strong customer orientation. As Chairman of the Executive Committee he kept asking questions—politely but insistently.

Career Information:

1948   Joined IBM as a marketing representative
1954   Named assistant branch manager, San Francisco
1956   Named branch manager, Chicago
1959   Named president of The Service Bureau Corporation
1964   Named president of the Data Processing Division
1966   Named general manager of the Data Processing Group
1967   Named senior vice president
1968   Elected to Board of Directors
1969   Joined Management Review Committee
1971   Became president of IBM
1973   Named chief executive officer (retained that title until 1981) and chairman of the board
1983   Retired as employee, named chairman of the executive committee

Other Affiliations:

- Director, Capital Cities/ABC, Inc.
- Director, DNA Plant Technology
- Director, Hospital Corporation of America
- Director, Merck & Co., Inc.
- Director, J.P. Morgan & Co.
- Director, New York Stock Exchange
- Director, PepsiCo, Inc.
- Director, Texaco, Inc.
- Trustee, The Brookings Institution
- Trustee, The Museum of Modern Art
- Member, Corporation of the Massachusetts Institute of Technology
- Member, The Business Council

Educational Information:

- University of California, Los Angeles, B.S., 1943
- Stanford University, M.B.A., 1948

Personal Information:

- Born December 14, 1920, Gooding, Idaho
- Married, has four children

196

Frank T. Cary

"*I* really didn't have time to have people educate me about manufacturing and engineering. I had a lot of good people helping me and learned to count on them. I also learned never to . . . assume anything or to believe that things would happen the way they were forecast. I was both curious and skeptical and always asked tough questions and expected others to do the same."

This is how Frank Cary describes his response to promotion to general manager of the newly formed Data Processing Group in 1966. IBM had recently announced a revolutionary new product line—the now-famed System/360—but the unprecedented level of technological effort required to bring these machines to market had strained much of the company's development and manufacturing management, leaving important segments of the organization exhausted. The situation facing IBM executives was little known to most outsiders at that time, but in later years many industry analysts agreed that Cary, whose career up to then had been largely spent in sales, marketing, and staff assignments, had taken on one of the most difficult management challenges in U.S. business history. Cary did far more, however, than to play the role of tough questioner.

Building a Team

"It was very important to build a feeling that everyone was working together as a team. We had functional divisions at the time. I remember we used to have division-manager meetings, and at first most of the division managers thought they were wasting their time. For example, if you were head of the service division, you had to sit through a broad agenda on all facets of the business—much of which might be of little proprietary interest to the service division manager. But without having all of the team there, I would have been the only one dealing with general management affairs, and I needed their understanding and help as well as their expertise. We had to pull together in a way that was right for IBM, rather than in just a functional way.

"I think the combination of being skeptical and working on team-building techniques enabled us to get things moving. The division managers began to understand and work on the larger priorities."

Moving Up—From Sales to Staff

Like all his predecessors as IBM's chief executive, Cary began his career in sales, when he joined the company as a marketing representative in Los Angeles in 1948.

"I was in sales at one level or another for my first 11 years, leaving sales to come east in 1960 to become president of the Service Bureau Corporation, which had been established as a subsidiary of IBM a couple of years earlier. It was my first general management job, and during the short time I was its president, it had its first profitable year. I remember Tom Watson giving me a gold watch on that occasion.

"I left that job to join the corporate staff, something I had never wanted to do, but after a certain amount of persuasion, I made the move. I was an assistant director of the corporate staff."

IBM's corporate staff played—and still plays—a critical role. A few years earlier, the now-famous IBM contention system had been developed, a system in which contention is encouraged as a way to test and retest proposals. Under this system, a functional staff head—for example, the staff director of marketing—would be responsible for reviewing the marketing plans and operations of all line divisions. During a division's presentation to the Corporate Management Committee, the corporate staff head had the chance to vote—to concur or "non-concur" with recommendations or conclusions. If he failed to raise issues and the plan later

FRANK T. CARY

failed, the corporate staff director would be held just as accountable as the division or line manager. If the staff director "non-
concurred," he had to justify his position in direct contention with
the divisional general manager. It is a process in which assumptions
and conclusions are questioned and evaluated continuously.

"Giving such a strong role to the corporate staff had been a
very major change in the way that the company conducted its

business. People were still learning the nuances of the line-staff operation, and it took a lot of effort to get it going smoothly."

Organizing for Growth

Meanwhile, a major technological development was under way at IBM. Some visionary computer architects had proposed an entire, program-compatible family of computers. Called the System/360, this family of computers was to become one of the most important in the company's history. *Fortune* magazine later described this "gamble" as a "billion-dollar, you-bet-your-company decision," an assessment that in retrospect might be considered an understatement.

"At the time there was a lot of concern that we had grown so much that we weren't responsive enough—particularly from a development standpoint—to the requirements of the marketplace. Management wanted to look at other ways to organize our business in order to make it more entrepreneurial and responsive, and to insure our rapid growth. So an organizational task force was established in early 1963 with the charge of proposing a reorganization plan, and I served on that task force. I thought the task force assignment would take at most 6 months, but we worked on it for almost a full year. The problem was trying to fulfill management's direction of organizing the business into smaller integrated units just at the time that the System/360 was in the process of being designed and prepared for announcement. We worked hard to do what management wanted, but in the end reached just the opposite conclusion: we recommended that IBM go to large functional divisions in the interest of getting the System/360 out the door. In other words, we recommended functional divisions as opposed to functionally integrated units. This is not what management wanted to hear, but there was really no choice.

"The whole development of the System/360 had to be very carefully and closely coordinated, as it was a family of closely related products. The same coordination was necessary within manufacturing, marketing, and service. To build contention into the organization, we combined development and manufacturing into one group and marketing and service divisions into another.

"We had wanted to make IBM's organizational units smaller and more entrepreneurial, but the times were wrong. The System/360 required such a tremendously coordinated effort that you simply could not ignore its profound requirements and expect to get it produced. It was an enormous undertaking.

"While it was a very frustrating time for all of us, the task force assignment was a great learning experience. During that year I interviewed almost every major executive in the company and heard probably every known organizational concept expounded. This gave me a tremendous foundation which was useful when I became president of the marketing division and throughout my career."

The Strains of Success

"Acceptance of the idea of a family of compatible systems was fantastic. We soon had an enormous backlog, and the pressure was really on to get the product out. But meeting the delivery schedules that had been committed strained our manufacturing and software resources. Both the market demand and the magnitude of the job had been underestimated, and by early 1965, it became apparent that we would not be able to meet some of our schedules. This, of course, created a great deal of concern within the company and generated conflicts between the two groups—development/manufacturing and marketing/service.

"Many of these conflicts were escalated to corporate headquarters. However, the staff contention system had never been meant to deal with the nitty-gritty of operating details. Our battles were forcing too many decisions to the top. To keep the business moving, we needed a way to get decisions made quickly below the corporate level.

"Top management decided that the two functional groups should be combined under one general manager who could deal with these conflicts."

Selected to become general manager of this new Data Processing Group, Cary faced a make-or-break challenge. Many difficult technical problems remained to be solved. Software schedules were in some cases meaningless. IBM's reputation as a company that delivered what it promised was in jeopardy.

"My main problem in becoming the general manager was that I didn't know very much about development and manufacturing. I had a lot to learn, and I had to get a lot of things done quickly. My recollection of those days is that they were very, very long. Some of us have laughed about how much time we spent in that general manager's conference room. We'd start at breakfast, later bring in the sandwiches and the apples, and then wind up there late at night. There were many endless days, but it was an exciting time too, because so much depended upon the success of that new organization. Billions of dollars had been invested in the new product line, and we were dedicated to making it successful. We had problems first in getting the hardware out, and then in getting the software out. All our attention was focused on meeting our original commitments and revising them only when necessary.

"As we gradually improved our performance—in the manufacture of semiconductors, in programming, in product testing, in productivity—things began to fall into place and began to sing. There was a lot of satisfaction in that."

Learning Through Asking the Right Questions

"The technique of intense questioning is something I learned in my earliest management roles, but I had to apply it much more strongly to the development and manufacturing functions to which I had had little previous exposure. When someone came in and started to make a presentation, I would stop them at the outset. I'd ask, 'What is it that you're recommending?' I made them explain in a way that was meaningful. I didn't listen to a lot of sales presentations about technology or processes that were foreign to me. I had to understand the facts, goals, schedules, and especially the assumptions.

"I found through experience that one of the most valuable management techniques is to keep asking for assumptions. For example—what are the assumptions behind the forecast? Pretty soon you bring the discussion down to a level you understand.

"There are great strengths in being a good listener and in visiting places where the work is done—asking people what their problems are, what they think needs to be done. And, it's really the only way that you can find out certain things in time to be helpful. If you wait for all of it to bubble up through the normal levels of management, it's often too late and the problem has been through so many filters that it often doesn't even sound like a problem.

"If you don't learn what the people on the line—developing, building, servicing, or selling the product—are doing and what kind of problems they're dealing with, you just can't have much of a feel for what's going on.

"I am a great believer in the importance of clear communication. The manner in which people communicate their ideas is a good indication of the clarity of their thinking. All of us do better when we have to put something down on paper. This discipline forces us to improve our thinking. When someone answers a question off the top of his head, the tendency is to be verbose and unorganized. But if you force people to discipline their thinking by putting their ideas in writing and then discipline it further by insisting that the idea be presented on a single sheet of paper, you improve their thought processes as well. I wouldn't read anything longer than one page. So, I learned a lot about people from the memos they wrote and the presentations they made."

Building Agreement

"All IBM managers are motivated to do a job; it's one of IBM's great strengths. The trick is a matter of knowing how to set the agenda—to get people working together.

"I had come from an environment—the corporate staff—where we were encouraged to operate in a contention mode. On the other hand, when it's obvious that cooperation rather than competition is needed, you put contention aside.

"When I became general manager of the data processing group, it was essential for the functional division managers to focus on solving the problems of the integrated business. So my agenda was designed to *eliminate* conflicts, and I think it worked very well.

"A very important part of management at any level is setting the agenda. I would select items that I thought important for all of the division managers to understand, and I'd have them sit through those discussions. We would talk about the functions that cut across all divisions—the financial management of the group, for example—but we would also talk about specific divisional problems. The general manager of the service division, for example, would report on things that were driving him crazy, and when the others listened to him, they would get an appreciation for his dependencies. Similarly, we'd hear about problems in development, manufacturing, and marketing.

"Since I did not want to be the only person worrying about the general management problems, I had to have each manager concerned about what was going on in the other functions of the business. Setting the agenda for the general managers' meetings to some degree forced them to pay attention."

Soon after Cary had this job under control, he became senior vice president and then executive vice president, serving on the Corporate Management Committee. In this capacity, he was responsible for IBM's research activities, its legal staff, and its international operations. This experience represented additional preparation for his becoming president of IBM in 1971 and board chairman in 1973.

Litigation a Major Challenge

In January, 1969, the federal government filed a major antitrust suit against IBM, litigation that would last for 13 years. It finally ended when the Department of Justice dismissed the case in 1982, after determining that its charges were "without merit." Countless millions of dollars and thousands of hours of management time were spent in defending that and a host of other antitrust actions. Although the burden of preparing the defense fell largely upon IBM's general counsel, Nicholas Katzenbach, it also weighed heavily upon Cary as CEO.

"When I got involved in all that litigation, I often thought back to my time at Stanford when I had taken courses in economics from a professor by the name of Theodore Kreps. Professor Kreps taught the concept of competition as a control mechanism, a control in the sense that an industry that is truly competitive is more likely to be innovative and serve the consumer.

"I never felt that IBM was trying to do anything other than to compete fairly. In every job I ever had, we had plenty of competitors to worry about. This gave me considerable comfort as we tried first one lawsuit and then another.

"The government finally agreed that it did not have a case. We also prevailed in all of the private suits.

"During almost all the time that I was CEO, we had to live with the government's constant scrutiny and the specter of being broken up. For example, when we got involved in Satellite Business Systems, because of our recognition of the importance of telecommunications, the Department of Justice fought it. We were a company under attack and on trial. We were trying to keep from letting those lawsuits dominate our business decisions. For the most part, we were successful, but clearly we didn't have all of the options we wanted.

"While we were able to keep the litigation from destroying us, we still had disappointments. Without doubt, the biggest disappointment—and the biggest shock—was when the unfavorable court decision came in on the antitrust suit filed by Telex. It was the second case that came to trial. We thought we had a good case and that we would win it; in fact we thought we were winning it as we watched it proceed during trial. It was tried in a district in Oklahoma which was overloaded with cases. The judge, who had been brought back from retirement, heard the case, and at its conclusion went off to the mountains for a long summer working vacation, during which he thought long and hard, and came to erroneous conclusions of law.

"The unfavorable decision would have cost us about $350 million. The shock of having thought one day that we would win—because the case looked so favorable from our standpoint—to hearing that kind of decision was immense. I went into hibernation. I said to myself, 'Could I have misjudged this so badly?' 'Did we make wrong assumptions?' A couple of days later I returned to the real world, convinced that we had not been wrong. I had talked with our general counsel and outside counsels, and we had concluded that the judge had simply made a mistake. We took the case to the Appeals Court and won it. But until we learned that we had won, I must say I had some very uncomfortable days.

"The timing of the Telex court decision could not have been worse. In the Fall of 1973, the price of oil had skyrocketed, sending an inflationary shock throughout the world, and certainly the stock market—including our stock—was adversely affected. Here we were, this big blue chip—a market bellwether —with a large adverse judgment, and we experienced a fantastic drop in our equity value."

The loss of the Telex suit took on additional significance (even though the decision was ultimately reversed) because it encouraged a significant number of IBM's competitors to file similar suits.

"Many competitors who thought they had a chance to win a claim filed lawsuits, encouraged by the prospect of receiving treble damages. We lost none of these suits; some were settled out of court and some were tried. But the main point is that we got through all this adversity, even though we had more than 20 lawsuits with which to contend. Everyone in IBM believed the company was right and that we would eventually win. And while we went through this highly litigious and most inflationary period in modern history, we managed to keep investing in the future."

Making Decisions

The burden of the antitrust suit and the pace of technological change marked Frank Cary's term as IBM's CEO and put a premium on sound decisions. Most major decisions, he says, are made incrementally. And, he adds, because of the heavy consequences such decisions may have, it is important to learn how to feel "really comfortable with an important decision."

"What I would often do is sleep on a decision—go over the various facets and possible consequences, gathering additional information, judgments, and insights—until the decision became comfortable. I never put off making decisions more than a day or two, but this process of reflection helped avoid consequences that I might otherwise have overlooked.

"In IBM we have a very thorough method for testing of decisions, because if you make a 'blooper,' it can be an expensive and public process as well. We have an interdivisional process in which every involved party has a chance to review and concur or non-concur. Theoretically at least, any major recommendation has had a lot of testing, and by the time top management approves it, it should be pretty good. All decisions can't be made that way, of course, as many must be made on the basis of relatively few facts and a lot of intuitive judgment.

"The CEO and the other members of the corporate office are people who must weigh things. Situations are very rarely black or white, but rather are all kinds of shades of grey. When a particular executive is said to have good judgment, this means that he balances things appropriately in the long-term interests of that company."

Assessing Technology

"In 1970, we had announced a successor family of computers, the System/370. It was an outgrowth of what had gone before, and did not begin to offer the degree of technological advance that the 360 had. It seemed to me that for the systems beyond the 370, we would need to invest a lot more in technology in order to produce a more rapid rate of change. We set up a task force to lead us toward really innovative systems in the future, but that task force ultimately recommended far more dependence upon technological advances and breakthroughs than we could gamble on. Everything would have had to come off perfectly on schedule, and to assume that all of this would happen was simply too great a risk. So instead, the task force's work became the basis for our technological plan. Following its technological recommendations drove us to higher levels of achievement, but we did not count on using any of these technologies until they were ready.

"While I was CEO, we invested billions of dollars mastering technologies that we now take for granted, technologies on which many of the new generations of products rely. People tend to remember more about the billions invested in manufacturing in the 70s.

"When people say to me, 'You did a great job in anticipating the company's manufacturing needs and investing in them,' they don't realize that the risky investment was first putting large amounts of money into technology—for example, pouring money into multilevel ceramics, into very large-scale integration, into liquid-cooled circuit technologies, and into new programming systems. The fact that we pressed for significant breakthroughs—and invested in them heavily—was fundamental to the cost and performance improvements that IBM was able to make with the introduction of the systems that are on the market today—for example, the 3080 family.

"The point is that there were about seven years of technological and manufacturing process development—and the machines that were shipped in volume starting in 1981 were dependent on those investments in technology that began in 1973.

"Once the technologies work, once the products using them can be designed, once a market forecast can be made, then deciding how much manufacturing capacity you need isn't really that tough. What's tough is making those investments in technology, betting on success in an environment of great uncertainty."

Charlotte L. Beers

Managing Partner, Chairman
Chief Executive Officer
Tatham-Laird & Kudner

*S*he keeps a hammer on her office coffee table—a presentation from once skeptical Sears executives who refused to believe a woman could understand hardware, but changed their minds when she expertly took apart and reassembled an electric drill before their eyes. She's the only woman who has risen through the ranks of advertising to become CEO of a major agency. Her management style is more intuitive than analytical—so she makes sure this is complemented by people around her who are more analysis-oriented. She prefers to stimulate people to do good work rather than issue directives—an approach which she doubts is effective. She finds it most important to create an environment in which people feel that they can make a difference. Impatient with bureaucratic hierarchies, she believes strongly in hands-on management.

In 1979, she took a faltering, insecure agency and made it one of the glittering stars of the advertising field. Tatham-Laird tripled its billings from $80 million to $240 million, achieved a 13 percent before-tax profit margin that is twice the industry's norm—and did it with a lean organization of only 325 employees. The 67th largest ad agency when she became CEO, Tatham-Laird is now 39th and moving up. Many would attribute this ascent to her strong drive and pursuit of excellence. As she says, "I guess I'm from the try-harder school."

Career Information:

1960 Joined Uncle Ben's Rice, where she moved from consumer research to brand management

1969 Joined J. Walter Thompson as account representative

1975 Made senior vice president

1979 Joined Tatham-Laird & Kudner and was named chief operating officer

1982 Named chief executive officer

1986 Added title of chairman

Other Affiliations:

- Member, Board of Channel 11 (PBS)
- Member, Board of School of the Art Institute of Chicago
- Member, Board of Xavier University
- Member, Board of Federated Department Stores

Educational Information:

- Baylor University, Texas, 1957

Personal Information:

- Native of Texas

Charlotte L. Beers

"*I*n my early days at Tatham, not enough of us were making things happen, so I was very much an agitator, a catalyst. If the work wasn't good enough, the point was really to challenge it, move it along to get something done. Today, in direct contrast, I spend hours and hours on a totally different task: trying to bring in the people who are right for us. During the past couple of years I have had to undergo a major personality change. At times it's frustrating, but the fact is they (the people at the agency) have to do the job now; I can't do it any more. I have to restrain myself. A year or so ago, I began to concentrate on new business and external matters. However, there is a sense in the company that my ability to flag something that's not right—or to signal an opportunity or weakness —is one of the strengths I have, so I'm encouraged to do this. At times I'll say, 'I want to see a review of this, because I am wondering if we've got enough focus.' As a result of that review, we may change the way we're doing things. On the other hand, if I were to do that very often, I'd just create a lot of wasted meetings, and I wouldn't be helping our people."

Charlotte Beers, chief executive of Tatham-Laird & Kudner, is the only woman who has risen through the ranks of advertising to the top job of a major agency. Since coming to TLK in 1979, she has led the Chicago partnership (incidentally, the only large agency in the U.S. that is organized as a partnership) into profitability. In recent years its billings have increased at about four times those of other advertising agencies, and its current before-tax profit margin is nearly double the industry average. Though responsible for a stunning turnaround in one of the most competitive of all industries, she gives the credit to her people.

"Talent clearly draws other talent. That's what happens *before* you can turn out great advertising.

"Bill Youngclaus, today the president of TLK, came aboard in the midst of a new business rush, but we were in danger of dropping a lot of balls. His background is also account work and big agency experience, but we're quite different. And those differences benefit the agency. He's gifted at causing an idea or spotting one. He cares deeply about our clients' business and they feel it. And he's making something happen around here. He works especially well with John McKee, an ex-actor and a top-notch group creative director. McKee is a powerful presenter. He and Bill are both philosophers who can get something done.

"The point of all this is that the talents here are highly varied, but complementary; but both these guys are intensely hard working, highly individualistic stars. We like the idea of an agency of stars. But it's not the easiest, most peaceful way to go. Much of the momentum we have was generated by teams of old TLKers and these kinds of new partners.

"Competitiveness in this business is odd in that people, agency to agency, can be great friends. We all have much in common, since we're in the pursuit of ideas—and those are elusive. There is great mutual regard for talent in this business, and in some ways that means you have more in common with your competitors than with your clients. But you clearly compete in win-or-lose situations with great regularity. One hazard of this business is that you could become pretty cynical as to just how long a client will stay with you; you have to be able to live with a continual sense of rejection. Almost nine out of ten new business presentations don't get you any business, though our agency's done considerably better than that. We had to!

"These presentations are expensive in money and in psychic cost. You have to train yourself to view them as opportunities where you have a chance to break the rules, to accelerate your thinking, to put your thoughts out there—and then go in understanding full well that there are many variables that you cannot control. Then, if you win, it's a plus—and if you lose, it's not unexpected. If you don't inculcate the agency with that philosophy, you find yourself dealing with an impossible

CHARLOTTE L. BEERS

report card. A credentials presentation can cost you tens of thousands of dollars of staff hours, and spec-create (speculative creative presentations) gets you into real out-of-pocket costs. The presentations rarely cost less than $25,000 and can go up to $150,000. Some agencies have gone to extremes, such as finished film, in an effort to win the client over. We would never do that; I don't believe in gambling today's profits on those odds. And although we are getting into bigger and bigger contests, we are not likely to be into a save-the-Ford-Motor-Company-account type of thing. Some of the more reputable clients will contribute dollars toward these new business presentations, but never as much as we spend."

213

Tatham-Laird & Kudner is clearly a brand-oriented agency. According to *Ad Week*, a CEO at a rival Chicago agency said, "Charlotte and her team are among the best brand builders in the industry. It's a real challenge competing against them because of their tenacity and their overall depth." To build and sustain a brand, there must be continuity, quality of talent, and meticulous attention to detail for a protracted period. TLK, she says, does not want to launch a product and have it succeed for only a couple of years, then launch another new product. Other agencies and other companies may deliberately do that, but getting a brand successfully and positively imprinted in the minds of consumers is not a stop-and-go process.

"We believe we must *build brands* and that the power of advertising lies in its ability to create not just a product success, but a *brand* in the minds and hearts of people. Having taken that as a goal, everything we do at the beginning of the process is to create a *brand*—not just to launch a product with its three or four finite attributes. Obviously, we bring product features into it, too. In the early meetings, the best thinking of the agency goes into the strategic process—to focus, to eliminate options, to decide where the greatest realm for a long-lived brand exists. It's a very sophisticated process when it's done right, and it is easy to misunderstand this. Most of our clients have product strategies, but today a strategy statement is such a broad-based mission that you could write 20 different executions and still be on strategy. As a result, you often don't have very hard-working advertising.

"We separate the creative process into two distinct parts: the creative definition of the problem and the creative solution of it.

"The heart of the strategic process, while defining the problem, is to eliminate all consideration of solutions. Few people know how to do this: no one wants to leave anything out. It is interesting to me that business people can be extremely tough-minded about how they allocate their physical resources, but when they must deal with a highly limited universe—such as a 30-second piece of advertising—they don't want to leave anything out. The creative opportunity lies in removing every piece of distracting information and thought; to agree, strategically, on what the problem *is*. You can define a problem in 20 ways, but we must agree on which particular problem it is that *advertising* can solve. When we are able to do this, we have housed the thinking in a clear understanding of what we want to do. This is very important.

"What kind of wonderful lift-off can we give that thinking, in terms of execution? This is the area of magic in an agency, and if you can distinguish the two, it's really exciting. You try not to trample on this second stage the way you did on the first. While this is done elsewhere, at other agencies, I think it's practiced more earnestly at Tatham than at most other places. Some agencies are more into the 'Let's execute a great idea,' and indeed certain kinds of advertising lend themselves to that. For example, if you are the agency for McDonald's, there's a certain weight and momentum already going for you. Our president, Bill Youngclaus, was formerly vice president of marketing at McDonald's and has a client background as well as agency. That's very important to us. He would say that even in the McDonald's circumstance there are very few new strategic decisions to be made.

"We are fortunate in having very elegant thinkers on the client side. That's partly because of the size of our clients but also because of their nature. If you have been at R. J. Reynolds for ten years, you are *very* sophisticated in the marketing process.

"We would never concentrate on the idea process of problem definition to the exclusion of the execution, but what is clearly becoming our trademark is *brand thinking*. We recently had a wonderful exchange with Procter & Gamble—the company which invented brands—and in this exchange, we redefined brand *thinking*. It was provocative for them and for us to realize that in today's world one has to rethink what a brand is, how it should be nourished and how advertising carries it. Products are getting better and better, but not necessarily better than one another. What makes a brand certainly includes legitimate product advantages, but also how you feel about it, how it's treated you, what place it's had in your home—and you ignore these kinds of issues at your peril. One of the great brands we've been lucky to work with is Mr. Clean, a very good all-purpose cleaner. The thing that makes this brand dis-

tinct and interesting is the friendship of 'me and Mr. Clean'—
our user and their friend Mr. Clean. Our newest Mr. Clean advertising acknowledges the consumers' role in all that; it's very
warm and charming work, not just a hard demo on how to
clean your house.

"In the first meeting we ask: Who is Mr. Clean? How does
he affect matters? What is his significance in your life? You try
to answer questions like that in the first meetings, as you lay
out a template for the copy.

"Finally, in brand thinking, nothing in the world can substitute for the creative people, the unique set of artists, writers,
and producers who bring brands to life. The reason I am in this
business is because I get to work with such idea people."

Early Experience at TLK

"Just a few years ago this agency was viewed as solid, stable,
and verbal—some would have said stodgy. I have a theory that
most agencies are in more trouble than they appear to be or in
more success than they appear to be—and there's something
like a two-to-five-year lag before the perception catches up
with the reality. Tatham has always had very talented people
and a remarkable client list, clients who are disproportionately
large for the agency's size. The people here had a kind of elegant opportunity to work on very big pieces of business, but
the agency had gone through several successions. At that time
(around 1979) the question was 'Who and what will we become?' Jerry Birn, who was chairman, was in the process of
answering that, but there was a sense among other agencies
that perhaps TLK would not continue to be vital, and the
clients' attitudes were beginning to reflect that.

"Birn's decision to hire me was an interesting one. He
could have sold the agency but chose instead to build, and his
courage was an inspiration to all of us. He had never seriously
interviewed a woman for a top job, though women have had
important roles in advertising for years in the creative area.
But to go outside to get a woman to come in and help build
—this was a remarkable action on his part, and he loved the
idea from the beginning. His joke is that he went out to hire

the best man that he could find and came home with me! Together, we were very lucky, because we had complementary
talents. One of the things you must have in this business, and
maybe in any business, is an understanding of what you do
well and a willingness to find someone else who can do the
things you don't do well. You need to find a harmony. I had
come from the account side—planning, putting ideas into action, making things happen. The creative people handle ideas,
imagination, and insight from a totally different frame of reference than do the account folks. In my mind, no agency should
ever try to make it without these two skills running side-by-
side. An agency dominated by account people and their type of
thinking—though there are exceptions—is not going to be as
healthy as an agency that has balance. Interestingly, the con-
verse isn't true, as there are boutique-type agencies with brilliant creative people at the top which do very well. But they
don't grow into major business enterprises without that balance. Some of them, like Chiat/Day, are sparking the rest of us,
and we admire them for that. But if small, creative-dominated
agencies try to grow into (and they may choose not to) being
competitive with JWT or other large full-service agencies,
they're going to have to change their character, by letting the
account-people planning function rise.''

In coming to Tatham-Laird, Beers had been wooed away from
a very senior position at J. Walter Thompson, an agency of massive size. Arriving there, she experienced a severe culture shock
and felt quite alone.

"People underestimate the importance of having a covey
of supporters and friends. My environment changed, and I by
necessity, underwent a dramatic personality change—becoming an earnest listener. I sure wasn't known for that at Thompson, where I was more of an impatient catalyst, making things
happen. There I felt the *worst* thing I could do was to listen
too long! But here I *had* to hear what people were saying and
weren't saying, so I spent a lot of time listening, trying to
understand where they felt short of talent or self-conscious or
uncertain, to see if I had strengths to fill in the gaps. And, if I

didn't, to try to figure out how we could fill them in. Then I did the same thing with the clients.

"The first thing I worked on was to try to help this agency understand how good it really is. It is good today and it was then. But they had been so close to their clients and had been reading some of the report cards that were questioning, 'Well, just how vital is the agency?' This was just a question, not a condemnation. Since I had the voice of an outsider and considerable personal conviction about what makes something good, I spent a lot of time giving them my honest assessment. I would refer to an earlier experience and would say, 'We could not have come to this quality of thinking this fast in my previous jobs.' And to clients, I would say, with a new and forceful voice, 'This is a very outstanding piece of work,' and they were inclined to agree! There is that wonderful time when you are assumed to be fairly objective and expert, and then there arrives another time when you come to be hopelessly biased in the interests of your own company. I think I used that time well in trying to raise the self-esteem of the organization.

"My second effort was simply to try to assess where there were gaps. The third thing I did was to make a lot of promises, yet being careful not to promise anything too far afield. I would say, 'Here's what we're about: we are going to excite the creativity that can come from a highly sophisticated strategic agency.' The strategic power of TLK was accepted, and we needed to lift the creative spirit. But also during that period we turned down some opportunities that we weren't yet ready for and also turned down some very senior people who were interested in coming here. We had to trust our instincts as to how well they would do in what was even to me an unknown environment.

"Before I arrived, the agency had lost a big piece of business, but the billings for earlier work continued for a while —as a kind of a false wind. We were experiencing a very low profit return, but we decided to spend the money on talent anyway. This took some courage, which we could never have mustered had Jerry Birn not said, 'Let's go build something.' TLK is privately held, so when you spend money, you take it out of the partners' pockets. We hired Bill Ross as chief operating officer, which is hardly a suitable title, as he's well-known for his creative reputation and stature. Making this statement turned out to be a wonderful communication about where we were going in terms of creativity. Soon, other great people began to join us.

"In those days, when we made presentations to clients, we had more ideas and ideals than we had facts or film. Once a client said, 'I don't understand this; here is a room of talented people, but all you have on your reel is slice,' some of which, by the way, was very good ('slice-of-life' is a term for packaged-goods advertising, a little daily vignette showing, for example, a woman using a product and talking about it); slice is very different, of course, from image advertising, which evokes more emotions. The client asked, 'What's happening here? You have all these interesting people, but nothing that exciting on the reel.' One of our people interrupted and said, 'Well, I came here *because* these people are here, and I think we're going to do something great.' The client wrote on a piece of paper, 'Talent follows talent,' and hired us!

"So now there was this cycle of new people coming aboard, and there developed a sense of belief, a willingness to struggle. Nowadays I need to restrain myself from having a disproportionate interest in those people who came aboard when doing so wasn't an obvious choice. We formed a core family, almost started a new company together. The next big cycle, then, was to merge those strengths and to build Tatham on the foundation of these new personalities and ideas. Something happened along the way: we had to develop our own language and culture. The business doubled in about 16 months because people got excited about our prospect and our potential. In a way, that slowed us down; as we had to handle all that business. Nothing was simple, since the first business anyone gives you is something that's in trouble. We had a very difficult time, and I kept wondering why it wasn't more fun to be so successful. We were all running around, doing what we had to do to get the work out, and trying to meet those greatly advanced expectations. There was a lot of trial and error in those years, and I don't look back on them as my fondest—despite the fact that we were getting headlines about how hot TLK was. Perhaps many managers go through this puzzling disappointment and anguish when you're on the way to success but haven't quite gotten there. We were not ready for all this new business —it almost happened too fast.

"I was on the phone or visiting with key clients a good bit of that time. Many were new to us and needed a share of my attention. I also spent hours and hours on the new advertising assignments, since we all went forward in a task force mentality to get those businesses launched. But a good third of my time was spent in talking to disgruntled and harassed employees, some of whom were working around the clock and others who were trying to figure out what we now stood for. The new Tatham was interesting, fun, alive, and extremely stressful. There was just no time to step back and be reasoned.

"Then we entered a period when we desperately needed to consolidate our gains and to see which of those were real. The 1984–85 period was very productive, as we finally found some time to try to imagine what we should be doing and where we should be going and, for instance, selecting out client prospects rather than having them select us out. We made some mistakes, and because we were becoming more noticed, we got invited to more new business than ever before. Today we would be even more selective and would eliminate the long shots far ahead of time, since we are still—and plan to remain—a very lean organization. All agencies—with one or two exceptions—have to be lean, since the profit return is not so lucrative that you can afford to maintain a large staff just on prospects. The cost of people is up 30 percent over four years ago, and the number of good people available is relatively small.

"In our industry, creative people tend to change jobs as an automatic way to upgrade, and people in other businesses are very puzzled about our willingness to let people do that. Having come from the business side, I have always been disturbed by the idea that we are occasionally just a stopping-off place. But the reason this happens is that the creative people tend to have less of an allegiance to the client. Often they can leave with no great risk to you—though some people are very key— and they sometimes change to seek an account which may provide a more harmonious environment. But another factor is that it's very difficult for a creative person to get something outstanding on his reel, given costs, the need for research, the seriousness of advertising decisions, and the methods by which advertising is screened and approved. So the creative person tends to think that if he or she had a better environment, then that fresh and one-of-a-kind piece of advertising could finally get on the reel. There is a constant quest for this. And sometimes a person who has been slogging along in an agency for ten years goes somewhere else and does a wonderful piece of film. Every creative person sees a message in that: 'I've got to keep testing myself!' While I am sympathetic to this, it is a disruptive factor.''

From Math to Aftermath

Daughter of a Montana cowboy and oil company executive, Charlotte Beers went to school at Baylor University and the University of South West Louisiana, graduating with a major in mathematics and a minor (somewhat accidentally, she says) in physics. For a short time she taught algebra and related subjects to petroleum managers in southeastern Texas oil fields but then went to work as a research analyst at Uncle Ben's Rice in Houston.

"In the era in which I was raised in Texas (not all that long ago) a girl was supposed to do a little work, get married, and live happily ever after. I had an impatience with that ideal and found a wonderful opportunity, going to work for a unique company, Uncle Ben's, owned by Mars Inc. Whenever people ask me for advice, I say, 'Try to go to work for Forrest and John Mars.' They are so totally supportive of women. At the time this didn't strike me as anything unique since I had always been treated as an equal. Later I understood it *was* unique. Second, they put a great premium on individual power; you don't have to talk about being entrepreneurial there—you simply *are*. Everything I was daring enough to try, they let me. They have relatively few people, give them no individual offices, pay them to come to work on time—a no-nonsense thing—and they pay you above the market average for exceptional work. I didn't catch on for a while that this is an unusual philosophy. I was young and frivolous, really more worried about whether my date of the previous night had sent me any flowers! They must have recognized my lack of seriousness, for they sat me down and gave me a Dutch-uncle kind of talk, saying that it looked to them as though I had some potential but it wasn't promising anything for them. It was a turning point for them to talk to me so frankly with concern. Immediately after, I turned around, started thinking about work and got into it. I fell in love with business in a way that's hard to describe. To me, the business of business is simply the most interesting thing you can do all day.''

At Uncle Ben's, because of her mathematics background and ability to do multiple regression analyses on the mechanical calculator, she conducted consumer and market research studies. She soon became expert at understanding the data and how one goes about asking the right questions. She learned the difference between what people say and what they mean and think and considers that knowledge a strong base for her later career.

"I learned consumer dynamics and converted myself from a mathematician. While I love the clarity and the sense of the puzzle which is math, I began to understand myself; I understood that I was not intended to work in an office by myself. I would always move around and find three people to talk to. I accepted Uncle Ben's as my family, and that work style stayed with me. I am simply not comfortable with any organization so large that I cannot embrace it and it can't embrace me; it all has to be personal with me. When TLK needed to enlarge offices, the first issue in my mind was whether we would be 350 people among some other 12,000. If so, we would not walk into those doors, for to me there is something diminishing about that. We are the primary tenant in this beautiful setting (the towering One Magnificent Mile Building that overlooks Lake Michigan).

"While at Uncle Ben's I was on the way to a more traditional path of women, and left to have my daughter Lisa. But then I was wooed back to do part-time work, for which I had no great appetite—just a need to defray some of my growing expenses. There was a new brand-management system going around at Mars, and after I had worked part-time for a while, they told me they needed a full-time brand manager. 'It can be you,' they said, 'but if so, you can't work part-time anymore.' I could not turn that down, it sounded so fascinating. In fact I got to be one of the first brand managers in the U.S. in the most traditional sense. They told me to think of myself as president of these two businesses (Uncle Ben's Quick Rice and Uncle Ben's Long Grain and Wild Rice), and I took that advice quite to heart. I became worried about the velocity of the rice, how it went through the shellers, where we bought it. In launching Uncle Ben's Long Grain and Wild Rice, I knew where the Indians grew the crop, I just knew everything. It was so exhilarating, and that became a very successful new product. What a great experience! I got to go through the whole marketing channel at a relatively young age—around 32—and helped a group of very talented people to launch this product. As you can see, I have been gifted with exceptional business opportunities where things opened up for me.

"So there I was, a bit of a maverick in the marketing world, accidentally finding myself by sheer luck in environments that were totally supportive. One thing I've learned from watching the creative people is that they have an instinct as to when the environment is supportive, and I have become highly motivated to create that kind of environment here—one that will nourish people.

"I went from Uncle Ben's to (J. Walter) Thompson, which was completely open about what I might do. Uncle Ben's was a client of theirs, and they had sought me out for my rather unusual background, a woman trained in marketing with a math background, looking like a possible candidate for an account exec role. At that time there were few women doing that. When I joined Thompson, there were more things that I didn't know about advertising than I knew. Now there are certain primary aspects of advertising that I would try to teach someone. If someone says, 'I want to be either on the client's side or the advertising side,' I have to assume they don't know anything about the business, since these jobs are totally different. But I got the chance to *live* the difference, so now I understand them.

"The biggest difference between the two is that in the advertising business you cannot separate the need to sell yourself and your ideas from the ability to deliver the written work on paper. People tend to react to you as to whether or not they like you and would enjoy doing business with you. Of course they judge you for your other abilities, but if you cannot articulate your thinking—forget it. Whereas, on the client side, you need not be that articulate, but you sure have to know your product. Actually, the day is gone even on the client side when you can be very inarticulate. Certainly the person who can absorb what others are thinking—and quickly and insightfully summarize it—has a real advantage and will move up in business anywhere.

"The thing that is thrilling about the advertising business is that if you can get a shot at doing something and you do it well, the rewards are exceptional. If you trust yourself, if you're daring about what you think you have to offer, an advertising agency provides a faster track than most places. But you do have to deliver. I got to be known as something of a troubleshooter at Thompson, and when something wasn't going well, they assigned that business to me. It was hard not to notice the person who was then the only woman in the room. I developed a sense of moving quickly to get things done. The most significant step in terms of my own career was when I went from account supervisor to management supervisor, a very big jump. I'm not sure whether Thompson had had a female management supervisor before that—there certainly wasn't one in Chicago. The people at Sears wanted more done by the agency, and Ted Wilson, manager of Thompson's Chicago office, did the unexpected and chose me. It was an unorthodox, gutsy move, since Sears was traditionally rather conservative and at that time male-oriented; there just weren't any women around. The product area that was in need of most urgent attention at that time was the portable electric tool division, a billion dollars worth of sales in a traditionally man's world. That was a kind of a remarkable vote of confidence that they gave to me.

"The portable electric tool people weren't too thrilled. They did want something to happen, but who was this Southern female who obviously didn't know a lot about the world of tools and men and so on? There was great wonderment. It was clear that I needed to have a right to speak, but they had no patience for long discourses on advertising and how it worked, and indeed no reason they should; they were better merchants than I could ever be. Then a wonderful thing happened. The buyer (a very important job at Sears) was Carmen Pizzi. The two of us were responsible for a major presentation on the portable electric drill, and because of the background I had in math and physics, I was a quick study on the drill. But I did understand what an armature was and the difference between brass bearings versus other bearings, and so on, so I said to Carmen, 'Nobody's going to listen to me unless I show something like this. Let me take your part in the meeting, and you take mine.' At the presentation, we both stood up, and I said, 'Today I'm the buyer on the portable electric double-insulated, variable-speed drill, and you will never be without one again in your home.' I proceeded to go, point by point, through exactly what made this drill significant, and by that time, of course, I had become a total believer. When I finished, they gave me a standing ovation, demonstrating a wonderful receptivity. Then Carmen got up and pitched the advertising. He was great, and they applauded him wildly, too! He omitted all the buzz-mumbo that ad people sometimes use and did a superb job of talking about why this particular advertising would work.

"He was the buyer for drills, lawn mowers, tractors, you name it, and the idea was that I would sit down with him and hammer out the marketing plan. I absolutely loved Sears: they stay really close to the consumer. After that chance to work together, we reached a great harmony on what could be done. I was fortunate in getting a couple of great people to work with me on the Sears account, and the interesting thing about taking over a business in trouble is that you can make a lot of changes and don't get narrowed down. During my time at Sears, we did the Great American Homes campaign for Sears Paint, and that's where some of the understanding of the power of a brand hit home."

In 1975, Beers was named Advertising Woman of the Year, following by one year Mary Wells Lawrence, who had established the Wells, Rich, Greene agency many years earlier. Beers reports that she felt she was in fantastic company but not deserving to be ranked with Wells. The award was given because of Beers' senior position as a woman in the largest advertising agency in the world. Many clients came to the award luncheon, and it was a great thrill for Beers, especially at her age, to receive this national award. It was a great thrill, too, for the Sears executives to see this woman (who had at one point stripped down the portable electric double-insulated, variable-speed drill, to demonstrate that she knew what she was talking about) be given this award as an advertising woman of note. Still, this seemed inadequate to them, so the next day they had a ceremony awarding her a handmade Craftsman hammer as the Advertising *Person* of the Year. The male sanctum had been successfully invaded by a thoroughly competent female person.

At J. Walter Thompson, Beers continued to accept increased responsibility, eventually becoming senior vice president, the first woman holding that position. Clients and others offered her several jobs, such as a vice presidency of marketing *and* (her emphasis) sales of a huge company. She turned this down, partly because she was not sure she could succeed at it, as her experience in sales had been very limited, though her regard for it is high.

"I knew I was a candidate for the senior vice president's spot at Thompson—I'm sure there were others—but I really wanted a woman to get that. That is the most feminist I think that I had ever been: I just thought it was well overdue for women to hold that title. It was very gratifying to receive that promotion, and there have been many senior women at Thompson since then.

"One of the problems with the traditional agency environment—and I can't say that we've conquered it here—is the constant need to move oneself up or feel a failure. In many agencies there are no middle-aged or older people, other than one or two captains. There's not as much honor in holding a job for five or ten years, in the client's eye, as in moving. That's a fault of the advertising business but one which probably will not change very much. The next step for me, therefore, had to be either head of the Chicago office or to take on a responsibility for some world-wide activity, and that didn't suit my personal life. Moreover, getting to know myself, I realized that I had a large need to interact with people, to have a kind of professional 'family relationship,' and that need does not lend itself to large companies. At about that time I got to that point in life where I needed to see if I could do something more or less on my own, rather than within a large, highly protected group. There are many times I wish I could talk people out of that feeling, because it is not for everyone, and it is not necessarily progress, but there is that inevitable sense of wanting to test yourself. Some have that need more than others, and I have developed more regard for people who don't want to do that than I used to have."

It was at that time, in 1979, that Tatham-Laird & Kudner asked Beers to join them to help build the agency.

"Tatham looked so very interesting: it was privately held, and ownership struck me as the most direct relationship. It had a wonderful foundation and opportunity for growth, and I thought that I could make a difference. Everybody who's here sooner or later likes the place, because they get a chance to make some difference, and I think this unique characteristic needs to be protected. I'm not sure how we will continue to do that if we triple our volume every four or five years, but we have to learn how. My number one concern is to make sure that people can have an individual impact on this organization even as it grows larger. When I arrived at Tatham, there was a certain sense of disorder or confusion, a lack of knowing just where we were going, and I'm not sure that I didn't create even more disorganization, even some degree of chaos. It sure wasn't the orderly world of mathematics."

Beers' Management Style

"Others could describe me better than I can, but I see myself as being much more intuitive than analytical, thoughtful, or reflective. As a result, I really need to have some thoughtful, reflective people around. Occasionally we will all say, 'Okay, we've got to trust our instinct here.' I never planned, for instance, to leave Thompson to go to a smaller agency where I could make a difference. Nor did I plan other parts of my career. A cycle just came around, and an opportunity—and I've never spent any time worrying about the fact that I didn't take other job opportunities that were offered me.

"I never tell anyone to do anything; in fact, I wonder if anyone gets away with that anymore; I don't know that that really works. In an advertising agency, the best thing you can do is to keep stimulating people to do the kind of irreverent, apart-from-the-norm work that is required. TLK can't do the same kind of average quality advertising another agency does, because we're smaller; for example, we don't have international offices. We have to be better.

"When you look for good people to bring into an agency like this, it's important to avoid people who like order and resources in depth, systems and process—people who find all of that comforting and necessary to their own sense of well being. We need, instead, to find people who are thirsty to make a difference, people with keen intelligence and energy. I am willing to put up with what others might call disruptive personality traits, if the talent compensates for that. We have collected a group of stars, people who are not modest and who push me and others for results, and I am not a very timid person. One interesting comment about Tatham—which I happen to like—is that it is no place for the timid. So we are definitely collecting people who believe that they have something to say and need a place where they can be heard. Now if the whole place were allowed to be like that, we would never get anything done. Someone in the group commented that we are not very good listeners, and that's probably true and to some extent, deliberate. If this goes to too great an extreme, then it's not just disorder, it's *chaos*. But out of a minimal-process environment I hope will come bigger and better and bolder ideas. We recently had a major meeting with our top 40 people in which we exchanged goals, visions, and ideas. That is a very difficult kind of meeting to pull off with a group like ours; I spent hours and hours on the agenda, trying to figure out how it could be done, and a lot of other people around here did, too. But at the end of the day, there was a physical, spiritual high. We asked, 'What is the brand TLK?' We used all our sophisticated brand thinking on our own agency, breaking into teams, with each team presenting the brand. It was funny and painful and thoughtful, yet there were some interesting common denominators from group to group—thank goodness we don't have *too* discordant a team! They said things like, 'A place you can make a difference,' 'an untraditional solution to advertising agencies,' and 'a high density of talent per person or per organization.' We began to get a physical—not just verbal—sense of who we are. Our next job is to replicate that, so that every person here understands our purpose and our point. Then, our clients should play the same thing back to us. They already do tend to find us to be a different kind of agency, but we need to get more playback from them.

"When I talk about not being very good listeners, I am referring to the internal, not external, communications. At the idea-generation stage, we move along rapidly, each wanting to push his or her ideas out on the table, and that's okay with us. This atmosphere has to be cultivated in the early stages—not at every stage, obviously. I'd rather know how people feel than just have a nice meeting. We debate, and anyone in the room with a good idea is as entitled as the rest of us. We try to create a peer atmosphere in idea meetings.

"When we're looking for top people, we need someone who is not going to be frightened by less protocol, someone who has confidence in the power of his or her ideas, because at some point in the business it won't be a person's title or responsibility, it will be the ability to keep up with the thinking that becomes critical.

"All of us have flaws or shortcomings, and it seems to me that I have to fight the tendency to be self-centered. There is a strength in being fast, to be able to reach a decision and to move on it, but the downside of this is that you may not have thought through the implications to other people. For instance, I may think that I am listening carefully and having a responsive meeting with a key person, only later to find that they felt I responded differently than I thought I had. I have to work at learning how not to miscommunicate.

"One thing for sure that none of us (and especially I) *don't* want is for this to become the Charlotte Beers Agency: we want it to become an agency of stars. So the very traits that permitted me to become more visible, noticed, those fast-moving characteristics, are now somewhat in conflict with the excitement of building an enterprise that has its own unique culture and language, and it can't be mine—it has to be theirs. So I am having to monitor my own behavior, having to give up those kinds of indulgent reach-for-attention behavior patterns that I used to have and which served me well in the past. I don't really need that much attention now, and it's just wonderful and probably a relief to the people around me.

"Insofar as values are concerned, it matters greatly to me that people are treated fairly. In this kind of business, my idea can cross yours; decision making can be usurped on the basis of what is—or simply what is thought to be—a better idea. Fairness is paramount in the way people are brought into TLK or encouraged to leave. If I think that someone is not going to thrive here, I believe it's fair to get them out quickly. I will turn the world upside down to get them another position, but I have to get them out. This is a very intimate business, one that can destroy your self-esteem, so I watch out for that very carefully. Then, too, I have to be aware of my personal behavior standard and try not to put someone into something they won't succeed at—even though they themselves don't recognize this. At times we spend a whole day critiquing people and their thinking, and we certainly cannot flinch on that —the quality of thinking. Therefore, you must put into the room with your best people, equal talent. The hardest decisions I ever have to make have to do with constantly upgrading the talent; at times you have to tell someone that he is not as good as he should be for the group, when all he (or she) has ever done is exactly what people expected of them, but then the ground rules were changed. This is very painful, in many ways quite unfair: you change the standards, and now they don't fit anymore. This is why the humane quality has to go side-by-side with the performance quality. We have no right to destroy anyone's estimate of himself. Yet the advertising business is so full of flukes; someone could leave here and blow the world apart, and I'd be delighted—perhaps I'd feel stupid as well, but genuinely delighted. Since we have this need to create a standard above the average, then it is not fair to bring in exceptional people and ask them to work with mediocre people. This principle is very important, yet very tough to put into practice, because day in and day out, all of us are capable of average or mediocre behavior. However, those two principles must go hand in hand. If not, you end up with an environment which is excellent but also ruthless. I guess I'd say that I believe in a very tough-minded standard, on the one hand, but a very tender sensitivity to the fragility of the person getting crushed. The creative people—who daily sell their hearts, their dreams, their ideas, their visions, from something deep within them—have improved my ability to be sensitive; they've taught me. As a result, I hope that this sense of compassion is or becomes a part of this organization. I try very hard to keep in perspective what matters, what the values of life are all about, what the human element is. There is a very successful advertising person with whom I have been compared—in terms of results—who has become successful and extremely wealthy in a way which has possibly disadvantaged others. It would bother me greatly for someone to say about me or the people in this agency, 'Boy, you made a real killing, look how successful they are (or she is), but also look at the wreckage around them.' Under these circumstances, I would have to consider myself a failure. Yet occasionally you do get susceptible to this; you sometimes make progress at someone else's expense.''

Advice to Young People

"What qualities do you need in the advertising business? Self-esteem and a zest for change. The world is full of change, and you have to like that better than you like order and predictability. Third, you have to be madly in love with ideas and develop the ability to express yours, appreciate others. Fourth, if you find advertising people the most stimulating group you can be with, then you're a surefire winner.

"It seems, too, you have to have an incredible resilience for dealing with and helping a wide range of personalities. You have to have a genuine liking and patience and interest in your client's affairs, because they'll figure it out if you don't. Then, you somehow have to have that undefined leadership quality to get to the top. I wish someone could explain leadership, but it seems to be related to the point at which decisions of some boldness are reached and acted upon. There are always one or two people in a room who seem to know how to do that, and the rest simply follow. I see this elusive quality of leadership in some people, regardless of their degree of performance and technical ability—they have a *need* to act and to bring the group along with them. If you are in our kind of agency, you can't get along without it. If you are in some other kinds of businesses, that same need could be a negative. I've recently read an interesting series of articles on leaders versus managers, and I am briefing the agency on it. Our people don't understand it and probably wish I wouldn't even talk about it. The purpose of this is not to put yourself in one camp or another; you have to do both. There are some heads of advertising agencies who are probably better managers and need to be, because they have vast business enterprises. But small, growing, entrepreneurial companies need a heavy leadership quotient. Lots of people talk about this, but I don't find myself very comfortable in doing so. The more I learn, the more I discover how fallible I am; and the less I want to be put in a position of pontificating about such an elusive and undefinable subject. Still, if you find yourself in a leadership position—or want to shoot for one—you do need to think about it.

"I'm thinking a lot about young people these days. Lisa is now 21. In talking to young people, I would say that a balance is needed. On the one hand you need a lot of self-confidence, but you also need to realize that you don't know as much as you think you do. I would treat the first job or the first interview as a job you simply had to have and would go in selling, treating every interview as though you wanted that job. I would go in explaining how you can fit into their company and make something happen, but you can't do that unless you've analyzed exactly what the company is and what they need—and even fall in love with it a little bit. This sounds cynical, but it isn't; it's a necessary practice to test out your own conviction. If you're not articulate, that would be the most trying thing in the world for you to do. But the first job interviews more likely fail because you haven't dared to express your feelings or even thought them through.

"Once in a job, if someone gets promoted over you who

has the sheer panache to make that happen, you might as well come to grips with the fact that your competition is not someone who can outthink you or even necessarily outperform you; it's someone who can outarticulate what they feel and how that can make the company better. True salesmanship has to rest on an honest feeling about your worth to this company. If you always start with this sentence, 'Here's what I believe the company should be, and here's how I'd like to help,' you'll be in terrific shape. The second thing, once you're in a job, is to deal with your managers as though they work for you. You manage *them*, you help them flourish, you create opportunities for them, you give them chances to be superior, and you always view them in the mind's eye as, 'These are people who magnify this company, and me.' I have always felt that everyone I was working for had to be managed by me in order to thrive, an interesting reverse way of thinking about things.

"Then there is the matter of disappointment. You will eventually realize that the most pivotal moments in your life *for good* come with someone knocking you in the nose, telling you you're not as hot as you think you are. So try to be open to constructive disasters! Don't sit around and let someone diminish you. Get out of that situation; nothing on this earth is worth it—not a personal relationship and not a business relationship. Somewhere along the way an assessment of what you know how to do and how the world values it has to come up for review. There are times in this world when what the world values is not what you know how to do best, and you just have to understand this distinction and not let the world judge you.

"I was always protected in the advertising business from the incredible ability of a client to say, 'That's not any good, and your thinking is not very good.' The reason I was protected is that I have never let someone else assess for me how good my thinking is. It's not that I'm not open to reviews, and I've listened to some people who I thought could outthink me, but I was always very careful to consider the source when someone criticized the work. Now if an outstanding client really reamed me over, I'd take that totally to heart; but if I were in the company of people who were in fact themselves unable or frightened, I would consider the source. If you don't, you're buffeted around by a lot of unnecessary stuff."

Richard A. Zimmerman

Chairman and Chief Executive Officer
Hershey Foods Corporation

*H*e presides over what was once a one-town company that meant chocolate and nothing else—but under his guidance is rapidly becoming an international giant in diversified food fields. He believes it is essential for a CEO to be broadly oriented toward general management; he himself rose to the top without any functional specialty. But marketing really turns him on, he says, and he sees selling brand image based on quality as Hershey's prime weapon in the highly competitive food industry. Integrity is the cornerstone of his management philosophy.

He heads up a company unique in several ways. More than half its shares are owned by the Milton Hershey School, established by the company's founder for orphaned boys. The school's trust maintains absolute control of the corporation and benefits from its earnings. Hershey became a well-known American institution without advertising—it never advertised until 1970. Diversifying rapidly, once all-chocolate Hershey has vaulted into the No. 1 market share position in U.S. branded pasta sales and owns the 700-restaurant Friendly Ice Cream Corporation. Says Zimmerman: "Our mission is to become a major diversified food company." With his transforming influence, he's taken Hershey a long way toward that goal.

Career Information:

1956   Joined Harrisburg National Bank & Trust Company as assistant secretary

1958   Joined Hershey Foods Corporation as administrative assistant

1960   Became assistant secretary

1965   Became assistant to the president

1971   Became vice president

1971   Became group vice president

1976   Became president and chief operating officer

1984   Became president and chief executive officer

1985   Became chairman and chief executive officer

Other Affiliations (partial list):

- Director/Trustee, Hershey Trust Company
- Director/Trustee, Milton Hershey School—Board of Managers
- Director/Trustee, Irving Bank Corporation and Irving Trust Company
- Director/Trustee, National Association of Manufacturers
- Director/Trustee, Pennsylvanians for Effective Government
- Director/Trustee, Business Council of Pennsylvania
- Director/Trustee, Grocery Manufacturers of America, Inc.
- Director/Trustee, Pennsylvania Chamber of Commerce

Educational Information:

- Pennsylvania State University, B.A., Liberal Arts, 1953

Personal Information:

- Born April 6, 1932, Lebanon, Pennsylvania
- Served as lieutenant in U.S. Navy, 1953–56
- Married, has three children

Richard A. Zimmerman

"*G*ood CEOs are disciplined. While their planning is fairly disciplined, they also know that a plan is not something that is just put on a shelf and brought out every once in a while to look at. In the best CEOs, planning is built into the psyche. Yet despite that disciplined approach, good chief executives never lose sight of taking that master stroke. There is always something out there they are constantly looking for and asking themselves, 'How can we achieve this, how can we get to that next point?' So while you always need to be moving along incrementally, you still need that master stroke that can reposition your company."

The Hershey Foods Corporation has been going through considerable repositioning over the past few years. No longer only a leading chocolate company, it is well on the way to becoming a major diversified food company.

"The food industry is changing as a result of three significant developments which are occurring simultaneously. First, an increasing part—over 35 percent today—of the food distribution industry has become foreign-owned. Second, there is a great deal of consolidation going on within that industry. Wholesale groceries handle perhaps 25 percent or more of our business, as do chains; and each sector is becoming ever larger. As a result, real marketing clout is essential. Third, food manufacturers are combining. Philip Morris and R. J. Reynolds, both now major manufacturers of food (due to their acquisitions of General Foods and Nabisco Brands, respectively), recognize the value of brand names. As a result, the character of our industry is changing.

"Brand names which stand for quality products become even more important when there are fewer manufacturers and fewer distributors competing for the attention of the consumer. Getting one's story across through effective advertising is essential. It has been predicted that our industry will see its first billion-dollar advertising budget this year; Philip Morris may be ahead of Procter & Gamble, which has always been the leader in advertising. That's a lot of money, in fact about half of Hershey's annual sales. Still, we will be putting over 5 percent of our $2 billion sales volume into consumer advertising alone, to say nothing of consumer promotions and trade promotions.

"That in itself is a big change for Hershey. Fifteen years ago our advertising budget was virtually nothing. Our largest division, the chocolate company, began advertising only in 1970."

> That this company was able to achieve a significant measure of success during its pre-advertising years is a tribute to the quality and reputation of Hershey Chocolate. Its decision to use advertising marks only one of the many changes that have taken place in the company over the past few years. Today Hershey produces a variety of high-quality food products, including pasta—of which it is the leading brand producer—and is a significant restauranteur as well, through its more than 700 Friendly Restaurants.

"We operate through three separate major divisions. While there are other divisions, such as our international and Canadian operations, our largest market is chocolate confectionery, which represents almost two-thirds of our total volume. Our second largest business is restaurants; Friendly's will be about a half billion dollar business this year. And in pasta, we have become the number-one domestic producer."

Strategic Positioning

"Each of these divisions is run fairly autonomously, so when we look at strategic positioning, we do so through the eyes of the divisions as well as from the corporate view. Each division has its own strategic plan, and they are very solidly integrated into our corporate plan. What we see in the divisions is an ab-

RICHARD A. ZIMMERMAN

solute concentration on low-cost production (this we *must* do, but *never* at the sacrifice of quality); and a continuous step-up of marketing activities. In other words, if we cannot extend our margins through better financial control and improved manufacturing expertise or better commodity buying, then we are very likely to increase our spending on advertising and promotion. That is the strategic thrust of each of the divisions.

"On a corporate basis, we would like to add to the dimension of the 'three legs of our stool,' if you will. One of those legs —the chocolate one—does about $1.3 billion of our $2 billion in sales. The leg representing restaurants is about $500 million. Then there is the very short leg, representing pasta, which produces between $160 to $175 million in sales. What we would like to do is to build upon that grocery products area, so we are out looking for potential acquisitions that will help us to build on our strengths there.

"At Hershey we take planning very seriously. Back in the mid-1970s, Bill Dearden, the man who was to become CEO within the next year or two (and Zimmerman's immediate predecessor), became deeply involved in studying strategic planning at the AMA Grove in Hamilton, New York. He brought his conviction back to the company and said, 'This is what we are going to be doing.' While we have altered and refined our original approach, we are still asking ourselves these very fundamental questions: What are our strengths; are they still present and valid in today's environment? Have we corrected our weaknesses, or at least as many as we can? Are our assumptions still valid? What objectives have we accomplished during this past year? Are our strategies in place to permit us to accomplish new objectives?

"One of our objectives has been rapid growth. *Forbes*, in its latest industry analysis of some 25 food companies, reviewed their five-year progress from 1980 through 1984. During that period, Hershey ranked second in sales growth, third in profit growth, and first in return to investors. We obviously are not going to rest on those laurels, but we consider that record evidence of the effectiveness of strategic planning. Strategically we plan to grow in domestic markets, and we believe that this will require not only good marketing techniques for existing products and the creation of new products but the acquisition of some solidly entrenched grocery product company or companies as well.

"It is very important to understand the business you are in. In chocolate confectioneries, less than 5 percent of the business is made up of imported products. A few years ago this was less than 3 percent, but the strengthened dollar has made it easier for others to export into our market. Our belief is that chocolate is a very personal thing. People like a particular style, a particular flavor, and it is our job to remind the American public that we make the finest chocolate that is available. We do have some special market products, some more 'prestigious' products, but we don't know how to sell $25-a-pound chocolate very well; we are much better at selling $3-a-pound chocolate, and that is what we are going to continue to concentrate on.''

Competition and Change

"I think that almost any business person would tell you that he has great competition, tough competition. But I'll stack ours up against anyone's!''

The food industry is highly competitive. In chocolates, for example, Mars produces such products as the popular Snickers and M&M's; in fast-food chains, competitors include McDonald's, Marriott, and a host of other companies. A number of these competitors are known for their astute management.

"In pasta, we have the leading brand share, but I don't know the total industry tonnage figures precisely enough to tell whether we produce the largest amount. There is a lot of private-label pasta, many different brands in a highly fragmented industry.

"The way our industry has changed manifests itself in new requirements. To succeed, a company must find a competitive edge. It must be a *quality* low-cost producer. It must be innovative in marketing techniques and have a strong emphasis on brand awareness and image. That is all we have to sell to the consumer, and they are inevitably tied together. You cannot sell brand image if your quality slips, and you cannot sacrifice quality just for the sake of being a low-cost producer. If you do, someone else will steal your market. The food industry is really not so different from any others, with one exception: the vast majority of our competition is domestic. There are not a lot of foreign entries in the food manufacturing field.

Whether or not this will develop, I am not sure. At the moment, foreign competition seems to be concentrating its investment on the food distribution side rather than on the food manufacturing side.

"Commodity buying is a vital aspect of food manufacturing, so much so that I personally chair the Commodities Committee, which meets weekly. While every food company places a lot of emphasis on commodities, most have a myriad of commodities, none standing out so distinctly as cocoa beans do for us. Since cocoa beans—a highly volatile commodity—represent such a large measure of the raw materials which we use, we have to stay right on top of the prices. In 1976, for example, cocoa beans were around 55¢ or 60¢ a pound; two or three years later their price hit $2.25 a pound. That's dramatic! Because we are going to need cocoa beans no matter *what* their price is—after all, in a very real sense, the continued employment of our people depends upon our getting them—we simply have to stay on top of this. But at the same time, as a percentage of our total cost of sales, our total expense for cocoa beans has declined—not because we are using fewer of them, but because the other aspects of our business are growing more rapidly. For example, our Reese's Peanut Butter Cup, which is 55 percent chocolate, is growing more rapidly than our standard 100 percent milk chocolate bar. In addition, we have been diversifying into other fields. In these ways we have tried to move away from being a completely commodities-oriented company, in order to be better able to control our destiny as we go forward, but this still requires very careful attention. But if there is a day in the future when I will not chair the Commodities Committee, I cannot as yet foresee it."

Hershey's Unique Ownership

An unusual aspect of the Hershey Foods Corporation is that more than half its shares are owned by a school. The founder of the chocolate company, Milton Hershey, had grown up in the Pennsylvania Dutch country of Mennonite farmers where the highest valued virtues were integrity and hard work. Believing that money should not be used for personal gratification, he and Mrs. Hershey, who had no children, founded the Milton Hershey School for Orphaned Boys in 1909, and in 1918 donated the company to a trust, so that its earnings could be used for the benefit of the school for orphans.

Although the words 'orphan' and 'boys' are both gone from its name, the Milton Hershey School still benefits from the corporation and offers education to biological and 'social' orphans, both boys and girls. Its trustee, the Hershey Trust Company, determined a few years ago that it wanted to maintain absolute control of the corporation, so today 50.1 percent of Hershey's shares are owned by the Trust for the benefit of the school. The town of Hershey is a unique community with a great deal of value beyond the Hershey Foods Corporation, *per se*, and the trustees thought it important to continue to carry out what Mr. Hershey had started in the early part of this century.

"We recently issued a Class B stock which has ten-to-one voting power, so that the Trust can continue to maintain control, yet simultaneously give the company the ability to issue additional shares of common stock for financial flexibility, for making acquisitions with cash and/or stock or combinations, or to go to the market as necessary. The Hershey Trust owns well over 95 percent of this Class B stock, although every shareholder was given the right to exchange their common shares for Class B shares (but at a discount or penalty in terms of dividend and with the right to transfer back to the common shares, so that Class B shares could be marketed if necessary). In doing this, we faced the prospect of possibly losing our listing on the New York Stock Exchange, which is currently debating whether it is permissible to have two issues outstanding with unequal voting rights. It would not be a happy prospect for us to lose our listing on the stock exchange, and the fact that we were willing to take that risk is one demonstration of the importance of having the trust company maintain its majority control."

At a time when many corporations are being criticized for having a short-term outlook, this unique ownership arrangement of Hershey provides a distinct long-term emphasis.

"Our company is really a part of the Hershey family. I sit on the trust company board, and when you come down to the essence of all that is Hershey, it is possible that the only organization that might be in existence 500 years from now is the Trust. The company's reason for being and our reason for being trustees is to maintain the school—that is what Mr. Hershey had in mind. And if we are going to do that for the very long term, we had better not try to run a company which is *status quo*; we need to run a company that will provide the best future for the Trust in the long pull. Whenever we do something in Hershey, I like to think that we have in the back of our minds the fact that ultimately the judge of our success will be— at least partially—just how well we preserve what Mr. Hershey had in mind when he founded the school.

"For that reason, whenever we bring customers to Hershey, we invite them to sit down at lunch with the kids. We are certainly not saying to them, 'Buy more Hershey products in order to support an orphan.' What we are trying to say is, 'This is part of our being, one of the fundamental reasons we are in business.' I get tremendous feedback from customers and our younger employees about how much that experience has meant to them. This is something that no other company has; it's unique to us. It is an extra dimension of the CEO of Hershey, and we can take a great deal of pride in the fact that 100 or 125 young people will graduate this year, and most of those boys and girls would not have had nearly as good a start in life as they are able to have because of the generosity of Milton Hershey, way back when."

One outstanding graduate of the Milton Hershey School is William Dearden, Hershey's former chairman and CEO and still a member of its Board of Directors.

Zimmerman's Career

"Life always has many twists. After getting out of the Navy and having a degree in corporate finance, I wasn't completely satisfied that I wanted to wind up in corporate finance, so I had an interview with Procter & Gamble and was offered a job. After thinking this over, I decided not to go with Procter & Gamble and went into banking instead. I really enjoyed banking, was in it for two years, but in 1958 I got a call that said, in essence, 'Hershey is looking for a few good people,' and if I were interested in talking with Hershey, they might be interested in talking with me. About two months later I decided to make that change and go with Hershey, a company that I had always admired.

"Soon after joining the company, I recognized that there was much work to be done. Hershey was not in the forefront of modern marketing or even modern production techniques. For example, when I joined the company every pound of product produced in the entire company was produced in Hershey, Pennsylvania. There was no advertising, our trade promotion was somewhat reactive, there was really no strategic planning —there were many things to be done. Still, I sensed that within the management of Hershey there was opportunity and an attitude of 'Let's get on with it.' I've never spent a single day at Hershey in finance or accounting or anything of that nature. Instead, I was put into various positions, including acquisition evaluation and planning for the building of new plants, which we did in 1962 and in 1964, and I became involved in those. I had a remarkable opportunity to be a generalist, for I was working with the assistant to the president and at times with the president himself. So I became a general manager almost from day one. And although I recognize how fortunate I was, there are times that I wish I had a defined speciality. People ask me, 'Did you come up through finance, or manufacturing, or operations, or sales, or marketing?' And I have to say, 'I didn't come up through any of those.' But since my degree was in finance, people assume that I came up through the financial side."

> In watching Zimmerman operate, one might assume that he came up through marketing. In fact, he says that if he had to do it all over again, he would go back and complete a MBA in marketing, a field which greatly intrigues him. At the same time, he has a great facility for handling numbers and an ability to penetrate quickly to the heart of an issue. Unlike most CEOs, Zimmerman held no line responsibility for the first dozen years of his career.

"I finally moved over to line operations in 1971, when I was named group vice president with the responsibility for all non-chocolate businesses. At that time, Bill Dearden was responsible for the chocolate business. This was another stroke of good fortune, for it gave me the opportunity to take a look at the frozen food business, the Cory Coffee Service, pasta—and to work with a Canadian company called *David et Frère*, which made biscuits and cookies. I had the opportunity to work very closely with the heads of all of those divisions, to learn something about many functional areas—everything from budgeting to marketing to manufacturing. Prior to that time I had focused on operations and human resources. But once I got into general management, I liked it and wanted to stay with it.

"In 1976, when Bill Dearden became CEO, I became president and chief operating officer. Then at the beginning of 1984, I became CEO, and when Bill retired last year, I became chairman and CEO."

Management Challenges

"In anyone's career there are some ups and downs. Over 15 years ago, I experienced one of those 'downs' that still bothers me to this day. We had a frozen meat company called Portion Control, through which we made airline meals, hamburger patties, and other products. We had acquired that business in 1970, and in 1972 it was assigned to me as group vice president. At that time we had embarked on a rather major expansion program, having added a plant and expanded another, and it was up to me to hire someone to run this operation on a day-to-day basis. I hired a great guy out of Sara Lee, and I still think he is good. Then price controls came along, the cost of raw materials was allowed to escalate, and beef prices went wild. Meanwhile, we were locked into school contracts and other feeding contracts, and we went through a period in which the best weapon the government had was *delay*. We'd go in and request a price, having given what we thought was a very good rationale, we'd leave, and we'd hear nothing. We would be asked for more information, told we'd hear back in another 30 days, and so on. To make a long story short, this operation was not profitable for the years '72, '73, '74, and

'75 by *very small amounts*; it always looked as though we would turn the corner just the very next year! One year, for instance, we lost something like $32,000, as I recall. I felt that we had a good management team, but we eventually wound up selling that business, really liquidating a good part of it, and in the final analysis didn't get much bang for the buck.

"What this told me was no matter how great a management team you have, you can get buffeted by outside forces that can just wreak havoc. I realized that while most things are under our control, there are some things that you had better be careful of, and you had better make certain that you know what your alternatives are, since there will be times in which you won't be able to control your own destiny. In this case, we simply couldn't get any price relief. Prices were absolutely dictated.

"At the same time, the rest of Hershey's businesses were satisfactory but not really outstanding. In 1974, we earned $1.01 and paid a dividend of $1.10. Then we had to cut the dividend because the price-control problem had hit our chocolate confectionery division, too. Cocoa beans were escalating, and we could get no price relief.

"Still, I suspect that part of the problem with the frozen meat-portion business was caused by the fact that this was a wholly new kind of business to us, one which we did not know very much about. We went in and built a whole new management team, and I have to think, 'Shame on us' for not knowing enough about the business or that particular management. As we began to make changes, there is no doubt, as I look back, that not only was the federal government affecting us, but we ourselves were not knowledgeable enough about that market to take the necessary steps. Some other companies survived in this business, and some didn't; there was a lot of fall-out and shake-out, but some *did* survive. Why we could not have been a survivor, I'm not really sure.

"Getting into pasta was a different matter. In 1966, we had bought our first pasta company, and that was during the period when companies were acquiring other companies almost just for the sake of acquisition. It seemed the natural thing to do, and looking back I don't think that we had a well scoped out plan to be in pasta; we had no fundamental strategy. As time progressed, we acquired several small pasta companies. The first one cost us only about $6 million.

"Well, we finally realized that we had to think this through. What should we do? We knew we either had to build the pasta business or divest it, so through the years we created a strategic plan that said, 'We are going to be in pasta, because it is a field of opportunity.' So we have become number one by careful planning and then by vigorously acting on that plan. We now feel very comfortable in pasta.

"First of all, we took a look at the total market. Pasta for years has grown faster than the dry-grocery product index. Second, we knew that pasta, once consumed even by people who like rice and beans, tends to get into their makeup. There was a time when pasta in our eastern Pennyslvania locality consisted only of noodles. Suddenly we began to notice that housewives there were making lasagna, and perhaps ziti and other interesting kinds of pasta. When we bought our first pasta company, per capita consumption in the United States was about eight pounds; today it is twelve, and we could see that trend.

"I was also involved in 1963 with the first acquisition Hershey ever made: H. B. Reese Candy Company, which produced Reese's Peanut Butter Cup. This was super. Bill Dearden had a lot to do with the sales and marketing, and even though I was only 33 or 34 years old when that occurred, I had the opportunity to be involved as a member of a small committee that helped to put it together and to work in human resources and some of the manufacturing areas. So I began to have these opportunities that panned out very well. The Peanut Butter Cup today is a huge seller, a $250 million brand all by itself."

Zimmerman's Management Approach

"I suppose that all of us are predictable to some extent. One thing I am given far too much credit for is a huge and great memory. Everyone keeps kidding me about this, saying, 'You pull things out of nowhere that we haven't thought about for 10 or 15 years.' Actually, I used to think that of *my* boss! I thought his memory was awesome.

"One thing which I have noticed about myself is that even though I have some financial background, I am not great with numbers. I enjoy them and don't fear them, but I don't consider that my strongest suit. What really turns me on is the marketing side. What I like our people to understand is that when we talk about a proposition, let's start out by talking about the market and the potential effect on the consumer. How can we enter that market? What is the logic? *Then* let's look at the numbers. Then we can *structure*. But first, let's ask *these* questions: What *is* this product? Is it *quality*? Are we going to be able to do something that *they* can't do—whoever *they* are, whether it be by an acquisition or something else? How are we going to *grow* this business? If we *can't* grow it, I don't want to be *in* the business, because we don't need any more static businesses. We don't even need any additional cash cows, since cash cows tend to diminish in value over a period of time, and we want things that are going to be growing. So the marketing aspects of anything that we consider, a new brand, a new product, a new geography, are *paramount*.

"Not long ago we licensed our Hershey brand name in Korea. This is a difficult situation for us, since we are not a Coca Cola; that is, we can't ship syrup. What we have to do is to satisfy ourselves that we are going to turn out the best chocolate in Korea under their laws and under their regulations that can be made. In the Philippines and Mexico, we have chocolate under the Hershey name. Now we have it in Korea. But in Korea, we have no fresh whole milk, and *that's* the *basis* of Hershey chocolate in the United States! So we have a different formulation there. Now the question is, are we going to get enough return in dollars to warrant that kind of a problem? Do we really want to turn out a product which has the Hershey name on it but won't taste like a Hershey bar in the U.S.? These are interesting questions. What you have to determine is: What is the market potential? Are we going to generate a sufficiently large revenue to warrant the plane trips, the special task forces, the headaches, the management disruption? Those are the kinds of issues that are fascinating to a CEO. You really don't get asked to make any easy decisions. Those have already been made.

"I think it is very important to understand marketing, and since I had no formal background in this, I do a lot of reading and engage in considerable discussion with good marketing people—and we are certainly blessed with them. We do a lot of 'What if' and 'How did you arrive at that conclusion?' kinds of things. Let's go back, I say, and see what would happen if I were to disagree with your basic premise. That kind of questioning is what I think is necessary if you are going to understand where the marketing folks are coming from. They spend vast amounts of money, and we always seem to need a little more margin to be able to be competitive. So you have to make sure that you are making the investments that need to be made."

Hershey's Values

"Hershey has four basic values. One is its people orientation, and another has to do with honesty and integrity. Those are *givens* inside the company; those we build upon and extend across all of our horizons, divisionally and anywhere else. We expect people to be honest and to have high integrity, and we expect that we are going to continue to have a people-oriented company. By this I don't mean smothering people with largess, but simply thinking about people as being primary and really our number one asset. In addition to those, we have two other important values: one is quality and value, from the standpoint of the consumer. That is an *absolute* marketing consideration: if we cannot satisfy that consumer, then we cannot succeed. Finally, we have a results orientation. I know that it is an old term, but we do believe in management by objectives. Each one of us has objectives that are measurable against our annual incentive plan. We have division and corporate objectives and individual ones as well. Part of my bonus is determined by how well I fulfill each of four or five prime objectives. We are results-oriented and expect good performance from our people. These are the four key values of our corporation that we have identified. In addition, we must always remember that the brand name and marketing considerations are also prime.

"As a matter of fact, we are just embarking on a major identification of those four values in a straightforward form so that everyone can understand them. Yet our mission statement, which was developed some time ago, embraces all of those aspects. What we now need to do is to enlarge upon them, to clarify them, and get them into a simpler-to-understand version.''

As Hershey continues to diversify, and as new employees join the firm, Zimmerman believes strongly that the values that have served the company well for its long history need to be uniformly understood, and this can be done only through careful and deliberate communication. Through acquisition, even some of Hershey's top officers have come from outside of the company's traditional culture. For example, for the first time, its chocolate division is now headed by a ''non-chocolate'' executive, a man who joined Hershey through a pasta company acquisition.

Results Orientation

"We believe strongly in management by objectives and execute this through semi-annual reviews. The mid-year review asks these questions: How do we stand? Are we on target? If we said we would complete something by April 30, did we do it? If we said we would complete something by the end of the year, are we on track?

"Or, on the other hand, we might ask, 'How have these objectives changed during this past period?' If an objective has changed, let's be realistic, own up to it now, and change it. Maybe we will eliminate it entirely. Perhaps the strategic situation has altered. But let's not pretend that nothing has changed, only to find out at the end of the year that we no longer can measure our objectives, since they are not relevant any more.

"On the average, I would say that I spend perhaps two hours—maybe as many as three—in the objective-setting session, but this varies considerably. More often, I will get together with someone who reports to me for the purpose of discussing potential objectives. Once we are seeing eye-to-eye, I will ask for tentative objectives to be submitted in written form. Very rarely do I accept these at the first submission, since I am not always sure I understand exactly what the words mean. We will discuss this again, talk it through, and perhaps at the time of the second submission we will have ourselves a contract.

"I fully expect that the objectives of those who report to me are a summation of objectives *from them* that they have already negotiated with the people who *report* to them. Therefore, putting my objectives together is very often the last step in the chain. I want everything to be in harmony as we come up through the various levels. Out of our whole group there are some 150 of us on an annual incentive basis and fewer than 30 on long-term incentive, but I want the performance of all 150 to be measurable against their own objectives and against divisional objectives simultaneously. Therefore, this process has to build.

"Organizationally, I have one line executive who reports to me, the president and chief operating officer, who in turn has all of the divisions reporting to him. The other people who report to me directly have responsibility for staff functions. Together, the chief operating officer and the corporate vice presidents who report to me comprise the group that we would be concentrating on in the objective-setting process."

Selecting People

Zimmerman reports that in filling six major officers' positions during the past two-and-one-half years, each job was filled from within the organization.

"We have a very good succession plan, and I assured our board of directors that we had the people on board to carry out the jobs of all of those people. One of them we lost by death, one of the most brilliant marketing men I have ever known, a 42-year-old man; this was a terrible tragedy. We replaced all of those people, and over the past 12 months there have been new people in each of these roles. It will obviously take two or three additional years before we really know whether we had the right resources and positioned them correctly, but the first 12 months plus have convinced me that I was not selling our board a bill of goods. We simply had good-quality people that we could move in. Every one of them was identified in our succession planning books. The average age of our corporate staff heads today is 46. Those who run the divisions are even slightly younger than that. These are all bright, young people, and I hope that our record ten years from now will show that in fact these people are as good as I think they are.

"We are not yet nearly to the point where I can be satisfied with the kind of cross-training that I want. Ideally, all corporate staff heads should come from divisional assignments or direct line assignments. For example, our chief financial officer —still in his thirties—came from having held that responsibility in our largest division.

"We do need more cross-functional training, if we can do this. Obviously, I don't believe in switching jobs just for the sake of doing that, and I would not want to switch the jobs of two people only to find them both uncomfortable in their new jobs and neither one productive. Still, I would like people in manufacturing to know something about marketing and both of them to understand a heck of a lot about finance, since eventually whatever we do results in numbers, and these are important for everyone to understand.

"When I select someone for a major responsibility, certainly there are some fundamental factors which bear on Hershey's culture. First, the person must have an integrity which cannot be questioned. The candidate must understand what results orientation is all about and of course should have a good track record. By this, I mean that he or she will have had to have been in some pretty solid battles and have come out in good shape.

"In addition, I think one looks for something that is almost indefinable; perhaps it is the breadth that a person brings. I admire and respect people who are great functional managers, but what I really look for in the high-potential financial or manufacturing person is that broad orientation to general management. In other words, there is that general demeanor that says, 'Even though I am a financial person, let me ask you this question about marketing.' And if it is a sensible question, you can see where he or she is coming from and that this is a broad-gauged sort of person, not just a functional specialist.

"We have also embarked on a two-week Hershey Foods management program—perhaps we are late in this—in which 35 of the very best and brightest of our people are engaged. At the end of three years, we will have over 100 people trained, each having been exposed to the finest faculty we could find. We hope that functional managers will broaden their perspective, and although our selection process is certainly not perfect, chances are that the vast majority of those who attend this program will in the long term be lined up for more responsible jobs in the corporation.

"Every one of us runs into problems which we don't expect. I admire the person who handles those tough ones. I also admire the guy who brings me something that he has put on paper which shows original thought. It is not too difficult to be the editor of a newspaper. The question is, 'Where were you when the paper was blank?' The man or woman who 'put it on the paper' or creates an original idea is the important one inside our business. Sometimes this might be me, but most of the time it is someone else, someone who is out there operating.

"Equally important is the manager who can take that idea and build on it, take it all the way to fruition."

Characteristics of Successful CEOs

"Among the CEOs I know, the most successful ones have a very positive outlook. Every CEO has to be a cheerleader. At times you may feel that you can list a series of disaster scenarios for your company, and certainly you are in the best position to do that; still, you have to be a cheerleader at least a part of the time. Of course you have to be realistic, but you should be able to say to people, 'This is what we have accomplished in the past—you and I and the people with whom we are associated—can't we move along and keep doing that? We have had some successes; that is why we are a part of this corporation. OK, we know it is going to be tough, but let's get at it!' You need always to be encouraging, and perhaps that is one of the most admired attributes that I see in most CEOs.

"Second, as I said earlier, good CEOs are disciplined. Their planning discipline is fairly precise, not that it cannot be altered. Still, a good CEO is always looking for something, searching for that master stroke. Sometimes this is as well-defined as a strategic plan, but many times it is not so well-defined. For example, our mission is to become a major diversified food company. Some might say that we are there now, and in some respects we are—compared to where we were ten years ago. But we still have some room to go. I never let any of our operating divisions or our staff heads fail to continue to be reminded that we want to become a major diversified food company. Are we doing the right things to get us there? Never take your eye off today's brands! For example, milk chocolate bars, almond bars, Hershey's Syrup, Reese's Peanut Butter Cups —those are the 'girls' we brought to the dance and who brought us to the dance. We are going to fill in our dance card to have the first and last dances with them, because they are the brands that we are going to be able to use to generate the capability—especially the financial capability—to move forward and do the other things we need to do. So we certainly need to fill the cards for the first and last dances with those we came to the dance with, but if we are not getting out there and dancing with another partner, I think we are a little foolish.

"It is important always to have that vision of where you want the corporation to go. And most good CEOs always have that vision.

"Then, too, a CEO needs to challenge his *people* about the future. You realize that quarterly earnings are important, and when you come right down to it, the public is measuring your corporation in only one dimension. The only common denominator we have with the steel business or aluminum or automobiles is in dollars. The financial community will evaluate us on quarter-to-quarter or annual earnings, and we have to accept that; good growth must go on simultaneously with looking for longer-term opportunities. But a CEO can't deal with the future alone, and a good one gets his people to think about it with him—or even to do a better job in thinking about it than he does."

Getting Feedback as a CEO

> Chief executives, Zimmerman says, often need to look for sub-
> tle clues rather than just to listen to what people are saying. Too
> often people may be concerned that they are saying the right
> thing. But what you really need to know, he says, often comes
> from second-hand sources.

"When we have a Hershey Foods management program or
quarterly meetings with our key managers, I often get feedback,
which I've learned to trust, from certain kinds of sources. Some
people will report back and say, 'Gee, that meeting was great
today—you should have heard what I heard in the locker
room.' You almost have to depend upon extraneous sources to
keep feeding you input. Recently after I gave a little talk, an
employee came up to me and said, 'You know, when we were
asked for some candid opinions about something that you
did in the past, I wasn't all that complimentary. But I heard
you tonight, and I'd like to take back what I said.' Of course I
didn't know what he had said, but I suspect that whatever he
did say was filtered and I never got it in full force. Obviously
this man had made some criticism about something I was trying to accomplish, and I might have benefited from hearing
about it earlier. In any case, you depend upon those indirect
kinds of communications and can never really get enough of it,
for you are never sure that you're getting as much correct information as you need.

"We spend a lot of time trying to communicate downward
effectively, holding meetings quarterly and much more often
than that if we have announcements. We have a fundamental
premise that we do not want any information to get into the
hands of the financial press or investor analysts that our people don't know either beforehand or simultaneously. If we
have an announcement that is important to our people—
perhaps about an acquisition, divestiture, or earnings—we get
our people together simultaneously. I certainly do not want
them turning on the radio as they are driving home at night
and hearing something that they should have heard from us.
At the same time, we always encourage written questions and
questions from the floor. And we try to be as candid as possible
in our downward communications."

One form of communication for which Zimmerman is well known is "Z-grams"—hand-written notes to employees that convey a thoughtfulness and an awareness of accomplishments throughout the organization.

"Still, we need the *other* kind of communications—'feed-up,' if you will. For that reason, last fall I spoke to 41 different employee groups—in the plants, in offices, in sales—wherever I could get at them. I only touched about 2,000 employees out of about 15,000 over a period of six months. Still, I learned an enormous amount from this experience. What I really wanted to know was what was on *their* minds. I wanted to demonstrate to the supervisors at the plant level and elsewhere that it's important to be listening to ideas. And I wanted to say to the employees who were generating these ideas that I expect their management to listen to *them*. What I found out was that in a lot of places our management is not listening as well as they should, and I will include myself. You hear this sort of thing: 'I had a great idea, but my supervisor said he had thought of that 28 years ago, and we tried it and it didn't work.' If we are going to get the best from our employees, I don't have a solid mechanism today by which I can get that best. What happens is if there is a problem on the line, out come all the guys in the white hats and the green hats, the mechanics and the supervisors, and they muscle aside the people who have worked that line for years, and they try to fix it. But I am sure that if we had asked those people on the line in the first place, they would *have* it fixed. So we are asking ourselves how we can do this better. All the way up throughout the organization, I am trying to encourage our managers to learn what these people have to offer and to call on their capable judgment and their thinking."

Being a Part of the Hershey Family

"It is important in our culture that there be an intense loyalty and devotion to the company. We have to remember that we really are a part of a family—the Hershey family. The trust company holds the majority control, and we are in business to help the Hershey School. If nothing else can give us a people orientation, that fact alone should do it. Mr. Hershey's idea was to help these orphans. Perhaps only a fifth or so of the students at the Hershey School are biological orphans, but the rest of them are certainly social orphans, kids whose parents are unable to give them proper care. The nature of the school has changed in that respect, but it still is true to Mr. Hershey's philosophy. His idea was that if we can give disadvantaged youngsters a break, if we can give them a better education than they would otherwise have, if we can give them more discipline, more character training, then we will be preparing them for a better future.

"Invariably a graduate will return after a few years and say, 'At the time I hated it, but now I realize the value of it and hope some day that I will be able to repay you.' They also say, 'You know, it was somewhat like a jail, because there was so much discipline.' We still have the kids milking cows. Not because we need them to milk cows—although our products certainly use a lot of milk—but it is the training, the discipline, the character building that is important. The students have to get up at 5:30 in the morning! In addition to that, they get good schoolwork, real preparation, and that whole aspect of our company's being gives us all a little extra dimension.

"We believe that the best thing we can do on behalf of the Trust—and in turn on behalf of the School—is to have the strongest, most powerful, best company we can possibly build, for that will guarantee the long-term future of the school. Incidentally, I have been on the board of Hershey Foods Corporation since 1970, and *never* have I heard the needs of the school come into the picture in terms of raising the dividends, for example. We simply try to do what is right for the shareholders of the Hershey Foods Corporation, one of whom happens to be the majority owner. At the same time, the chief operating officer and I sit on the Hershey Trust Company board, and in that role we exercise our fiduciary responsibility. In that capacity we also try to do the best we can for the Hershey Foods Corporation, for to do so will best ensure the longevity of the school."

Advice to Young People

"First of all, I would advise any young person considering a business career to do it. Go for it; that's where the action is, and it's fun. If you don't get any kick out of it, then don't do it. But there is great opportunity in business. With regard to career planning, I don't think people should be naive enough to think that they can achieve something long-term if they don't do some planning for it, but I certainly would not get hung up on planning for one's own future. All of us are measured, I think, on the basis of how he or she performs today, this month, this quarter, this year. And by this, I don't mean just financial results. If the person is in a senior management position, he should be asked what input he has provided for the future. If he is in a junior position, then you might want to ask, 'What did his marketing plan do for Reese's Peanut Butter Cup? Did that promotion work? What kind of advertising were we creating? How much of a hand did he or she have in it? Was the thought process solid and clear?' I think it is more important to do today's job inordinately well than to worry too much about career planning. Doing today's job inordinately well will set you apart from the others.

"With regard to education, I must say that I am opposed to colleges and universities becoming trade schools. I admire young people who bring technical expertise to us from their education, but I have noticed that those who are trained in too narrow a technical field sometimes have difficulty in getting their arms around the larger problems. I guess I am a supporter of the liberal arts. Our current chief operating officer was a history major at Yale with an MBA in finance on top of it. That liberal arts background, which happens also to be mine—so perhaps I am biased—is certainly valuable the higher you go. It may not help much at the entry level, but a combination of a liberal arts foundation and a technical specialty or an MBA or some other kind of expertise is built on top of it, seems to me, ideal.

"Then to the young man or woman who has just entered the job market, I would say that there are times when they will confront difficulties. On my very first job I moved into a banking situation where I was looked at as a smart young college graduate—not because I was a smart aleck, I hope, but because I was college-educated. I decided to do two things: first, to 'kill 'em with kindness'—ask for advice; everyone likes to give advice. Second, I realized that once in a while I would have to trample on someone's toe, and I tried to remember to wear those velvet slippers. Why hurt anyone? There is no need to do so. Ask for advice, watch how people behave, and remember to be courteous. Why not? It doesn't cost anything. In addition, you should try to buy into your company's value system. If you can't, then get out, and quickly. Why accept something which is not your standard? But if you *can* buy into these values, then be willing to defend them.

"And always be striving for that next educational experience. If your company has a program of sending employees to three-day seminars or to the Advanced Management Program at Harvard or wherever, take advantage of it. Obviously, don't bedevil your superior, but ask him or her just what the opportunities for further education are.

"To prepare for a major job, I would say this: don't fail to read. I think that reading is very important. I happen to have an interest in World War II and have a whole library on that subject. So I read extensively on that. It certainly teaches me nothing about business, but it is a great diversion. So I will be working on two books at the same time, a business book and another one. In my briefcase, when I am traveling, I will have a couple of books. Whatever your interest, do not fail to read."

William J. Kennedy III

Chairman, President, and Chief Executive Officer
North Carolina Mutual Life Insurance Company

*B*ecause child labor laws were not enforced in 1933, he "learned the work ethic quite early" by becoming an office boy for North Carolina Mutual at the age of ten. Now he is leading the company—already the nation's largest black-owned financial institution—in a strong drive to grow through innovative insurance products and diversification. That drive, he says, makes him feel "more stretched than ever." But working hard goes along with his basic commitment as a CEO: To set high goals and then get the total support of his people for achieving them. No ivory tower CEO, he believes in leadership by "getting out in front." When he looks for top people, he stresses loyalty to the company and a feeling of responsibility to help build it.

He heads a company with 1500 employees and 950,000 policyholders. Started in 1899 for blacks who could not obtain insurance from white-owned companies, North Carolina Mutual still sells "industrial insurance" based on weekly premium payments—but to stay competitive it has developed a wide variety of other insurance products. Kennedy's diversification drive has led also to subsidiary companies in real estate development, mortgages, investments, cable television, and cellular telephones. On top of that, North Carolina Mutual is developing a money-management company.

Preserving the status quo is alien to Kennedy's philosophy. As he puts it, "You have to keep up if you don't want to fall behind."

Career Information:

1950 Joined North Carolina Mutual as administrative assistant

1952 Became assistant to the controller

1956 Became assistant vice president

1959 Became controller

1961 Became assistant secretary and controller

1965 Became assistant financial vice president-controller and member of Board of Directors

1966 Became financial vice president

1969 Became senior vice president

1972 Became president

1975 Became vice chairman of the board, president, and chief executive officer

1979 Became chairman of the board, president, and chief executive officer

Other Affiliations (partial list):

- Member, Board of Directors, Pfizer, Inc.
- Chairman, Board of Directors, UNC Ventures, Inc.
- Member, Board of Directors, Mobil Corporation
- Member, Southeast Regional Advisory Council, Boy Scouts of America
- Member, National Association for the Advancement of Colored People
- Member, Durham Chamber of Commerce

Educational Information:

- Virginia State College, B.S., Business Administration, 1942
- University of Pennsylvania, M.B.A., Insurance, 1946
- New York University, M.B.A., Finance and Investments, 1948
- Additional graduate studies at New York University, 1948–50

Personal Information:

- Born October 24, 1922, Durham, N.C.
- Served in U.S. Army with final rank of lieutenant, 1943–1945
- Married, has one son

William J. Kennedy III

"*A* company can't achieve anything unless the people around you know what you're shooting for. First, our goal was to be the best black-owned life insurance company in the United States. We think we are the best, as well as the largest. So we achieved that. Then our goal was to make it into the top 10 percent of all life insurance companies in the United States. We finally achieved that, and now we want to get into the top 5 percent. To do this we must make bold steps, but I'm a very positive thinker—everyone who knows me will tell you that—and I believe we can do the job."

As chief executive of the nation's largest black-owned financial institution and by some measures its largest black-owned business, William Kennedy stresses that in its drive into the upper echelons of the life insurance industry, North Carolina Mutual's principal competitors are not other black-owned insurers but white-managed companies. With assets of about $200 million and income of nearly $90 million, North Carolina Mutual had, as of 1984, nearly $8 billion of insurance coverage in force; while this is but a fraction of the more than $400 billion of coverage underwritten by the largest U.S. carrier, it is twice that of the next largest black company.

"We know we can't compete with New York Life, Metropolitan, or the Pru, but we could get to be a $10 billion company by taking sufficiently bold steps. The opportunity is there. We were very pleased when we went from $1 billion in coverage to $2 billion in a very short time, but I told our people we could go much further—and we reached $5 billion within the next five years. I try to shock people by setting surprisingly high goals. That's the job of a leader: to get his people to raise their sights—to visualize future possibilities and then to believe in them. The leader must make clear that what you *want* to be done *can* be done."

North Carolina Mutual has come a long way from its modest beginnings. During the 1890s it was the custom of Durham's black community to collect money at funerals to aid the surviving family members. Seven leaders of the black community and particularly two of them—Durham's first black physician and the owner of six barber shops, mostly for whites—founded the company, which began operations in 1899 as The North Carolina Mutual and Provident Association, providing insurance to blacks, who at that time could not otherwise obtain it. For many years the company's principal product was "industrial" or weekly-premium life insurance, a policy that originated during the industrial revolution in England. "Industrial" insurance was sold individually to factory workers who were paid weekly.

"In the old days many of the agents would stand outside the factory gates on payday, and as workers came out, they would collect the premiums, knowing that the workers' first stop would be the bar, and by the time they left there and bought some groceries, there would be no money left. In the South there were and still are door-to-door insurance agents who collect premiums for what some call insurance 'debit business.' The agent would be debited every week with the business in his territory, and as he collected the premiums, he would receive credits. The word 'debit' was also used to refer to the agent's territory. In the industrial-insurance business, you have to have small territories, since you can't afford to have an agent running all over town trying to collect small premiums."

Although North Carolina Mutual has expanded and diversified in a number of directions, over half of its premium income from individuals still comes from weekly premium insurance.

"There is still a market for this among industrial workers, construction workers, domestics, low-income people of virtually any occupation. And don't forget, most of the nation's

Photo: Alvin Lester   WILLIAM J. KENNEDY III

largest insurance companies—Metropolitan, John Hancock, and Prudential, for example—got their start this way. Although they have stopped selling this kind of insurance, they still have sizable weekly premium debits.

"There have been enormous changes in life insurance over the past 20 years. Before then, the industry was fairly stable. Then came innovations: Prudential introduced its family policy and became the largest life insurance company, overtaking Metropolitan in about three years. Then the mutual fund companies began to say, 'Buy term insurance and invest the difference,' and of course they wanted you to invest the difference in their mutual funds. Later came the universal life contract, which gained great popularity because, in addition to basic coverage, it offered attractive benefits tied closely to returns from annuities and other interest-bearing instruments. But its popularity has peaked, and today it is probably trending down as a percentage of total insurance.

"Much of this change is related to the interest patterns of the country. The money-market concept has had a tremendous impact on the insurance industry, and innovations are going on all the time. To succeed in this industry you need a variety of products, and this takes continuous innovation if you hope to stay competitive. Most life-insurance companies have some special wrinkle that separates them from the pack. One interesting example of this is flexible-premium annuity contracts, some of which are used for individual retirement accounts. Changes in the tax law also shake up the way we have to do business.

"You need innovations in marketing as well. I have been pushing toward more direct-response mass marketing through direct mail, some newspaper advertising, and some television (as much as we can afford), for example. We sell through our own representatives, through general agents, through the media—any way we can. You have to keep up if you don't want to fall behind."

Dealing with Racial Bias

Unlike the early years of North Carolina Mutual, when blacks could not obtain coverage from white insurance companies, the large insurance companies now represent the company's chief competition. But even today, Kennedy stresses, it is very difficult for a black insurance company to sell insurance to white people.

"So we decided to acquire two white-managed subsidiaries. One of these, American Citizens Life Insurance Company, is a full-fledged life-insurance company located in Washington, D.C., but it is really our mass marketing arm. It services the business and writes up the contracts, and in turn we accept the risk and carry all the reserves. Through this company and another white-managed subsidiary, American Capital Life Insurance Company, also based in Washington, we are selling a considerable amount of insurance to white people, something we could never have done directly through North Carolina Mutual.''

The history of NCM is in a real sense the history of the black struggle. Founded in the post-Reconstruction era, the company has long been a symbol of black progress. After visiting the company in 1910, Booker T. Washington wrote about it in a then-popular white periodical which praised Durham as ''the city of Negro enterprise.'' Two years later, W. E. B. DuBois also visited and praised the company. By 1913, North Carolina Mutual had helped to start a college, a hospital, a library, a bank, and three weekly newspapers to serve the black community.

During those early years, prejudice hounded even the technical operations of the company. Since there were no black actuaries, Kennedy says, NCM retained as consultant a white actuarial firm that ''apparently did not care just what they did for North Carolina Mutual.'' Policies based on their actuarial advice caused the company a great deal of trouble: the benefits were worth more than the premiums. As a result, North Carolina Mutual sent Asa T. Spaulding to school, and he became the nation's first black actuary. Spaulding, who later became NCM's fifth president, observed that during the time of its founding the whole idea of blacks trying to run a life insurance company was ''not only questioned, but openly ridiculed.'' This prejudice on the part of whites continued. Even some black people did not want to do business with a black company, according to Kennedy. Over the years, he says, they had been brainwashed to feel that whites could do a better job in any area. He quotes an ironic Southern saying: ''The white man's ice is always colder than the black man's ice.'' Even in acquiring land for its headquarters building, the company had to go through a white third party.

In 1966 North Carolina Mutual constructed a 12-story building in Durham for its home office. *The New York Times*, featuring the building on the first page of its Sunday real estate section, described it as ''the tallest office tower in Durham and . . . the tallest office tower in the country using a combination of pre-cast concrete sections post-tensioned at the site.'' Vice President Hubert H. Humphrey gave the dedication speech at this award-winning building.

Like its headquarters tower, North Carolina Mutual has managed to stand tall through the eras of the Depression, integration, affirmative action, and white backlash. Today a special challenge lies in the recruiting and retention of competent black professionals and managers whose talents are competed for by the nation's largest financial institutions and other corporations.

Kennedy's Career

When asked what he was doing before joining North Carolina Mutual, Kennedy says, "There never really was any 'before!'" At the age of ten he began working for the company during summers as an office boy.

"In those days the child labor laws weren't enforced, so I learned the work ethic quite early. I was an office boy for about five years, then began running printing equipment, working in the supply department, then working in the benefits section where I did some calculations. As I gradually improved my education and acquired the ability to do more things, I was given more responsibility."

Kennedy graduated from Virginia State College with a degree in business administration and attended The Wharton School of the University of Pennsylvania for one year, after which he joined the Army during World War II.

"I was shipped down to Fort Benning in Georgia, where I spent 18 months in a special training regiment which had been set up to train illiterate soldiers to read, write, and do basic arithmetic. Many of the blacks who had come into the army out of Mississippi, Alabama, Georgia, South Carolina, and even parts of North Carolina had no education. When I got to Benning, since I knew how to type, I immediately became a company clerk. In 1944, as the Army became desperate for manpower, they began to assign the permanent cadre of the regiment to trucking companies which were formed to be sent to Europe. I certainly did not want to be in a trucking company, so I volunteered for Officers Candidate School. After being commissioned a second lieutenant in the medical administrative corps, I was assigned to a station hospital at Fort Huachuca in Arizona, where I ran the officers' mess hall until the end of the war.

"When I got out of the Army, Wharton School let me re-enter even though the term was already under way. I arrived at Wharton on the first of November and finished my MBA in insurance that next February.

"I came back home to Durham with the intention of working for North Carolina Mutual, but when I got there, I quickly recognized that there was a need for someone with formal training in investments and finance. So I enrolled at New York University, where I earned another MBA and continued working toward a Ph.D. until I had used up all my GI Bill credit. I managed to finish everything toward my doctorate except for the dissertation, and I thought—rather naively—that I could find time to do that later.

"Meanwhile, however, I had gotten married in New York City, and after we moved to Durham, I found myself working at two or more jobs. One job was at NCM, and another was teaching graduate school courses in the evening at what is now North Carolina Central University. Soon I also started an accounting business on the side and was at that point simply too busy trying to earn enough money to support my wife—and, by then, our child. As I look back, I am sorry I didn't finish my Ph.D., but I doubt that it would have helped me in my career. On the other hand, it would have given me some personal satisfaction. As I look at my own son now, I am constantly at him to finish whatever he starts!

"My job at North Carolina Mutual was as administrative assistant, helping out both the controller and the treasurer. I had a good accounting background, so I was assigned to internal auditing and was also helping with the company investments. As it happened, most of the people in the investment department wanted to attend a meeting of the National Insurance Association in Los Angeles. In those days this involved a long train trip, so during their several-week absence the whole investment portfolio was turned over to me to handle—and this was during my first two weeks back on the job! That experience had a lot to do with my gaining confidence on the part of the company's management. About three years later I was put in charge of the home office auditing function, my first supervisory job, and three years later I moved back to the investment side.

"The internal auditing job was excellent because it gave me a good view of the whole operation of the company. In addition, when I went back into investments, I had the opportunity to work with Mrs. Viola Turner, then the assistant treasurer. I also worked closely with then-controller Asa T. Spaulding, retaining a supervisory role over the audit function as well as handling millions of dollars' worth of security transactions for the company. Not only that, but shortly after I returned, the assistant treasurer who handled the company's taxes became ill, and there was no one else who knew how to handle this. I volunteered to try to do the job, dug into it, filed the tax return and eventually handled all the taxes—municipal, licenses, fees, everything. Being involved in all three functions at the same time was a real challenge, but I learned a lot.

"A few years later, Mr. Spaulding moved up to the presidency, vacating the controller's job, and I was given that. The by-laws required that there be an assistant secretary on the executive committee, so I was named assistant secretary and controller. This gave me unusual exposure to what was going on throughout the whole business. When Mrs. Turner retired in 1966, I was named financial vice president, with responsibility for both the treasurer's and controller's functions. A few years later I became senior vice president and in 1972 president and chief executive officer.

"I cannot overemphasize the role that Mrs. Turner played in my professional life. She taught me how to trade securities in a very sophisticated way. When I started doing investment work, I knew all the technical things, how to compute yields, how to analyze, how to do all those things you can learn at school. But I didn't know how to talk to brokers and how to negotiate prices. But I learned by just listening to her handle those brokers over the phone, seeing how she got the so-called hot issues as they were issued, the issues the brokers didn't want to sell you very many of because they had a need to spread the available shares around a lot of customers. She always got more than her share because she knew how to do it."

New Opportunities for North Carolina Mutual

"There has never been a time when I haven't felt stretched, and I guess I feel the most stretched right now. There are so many challenges and opportunities for the company, so much to take advantage of.

"About 15 years ago we began a major marketing program for reinsurance. A number of major U.S. corporations had started taking some initiatives to help black suppliers, and we came up with the idea of going to some of these giant companies that were carrying group insurance with the large carriers such as Prudential, John Hancock, Massachusetts Mutual, New York Life, and so on. General Motors, for example, had had its group life insurance with Metropolitan since 1915—never with any other carrier. We wanted to try to convince them that we deserved some of that business, so we talked with the General Motors management. At that time about 40 percent of the GM work force was black, and we suggested a simple way for them to help us would be to direct one GM prime carrier to reinsure a portion of its group insurance with North Carolina Mutual. General Motors gave us about $125 million worth of its group insurance, which was about 1 percent of the total group insurance the company had in force. Since that worked well, we went on to Detroit Edison, to S. S. Kresge, from one company to the next. Then we just got out the Fortune 500 list and started working this whole list until we had 100 of those companies sold on reinsuring a portion—even a small portion—of their business with North Carolina Mutual. A lot of other black insurance companies later followed our lead.

"Now we are in the process of developing a money-management company. There are no black money managers of any real consequence in this country—the largest one I know of handles about $32 million. So we have decided that there is no reason why we should not have an opportunity to manage some of the money for the larger corporations, and we are going to try this."

Kennedy has also pushed diversification, and North Carolina Mutual now has subsidiary companies in real estate development, mortgages, investments, and communications. The communications company owns two small cable systems in South Carolina and is involved in a joint venture in cellular telephones with other companies. The cellular telephone group currently holds franchises for Detroit, Houston, Toledo, Honolulu, and several other cities. It is these and other opportunities unrelated to insurance as well as the money market challenge that cause Kennedy to feel "more stretched than ever."

Kennedy's Management Approach

"I have never resisted doing anything that I would ask anyone else to do. Perhaps I've gained some respect and recognition for this.

"Some people in management are rather autocratic. My approach has never been that way. I've always sought to get people to cooperate with me, and I've never minded getting out in front. That is where a leader belongs."

When employees were asked to help move into the new office building over a weekend and to work late hours to keep on schedule, Kennedy—then the company controller—says he worked three shifts around the clock, side-by-side with each shift of workers. Several years later, he took an equally out-in-the-open stance with union negotiations.

"When I became president, I had to confront a union problem in our home office building; the AFL-CIO Insurance Workers of America had just come in and organized our company. The first thing I did was to talk to the employees about the union and the fact that it really wasn't necessary; that North Carolina Mutual over the years had been fair to its employees, and there was nothing to be gained by a union. Then, we bargained with the union and bargained so hard that the employees were worse off with a union than they were before they had had it. We put in work rules; we had never had firm work rules before. We installed lots of things—new requirements—that they had not anticipated. Then they didn't get any increases in compensation. During the second year I was president, they called for a new election, and we were able to persuade the employees to vote against the union. In this way we got the union out of this building and haven't had a union here since. We felt that this was a great achievement: we developed a spirit of cooperation among the employees as opposed to an attitude of antagonism with management. This spirit has lasted throughout my administration: we still have a feeling of to-getherness as opposed to a feeling that I should tell them what to do."

Kennedy considers loyalty to the company a prime prerequisite of leadership and gives it strong consideration in his appraisals of up-and-coming managers.

"When I go to select someone for a top job, one of the qualities I value most is loyalty to the company and a feeling of responsibility to help build it. That has been a pervasive philosophy at North Carolina Mutual over the years, and we have been very fortunate to have a series of good leaders. We often talk about the fact that in many of the smaller life-insurance companies—the stock life-insurance companies—their founders and members of succeeding management become rich; they become millionaires, since they own a large percentage of the company. In many cases the small stock companies are owned by a small group of people, usually one family, and these families become quite wealthy. We point to the fact that at North Carolina Mutual no one has ever become a millionaire by being its president, and this has been true over the years. The dedication and the focus of the presidents of this firm have always been to build a company, as opposed to helping themselves. There is a feeling that we should share the fruits of the company as well as the labors that go along with building it. I think we have proof that this works. For example, around the time I joined the company, Atlanta Life—a black-owned stock company—was about the same size as North Carolina Mutual. We just began to outgrow them and outgrow them until now, when we are approximately twice as large as they are. And this is true even though Atlanta Life is located in a much bigger city.

"I believe that the feeling which has existed here for many years is one which should be fostered: that personal considerations should be subjugated to the need to build a company."

Special Challenges for Black Companies

"Until recent years we have had a good record of retaining our people. Our home office operation has lost hardly anyone to a competitor. But since integration, and particularly since the Research Triangle area in North Carolina developed, job opportunities simply abound. The unemployment rate in Durham has for a long time been very low, so retaining some of our best people is a challenge.

"Many of our people are well trained, since we put a lot of emphasis on continuing education and self-improvement; many have MBA's and law degrees, several are CPA's, and one is a chartered financial analyst. These people continue to get overtures. For example, we made it possible for a young man with a CPA, whom we hired from a black accounting firm in Detroit, to go to law school. As soon as he finished his degree, a law firm offered him twice his salary to come back to Detroit. The only thing I could sell him on was the future of North Carolina Mutual, the fact that it was going to continue to be here and that the opportunity for him would be tremendous. On the other hand, I said, if he were to go into this large, predominantly white law firm—that probably wanted to get him just in order to be able to say that they had a black on the staff—I wasn't at all sure how much he would really get into the full operation of that law firm. I convinced him that he ought to stay, and now he's senior vice president and chief administrative officer of North Carolina Mutual.

"Similarly, the vice president-treasurer is a very well educated person who in fact completed the Fellow Life Management Institute exams in record time, taking all of them in one sitting and passing them—ten in all. No one I knew had ever done that before. Then he studied for the chartered financial analyst designation, and after five years' experience—which is the minimum required—he passed all the exams and completed the other requirements. Then he decided to go to law school. We helped him get his law degree, and he passed the bar examination on the first try. This man was offered substantially more to join an investment banking firm in New York City, so I had to sell him, too, on the future of North Carolina Mutual."

Advice to Young People

"If I were talking to young men and women—and I often do at various schools from Harvard to Wharton to Duke to Morehouse—I would say this: 'The first thing you need to understand, once you get your MBA degree, is that you are really not prepared to be the president of a company either now or next year. So you might as well make up your mind that you have to put in a certain number of years of apprenticeship to get those things that you can't get from graduate school. If you can keep this in your mind and are willing to make some initial sacrifices, then the effort will pay off in the end. The things you gain in experience, like your education, are never lost. You can spend money—even a lot of it—and lose it quickly. But nobody can take your experience and education away from you: *you* become a valuable asset. Now, if you say that you want to start your own business, this is admirable, but even in starting a business, you need to know what is really involved in running a business; and the only way you can find that out is to get into a business that someone else is running and observe what is happening. Otherwise, your chances of success will be much less.'

"I frequently say to members of black MBA groups: 'I'd like to have you consider working at North Carolina Mutual. I recognize that opportunities abound for you now to go into almost any area you'd like to go into. When I was young, this was not true for me. When I finished my second MBA in 1946, I tried to get a job in New York City. There was no job I could get. I went to life-insurance companies and told them I had a master's degree in life insurance and another master's degree in investments and finance. But nobody would hire me, because I was black.'

"This stays on my mind as I talk to young people now. I say, 'You have a different situation: you *do* have the opportunity to work for IBM or General Electric or the Ford Motor Company or General Motors, and you can work your way up through the echelons of those companies.' However, I remind them that very few blacks have ever worked their way up to the high echelons of any of the major companies. If you look carefully, you will see that the only black vice presidents who move through those levels are vice presidents for special markets, which means that they are really 'showcase blacks.' There are a few—very few—exceptions to that, for example, a man named Otis Smith. Smith was a lawyer in Detroit who became a Supreme Court justice for the State of Michigan. He got a job in the law department at General Motors and eventually worked his way up to become general counsel. But that does take a few credentials, especially if you have to become a Supreme Court justice first!

"So this really is something to think about. I tell them, 'Think about how long it might take you in an integrated corporation to work yourself up to the top, when the majority of candidates for the position you want are white, and *they* have a hard time *themselves* working up to these major positions. The average time it takes to become a vice president in a big corporation is 20 years; it is a rare exception for a person to get there quicker than that. But if you think in terms of coming into a black-operated company, whether it's North Carolina Mutual or any of the other 35 black life-insurance companies or the 30 black banks or the 40-or-so savings and loans or any of the black companies in the country, I say the competition is not impossible. If you can go in and do a good job, you can expect to move rather rapidly.' I point out to them the experiences of people who are coming into North Carolina Mutual. The controller here, for example, is a sharp, smart young black who was a CPA working for Deloitte Haskins & Sells. I hired him as assistant controller, and in two years' time he's vice president-controller, because I learned that he could do the job.

"'But, if you as a young black man or woman really want to go to work for one of the larger companies, then that is what you ought to do. There is absolutely nothing wrong with that. In fact, some of the people I have brought into North Carolina Mutual have been hired because they have had the exposure in large integrated organizations and have learned a lot of things which they can teach us when they join North Carolina Mutual.'

"I am in the process now of hiring a man who is vice president and chief actuary for a large, billion-dollar, white life-insurance company—even though he's black. He can bring all sorts of advantages to North Carolina Mutual in terms of know-how about what's happening in the insurance industry today.

"We maintain educational programs for people at the lowest levels of the company, constantly urging them to improve their capabilities. I think we give pretty good on-the-job training here, too. Just as Viola Turner was my mentor, I also try to be a mentor. So I say that you can learn a lot in an organization like this, where there is real caring.

"Another thing I say is that I believe in working hard. I've always been willing to put in excessive amounts of time on whatever I was doing, never quitting on a job until it was finished. Then, I try never to take the credit, but to share it with everyone who helped to get the job done. When I was in internal auditing, I worked for a man named J. J. Henderson, who had worked there since the middle 1930s and was an assistant treasurer. While we worked together on the audits, I did most of the work, developing the audit plans, for example, since I had had training for this at school. But whenever we filed an audit report, it was always signed by J. J. Henderson and W. J. Kennedy, not by W. J. Kennedy alone.

"Years later, when it came time to select a president, I was a candidate among three senior vice presidents; the other two were older and had been on the board of directors longer than I. I believe that I was selected as president because I had the strongest supporter: it so happened that Mrs. Turner was on the Board of Directors as the senior financial person in the company. She was able to convince the nominating committee that I should be selected, rather than the other two. She knew my work better than anyone else, and she knew what I had accomplished over the years and was convinced of my dedication to the company. She also pointed out that because of my relative youth, I had a longer time to get my program installed. So, she was really the one, the person who had worked with *me*, who convinced the company that I should become president. At that point J. J. Henderson, who then was vice president/treasurer, gave me his full support, too.

"I certainly was not out campaigning for the presidency, and in fact it came as something of a surprise to me that I would be selected over the other two candidates, both of whom were very competent. Most people who know me would probably say that I got to this position through a combination of knowing the company through and through—partly because of the exposure I'd had in working in so many different areas, including internal audit, and being the assistant secretary of the executive committee—and my willingness to work hard and to be fair to people.

"I have never mistreated anyone along the way, and that is important too. I like to tell young people that you have to have 'pull from the top and push from the bottom' in order to make your way up that ladder of success. I have very little tolerance for office politics. If someone comes to me to tell me of the deficiencies of another person, I tell them that I do not want to hear it. If I cannot see the deficiency for myself, then it is not there so far as I'm concerned.

"And of course, I always say that you should not be too worried about making some bad decisions once in a while; everyone does this from time to time. I was on the executive committee when we approved getting into what we call school accident business, and we nearly lost our shirt, perhaps a couple of million dollars in all. While I was not the chief executive at that time, I was a member of the company's power structure, a senior officer, and I was convinced that this was just the thing to do. Yet I was just as wrong as the others, so I share responsibility for that poor decision."

Tough Decisions

"About three years ago I had to convince the rest of our management that the time had come to look at our organization from a very objective, productivity point of view. Our competition was severe, our expenses were running higher than the industry average—things were getting critical. We had to recognize that we had more people on board than we actually needed, and I had to work very hard to convince our people that we should bring in some productivity consultants. I took a certain brunt of criticism for this, but we ended up reducing our home office staff by about 30 percent. This was a very significant move, as it helped to reduce our operating costs to the point where we could look at profit again as opposed to looking at a loss from operations. We also reduced the staff in our field offices, and very likely this never would have happened if I had not forced it through.

"This reduction in force was a very tough thing to do, because having been around the company for a long time, I knew everyone by his or her first name.

"The job of a CEO is to face those tough decisions and also to confront opportunities. One of the most significant opportunities was becoming a major reinsurer. That move alone doubled our premium income. I have also pushed hard for innovations in mass marketing and improvements in product lines, the suggestions for which have come primarily from our marketing people. Getting those new products out there—getting them developed—has been a real job. Trying to get the company on a sounder financial basis has been another challenge, as we—as others—have always had trouble in accurately computing reserves every year to determine what our liabilities really are. I have been putting a great deal of emphasis on that. I am a stickler for doing things correctly, and I believe that the focus I have placed on maintaining appropriate and correct records and clear standards of performance has helped us to manage the business in a more orderly fashion.

"In any company—and particularly in older ones—there are a number of people who have permanently retired on the job. In years past, they have done their job, but in recent years they just have done nothing to move the company forward. I have taken the position that we have to work with these people as hard as we can, and we must try to change them or get them to change themselves. But if no change is forthcoming, then we have to move them.

"This is something which North Carolina Mutual had not done very well in the past; a person got into a job and was generally there for life until he retired. In the last five years we have had a considerable change in the management of our field personnel, and I have had to become very hard-nosed about the fact that we cannot tolerate having people in jobs where they can negatively affect the overall growth of the company if they are not performing, if they are not contributing their part.

"I used to make a speech in which I likened North Carolina Mutual to a big ship. On visits to district offices I would remind the people that ships move forward with propellers and are held fast by anchors. I would say that I look at every person in North Carolina Mutual and try to determine if he is a propeller or if he is an anchor. I would say that we are going to cut all these anchor lines and we are going to turn these propellers loose to let them push this company forward. So each person has to decide whether he is an anchor or a propeller. And if *he* can't decide, *we* will do the deciding for him. The ship of North Carolina Mutual, I would say, is going forward, and we are not going to have any anchors hanging on—just propellers!

"We have a lot to do in the future to keep this company moving, and there has to be diversification in its activities. The companies that we recently started represent the new activities that we feel will be beneficial to the future."

At the turn of the century, the motto of North Carolina Mutual's predecessor company was "A Soul and a Service." Its recent advertisements point with nostalgic pride to these words. But over the years, "A Company with a Soul and a Service" has been more than a slogan, the ads proclaim: "It's been a way of life."

Henry B. Schacht

Chairman of the Board and
Chief Executive Officer
Cummins Engine Company, Inc.

*H*is colleagues consider him a brilliant leader—but he is self-effacing to the point where he always says "we" instead of "I" when talking about the progress made by Cummins from a $150 million company in 1964 to one with sales of $2.5 billion today. "Collective responsibility" is a keystone of his management philosophy. He credits the team approach for Cummins' forceful, innovative response to the onslaught of foreign competition on its worldwide sales of diesel engines for heavy trucks and off-highway heavy equipment.

He became CEO in 1973, with the conviction that Cummins could no longer remain competitive by relying on traditional manufacturing methods: stable work rules, high-inventory management, economic lot quantities. Now Cummins is moving toward flexible manufacturing techniques that enable it to respond more quickly to customer needs. It has reorganized its human resources to improve its productivity while reducing its workforce. And it is taking new directions in marketing by working closely with customers during the design stage of their new products, to determine what kinds of engines they will need. Schacht acknowledges that it's tough to make radical changes—because employees may feel that their previous work is being condemned. That's why he make every effort to convince Cummins people that these changes aren't the end of the world, but the beginning of a new world.

Career Information:

1956 Joined American Brake Shoe Company

1962 Joined Irwin Management Company

1964 Joined Cummins Engine Company as vice president – finance

1966 Became vice president and central area manager – international

1967 Became group vice president – international and subsidiaries

1969 Became president

1973 Became president and chief executive officer

1977 Became chairman of the board and chief executive officer

Other Affiliations:

- Director, CBS, Inc.
- Director, AT&T
- Director, Chase Manhattan Corporation & Chase Manhattan Bank, N.A.
- Director, National Executive Service Corps
- Director, Clean Sites, Inc.
- Trustee, The Brookings Institution
- Trustee, Committee for Economic Development
- Member, The Business Council
- Member, Council on Foreign Relations, Inc.
- Member, Advisory Board, Yale School of Organization & Management
- Member, The Associates, Harvard Business School
- Senior member, The Conference Board

Educational Information:

- Yale University, B.S., 1956
- Harvard Business School, M.B.A., 1962

Personal Information:

- Born October 16, 1934
- Served in U.S. Navy, 1957–1960

282

Henry B. Schacht

*"I*t has always seemed to me that the smartest thing you can do is gather around the best people you can possibly find, people who—if you can do it —are better than you. All my experience suggests this is right."

Henry Schacht has followed this team-oriented operating philosophy since the early 1960s when, at the age of 31 and barely a year into his first industrial management job as financial vice-president at Cummins Engine, he was asked to take over the company's troubled European operations. Before accepting the assignment, he flew to London for an on-the-scene look at the problems, then returned to Cummins headquarters at Columbus, Indiana, with one basic request.

"I asked the president for three of the best people I knew of in the company—one in finance, one in marketing, one in manufacturing. The three of us went back—a personnel guy and an administrative guy were already there—and spent two years getting things sorted out. We started by asking: 'What is it we need to get done? What are the priorities? Who's going to work on what?' But there was no magic. I know only that we had good people and a discipline to approach the situation, plus a high degree of good humor and a good sense of our own fallibility."

The European assignment—to restore five money-losing manufacturing operations to profitability—was a crucial learning experience for Schacht. It gave him his first operating experience in a large, complex, interdependent business organization, and he returned from Europe in 1967 to become head of all of Cummins' international operations. Two years later he was made president of the company—then, as now, a leading international producer of diesel engines—rising to CEO in 1973 and chairman/CEO in 1977. Significantly, the team approach that Schacht used to help straighten out Cummins' international operations in the mid-1960s clearly dominates the corporate culture and management style of the 22,000-employee, $2.5 billion organization today. When discussing Cummins' corporate operations and performance, Schacht studiously avoids saying "I," "me," or "my." He says "we," "us," and "our," and refers repeatedly to "collegiality" and the "collective responsibility."

"You've got to understand that those of us who came to Cummins in the early years worked for a man named J. Irwin Miller, a founder of Cummins and former president and chairman, whose philosophy was: 'Try to attract people, the very best you can, and hold them to the highest possible standards.' Miller also said, 'Always be a good listener, take the best of the ideas, and never be afraid to say no when it's time to say no—but always do it on the basis that there is no omnipotent he, she, or they.'

"Remember that, in fact, when you talk about 22,000 people, you are talking about 'we.' If you start talking about 'me,' then you aren't going to get as much collective wisdom as you will if you think in terms of how we should organize to do something in a way that is absolutely competitive, clearly meets the standard of absolute requirements, and is better than the other guy. That's what our system thrives on.

"When you get into large, complex, interdependent organizations, you are by definition in a 'we' posture. I think you are far more able to reach efficient operations on a collective basis than you can on an individual basis. All the evidence I have seen over the last 25 years suggests that's so. Maybe that's what happens in an interdependent company where the manufacturing guy is at the mercy of the engineer, who's at the mercy of the other guy's product planner, and where everybody's at the mercy of our ability to market."

Schacht suggests that to "maximize human behavior, it's necessary to set performance standards consistent with the needs of the organization."

284

HENRY B. SCHACHT

"In other words, if you can say *we* have certain ethical limits beyond which *we* just simply are not going to go . . . If you can say *we* have certain ground rules on which *we* all agree . . . If you can say here's what *we* are trying to do and if everyone works at it as hard as they can with some sense of good humor and understanding of individual human fallibility—and with some sense that it's all worth it—then *we* will get further than if we operate as a loosely connected group of imperialists who say, 'I know best, do what you're told, get out of the way.'

"At Cummins we work very hard at a sense of collective responsibility—collective performance. But that doesn't mean there isn't individual responsibility within that. Nor am I implying that there is no individual sense of accountability within a general sense of sharing, direction setting, and performance. That blend goes back and forth, and some are uncomfortable with it. Within our top-management group we have a shared goal of what needs to be done, a shared perception of what's been pounded out over a long period of time—about what the world is like and how you must behave to be successful at it. There is a degree of understanding of each other's strengths and weaknesses and a sense that if you are about to say we ought to do 'A' and your colleague says he doesn't agree with you, you probably ought to stop and listen—and find common ground."

Meeting the Global Challenge

Schacht says the team approach and spirit of collegiality are basic to the Cummins' response to competitive pressures, because only as team participants can managers fully and effectively articulate major problems and develop joint strategies involving not only other managers, but all members of the organization. An example is how Cummins has responded to basic social, technological, and foreign manufacturing challenges that beset U.S. industry starting in the late 1960s.

"The first thing you must understand is that your management team, however you define it, has to understand and believe what the competitive issues really are; you've got to make sure you're looking at the right standards. We've always prided ourselves as being fiercely competitive, and as a manufacturer of intermediate products—I think we're the largest major component supplier still around—we are an unlikely company. I don't know anybody else who comes even close to $2.5 billion in sales that does not make an end product. We live in a position that is tenuous at best, but this has brought us great advantages, because we don't take very much for granted. We spend a lot of time thinking about competitive pressures and where we could get knocked out.

"In the late '60s it became apparent to us that our manufacturing system was increasingly wasteful of our human resources, and that there had to be a better way to organize human beings. We had basically organized them as though they were machine replacements rather than intelligent beings who weren't doing just physical work. We started with our early plants by rewriting the rules of how human organizations should work together.

"In the late '70s we became very much aware that the product cycle was changing substantially, and we put a billion dollars in new products. And in the mid-'80s it became increasingly apparent that we were going through a period of globalization (in products and markets) and that the cost, quality, and delivery factors of our manufacturing process had to be rethought.

"Since our management approach is collegial rather than individual, our top 10 or 15 people came to these awarenesses together. The next step was to get the 22,000 people in our workforce thinking about such problems. Our chief operating officer, Jim Henderson, undertook this task and has spearheaded the entire effort. He develops quarterly, sometimes monthly, videotapes—an enormous amount of documentation—and through them makes regular contact with our whole workforce. Using Jim's tapes, we have taken our people through our view of the competitive threat from our foreign competition, we have shown them Japanese products, and we have shown them Japanese warranty and cost curves, plotted against our own. We want every person in the company to have the same degree of knowledge as the senior management, even if it's painful and scary as hell. We spend a lot of time and effort trying to communicate that fact along with what our standards of cost, quality, and delivery must be and how important it is that we change.

"Jim's quarterly tapes last roughly an hour and have lots of visuals. We show them to groups of not more than 100 people, and we make sure that someone is available to answer all questions. Our senior management audience of about 100 people meets quarterly for two days, and twice a year we have planning conferences attended by some 600 managerial folks. We work hard to make certain that everybody is convinced and everybody understands.

"The chief operating officer and others on the management team spend a lot of time getting feedback on our efforts. Some of the feedback is very direct and pointed. Sometimes we get our point across and sometimes we more than get it across. Sometimes we can't live up to the things we say we're going to do. It is always a struggle.

"One example of our difficulties is highlighted when we go through a period when we have to lay people off. How do you convince people to increase their productivity—when after they boost individual output, they may lose their jobs? The answer is, you can't.

"We have also reached the point where we have to say that we cannot protect our people from the ups and downs of the economic cycle. Swings of 80 percent in our demand are not unusual, and people in our business accept that, I think. At least it's not new to them. But they *won't* accept the fact—and I don't believe they should—that if they work harder and are more productive, they're going to be laid off.

"In response to this we have committed an effort to provide new work and new jobs. We've got a pretty good idea of what our markets are going to look like, and we know what our cost, quality, and delivery targets will be in terms of man-hours per unit produced. Therefore, we know how many extra people we're going to have for each of the next five years. We've set up a whole unit of people to get that much new work into the system. In five years the engine-business unit will shrink in terms of personnel, but those people will be put into the new units working on other services and products.

"Manufacturing employment is the biggest single challenge we have. We will be struck dead in our tracks on productivity if the result of gains in productivity is worker layoffs."

Technology, Technology, Technology

Just as Cummins is calling on its technological strengths and new product ingenuity to meet the global challenge of foreign capital goods manufacturers, Schacht says, all U.S. manufacturers must mount similar technological counterattacks.

"In the last ten years, and mainly in the last five, U.S. industry has moved from an essentially secure domestic domain to one facing the challenges of international competition. Even those of us with substantial international operations operated on the basis that our domestic markets were essentially domestic and our international markets were essentially international. But now we have experienced a globalization of world markets and are learning what the challenges of global competition really are.

"What we find is that over the last 20 years the emerging nations of the Far East have amassed a formidable capability to compete in the arena we used to call our own. They have a ready supply of increasingly skilled labor that is willing to work for wages that are a fraction of ours. Furthermore, we have provided them (both consciously and through a series of historical incidents) an infrastructure that supports manufacturing in a very favorable environment. We have also supplied considerable technology. So now, when you cast your eye toward the Far East, you find a ready supply of very, very good labor—technically competent labor—at wage rates far below ours and with a skill base that is increasingly close to ours. You find infrastructures that can raise and deploy capital in quite formidable ways. And you find an open trading system that encourages others to ship goods into markets which they previously either weren't able to reach or hadn't even thought about shipping goods to."

Schacht emphasizes that in this globalization of markets, the U.S. market is not the only target.

"Japanese shipping into Latin America wasn't a phenomenon that we saw much of in the '50s and '60s. Nor did we see the Japanese and other Far Eastern suppliers in Africa, the Middle East, and the Near East anywhere near the way we do now. They are truly global competitors, operating from a base that we either helped put in place or directly developed for reasons that were quite rational at the time."

For Schacht, the intensity of the new global competition and the openness of U.S. markets to foreign competitors dictate a clear response: compete on terms that stress your own advantages.

"A U.S.-based manufacturing company must ask itself two questions: What are the terms of the competition we are likely to see over the next 20 years? And, how does one go about positioning one's company so it can compete successfully in this global marketplace?

"I think the answers are fairly straightforward. If you are going to compete, you must try to play in a game where the rules are most favorable to the strengths you bring to it. The United States brings to this game a formidable technological base, an astonishing array of skills that are basically derived out of a massive home market; a strong competitive instinct; and in general an adaptability and a sense of good humor that I don't sense in other parts of the world. By this I mean we are still young as a nation, still vigorous and relatively pioneer-like in our outlook (although some of our ossified institutions would not stand up to that test), and still willing to change what needs to be changed—in short, we are a very pragmatic country with a very pragmatic set of approaches to most problems. We haven't until recently fallen victim to our own theologies; we have a marvelous ability to mouth them . . . and then get on with whatever it takes to sort things out.

"What this says is that if you have this kind of heritage and these kinds of instincts, then you have to think about three things: technology, your manufacturing skills (which I would reduce further to cost, quality, and delivery), and the liveliness and intensity of your marketing effort. In these three broad, unsurprising elements lie the answers to how you can compete in this global economy."

Schacht says, however, that for U.S. capital goods manufacturers, technological advancement must be the principal driving force of their competitive strategies. Quality, price, and delivery mean nothing, he explains, unless you shorten product life cycles while producing a "better widget."

"We must not allow the Japanese and the emerging nations of the Far East to compete on the ground of our static technology. If we allow our technology to remain static, then we will be in the commodity business—and the commodity game is not well played from a high-cost base. We must accelerate our investment in technology and translate that investment into an increasing flow of new products. We must make those people who want to increment-us-to-death on cost play our game. The Japanese and others have not yet shown the ability to revolve their capital goods offerings quickly. They have clearly done so in electronics, but in the basic hardware business— whether it be aircraft, diesel engines, or whatever—they have been most successful where the leader has, for whatever reasons, found it comfortable to stand relatively still in technology. Give the Japanese a standing target in terms of technology, and they'll put that technology in place and eight-percent you to death.

"I don't believe you can play a set piece against a lower standard of living in an equally capacitized set of countries. First and foremost, the way to compete in this world is technology, technology, technology. And if you conclude that technology doesn't work, then you had better not produce in the United States. Produce where they (the competition) are and then try to ship back to the U.S. There is no inherent advantage in producing here, if you don't bring anything more to the marketplace than cost, quality, and delivery. Capital goods companies must learn to shorten their product life cycles and increase their flow of new products."

Schacht believes that, along with accelerating their technological output and new-product flow, U.S. manufacturers must initiate a thorough overhaul of their basic manufacturing skills and processes. Rethinking manufacturing costs, product quality, and delivery is a key step in this direction, he says, but it's only the beginning.

"It's vital to rethink cost, quality, and delivery. And my guess is that there are two phases to that effort, one of which we in this country are in the process of completing—and that is, squeeze it all out. Take the system we have built since the '40s and just wring the hell out of it. Get more efficient, reduce the number of management layers, get rid of the excesses—the fat that accumulated in the protected years of the 1950s and 1960s—and make your current approach to cost, quality, and delivery work better. Do all the things you should have done before, be more effective and more efficient, do with less, work harder, and drive your productivity goals back into the 2 or 3 percent area from the minus. However, my guess is that when you're through with all that, you've still got a no-go.

"If we as U.S. manufacturers are honest with ourselves, and if we look at what the people in the Far East have done with their decisions about how to array people, physical goods, and money, we will find that our system of base manufacturing—very stable work rules, very high-inventory management, economic lot quantities, and all the rest that went into the manufacturing teaching of the last 35 years—is sunset. It just doesn't work.

"When we compare the cost, quality, and delivery capability of our Japanese competition against our standards, we are embarrassed. We aren't even close. And there is no way squeezing harder or running harder can make the system we have set up in our own manufacturing system more efficient. We've got to rethink the basic tenets of the manufacturing process. This means moving away from a system that is essentially driven by relatively inflexible, high-cost machinery with the long setup times that drove us to economic lot quantities, large inventory investments, and long runs. This system will not work against the Japanese or our other Far Eastern competitors. They don't think that way; they don't operate that way; and they have proven you don't have to do it that way. They go the other way—they say, 'We'll produce components as required by our assembly lines'—and that means highly flexible machinery, plus no inventory.

"When they need a gear, they produce it. And they produce it three days before they need it, and it all comes together. They have less product proliferation than we do. And with less inventory, they have less investment. They have a devotion to flexible humans—they use workers as we ought to use them, not as substitutes for machines—and they do it with major investment in low-cost machine tools and tooling.

"Thus they are more 'Rube Goldberg' than we are. It's a myth to say that they are the great investors in high-cost numerical controls and other fancy equipment. That's not what their plants look like—some do, but not many. Most of their production facilities are highly inventive, highly ad hoc; they solve the problem on the floor, and they drive, drive, drive, drive."

Schacht rejects any suggestion that we can solve most of our problems simply by installing fancier machinery and more giant computers.

"Our competition doesn't change the technology, and I think that's one of their big weaknesses. However, we've got to learn to be more like them. We've got to get along with half the number of people we've got, just to produce the same quantities.

"Bigger computers are not the answer. We use bigger computers to drive our system more efficiently, but we've already concluded that no matter how efficient our system is, it is not inherently effective. So at Cummins we are in the process of dismantling our cost, quality, and delivery system and reinvesting in our factories with very flexible human agreements as to how we work with each other. This means very low levels of inventory and very flexible machinery that is driven basically from a short-term demand forecast that presumes the factory can deliver to order—rather than long-term with everything produced in economic lot sizes and then put in high-base storage. [Under the old system] we needed big computers to schedule production and bigger computers to find it afterward. But we can't build the darn thing right any time, simply because the customers don't think that way. They want what they want, not what we can build. So now we build engines to order, but we never get them built quite right—we always build them 90 percent right and then go find the other part.

"This is a vast oversimplification of the problem, but we know that our costs on a real-time basis are essentially 30 percent higher than those of the Japanese, and we believe we're the low-cost producer in the United States and Western Europe.

So we've got to change every plant to a new standard of cost and delivery. As to quality, we found that when we looked at the way the Japanese thought about quality and the relationship of cost to quality, we were not even in the same game—or in the same league.

"This means that even after you accelerate your technology and introduce new products with increasing frequency, you still must remake your entire manufacturing plant—even though you thought you were the best there was to start with. And you must convince your people that what you're doing is not a condemnation of their life's work. Instead, it's a revelation that there's another way to do something, and we are convinced that rather than reaching the end of the world, this is the beginning of a new world."

New Directions for Marketing

Marketing has also taken on a new dimension for capital goods manufacturers, according to Schacht.

"We've learned that you've got to market like hell in ways that we have not really thought about for some time. We must intensify our marketing, so we can deliver to the customer precisely what the customer wants—on time, every time—and not what we would like to deliver at our convenience. That sounds simple, but it isn't; it requires a whole new frame of mind.

"In the capital-goods business, essentially we haven't been intense marketers; we have been one manufacturer talking to another. That's not good enough. We need to get into the customer's forward-product plans just as if we were an integral part of his business. This requires a mutuality of interest between vendor and buyer that is the antithesis of the familiar relationship between the industrial purchasing agent and vendor —a bunch of hard-nosed purchasing agents trying to get the last inch out of a bunch of salesmen who are trying to give them as little as possible. We've got to scrap this uncooperative relationship and agree on what a price ought to be on a world-based standard and how we are going to get there. We're slowly beginning to think that way."

> Intensifying the marketing effort means that senior executives have to spend more time with their customers. For example, Schacht spends about 35 to 40 percent of his working hours in direct contact with top officials of Cummins' customer companies. His goal: to move the marketing effort into the first stages of product planning.

"This means sitting down with the senior customer people and saying: 'Look, we need to redefine the terms of trade from scratch. The current way we're doing business is sort of a love-hate relationship. You can't build trucks and construction equipment without engines, and we can't sell engines unless we become an integral part of your product. Today you've got three engines, two transmissions, and two axles to choose from, and your vendors are beating each other up. It won't work that way any more.'

"We also tell the customer: 'You've got to decide which of us you want to work with (we hope it will be us, but it could be somebody else). We'll sit down with you and you tell us what our product has to look like in 1990. If we don't do that, the 1990 product is going to be either European or Japanese.'

"This means that I spend a good bit of my time on what I call the intense marketing side—making sure that we become an integral part of our customers' forward plans, rather than just a purchasing agent's decision to buy Brand X or Brand Y. I think this increasingly is going to be the way industrial products are brought to market. I think you will find fewer choices offered for products and vendors, yet far more partnership relationships. You will find much more emphasis on product planning as opposed to selling—with much more give and take early, rather than late, in the process. And rather than our designing engines and then convincing you, the customer, to put them in your equipment, we will have to try to find out what it is that your equipment needs to do to compete with the Japanese and Germans in all markets. Then from this knowledge we will determine how we can maximize performance, through the technology we can bring to the engines, instead of just saying, 'Here's my engine . . . you ought to buy it rather than our competitors'.' We're moving the entire marketing effort out of the purchasing agent's arena and into the product-planning arena.

"I believe strongly in industrial marketing, which is very different from consumer marketing. In industrial marketing, by and large, you deal with a finite number of customers where your technology and product have a finite place to go— whether you're selling trucks to a highly definable population of fleets, construction equipment to a highly definable population of large contractors, or an intermediate product to a highly definable group of equipment manufacturers. It's not marketing that involves shelf-space advertising, consumer loyalty, nameless-faceless customers. These are real people, and your chief executive had better spend a good bit of time with them."

According to Schacht, U.S. manufacturers have had to shift their marketing efforts to a more closely coordinated designer-to-designer effort to meet foreign competition.

"U.S. manufacturing was essentially a closed system for decades. As long as it was Chrysler versus Ford versus General Motors, they all had the same system—three engine suppliers, two transmission guys, three axle guys—nobody cared. We competed for 25 years on a relative-cost basis in this country, but no more. We now compete on an absolute-cost basis, and when we look at absolute costs, we don't stand the test, relative to the rest of the world. We're still competing against Detroit Diesel and Caterpillar, of course, but the Europeans and the Japanese have breached the system. The ultimate test now is the cost of the engine in the Japanese product or the engine in the Volvo or the Daimler-Benz. And we don't meet the test."

The Importance of Balanced Management

While the Cummins management culture reflects a fundamental emphasis on collective responsibility for corporate performance, it still requires thorough assessment of individual accomplishment. Senior managers and their key staff people meet regularly in one-on-one conferences to review progress toward what Schacht emphasizes are "shared" understandings of personal and corporate objectives.

"The ultimate responsibility for performance appraisal for the top half-dozen people rests with the chief executive and the chief operating officer. In December, we provide our Board with our annual assessment of how the most senior people are doing against what we all agreed we ought to try to get done during the year. We report how the two of us are doing against what we said we'd try to do and review which of the top 50 people are most likely to be able to take on more responsibility.

"In January, the chief operating officer sits down with his staff—the top ten or so people in the company—and they reach a shared set of understandings. Each quarter they review how they are doing against what they thought they would be able to do. Each has his own personal sense of what has been done and what needs to be worked on; each is aware of his own strengths and weaknesses, as perceived by the chief operating officer.

"I believe that management succession should be a long relay race and not an over-the-cliff event. It's terribly wasteful of human talent to set up side-by-side races of competent people in which you develop win/lose situations and force someone up or out. I just can't believe that's the right way to do things, so we try to focus our thinking about management succession in terms of long relay races.

"Jim Henderson, our chief operating officer, and I have been in the same relative positions since 1969—that's 16 years, and we're both 51. Our chief financial officer has been in his position for 15 years, during which period our company has doubled and almost doubled again in size. We've had many reinforcing experiences that this is a good way to work together. Irwin Miller, who made his choices and bets, rightly or wrongly, relatively early, still brings insights to the business. I see him three or four times a week and find that it is absolutely one of the most important things I do. I learn every time; I'm still learning and hope I will always learn."

Schacht's Early Career

"After college, I worked for a year, spent three-and-a-half years in military service, then went right to graduate school, which I found to be the most intellectually challenging two-year period of my life. Then I joined a company called the Irwin Management Company, a personal holding and investment company for the Miller family, spending two years there in a highly analytical job, first in charge of their venture capital portfolio and then, after their investment manager left, the stock and bond portfolio. When (in 1964), they asked me to go over to Cummins, I said yes—for what I found interesting was not the physical act of investing and selling but the management task that I saw other people doing in the companies in which we were investing.

"I went to Cummins as its first vice president of finance, so the task—the company then had $150 million in sales compared with sales of $2.5 billion today—was to try to build a finance function. But after being there only a year, I was made head of the European operations, which were losing a lot of money."

> Schacht took the critical European job with little or no on-the-job managerial training beyond his nearly four years as a naval officer in the late 1950's. Although his responsibilities in the service were "nothing" compared with what Cummins later handed him, he regards his Navy years as one of his "most important experiences."

"The military gave junior officers at that time an enormous amount of responsibility. You learn many lessons by being in command of those who have more experience than you. What is critically more important is getting your mission accomplished, when, as a junior officer, you have 50 or 100 enlisted people working for you; the only thing you contribute is some ability to sort things out. You certainly don't bring experience or institutional memory; you certainly don't bring wisdom in any sense. But you're in charge, and you're responsible. The military has a habit of being unforgiving of those who don't exhibit some degree of ability to carry out command responsibilities despite the fact they're only 21 or 22. Learning to work in that environment—being responsible, being a long way from anybody who could be viewed as a support function—was very important for me. I grew enormously.

"I think this reinforced for me that the people with whom you work are your biggest allies, that they are human and dependent on you, that there is a high degree of interdependence in any human organization, and that even the most experienced people need support and leadership. I learned that if you are willing to take on that burden, they will respond to it; that people can be motivated and led, but not against their will; that there is much wisdom residing in people who may not have had the advantages of education and travel; finally, that they're just as bright and just as able and, in their way, sometimes very articulate. There's a fundamental good nature in human beings that those who aspire to and succeed in command positions sometimes forget."

Advice to Young People

> Graduating business school students often ask Schacht for advice on how to make a job choice or otherwise point their careers in the right direction. He offers clear advice.

"I tell them not to worry, to have confidence in themselves, to ask themselves a series of fairly straightforward questions, and to do what seems right at the time. Then I say: 'Go where your heart takes you!' After all, the world does not lend itself to the kind of planning that they've just spent two years in business school thinking makes all the difference. It does make a difference, of course, but insofar as career choice is concerned, it's best to go where you will be comfortable. You may not get it right the first time, and if you don't like it, then do something different. Trust yourself!

"Making a job choice really isn't that tough. Start by setting up a series of negative screens, the first of which is to ask yourself: 'Does the product of the company turn me off?' If the answer is yes, forget it. There are infinite fish in the sea.

"The second negative screen is location. If you don't want to go to work in Columbus, Indiana, for example, don't come to me and say I love everything about your company but Columbus—but you can send me to London, New York, or Dallas. You may think your choice is great, but it won't be—because if you're as good as you think you are, all roads, in this instance, lead to Columbus, Indiana. Why get yourself in a position where the more successful you are, the more likely you are to have the one thing happen to you that you already know you can't live with?

"The number three screen is ethics. Is the professed and observable ethics and value system of the company compatible with your own? Every company has one; it's not hard to find—just ask people. If the people in the company give you a blank stare, that will tell you something. Think about your own value system. What would you have done if you were Ehrlichman or Haldeman (officials in President Nixon's White House staff)? They were good guys; they weren't evil people. But they didn't ask themselves key questions soon enough or fast enough—or get put to the test early enough. Ask yourself: At what point will I walk away? What is my price? What won't I do? Make sure that your answers are compatible with expectations.

"Once you resolve these answers, ask two other questions: What is my first job? Who will be my first boss? Look at the job on the basis of 'Is it something I'm really going to have fun doing?' If the answer is no again, don't take it—because you won't do it very well. A first job should act as a springboard so you can go through the organization like a hot knife through butter. But first, do that job well.

"As for the first boss—you have one question to ask: Will he or she continue my educational process and be willing to listen to me? If the answer to this question is no, you will be frustrated beyond belief.

"Of all the jobs you've managed to look at, if you find you have five yesses to these questions—my guess is you've got one or two—then you should put the prospective jobs side-by-side and do what your heart says you ought to do—and then forget it. Don't look back."

Portia Isaacson

**Chairman and CEO, Intellisys Corporation
President, Isaacson, Inc.**

*S*he enthusiastically touted the personal computer market when nobody else was taking PCs seriously—and parlayed her prescience into a highly profitable consulting service. As CEO of Future Computing Incorporated, she provided authoritative marketing information to hundreds of corporations (some of whom had previously scoffed at her predictions) for very healthy fees. Within four years of starting Future Computing with $16,000, she sold it to McGraw-Hill for around $40 million. Now she has two new start-up companies. Intellisys Corporation is producing software for electronic homes. Isaacson, Inc. provides planning and implementation services for mergers, acquisitions, and divestitures in the computer and electronics industry.

She is the quintessential entrepreneur—defined by her as an opportunity-seeking mechanism. Her management style is to let her people be creative in a high-energy, do-it-now environment. She constantly pushes them to do things that "can't be done."

She says she learned entrepreneurship from her father, a small Oklahoma dairy farmer who was always trading or dealing for something to make a little money. Her advice for future entrepreneurs: Position your enterprise to set it apart from competitors—and maintain a focus on one vital area rather than spread yourself too thin.

Career Information:

1965 Joined Central State College (Okla.) as teaching assistant
1967 Joined Bell Helicopter Company as scientific programmer/analyst
1968 Joined Lockheed Electronics as scientific programmer
1968 Joined Computer Usage Company as analyst
1970 Joined Recognition Equipment Incorporated as senior systems software programmer
1971 Joined North Texas State University as instructor
1974 Joined Xerox Corporation as engineering specialist
1975 Joined University of Texas at Dallas as assistant professor
1976 Became partner and vice president of Binary Systems, Inc. Still retains this position
1977 Became private consultant
1978 Joined Electronic Data Systems Corporation as fellow-vice president, Business Systems Division
1980 Founded and became president of Future Computing Incorporated
1985 Founded and became president of Isaacson, Inc.
1985 Founded and became chairman and chief executive officer Intellisys Corporation

Other Affiliations (partial list):

• Director, Future Computing Incorporated
• Director, Microsoft Corporation
• COMDEX Advisory Board, 1982
• IEEE Computer Society Governing Board, 1980–82
• MECC Computer Literacy Project Advisory Board, 1981–83
• Managing Technical Editor, IEEE *Computer*, 1978–81

Educational Information:

• East Central University, (Okla.), B.S., Physics and Mathematics, 1966
• North Texas State University, M.S., Computer Science, 1972
• Southern Methodist University, M.A.S., Computer Science, 1973
• Southern Methodist University, Ph.D., Computer Science, 1974

Personal Information:

• Born September 7, 1942, Oakland, Calif.
• Served in U.S. Army as WAC-Specialist 4, 1960–62
• Married, has three sons. Major outside interest is fashion.

302

Portia Isaacson

"*I* have finally learned that I am an early-phase person. Thank God I found that out—for years I just thought that I couldn't hold a job; now I know what I am good at: starting things. There are some people who can run companies and do a great job of that for an extended period of time. And there are some other, very special people who can go in and turn around companies which are failing. I know a number of them—these people are very admirable—but usually they are people who can't run a company for any period of time, or don't want to. The turn-around specialists are often workaholics—as I am—and as soon as one company starts turning around at all, they're off to turn around another one.

"Why is it that some individuals—not very many, I've learned, but I am one of them—are willing to take a piece of blank paper time and again and mark it out and say, 'This is what we are going to do!' They drive a stake in the ground and take the responsibility and the risk (and that's the issue) of really having it not work. After all, most new companies and new ideas don't work. Doing blank paper is one of my key characteristics. Another is the ability to think big, I mean BIG. When I started Future Computing, some people said to me, 'Portia, what makes you think that IBM, AT&T, and even Apple will ask *you* about personal computers?' It never occurred to me that they wouldn't! It never did! I am sure that to many people the act of my starting up Intellisys is equally bizarre. The idea of electronic homes is new today, just as personal computers were new when I founded Future Computing. After all, I could be really embarrassed. Here I am, raising flags, talking about electronic homes; we're already on network teleision, and my shower doesn't even work! I could fail really visibly, but I guess I don't care. I don't think about that at all. It simply does not occur to me that we could fail. What does occur to me is that there will be a lot of problems, new ones every day, but I really like figuring out how to solve problems. That's the kind of manager I am, and I've heard that that's not too good! But as long as I have a problem and I know what it is, I can fix it. And at the same time, I'm starting up this other new company—Isaacson, Inc. This is what I love to do, and I'm good at it. I guess I must just have a need to create new things."

> Isaacson's vision of her new start-up company, Intellisys, is a firm that will provide software to enable personal computers to manage centrally all home-based electronics: audio and video entertainment systems, lighting, heat and air conditioning, highly sophisticated telephone communications systems, security, swimming pool controls, energy systems, some discrete appliances, and anything else that comes along that is electronically manageable. Her new home in Dallas serves as a prototype and test bed for this software, which will be sold not to consumers but to original equipment manufacturers, suppliers, and construction companies.

"I've been thinking about the electronic home for at least ten years. In fact, about ten years ago I wrote a paper on this concept. I have been involved in the development of the personal computer industry for some time now, and electronics in the home is one of the things that you tend to think about as a possible future, but one which is not terribly central to the personal computer industry. In a way, it's really just a pet project of mine. When I sold Future Computing to McGraw-Hill, I realized that I had finally been a very successful entrepreneur. I have noticed that all entrepreneurs who sell their companies do something a little strange when they come into all that money. Instead of buying a $2 million airplane, I built the electronic home I've always wanted. The part that's missing—an important part—is the software. If you're willing to spend the money, you can buy individual subsystems such as one that will control centrally a very sophisticated lighting system. You can buy integrated entertainment control systems. But I have decided to come in on top of that with a little bit of custom hard-

PORTIA ISAACSON

ware and a lot of computer software to actually manage all these systems. Having built this home and gotten into developing all this software, I saw an opportunity. An entrepreneur is an opportunity-seeking mechanism. So, I said, 'Ah! There's one! I think I'll do this!' You need one central computer to handle all the control functions, and you can have a lot of other optional computers that simply provide a human interface to the central system. For example, there is a control tower which is actually a light pen and a digital television, with an IBM PC underneath it which is connected to a local area network outlet in the wall, allowing it to communicate with the central computer. A voice-activated human interface can be provided through the telephone system. You can have a lot of computers to serve that human interface function, and all of this is optional. Of course what is not optional is the central computer that houses the operating system. We do this through an IBM PC AT, with a hard disk and a lot of communications capability. Electronic gadgets in the home have been proliferating for a long time. Not everyone can afford all of this stuff—but many people do go for it—and eventually there's a clutter of remote-control devices, complicated intercom systems, telephones that do all sorts of things, burglar- and fire-alarm systems, and there's really no need to deal with all of these things separately. The PC can do it for you, but only if there is software to do it.

"Intellisys will become a very big software company. There are no competitors today, and there won't be any. The market needs only one such company, because of the need for standards, and we intend to be that company. We are very well positioned, as we know all the manufacturers extremely well because of my past relationships at Future Computing, so we should be able to pull off being *the* only one. In fact, to start up this kind of company from scratch, you probably could not raise the money you need. I will be raising venture capital for Intellisys within the next six months, and by then we will have working products, a laboratory right in my home which will have a very high national profile.

"Intellisys will be another high-growth company, and I do not want personally to manage that kind of enterprise right now—the kind of company where you have to get real focused and be obsessed to do it. So the first thing I have done is to bring in an outstanding president, Don Bynum, who at one time headed TI's home computer business. I also have a very strong marketing vice president who worked for me at Future Computing in that same capacity, a woman who really knows a lot about the consumer electronics market. Both have textbook entrepreneurial characteristics; they represent a very strong management team, and I am trying to stay out of their hair. After all, I am starting another business called Isaacson, Inc.''

Isaacson, Inc.

''The second business, which I plan to operate in a hands-on way, is being set up to do mergers and acquisitions and business brokerage. This is something I have done or at least dabbled with in the past at Future Computing. Through having helped put together a couple of really big deals within the personal computer industry, I learned that I am basically a deal maker—that's what I like to do. So in this company I will operate it personally with only two employees. My plan is to keep the staff very small, work on a very small number of transactions—probably no more than a half dozen at a time—deals that I can add value to. All of the transactions will be in the computer, communications, electronics industry, but at the moment I am swamped with computer retail chains. So Isaacson will be involved not just in technology companies but in distribution businesses.''

In 1976 Isaacson and her husband opened The Micro Store, the first retail computer store in Texas and one of the first in the U.S. Later, while running Future Computing Incorporated, another company she established, she worked closely with Sears, an early client, in developing the business plan for Sears' business system centers, which sold personal computers. Through these experiences, she gained a wealth of background in PC distribution. It is partly this background that has propelled her second new start-up company, Isaacson, Inc., so quickly into "deal making" with PC distribution businesses. Both Intellisys and Isaacson, Inc. are highly focused and well positioned.

The Positioning of Portia Isaacson

Isaacson's elegant electronic home in Dallas contrasts greatly with the environment of her youth, a poverty-stricken dairy farm in Oklahoma.

307

"Nothing was doing very well in those days, that's for sure. My father is a very work-ethic German, honest as the day is long, always holding three jobs at a time, and making deals—always horse trading. He moved houses, worked on the farm, drove a milk truck, did whatever there was to be done, working from very early morning to very late at night. My work-ethic values came from him and probably my entrepreneurial instincts as well. Every day he was trying to make some kind of deal or to start some little business, and he certainly was a fine role model for me.

"Something else I got out of that experience was a lot of anger. Many successful people, I think, have had a lot of anger at one time. Mine came from the poverty and a very troubled family life. My parents were finally divorced (thank God!) when I was about ten, and I soon acquired a terrible step-mother whom I absolutely hated. But most of my anger came from the fact that my world was the world of books, which opened my mind and eventually the door to the rest of the world for me. Where I lived in my head was not where I lived physically, and I was intensely angry, simply because I could not have a better life. Through reading, I developed a deep-seated desire to become a scientist. I probably read every biography written about Marie Curie. I was impressed with the fact that we had similar backgrounds, both very poor. Her accomplishments expanded my concept of what might be possible, and she became a role model for me. I wanted to become a chemist, but I couldn't go to college. I couldn't figure out how to get there. I had been recognized as a science-talent student nationally and had the opportunity for wonderful scholarships, but no bus fare to get there. So I became unjustifiably angry. In addition, our family was the poor of the poor, never invited to the good parties, and this made me angry, too. I compensated by being smart, winning competitive speaking awards—my first at age seven. I really excelled in debate and extemporaneous speaking. The night I graduated from high school as valedictorian, with only $25 in my possession, I simply left, thinking, 'I'll never see you again, and I'll show you!' Years later, I was still angry but didn't quite remember why, and it is only in the past few years, after becoming comfortable with my success, that I have been able to restore family relationships, which are now very pleasant.

"I was thinking about this recently when I was getting ready to talk to some students at my son's college. I thought about positioning, and I told them this: 'You are your first product, so positioning yourself in the market as an individual is extremely important. You need to approach this just as you would approach positioning any other kind of product. It is very important to be unique, to have skills, to have something about you that, first of all, has value and second, has the kind of value that if people want it, you represent the only place they can get it.' I remember thinking back and remembering that I originally majored in physics just for that reason. I thought that anything that difficult simply had to be in demand, because there were not that many people who could do it, and very few girls who would even try.

"Early in my career being a woman worked to my disadvantage, but later it became a tremendous advantage as it simply made me more special, unique. If you are the only person who has something which is needed, you can charge anything you like. I am not a big fan of the generalist type—someone said that an MBA is hazardous to your wealth, and I think that's probably true. While a business background is good, what I like to see kids do is to get a technical background, if they can handle that, at the undergraduate level, along with some business and economics—the nuts and bolts of the world —and then go on and get a technical masters, but with some work in between their undergraduate and graduate degrees. There's a risk that you won't go back to get that masters, so the wisdom of this could be argued either way. My oldest son is a college senior with a computer science major and a strong business minor, and he is thinking about staying one more year to finish out a business major too, then take a master's degree in technical communications. He also thinks he might want to live in Japan for a year. I think that's a brilliant plan, in terms of creating uniqueness.

"The other thing about positioning yourself is that you should not just sit down and say, 'I want to make a million dollars, so what do I do?' The right approach is to ask what value you can offer, what value you can create. The whole approach to life should be your value to the market, because value is where rewards come from. Marie Curie made a great scientific contribution to mankind by discovering radium. In some sense I wanted to find my own radium, to do something great for mankind. Then and only then would I get the recognition I needed (as a child), and then I wouldn't be angry any more. *That* would show them, if I made some great humanitarian discovery, and that is why I wanted to be a scientist. What you need to do is to offer value to the world. The businesses I have created represent my radium.

"I had to drop out of college one course short of my bachelor's degree in physics and took a job as a computer programmer just to pay the bills; by that time I had been married and had three children. That turned out to be a tremendously lucky break for me. I loved programming and did it for eight years before going back to school. I got into highly technical systems programming and decided that to position myself better, I needed some graduate training, so I went to graduate school to get a master's degree. I noticed that I had reached a stage in my career where I was always a project leader but never quite a manager, and I thought that perhaps girls had to overcompensate. Like my father, I've always done three things at a time, so when I started back to school, my income went up because I started to do some consulting on the side. I made more money consulting part-time than I had ever made in a full-time job, so I went ahead and got two master's degrees and a Ph.D. in computer science at SMU.

"I tend always to be obsessive, and I was really obsessed and having fun on my Ph.D. and at that same time working at Xerox. By the time I finished my Ph.D., I was managing a software development group there, and, through that, got into deal making. The particular project at Xerox was a huge one, the development of their big laser-printer system, the 9200. I was helping to design this system, which had highly sophisticated internal computer architecture requiring multiple minicomputers, and was assigned to negotiate with potential minicomputer suppliers; to do so I had to understand the technical details of the design in order to talk intelligently with the minicomputer firms. I wound up with many people reporting to me on a dotted-line basis, and at that time the press reported that this project represented the largest procurement of mini-computers ever made. I was working with attorneys, business-people of all kinds, and it was really fun. So by the time I finished my Ph.D. I had lost most interest in technical matters and became somewhat entrepreneurial. Xerox moved that part of their operation to El Secundo, which was why I left Xerox, and it was shortly after that that I opened the computer store. By that time I was also on the faculty of the University of Texas, Dallas, and had in addition been selected to chair the National Computer Conference. This is what made me 'famous' in the computer industry.

"Everyone thought this was so bizarre. I am probably the only past NCC chairman whom you could even name. The press just loved me because all I wanted to talk about was per-sonal computers; this was almost ten years ago, and everyone thought it was really funny. PCs were not considered legiti-mate at the time, and everyone thought it quite strange for a 'girl' to be chairing the National Computer Conference—the first woman who ever had done so. Here I was, chairing the straightest computer conference in the world, a legitimate chairman with a Ph.D. in computer science, but all I wanted to talk about was personal computers. As a result (and also because I have been an accomplished speaker since childhood) I was invited all over the place to give lectures, always the after-dinner entertainment—giving everyone lots of laughs, since few people other than I took the PC seriously. This assignment gave me a very high profile, and I became known for having predicted a lot of things about personal computers which, year by year, came true. But at that time no one believed this could ever happen. Five years later, when I launched Future Computing Incorporated, which concentrated only upon personal computers, they remembered me and said, 'She was right.'"

Intrapreneurial Experience

"At that point I wanted to start up a consulting business, so I left my teaching job, and Ross Perot, the founder of Electronic Data Systems, became my biggest client. Ultimately, he hired me to work with him. Now I would know how to say no, but I didn't really know this at that time, around 1978. I had wanted to do what I ended up doing later—to start my own company —but I found that the only companies that would pay me anything then were companies such as IBM and AT&T, and they just wanted me to give lectures that were mind-expanding, to present futurist-type messages within their companies. I couldn't really make a very good living doing that, but it turned out that that's what Ross Perot wanted me to do, too, to mind-expand the EDS people, which—at least in the case of personal computers—was probably not possible. I had gotten along with Ross really well, and he simply insisted that I come to work for him. We had several meetings before I finally accepted the offer I couldn't refuse, and he made me an "EDS fellow," along the lines of the IBM fellows, which meant that I was on his staff with no defined responsibilities. About a year later I attempted to start a business within EDS (this was the second business I had started, the Micro Store having been the first).

"It was in 1978 that I started a business within EDS which was to produce broadcast-quality, videotaped training material on personal computers. I was too early, getting to the market about four years before it even existed. In addition, my business plan called for selling videotapes for about $200 a pop. I wanted to just sell them and shove them out the door. Unfortunately, the person I reported to believed I should follow the pattern of another successful training company which only leased videotapes. I was literally directed to lease the tapes rather than to sell them and could not find any way to get my manager's decision reversed, no matter how much I documented my point of view. I knew that it was simply not possible in those days to lease a videotape library to the market that I wanted to reach, that is, the market for training within computer retail stores, where the tapes would have to be used over and over. Since I could not get that decision reversed, it was my opinion that the business was destined to fail; and it did. At that point I got EDS's permission to try to sell the business, which was the first time I had ever tried to sell any business, and I could not accomplish that either. Ultimately the tapes themselves were sold by EDS, but that was after I left. There were four other businesses which EDS had started at about the same time, each having something to do with the personal-computer industry, and each was failing for similar reasons. Arbitrary decisions that really did not fit the market's concept—such as the lease vs. sell issue (which was fundamental to the business I was trying to start)—wouldn't let them work right. But in the case of my effort we had recovered some of the investment—which was not a large one—so I didn't feel too bad. What I did feel bad about was the disappointment of the people whom I had brought into the business. For most of them there was no other place at EDS, as they would not fit into the very specific culture of that company. In looking back, I realize I made much too strong a promise to those people, a commitment to find all of them jobs—and I did not leave EDS until I had done that. Since then I realize that one should not take that much responsibility for other people's lives. That was a very hard time for me, yet a great learning experience. I learned some key things by doing a lot of things wrong in the business I tried to create at EDS.

"One thing that helps make you successful, I think, is having some experience with failure. I don't deal with failure very well, though I certainly have had a lot of practice at it, since I'm always pushing limits. In fact, I have a theory, which I am trying to document, that very successful people have probably had more experience with failure than anyone else. When I say that, I am focusing on entrepreneurs, for it's not really true that most entrepreneurs 'luck' into a success, getting it right the first time. Usually, they have tried a lot of things and finally one worked, or they finally learned how to make one work. I also learned that cultures are quite different. The kind of marketing that I was trying to do just would not fit into EDS. At marketing in a broader sense, they are fine. I greatly admire EDS and its very strong culture, but it is one that I did not fit into. I also learned something very important, just from having worked for Ross Perot. With him, nothing is impossible. Nothing. My office was down the hall from the board room where they planned the raid to successfully rescue their executives in Iran. I have never had a small idea since I worked for Ross Perot. I became, like him, an 'intergalactic thinker.'"

Future Computing Incorporated

"I finally founded the consulting firm I had had in mind for so long. My failure in starting a business at EDS had taught me the most important thing: Marketing is king. This definition has been attributed to Buck Rodgers, formerly of IBM: Marketing is always having the product that the customer wants; sales is making the customer want the product that you have. I thought this was wonderful. So I learned to do marketing in that broad sense.

"Future Computing is an information-service company, but very unlike most companies that would be labeled that way, because it's very product-oriented, more like a publisher, with less than 10 percent of its revenue coming from consulting and the rest from leverage-type products. This approach was critical to making it into a business that could be sold. My strength as an entrepreneur, that opportunity-seeking mechanism, is in marketing—that is, in always having the product that the customer wants and needs. What made Future successful was, first of all, that we were really close to very important companies in the industry, and I listened very closely to them. If two companies asked the same question, I published the answer. You have to be sensitive to the needs of the market and to respond fast. This is what we did, and Future really grew. The fun part of building Future Computing was that we always funded it out of the customer base, no outside funding whatsoever from day one. It's not too easy to build a company to nearly $10 million in annual sales with no outside funding. The first year, back in 1980, we ran totally a consulting business. My plan was to use the consulting revenues to launch products, and the easiest product to start was a newsletter. This was followed by seminars, then research reports, and ultimately a very high-ticket annual subscription service. Once we reached about $4 million in sales, cash flow became very tricky. So what we got our customers to do was to give us money up front. Friends would ask, 'Portia, how do you get companies to send you $15,000 and let you send them anything you feel like sending them during the year?' Well, they did it, that's how we funded it, and it got bigger and bigger.

Now there are many companies that pay Future $100,000 in advance for research that Future will decide to do during the year, based upon what's happening in the market. You really cannot specify in advance in a market that volatile exactly what these companies need to know. A part of this is based on trends, but the key is to determine what these companies need to know in order to compete successfully. We became very good at documenting the structure of an industry that is incredibly complex; for computer companies, it was horribly complex, for many of them had never dealt with independent distribution companies and independent software companies. The personal-computer industry is structured like consumer electronics, where there are movie-makers and retail chains and zillions of little companies that these huge companies have to do business with, in what is a completely foreign territory— another planet—to them. So the structure of the industry and the nature of the deals they needed to know about would be the basis of some of the things that Future would study and publish, for example, 300 pages of analysis of terms and conditions, or how to do business with computer stores, all the way down to absolutely gory stuff. Much of what Future does is not classical quantitative market research, although they do some of this, too—user surveys, customer surveys, and so on. But the nuts and bolts of Future's business is based on understanding in great detail the changing industry structure. In addition, Future has a very sophisticated laboratory in which products are tested on behalf of manufacturers in order to render an opinion as to their marketability. There's one lab which tests products for compatibility with the IBM PC. Future provides in confidence a 20- to 30-page document telling them why their computer is or is not compatible, containing recommendations as to what should be done about the findings. Every major PC manufacturer uses that service. There is simply no significant company in the personal-computer industry that is not a client of Future Computing, almost in proportion to their market share. Future is a strange company, as it is capable of sophisticated market insight in a sophisticated technology-driven market. Its professionals are all like me—Ph.D.'s in computer science who have become basically marketeers.''

Working with People

Isaacson is an outgoing, self-assured, and naturally friendly person who exudes ebullience and great good humor. During the course of the interview, which took place in her electronic home, service people were arriving and leaving, electronic systems were being installed, and a marketing meeting of one of her new start-up companies was taking place in the dining room. Her attention seemed to be focused sharply on all of the activities simultaneously taking place, as she moved from one activity to the other.

"I absolutely do find a sharp distinction in dealing with people who have Ph.D.'s in computer science and other people. The Ph.D's definitely fit the mold we've all heard about. Their hours are not regular, they work at an extreme pace for a while and then don't show up until 10 a.m.; they are more relaxed in the way they want to dress and have very big egos. I call them babies. Yet in some respects they are not unlike sales-people, particularly in the way you need to coddle them along. While there are exceptions, many are prima donnas. I am very comfortable with these people, so they like working for me. I somehow manage them without their knowing that they are being managed.

"I don't want to know any details, and if they want to talk to someone about their projects, I am not the person to talk with. I deal with them on schedules and try to give them some of the contacts within and without the business and help them to build their self-esteem. I always try to find what they really want or something they would really like and periodically do some unusual things. I'm a big fan of the unexpected gesture, a ticket to London, for example. Last year I bought a car for one of our people. That was an exceptional situation, and that's why I did an exceptional thing. But I think this approach works just as well with salespeople. For example, I let someone drive my Porsche for a month because he did something really neat. Letting such people have an unstructured environment is really important. I communicate that simply by not reacting to their strangeness too directly. They know that I think they are okay so long as they deliver. But they also know that I know whether or not they are delivering.

"The secret to the success of Future Computing is probably in the people I recruited as the nucleus, the ones who started with me. They love to work there; it is a think tank, a creative place. People have come back to work for me again and again after they've gone out to some other job. They return, saying, 'There's no other place with as much fun as this.' What they mean, I think, is that around me there is always a very high-energy, creative, do-it-now atmosphere. I am always pushing. Whatever I want, I want right now, and there are always at least 15 things going on. While they're busy with something else, I walk in and say, 'Guess what we're doing today?' There was a big joke for years at Future about Monday mornings, because on weekends I'd get to think. So every Monday morning Portia would always come in with *something*. They would make bets on which department I was going to attack first.

"I tend to give direction from a distance, painting a broad picture on the wall and asking my people to go away and fill in the details. When they bring it back to me, I might say, 'Well, I like all that—it's just wonderful—but this piece right here needs fixing.' I never deal with details, yet I never fail to give direction; my theory is to do something, even if it's wrong. My style allows people to be creative in a high-energy environment.

"For example, when we designed my electronic house, we spent weekends in marathon sessions. I wrote the initial 30-page document, holing myself up for two weeks to define the overall functional specifications. I didn't know whether some of the things I had in mind were feasible. I also didn't care. Then I got together with my team, consisting of a super software guy, and an electrical engineer who was going into all the little custom microprocessor details, a telephone specialist, and an audio/video expert. They would give me all the reasons we couldn't do what I wanted to do, and I'd insist that we would do it anyway. They would come up with design ideas on the fly, and my job was to keep pushing them beyond what they thought their limits were, to give them some of my intergalactic energy. As a result, we wound up with something much better. My philosophy is that I simply don't accept the fact that 'we can't do it.' Anything is possible, and it's up to *you* to figure it out. After that, we might reject it, but in the meantime, let's try it. People like working in this optimistic environment."

317

Selecting People

"When I think back about the people whom I have hired, there have been a lot of different types. Still, I look for certain characteristics for specific jobs. One area I have mishired in for years is the operations and financial area. I messed that up so many times, probably because it's an area in which I have an inadequate background, so I cannot recognize the right traits. In looking for marketing people or technical people, I probably look for a little bit of me. I believe in very long interviews, several of them over a period of time and, if possible, one over a meal. I need people who will be able to deal with me, since I tend to intimidate some because of my high-energy level.

"In high-growth situations, when a company is just starting, there may be as many as 20 people reporting directly to me. In that situation I have to be involved in details—though I have reached the point that that is not what I want to do. When a company matures, I want a small executive committee and a strong vice president who can supervise the day-to-day operations so that I can do future planning.

"When I hire a financial person, since this is not my strength, I select three people outside of my company in whom I have great trust and ask them to make all of the hiring decision except for the essential part as to how and whether I can relate to the individual. I recognize that I am totally incompetent to judge the skills and technical competence of these people, so I call on others to do that, and I look for the people skills."

Working in a Mature Company

In 1984, Isaacson sold Future Computing Incorporated to McGraw-Hill. A number of other companies had approached her, but she chose McGraw-Hill because of its management expertise and its willingness to allow her to retain considerable control.

"I have become absolutely, academically fascinated with the different phases of an entrepreneur's life. There is the particular time when the entrepreneur decides to sell, the process of making that decision, the deal itself and then the inevitable adjustment process. I was looking forward to staying with McGraw-Hill after they acquired Future, and in fact I took on as a mission to learn how to become a good corporate player; I had not learned that at EDS and considered it something of a failing on my part. I was always impatient with companies that did not think as big as I. I was and am impatient, never having held a job more than two and half years before I started Future Computing. Every company I left would give me glowing references, but they would add that I was very impatient. I cannot move a big company to do things as I would like to have them done or as fast. But at McGraw-Hill I felt I was ready to be a corporate player. It was the right kind of company, consisting of about 50 different businesses, many of them around $10 million, each with its own identity and each with its own president or general manager. It was a structure I thought I could go into and still maintain a lot of independence. But I just did not fit. Shortly before I decided to leave McGraw-Hill, I was offered a significantly expanded responsibility there that would have had three other companies reporting to me, with the whole business area totaling about $60 million. But I had already concluded that the box was too small. I was boxed in, with a limited ability to make independent decisions, even though McGraw-Hill was very good about trying to accommodate me.

"Actually, the box was getting too small for me even before I sold Future, for I had recognized that by then I had 140 people and needed a very strong management team. Obviously, if you're going to have a strong management team, you have to let them manage the company, and I wasn't sure how I felt about that. In addition, Future had reached the stage where it was not being recreated on a daily basis. In the early days I had launched a new business area almost every day, it seems, identifying a new opportunity, putting up the blank paper on the wall and letting my people fill it in. But with 140 people and $8 million of sales, you don't do blank paper every day. Instead, you walk in and review last month's financials, make a few adjustments here and there, work on next year's strategic plan, and that's it. For me, that was a part-time job. In the early days, I had ten clients with whom I was working, helping them create businesses. So I got into the habit of creating businesses and became addicted to it.

"If something wasn't working, I changed it. Creating a business from scratch, which really means putting all the people in the right places and thinking about the work chart of the day, visualizing products, making them work—that is the most creative thing I can imagine and not unlike what an artist does in creating music or a painting. The whole thing comes out of your own head. It's the ultimate ego trip, building something in your own mold that lives and breathes, an organism that serves a market. You get so hooked on the creative process of doing this exactly your way that later, when the company gets bigger and you can't be that creative anymore, it's a totally different experience. I really admire the person who needs to come in then and fine-tune it, and God, does it ever need fine tuning by then! But that's not what I'm good at.

"I have started three businesses: the Micro Store, the tape business at EDS, and Future Computing. Now I'm starting two more (Intellisys and Isaacson, Inc.). What really got into my blood was not just the start-up bug; it was also my experience around 1980 when many large companies were just entering the personal-computer industry. Of those companies, there's not a single one with which I was not personally and deeply involved in helping them to create *their* businesses. They called me in because I was supposedly the expert on the market they wanted to enter, but what they liked about me was that I always wound up helping them to create their businesses. At Sears, for example, I made several presentations at high levels about how I thought Sears could enter computer retailing. They decided to do it and retained me to work on their business plan, and I literally wrote it. When I walk into their business systems centers today and see that they're still following my plan, I get an incredible feeling. Then I helped them select the people who went into their organization and dealt with their potential suppliers on their behalf. I have had a hand in helping to create 30, 40 or more businesses other than my own, working with software publishers, computer manufacturers, even with an encyclopedia company on the concept of selling computers door-to-door.

"As you see, I can't even talk about mature businesses; I keep going back to concepts and start-ups. I am still vice chairman of Future but quite inactive there. The title symbolizes that my leaving McGraw-Hill was friendly and constructive."

Starting the New Businesses

"At Intellisys I have made a conscious decision that this company is going to do only one thing: it's going to be a software company. And I recognize that I do not enjoy doing just one thing, even though this company is going to grow rapidly and will require ten times the energy of a full-time president. Intellisys needs someone who wants to be obsessed by building that kind of business, and since I've made the decision that I don't want to do this personally, the first thing I did was to find an outstanding man whom I have known ten years to run it and run it well.

"Meanwhile, I have started Isaacson, Inc., and I'm personally going to run that business. I have hired a perfect assistant and need now to find the ideal financial person to help in this mergers and acquisition business. The assistant I've hired is someone I can count on; I can send him to clients to represent me. Even today, there are many people who become a little nervous about dealing with a woman, so I need to back myself up with a really straight, three-piece-suit kind of guy, so the potential client will say, 'Well, if he works for her, then she's probably O.K.'

"When you have your own business, you know that people are choosing to do business with you. It's not like working for a big company where you always might wonder about that. At Future about 70 percent of the managers are women, very strong and well-credentialed, MBA after MBA, aggressive, bright, and young. I never particularly thought about hiring women, having mostly worked with men. What perhaps happened was they saw me as a role model and some of the other great women as role models. Also, I mishired a couple of men who were not comfortable working around that many bright, talented, aggressive women. Both of the mishired men were terrific guys who didn't understand that they had that problem, but that's why they left the company. We just made them too nervous.

"I have always had an absolutely obsessive focus, obsessive to the point that people have wanted to cage me up at times. When I start doing something, that's what I do, shutting out everything else. When I was working on my Ph.D., I think I forgot my kids' names. This absolutely obsessive focus is not necessarily a positive trait. It drives some people away, but the ones who stay are ones that I may rehire at my next company, those who like the environment I create. Being a compulsive workaholic, I have to be very conscious about not demanding that kind of behavior from other people. I am sensitive to the fact that some people like balance in their lives—even though I guess I don't—and any successful person must understand and be sensitive to the values of those who work for them.

"Within ten years, Intellisys should be more than a $100 million company, and I'd like to see Isaacson, Inc. do about $5 million a year, with almost all of that being profit. It's an interesting kind of business, one in which we may do only three deals per year, but they could be really big ones.

"The mergers and acquisitions that we hope to handle should make sense from a marketing synergy viewpoint. I believe that's more important than common technology or backroom issues. Besides this, the compatibility of the companies' cultures is an absolutely critical point.

"I have learned enough about myself to know that I am a great team player so long as I am running the team. I have had a lot of careers, in addition to starting five companies, and I may have a lot more of them. As I say, I usually do three things at a time, and at this point I have a lot of years left—maybe 20 —so I'm about half way to wherever it is I'm going. Right now, however, I'm totally obsessed with these two companies I'm starting, and I plan to stick with them. Yet every once in a while a new idea pops into my head. An entrepreneur can't help but be an opportunity-seeking mechanism."

Ichiro Hattori

President
Seiko Instruments & Electronics Ltd.

President
Seiko Epson Corporation

*I*n 1969 his company developed the first
quartz watch and swiftly took over leadership of the world's watch industry—but
even at the peak of success he recognized
that market saturation could threaten Seiko
with disaster. His answer was diversification. Now Seiko watches have been joined
by scientific instruments, robots, semiconductors, electronic components, computers,
computer graphics systems, printers,
shavers, and spectacle lenses. Diversification
was not an easy task, he says, for the complicated Japanese corporate decision-making
process depends on achieving a company-
wide consensus on major changes.

Now he is moving to internationalize
Seiko's operations—including building a
plant near Portland, Oregon. Back home,
this grandson of the company's founder is
planning to bring more women into management and working to develop an effective management team by basing promotions
on ability rather than seniority. Very aware
of U.S. corporate culture, he believes that to
remain competitive, Japanese companies
must adopt some of U.S. management's flexibility in selecting and assigning the best
people to important jobs.

Career Information:

1954   Joined Seiko Instruments & Electronics Ltd.

1967   Became senior managing director

1979   Became president

1980   Became president of Seiko Epson Corporation

Other Affiliations (partial list):

- Member, Board of Directors, Japan Center for International Exchange
- Director, Association for Promotion of International Cooperation
- Vice Chairman, Japan Clock & Watch Association
- Member, Japan Federation of Employers' Associations
- Member, Pacific Advisory Council, United Technologies Corporation
- Member, International Advisory Board, Security Pacific National Bank
- Member, Board of Trustees, Aspen Institute for Humanistic Studies

Educational Information:

- Tokyo University, B.A., Law, 1954
- University of Zurich, Economics, 1956
- Yale University, M.A., Economics, 1957

Personal Information:

- Born February 27, 1932, Tokyo, Japan

Ichiro Hattori

"*I*n American society, it is taken for granted that one should express himself in order to be appreciated. In Japan, however, outspokenness is sometimes not considered a virtue, and vocal communication, therefore, is somewhat limited. For this reason a manager in Japan must work harder to understand people, to hear even what they *do not* say—to understand what a person wants, even though that person does not say what he wants.

"This is even more true of the chief executive officer, for the chief executive's position in any country is somewhat intimidating, and hence he may not get to hear what he needs to hear."

As the chief executive of two companies whose growth and prosperity are directly dependent on their ability to apply rapidly changing technologies to swiftly shifting consumer and industrial markets, Ichiro Hattori draws heavily on his communications skills—especially his ability to listen.

"At Seiko we believe that our top managers enjoy very effective communications, so we need no additional emphasis at this level. But at the factory management level, good listening is very much stressed. As you know, listening to employees is a traditional aspect of Japanese management. It is mentioned in most of the books that Americans read about Japanese management."

The world-famous Seiko watches, among other precision products, are made by Seiko Instruments & Electronics Ltd. and by Seiko Epson Corporation, both headed by Ichiro Hattori. Seiko clocks are manufactured by a related but independent company, Seikosha Co., Ltd.; both the watches and the clocks are marketed throughout the world exclusively by Hattori Seiko Co., Ltd., though many other products of the three manufacturing companies are marketed directly by them. These four central companies make up what is know as the Seiko group.

Seiko I & E, which over the past 15 years has become the world's leading watchmaker, also operates seven Japanese-based subsidiaries and four overseas subsidiaries in Hong Kong, Singapore, West Germany, and the United States.

To achieve its pre-eminent position, Seiko Instruments & Electronics pioneered in both electronic and mechanical miniaturization. In 1969 it produced the world's first commercial quartz wristwatch and in 1984 the first truly capable wrist computer. Beyond such miniaturized products, which include highly advanced electronic components, the company produces and markets sophisticated computer graphics systems, scientific instruments, machine tools, and robots—both for scientific analysis and for factory automation.

Seiko Epson Corporation, formed in 1985 through the merger of two former Seiko companies, Suwa Seikosha Co., Ltd. and Epson Corporation, develops, manufactures, and markets personal computers, printers, semiconductors, portable television sets, shavers, synthetic jewels, and numerous other products.

It is through Ichiro Hattori and other members of the Hattori family that Seiko has achieved its remarkable worldwide success.

"We know something about the business of watchmaking, for we have been at it for a very long time. The history of our company goes back almost 100 years. In those early years we made only clocks; we have been making watches for perhaps 60 years.

"Until about 1970 our chief objective was to become equal or superior to the Swiss watch industry in terms of quality and reputation. We worked very hard toward this end, but it was not really possible for us to achieve this goal until about 15 years ago, when we pioneered in the invention of the electronic watch. Virtually all watches today are quartz watches, since they keep far better time than do mechanical, spring-wound watches."

Winning Over Switzerland

"Our company reached its success in a somewhat different way from other Japanese companies, particularly those whose

products are based upon mechanical technology, for example, cameras or sewing machines. The Japanese camera industry, pioneered by such companies as Canon and Nikon, became the world's leader around 20 years ago. Their products—and later, others—became more famous than products of German camera manufacturers. They became world leaders through rationalization of manufacturing. As a result of very hard competition within the camera industry, they learned how to make cameras better than German makers could. The approach they used, however, was not available—not even possible—for the Japanese watch industry. As hard as we tried, and we thought we tried very hard, we were never able to achieve a reputation exceeding that of the Swiss or to become better known than they in the world market, until the invention of the quartz watch. This was a revolutionary event.

"I think there are at least two reasons for this difference. First, at that time the Japanese camera industry was already far more competitive in the worldwide market, so perhaps it had more incentive to put in major efforts, major energies, to improve its product. Unlike the Japanese camera industry, our watch industry was perhaps a little more complacent. Second, during the postwar era the Swiss watch industry enjoyed a much stronger worldwide position in the market than did the German camera industry. In any case, the reason that Seiko was able to become the world leader in watches was the invention of the electronic watch.

"Just as important, however, was the fact that Japanese watch companies had the foresight to believe that the quartz watch would be the watch of the future. European and American watchmakers did not recognize this and ignored the importance of its future possibilities."

Complacency, Hattori says, has always been somewhat intrinsic to the watch industry. The Swiss watch industry was a monopoly until about 20 years ago, and Americans were importing large numbers of watches from Switzerland.

"This, by the way, is the reason that the watch market has not become an issue in the trade discussions between the United States and Japan. Seiko took the market from Swiss manufacturers, not from the United States."

The scientific principle underlying the electronic watch is certainly not new, having been understood for at least 40 years. For many years quartz clocks had been used in military applications and in radio broadcasting. Radio stations used such clocks, as did others who had a need for highly accurate timekeeping. Prior to the advances made by Seiko, however, these instruments were bulky. With the development of semiconductors and other forms of miniaturization, the idea of reducing the size of a quartz clock to that of a watch became a realistic goal.

"To accomplish this required several inventions. If a time-piece were to be reduced to the size of a wristwatch, its electric motor would have to be miniaturized. The battery would need miniaturization, and so would the circuits. Miniaturizing the circuits turned out to be the most difficult step. The early quartz clocks had used vacuum tubes, but even with the invention of the transistor, there were still serious problems: the transistor, small as it was, was still too large for a wristwatch."

No Free Ride

"Here is an interesting story: when the semiconductor industry was being born in Silicon Valley, there were many small companies. One of them was attempting to develop a semiconductor circuit for a watch application. The inventor approached both American and Swiss watch companies, but no one would bother with him. Finally, he contacted some Japanese watch companies, and the Japanese agreed to invest some money toward the development of this circuitry. This bit of history reveals how the American and European watch companies ignored the possible invention of an electronic watch. Only the Japanese companies had that dream.

"I often tell this story to Americans who complain about the so-called 'free-ride' of Japanese companies. From our point of view, this was one time when there was no 'free ride.' The Europeans and Americans simply *missed* that ride! After all, the invention had been offered to the Americans and to the Europeans before it was brought to our attention in Japan, but no one in either place would take him up on his offer."

> Seiko provided the first development contract for that American invention, and it may have been its most profitable investment. It was certainly one of the most profitable in recent technological history.
>
> Eventually semiconductor companies in the United States tried to break into the electronic watch market. Millions of dollars were spent by engineering-oriented companies such as Texas Instruments. In this case, however, they lacked knowledge of the consumer market as well as the years of experience that Seiko had in creating watches of beautiful style.

"Watches are often purchased as gifts. They therefore need to be beautiful, fashionably designed; they need to have the appearance of other precious gifts."

> Seiko is a highly market-oriented company, a tradition stemming from its early roots. Its first company (K. Hattori & Co., Ltd., now known as Hattori Seiko Co., Ltd.), founded over 100 years ago, was a "store"—an importer of watches and clocks from Europe for distribution in Japan. Later, it created a production arm, organizing companies to manufacture clocks and then watches.
>
> The original company, however, has retained its marketing mission. Much later, the manufacturing companies began to diversify into other kinds of electronic products. Today, watches and clocks represent less than half of Seiko's business. For example, about one-third of the sales volume of Seiko Epson Corporation comes from personal computers and related products. The original company, renamed Hattori Seiko, still survives, providing a strong marketing influence to the entire Seiko group. The two United States subsidiaries, Hattori Corporation of America (which concentrates on watches and clocks) and Epson America Inc. (with emphasis on personal computers) together yield nearly $1 billion in annual sales.
>
> Ichiro Hattori is a grandson of the company's founder, and two of his cousins are currently active in the management of the Hattori Seiko Company. Ichiro Hattori joined Seiko I & E in 1954, shortly after which he undertook graduate studies briefly in Europe and then at Yale University, where he earned a Master's degree in economics. Returning to Seiko, he worked primarily in corporate planning, though he also gained hands-on experience in negotiating with customers and in the export field.

"Since 1970 I have been primarily involved in pushing the company into diversification and, to some extent, in trying to internationalize the company by looking for appropriate locations for factories overseas. We now have plants in Southeast Asia—Singapore, Malaysia, Hong Kong—and are presently building a factory near Portland, Oregon."

> Some overseas companies, for example, Michelin Tire Company, believe it important to transplant, at least to some degree, their companies' cultures into their American operations. Hattori, however, has other priorities.

"A high level of quality consciousness is, of course, essential for us, but that is nothing new. One has to have this if one is to manufacture watches and clocks and the other kinds of products we make; that goes without saying. But beyond that, I really do not feel that we need to worry too much about explaining the Seiko culture or trying to transplant it. I think it is more important, in going to the United States, simply to develop a very good operation there, a good organization—American-style. Of course there are good companies and bad companies in America, just as there are in Japan. We will work very hard to build a good organization there."

> The Seiko companies have always been managed in a shared mode by various members of the Hattori family. For some years Ichiro Hattori's father was president of Hattori Seiko, sharing the management responsibility with a brother. After the death of that brother (Ichiro Hattori's uncle) and the subsequent death of his father, a cousin became president of Hattori Seiko, and from that time on they and another cousin have shared the leadership responsibility. Ichiro Hattori became president of Seiko I & E about ten years ago, having been a member of its board of directors before that, while his father was still alive. Today the Seiko group of companies is managed in shared fashion by the third generation of Hattoris. This is not an unusual arrangement in Japan; in fact, Hattori describes it as "quite normal."

"We see a lot of each other, talk to each other, spend time communicating, meet together at board meetings, and so on. But then when we take vacations, we go our separate ways!"

Strategic Planning

"In long-range planning, it should be quite apparent as to which business sector is a growing area and which is not. For example, electronics is growing; steel is not. This was obvious to us, so the question became, what should we do? The watchmaking industry had long been dependent upon precision mechanical technologies—and still is. That particular kind of technology is essential for watchmaking, but it does not lend itself to diversification into other kinds of products. The Swiss watch industry had, as we had, strong expertise in precision mechanical technology, but they were unable to—and perhaps did not venture to—diversify into other fields. This factor may account for the former monopolistic or oligopolistic nature of the Swiss watch industry. Possessing all of that specialized technological expertise, the Swiss were simply unable to transfer it, to use it elsewhere; but at the same time, they had such strength in it that others found it very difficult to compete with them. The technological wall was very high.

"That meant that there was a large gap between the technology of our watch industry and that of other industries. We saw that the future was in electronics, but we did not have that capability. So we had to start doing something about this, by taking licenses and by other means. We acquired licenses in drafting equipment and computer controls. We developed electronic plotters, equipment for CAD-CAM, although it was not called by that name then. In another of our companies we developed a small electro-mechanical printer which later became the printer for the Epson computer. From then on we started developing a business in that general electronic control and computation area.

"But on the traditional side—our business in watches and clocks—it took us a very long time to convince our employees of the need for diversification. At that time the electronics business was booming, and we had the advantage of the then-recent invention of the quartz watch.

"Because we pioneered with the quartz watch, we suddenly became the world leader in watch technology. Our sales of watches were growing very rapidly, as we began to take over the market share held by the Swiss watch industry. Still, even then it was obvious to us that the market would become saturated at some point. If we were to do nothing about this—if we could not develop new technologies for new products—we would sooner or later arrive at a dead end. If the watch market did not keep expanding—and we recognized that, like everything else, it had a limit—and if we wanted to do something else, we did not have the technologies to move forward. Had we been in America, we might have merged with another company, but it does not work that way here. We could not acquire another company; we therefore had to acquire new technological capabilities, and we had to do this considerably before the watch market reached saturation.

"Our employees, however, thought traditionally and believed that the watch market was forever. I too believe there will always be a market for watches. Still, you have to stay competitive, especially cost-competitive, with watches that come from other places—Hong Kong and Singapore, for example. To do this requires that you rationalize your manufacturing process. It means that you will have to lay people off, unless the volume grows very rapidly, which of course we knew it would not do. This, then, was the message that we had to get our employees to understand."

Communicating

"There is certainly no magic in trying to get across a message like this. You have to talk about it all the time, write about it in many memos, publish persuasive articles in company periodicals. Because we realized this about ten years before the watch market became heavily saturated, we had time to take action. On the other hand, it required a lot of time.

"Initially we moved slowly, but in about five years we were able to get something going. In Japan it takes more time to do something like this than it does in the United States, for in the U.S. you can hire lots of top-level employees, technological experts, release people if necessary, and even buy companies. The content of a company can be changed much more quickly there than here.

"Also it is not appropriate in Japan to lay people off unless a company is actually confronted by a real crisis. You cannot pre-empt disaster by doing this. The disaster has to arrive first, then this may become appropriate and necessary—but only after a substantial loss for two years in a row, for example."

In communicating the serious need to revitalize Seiko by diversification, Hattori naturally began with top management. Once they were convinced, he and his team began to communicate carefully with larger groups of employees. A traditional approach in

Japan is the format of a symposium on the future of the company, held once or twice a year. At Seiko, these symposia are held for groups of as many as 350 managers. He recalled three successive symposia, one on total quality control, one on long-range planning, and the third on the annual objectives of the company.

In describing the complexity of the Japanese corporate decision-making process, Hattori has pointed to the key role that communication plays in gaining consensus. For example, in the normal course of events, when top management considers a proposal from lower level managers, it avoids making a unilateral decision, but instead moves first to ensure the development of a company-wide consensus. Top management's suggestions about the proposal are passed down to the initiating department, which is then requested to prepare plans for implementation. First, however, these plans must be reviewed through meetings at various levels throughout the company. When consensus is reached, a decision follows. Although to Americans this process may seem slow or cumbersome, a distinct advantage comes during the implementation phase; for by then the employees who will be involved in the project have been fully informed and in fact have "bought into it."

The decision process is perhaps even more complicated when major changes in products or company activities are involved. In a recent discussion of product diversification, Hattori wrote:

Once corporate employees agree to the need for new projects, the decision making begins with operational goals and plans. In the case where plans entirely new to an enterprise and its employees must be implemented, such as for multidivisional operations, there is a need to enlighten the corporate employees' community on the general strategy. The objective here lies in making every employee aware of the changes in the environment that have created the situation in which an enterprise is compelled to alter its course of operations. Without informing company employees about the strategic view, an enterprise cannot hope to obtain the cooperation of its subordinate organizations or expect it to formulate operational plans based on correct perspectives. Often the subordinate organization's staff is too busy with its routine assignments to grasp the actual situation in which the company is placed.[1]

"I have been asked whether I believe books on Japanese management for the American and other markets are oversimplified, and of course they are and need to be, since when one is being introduced to a new subject, that subject must be simplified. Later the finer points can be learned. But certainly careful listening is an essential part of Japanese management."

Ichiro Hattori's Contributions

Hattori insists that he possesses no particular management style that is unique or distinctive from that of his cousins or colleagues in other industries. Style, he says, is not nearly so important in management as content and emphasis. His management emphasis over many years has been a steady push toward product diversification and internationalization. In addition, he has worked hard to develop an effective management team and a pool of potential senior managers.

"In Japan, it is not just the quality of the top people but rather, and *especially,* the quality of the higher-level middle managers that is key to a company's success. In the case of Seiko this would comprise about 200 managers. A special 1 percent, he says, are the key to success.

"At Seiko we emphasize training, but this is traditional among established Japanese companies. We do nothing unique or particularly unusual. Perhaps some of the newer companies, like Honda, may operate in a somewhat different way, but we follow the training tradition common to the older companies.

"Besides diversification and internationalization, I am emphasizing one additional consideration—an effort to assure that we are promoting the right people. It is so easy to fall back on the old custom of promoting people based upon their seniority. But if you continue to do this, you may lose out on manage-

[1]Ichiro Hattori, "Product Diversification," *The Management Challenge: Japanese Views*, Edited by Lester Thurow, p. 119.

335

ment potential. Therefore I am now concentrating on making sure that we develop a system to get the right people promoted.

"This whole aspect of management is much more difficult in Japan than in the United States, for in the U.S. you can try out a new man, and if he does not prove out, you can then just reassign—or even dismiss—him. But in Japan, where we follow a very stable employment practice, if we promote someone who turns out to be unsuccessful, theoretically we can replace him with a new person, by demotion or dismissal. But in reality this is very awkward, almost impossible. So my first step is to try to create an atmosphere in which it is possible to replace a person with someone else, when conditions require it. That is not an easy thing to learn how to do, but if we do not do it, then we will forever risk losing the kind of talent and expertise that comes from the ability to freely and intelligently select and assign the right people—the best people—to important jobs. In the end, I believe that this aspect of Japanese management—and how it is handled—will affect the competitiveness of Japanese companies."

Seiko has a formal performance appraisal system; hence there is an opportunity twice each year to determine whether a man or a woman is promotable. If an employee gets an outstanding appraisal on three successive occasions, then special attention is paid to that person. Top managers have the responsibility for reviewing those who are promotable and for selecting and appointing managers. This performance appraisal system is helping Seiko to build up a pool of potential management talent.

"Women have traditionally not occupied positions of significant management responsibility in Japan. Within the technical area, we do have a number of outstanding women at the group-leader level. We still have no women at the upper middle-management level, and we have to encourage this. However, since we do not have a well developed pool or base from which to draw, it is still quite difficult to find outstanding women who can take on significant managerial roles. We need to broaden our search, possibly even to go beyond the pool available within our own organization. There are, after all, a number of very capable women who hold managerial jobs in the government bureaucracy, and that would be one good place to look. We have not done this before, but I think that it can be done."

Advice to Young People

"If I were talking to young people at a college or university, I would tell them that they should become an expert in some specific field before trying to become a general manager. I don't think that you can succeed by just being a generalist; the important thing is to become an expert in some area—*any* area which is within the company's management domain. Secondly, I would say that one should learn to communicate with people at a very deep level, not just superficially. One has to learn how to communicate and to really understand other people in order to become a good manager.

"This is even more true in Japan than in the United States. In America, because of the many differences among the various ethnic groups and the necessity to understand each other, the expression of one's point of view is very much valued. Therefore, the ability to understand other people is not so difficult, since people there are outspoken. Here, they are more reticent to speak up.

"It is even more important for a chief executive officer to know what people are thinking. He will not learn this automatically. Therefore, part of my job as president is to draw people out, to hear what I need to hear. So one bit of advice I would give to a young person is to learn to understand people very well if he or she wants to be successful in management."

Anthony J.F. O'Reilly

President and Chief Executive Officer
H. J. Heinz Company

*E*arly on he was an Irish rugby star, then a Dublin solicitor. Now he is CEO of a $4 billion U.S. corporation. He made this remarkable transition by moving in 1969 from the leadership of the Irish Dairy Board and the Irish Sugar Company to become managing director of H. J. Heinz, Great Britain. Ten years later, he was named CEO of the whole company. However, he remains an Irish entrepreneur—as chairman of Ireland's largest newspaper business and of a Dublin-based oil and gas exploration group. As O'Reilly says, he is blessed with a "very high energy level."

As Heinz CEO, one of his strong suits is spotting demographic trends and positioning the company to capitalize on them. A dramatic example is Heinz's acquisition of Weight Watchers, based on demographic studies showing that the calorie-counting trend would grow into a huge potential market. He calls the decision a "home run"—a characterization supported by the fact that Weight Watchers' low-calorie products now provide over 12 percent of the company's total profit. At the same time, realizing that Heinz could no longer enjoy a "free ride" on inflationary trends, he generated a "Low-Cost Operator" culture that sharply reduced costs and added to profit margins. He sees continued growth ahead, based on his determination not just to be prepared for the future but to shape that future.

339

Career Information:

1958 Joined Weston Evans (England) as industrial consultant
1960 Joined Suttons Ltd. (Cork, Ireland) as personal assistant
      to chairman
1961 Became director, Robert McCowen & Sons (Tralee)
1962 Became general manager, An Bord Bainne/Irish Dairy Board
1965 Became director, Agricultural Credit Corporation Ltd.
1965 Became director, Nitrigin Eireann Teo
1966 Became managing director, Comhlucht Suicre Eireann Teo
      and Erin Foods Ltd.
1967 Became joint managing director, Heinz-Erin Ltd.
1968 Became director, Allied Irish Investment Bank Ltd.
1969 Became managing director, H. J. Heinz Co. Ltd., U.K.
1970 Became director, Thyssen-Bornemisza Company (Rotterdam)
1971 Became senior vice president, North American and Pacific,
      H. J. Heinz Company
1972 Became executive vice president and chief operating officer
1973 Became president and chief operating officer
1979 Became president and chief executive officer

Other Affiliations (partial list):

- Partner, Cawley Sheerin Wynne & Co., Solicitors, Dublin
- Chairman, Fitzwilton Ltd., Dublin
- Chairman, Atlantic Resources, Dublin
- Chairman, Independent Newspapers Ltd., Dublin
- Member, Board of Directors, Mobil Corporation
- Member, Board of Directors, Bankers Trust New York Corporation
  and Bankers Trust Company, New York
- Senior Member of Board, The Conference Board
- Chairman, Ireland Fund
- Member, National Committee of the Whitney Museum of
  American Art
- Council Member, Rockefeller University, New York

Educational Information:

- Belvedere College, University College Dublin
- University of Bradford, England, Ph.D. (Agricultural Marketing)
- Wharton Business School Overseas

Personal Information:

- Born July 5, 1936, Dublin, Ireland
- Married, has six children
- Outside interests are tennis and opera. As youth, played rugby for
  Ireland 29 times and British Lions 10 times

340

Anthony J.F. O'Reilly

"I like to analyze a situation very thoroughly before I make my move. As a football player that is one thing I did: I always hung back. While this has surely caused me to miss some opportunities, I have made very few major mistakes. By taking this approach, I think that I have kept the mistake factor at a tolerable level and have made a few touchdowns as well."

Since becoming chief executive officer of H. J. Heinz Company in 1979, Anthony O'Reilly has had to face many more competitors than his football analogy would suggest, as the food industry is characterized by intense across-the-board competition. From his earliest days as CEO, O'Reilly has been making the company more competitive, by acting on a thorough knowledge of demographic and economic trends. Five years into his job and convinced of his ground, he set into motion a major cost reduction program.

"In early 1984 I gave a paper to our assembled management from all over the world entitled "The Party Is Over." The party to which I was referring was the party of inflation, which had long been a benign influence for a great number of companies —particularly those with strong brand identities, which are, in a sense, import-repellent and enjoy a good deal of consumer loyalty. This factor had enabled us to pass along the worst excesses of inflation to the consumer and add our margin thereon. As a result, the 1970s showed very substantial nominal —as opposed to real—earnings growth for the food-company sector, and this was true in particular for the H. J. Heinz Company. While we enjoyed a compound growth of 17 to 18 percent—underwritten by 8 to 10 percent inflation—the underlying unit volume growth was quite low, only 1 to 2 percent.

"In making this presentation, I was drawing to the attention of our management the fact that the Great Underwriter had fled, exorcised by the combined efforts of Mr. Volcker and Mr. Reagan. Since our fortunes have now become very much more dependent upon real growth and true economies, I pointed out that we needed a change in our culture. By 1984 the times were demanding that the company become a low-cost operator. What was needed, therefore, was a thorough examination of the whole culture of Heinz. We needed to understand better how we did things—*everything*. This was particularly true in areas where there were unconscious conspiracies. One such unconscious conspiracy was the one between the outside advertising agency and the brand group, where more had come to seem better. In that very imprecise world of advertising I demanded a lot more for the buck than we were getting. For example, I insisted upon more 15-second commercials, rather than 30-second ones, since our research shows that the former has about 80 percent of the effectiveness of the latter. Because we spend over $300 million a year on media, this is not a trivial matter.

"It had become very clear to me that we were going to have to take a look at de-manning in a very significant way, particularly in the United Kingdom, where Heinz had been a people-intensive business for a great number of years.

"It was extremely important for us to start to recast the nature of the Heinz business for this post-inflationary period, and we came up with a phrase. We called the first year of this effort "The Year of the Operator," demanding that we become the low-cost operator in every sector we were in; and if we could not do this, we would simply get out of that sector. We wanted to be the number one or number two brand as *well* as the low-cost operator, and we went to rather extraordinary lengths to try to find out who was producing what cheaper than we were. In certain cases we found—dismayingly—that we were not the low-cost operator; we discovered in certain parts of the world that we were prosecuting a management style which was generous and affluent, having been grounded in those times when there was real growth—for example, and particularly, in the post-war markets of Europe such as Great

ANTHONY J.F. O'REILLY

Britain and Italy. As the population grew and rationing no longer existed, we enjoyed real volume growth in the food industry. But now that the unit growth had declined, we had to go to "The Year of the Operator," a demanding and challenging new year in which I demanded a full 2 percent improvement in operating costs—in *every* kind of operating costs.

"The meeting at which I reported that the party was over was a multifunctional one. Heinz is a highly decentralized company, so we rarely pull everyone together—people from marketing, distribution, production, operations, research—from all over the world. It was probably the most important meeting that we have ever had. Because of this message and the conviction behind it, we experienced a substantial kick in our profitability, and this has enabled us to do quite a lot of new and exciting things."

343

| O'Reilly had ended that speech in this way:

> We can, as a company, *do more with less*. For the consumers of our goods and services, there will be *more* variety at lower relative costs and thus for all our constituents, our workforce, our management, our consumers and our shareholders there will be increased prosperity in a manner which displays Heinz and the capital system in its most attractive and effective light.

"Among the steps we took was a considerable de-layering of management, pushing decision making further down. After all, why should we need assistant product managers in product areas that have been around for years and where the product life cycle has become a rather gentle curve? In ketchup, for example, one doesn't need to have a high degree of product innovation every year: ketchup is ketchup, and our innovation focuses on packaging developments, such as the astonishingly successful 28-ounce plastic bottle and "lite" ketchup for the calorie-conscious.

"We have during this past year managed to get an extra 1 percent operating margin from what we call the LCO (Low-Cost Operator) drive within the company, even though our margins have been quite tight and volume has been quite slow. Our five-year business plan, which is the central part of our planning process, indicates that by 1991 we should be achieving about 1.8 percent improvement in our operating income. None of these things happen immediately; each has a gestation period of perhaps two to three years. But they do happen. When I was managing director of our British company, we had 10,000 people producing 120 million dozens of units. The British are producing about the same dozenage at the moment, but with many fewer people—only 3,800. In short, we have become much more capital-intensive.

"Most important, our plans now show that we should be able to improve our overall margins from about 12 percent up to nearly 14 percent by the year 1991."

O'Reilly dramatically emphasized that the "easy pickings" of the previous ten years were no longer available to Heinz or to its competitors, and he considers the emphasis on the low-cost operator to be the most important strategic move that the company has made in the past 18 months. Results show that his strategy is paying off.

Need for Strategic Investments

"I had no intention of passing on this increased largess to the marketplace. My view is that if we as a company can grow at 6 to 7 percent above inflation, we will then be doing our job for our shareholders, and that's about the organic rate at which a good company can grow. If we were to move our 12 percent operating margin up to 14 percent, we would then plan to spend the extra 2 percent on what I call the new "two-year-olds"— the best young racehorses that we thought might run well.

"We sometimes call our investment strategy the 'fats and cats strategy.' Weight Watchers is at the core of the fats emphasis, and we have become very interested in the entire pet food industry, which is a dynamic and growing one."

O'Reilly's pet food market strategy is "cats"—rather than "dogs"—because, as he has said:

"The dog may be man's best friend, but happily America is going rapidly to the cats. The result is that cat food, as a percentage of all pet food sales, stands at 36 percent and rising— rising, in fact, ten times as fast as dog food."

"Our strategy is to look at all of the products within those two areas that present opportunities for heavy marketing. We have been investing very heavily, for example, in Weight Watcher desserts, Weight Watcher entrées, new Candlelight dinners—a submarket within Weight Watchers—and in gourmet cat food. The market has been responding very amiably. We are also in dry baby food, a tougher road to travel, but we are working away at it and spending a lot of money there. By plowing that extra 2 percent into the business to stimulate consumer interest, we will be able to improve the vitality of our brands and the ultimate quality of our earnings.

"We count heavily on demographic studies, and through these have concluded that wellness is becoming an increasing concern, particularly among Americans—though we are having enormous success with Weight Watchers in France, Germany, Great Britain, and Switzerland as well. There is a clear demographic trend toward calorie counting and body watching. We think that we will perhaps be able to export to Europe many of the caloric food concepts that are now so successful here in the United States. Of our total profitability this year, over 12 percent will come from Weight Watchers.

"We are looking at other parts of the world as well: we are now in China, with a baby-food plant nearly completed. The government has given us a five-year exclusive for baby food, and even allowing for the limited buying power of the consumer, there are 16 million babies born each year in China, as compared with only 3 million American babies. So we are quite excited about the potential number of little mouths there to feed. We are just going into Korea and have mounted a major campaign in Japan. We are interested in that entire Asian crescent, not for immediate results, since we simply don't know whether some philosophical revolution will take place halfway through our marketing formulations or whether we will find that we can't get our money out because the rules of the game have been changed. Certainly as far as we are concerned, we have been delighted with the way the Chinese have treated us. The whole baby-food project is now under way; we have 60 percent control of it and very aggressive, profit-oriented people working with us on the Chinese side. We managed to mount this whole thing in two years, which is remarkable in a bureaucratic world like China."

Career Changes: A "Random Walk"

At one time O'Reilly visualized a long-term career in the law, having taken a degree in civil law at University College Dublin, then qualifying as a solicitor. He did practice law for a while, worked briefly for the government, and was a management consultant for a short period. But at age 25, an unusual opportunity in agricultural marketing came his way. It was a turning point.

"The Irish government had introduced a new economic program for the development of the agricultural industry. At that time I was in a very good law practice, having done very well academically, winning first place in my final exams, and no doubt would have been in the partnership. But the government was setting up a dairy board, and I was asked to become its first chief executive. I became quite excited about all this, risked my career—but at the time did not know the extent of the risk I was taking. The innocence of youth confers a certain invincibility if you are half right on your actions, since you are not fully aware of the pitfalls; later in life I became, as a businessman, much more cautious and probably less effective in certain areas as a result. But at age 25 I had the intestinal fortitude to risk it all without really knowing what it was I was risking.

"Once I was head of the Dairy Board, its principal shareholders—the government, the farmers, and the cooperative societies—gave me *carte blanche* to help develop the marketing of Irish dairy produce. I launched something—now over a billion dollar enterprise—called Kerrygold, an international brand of butter, cheese, milk powders, and all other sorts of dairy products. It has since become a worldwide brand.

"I spent five years with the Dairy Board as its CEO and later was asked to switch over from that to the Irish Sugar Company, the largest agribusiness owned directly by the government. I was reluctant to do that, since I was very happy in the dairy field, a very international industry with a lot of movement, a great deal of travel and good will, and great congeniality. However, reluctant as I was, I decided to make the change and became managing director of the Irish Sugar Company. It had an extraordinary affiliate, called Erin Foods, which somehow managed to lose over two million pounds on sales of less than two million pounds, which seemed to be an accomplishment worthy of inclusion in Ripley's 'Believe it or Not.'

"The first few weeks I was at Erin, we actually had negative sales—which I thought a remarkable achievement; in other words, more was coming back from the previous year than was going out in the current one. Quickly I realized that this was a complete mess and looked around for an associate company for Erin. After talking with 19 different companies in Britain, including the H. J. Heinz Company, always very strong in Great Britain, I formed a joint venture with them in 1967 called Heinz-Erin. One year later I was offered the position of managing director of H. J. Heinz, Great Britain—the jewel in its crown, which at that stage comprised nearly 50 percent of Heinz's total worldwide profits.''

O'Reilly took on the job of managing director of H. J. Heinz Co., Ltd., U.K., in May of 1969.

''After being managing director of Heinz in Great Britain for two and one-half years, I was asked, in 1971, to come to America as a senior vice president and in the following year was made chief operating officer, then president in 1973; I have been chief executive since 1979.

''I had the good fortune to work with Burt Gookin, a man who left an indelible stamp on the H. J. Heinz Company by effecting a major cultural change. A tough accountant by background, he successfully exorcised feudalism from the company. Such feudalism is a factor in the evolution of all family businesses, and to say this is not to make any criticism but simply to state the reality. Gookin professionalized the company by bringing in outside people, changing the structure of planning, and introducing a very sound system of compensation, thereby legitimating the philosophy of high reward for high risk.

''You do not get very much money for coming to work at Heinz, but you can earn a lot if you produce results. My total compensation, which is quite large, is dependent upon results, which are very strictly calibrated by the Compensation Committee and by the Board of Management, and the same is true for all of the principal officers of the company.

''My chief contribution has been in marketing and margin awareness, since Burt was basically not a marketing man. What I have been trying to do is to get those margins up and to spend at least half of the increased margin back against the consumer. The arithmetic is very simple. Having taken the gross margin, which is where you always have to start, from 30 percent of net sales to 38.5 percent, we have spent half of that 8.5 percent increase back against the consumer. Our marketing expenditure was less than 3 percent of sales in 1975 and almost 8 percent of sales in 1985.''

Looking Back: Lessons from Kerrygold

"The Dairy Board and Kerrygold had been a tremendously interesting experience for me. Fundamentally, I had pooled together 110,000 farmers, with perhaps five dependents each, so their families represented about 600,000 people in a country of 3 million souls. Being the principal executive and spokesman for this group, I told them that we were going to confront the international consumer and we would do it through the agency of this brand, Kerrygold. We would try to secure a premium for the brand that would exceed the cost of its creation, hence improving the net return to the farmers.

"I will always remember the head of quality control at one of our major cooperatives who was not in favor of our branding experiment. He said to me, 'Young man, you are bringing the Irish farmer face-to-face with the British housewife, and they are patently unsuited to one another.' Despite his and others' skepticism, we made a great success of Kerrygold; and, of course, there was something very *machismo* in having an Irish brand all over the world. It was very exciting to beat the Danes and the Dutch and the New Zealanders and Australians for the affections of the British housewife, and though we did get a premium, there were enormous costs involved."

> Later, while O'Reilly was at Heinz in the U.K., his intense curiosity and apparent need to understand the measure of his earlier success at the Dairy Board led him to take an unusual step.

"I had always wondered whether and to what precise extent it was true that the farmer's lot had been improved economically by the Kerrygold brand. So in 1970, when I went to

Britain, I gave a number of lectures about this, and the Kerry-gold brand became a kind of classic case study in marketing. Though I had no previous brand-marketing experience in 1962, when I launched Kerrygold, I had had the right sort of agency in Benton & Bowles, who helped us to apply straightforward, uncomplicated Procter & Gamble marketing tactics to butter, cheese, and all the other products, and the market had responded. In contrast, most agricultural marketing boards were quite deficient in marketing. Though there were Dutch, Danish, and Australian marketing boards, they were essentially subsidy-control mechanisms, organizations for the structuring of farming and the allocation of quotas and subsidies within their particular countries. After having talked so much about this, I was persuaded by some professors of the University of Bradford, which had a very good agricultural marketing school, to set down the story of Kerrygold and to analyze rigorously whether it had really been the success that I thought it had been. On and off over a period of nine years I wrote my Ph.D. dissertation and agonized over what it revealed, finally and sadly coming to the conclusion that robbing the public purse was a substantially more rapid way for the farmers to enrich themselves than by using good, rigorous marketing practices. Although we had added perhaps 2 or 3 percent to their incremental income (in real terms per annum over the ten-year period from the beginning of Kerrygold to the time I began my inquiry), the fact was that most of the improvement came by plundering the public purse, either through the EEC mechanism of CAP (Common Agricultural Policy) or through the domestic leverage of their political power—600,000 out of 3 million souls. In sum, the basic incremental increase of their wealth had come from that political leverage and from government subsidy rather than from sophisticated marketing practices.

"The result of this was that I got my Ph.D. and unhorsed myself in the process. It had been very exciting, very absorbing to have had this great impression of my having greatly enriched the Irish farmer over this period of time, only to find at the end of it all that I had only modestly improved his net worth and to have to admit that plunder and political privilege were the real paths to fame and fortune for the farmer in that period.

Now with the CAP diminishing in political power, it is possible that marketing will again become the engine of growth as it always should have been.

"Yet Kerrygold had been a wonderful period of my life. My wife is an Australian; we were having babies and loved traveling around the countries to meet the farmers, going to dances, and so on. One farm leader, John Feely, said to me, 'Don't let me ever hear you use the word productivity to farmers again. The important thing is the *price per gallon.*'

"Looking back on my career, it became clear to me that I had taken a much greater risk than I had anticipated at the time. It was a great challenge to me. But from then on, my career became a kind of random walk. I have always been a believer in the concept of doing the job you are doing as well as you can do it and not to worry about the next job. It is amazing what will follow; the consequences of good performance are incalculable but generally productive. I never sought the job with Heinz nor asked for a job from anyone. The only job I ever really wanted was the one at the Dairy Board, and I let my name go forward for that. I keep telling my children, 'Just do what you are doing, live up to your ability, and the rest will take care of itself.'"

The Irish Entrepreneur

O'Reilly is an unusual, perhaps unique, CEO of a large American corporation in that he operates successfully both as corporate CEO and as independent entrepreneur.

"When I agreed to come to America, my new job at Heinz was both a challenge and a loss, because I was leaving Ireland, for which I have deep affection. I believe that we are all a prisoner of our roots, and I certainly admit to this. In leaving Ireland I made a number of investments, some of which have proven to be very fruitful. As a result, I have probably built up an estate outside Heinz larger than the one I have within it. Dealing with this became a challenge. While it makes me feel independent, it also frays the nerves and reduces the life span, I am sure, through all the shuffling back and forth across the

Atlantic. And there are moments of crisis, too. I have the controlling share in the largest newspaper publishing business in Ireland—a $100 million business of which I own about 35 percent. It has a market capitalization of about $75 million and is a very important piece of my Irish investment program. I also control an investment company in Ireland and am chairman of what I hope will prove to be Ireland's first small-to-medium-size oil company. Recently we found oil off the coast of Waterford; we flowed about 10,000 barrels two years ago but have had a couple of dry wells since and a bit of decline in public confidence. But we are back again with a well we have drilled out with Chevron, BP, British Hydrocarbons, Union Oil, and another Irish oil company, and there has been a further discovery, moving approximately 2,000 barrels per day of quality crude.

"As a result of what I have experienced in this arena, I am able to look at myself as wearing two hats, an entrepreneur in Ireland and a professional manager of a large public corporation in America. I observe that I am more risk-averse in Heinz than I am with my own money—an interesting self-revelation. I suppose that I feel I have a right to lose my own money, but within me there lurks a vestige of my lawyer's sense of the fiduciary. I feel that I am more of a trustee as manager of Heinz's assets, and of course, Heinz is historically a conservatively managed company. One simply does not have to take enormous risks to achieve a level of acceptable prosperity at Heinz that one might have to put into other business ventures. In contrast, I had to take a number of real investment risks in order to get away from the power of the trade unions in controlling prosperity in the newspaper industry in Ireland—for example, the company had to establish an international presence with magazines in London, outdoor media in France and Germany, radio in California, and so on. You have seen what trade unions have done on Fleet Street in London, where they have wrecked a number of formerly quite prosperous newspaper groups.

"In any case, I seem to be able to separate these two roles quite clearly to date, although at some considerable expense in terms of personal wear and tear and reduced time with my family."

Risk Taking at Heinz

"Still, there are areas at Heinz in which I see legitimate need for risk taking, and indeed I encourage it. There are some areas in which we need to spend heavily, and I will not hold one of my colleagues guilty of a heinous crime if he fails in an area of affordable investment which we think is demographically sound—a market-opportunity area such as cardio-fitness centers, or the pet-treat market, for example. This is a market which is growing dramatically—ultra-gourmet treats and all those little extra pieces of love and attention that can be tangibly given to the pets to eat. In regard to expenditure by Heinz in those market-opportunity areas, we are very heavy investors and, I think, entrepreneurial. If those in charge for the company are successful, they will become the new legends of their time within the culture of Heinz.

"We do have to encourage risk taking. It doesn't happen automatically. We encourage this, first of all, by infiltrating through our organization to identify the 20 fastest 'two-year-old horses.' We want to know which five of them will run in Churchill Downs next year. We want to know where each horse is. We say, 'Come on, guys, show us—parade your wares before us.' We see ourselves as the friendly cross-examiners and the enlightened merchant bankers, so to speak, from world headquarters. We try, too, to make these risk-takers visible within the company. We extol their merits and simply are not into Monday-morning quarterbacking. People make mistakes — everyone does—and it's almost a *sine qua non* that one must have made a major mistake of some sort before he or she gets to a high management level within the company. Obviously, the bad banker is the banker who has too good a loan record, the one who has never had a bad loan. This means that he has probably never gone out to get the high-margin business. We feel that the same rules apply to marketing people: they have got to show enterprise, they have got to throw themselves wholeheartedly into a multiyear program. We will finance the program and will not recriminate if, at the end, a certain product which they and we thought had promise doesn't work.

"One good thing about us, I think, is that we are persistent. We will not go into a fight unless we think we can stay in the fight for five years. We are not only persistent but constantly Socratic as well. For example, there was a marketing proposition which sharply differentiated canned specialty pet food from dry and semimoist pet food. Morris, the finicky cat, was the great spokesperson for canned specialty pet food but not for semimoist or dry. For seven years we tripped along with no brand share to speak of in semimoist and dry cat food. Finally, after great internal debate, Star-Kist switched the marketing proposition and made Morris the umbrella 'spokesperson' for all discriminating cats on behalf of dry, semimoist and moist food. Our numbers bounded through the roof. Our persistence has paid off, and now we have a 17 percent share of the semimoist and over 10 percent of the dry. We changed the product, we changed the package, and most important, we changed the marketing copy claim—a very interesting lesson for all of us.

"While I am generally very sympathetic to the marketing function—since this is something I know a bit about—I also emphasize the low-cost operator. I have a desire to make sure that we are not just good at marketing but that we actually provide a low-cost base. I think people would say that I do not worship at the alter of Nielsen and that if there is profit pressure, the first budget that will be cut may indeed be marketing. We simply don't deify the holy gospel of marketing, which some companies tend to do. Procter & Gamble people may feel that their marketing budgets are safe. Ours are certainly not.

"I tend to be analytical and at times cautious. And while perhaps this trait has made me miss some opportunities, Heinz has made a few home runs since I've been here as well. Acquiring Weight Watchers five years ago was certainly a home run. My natural *milieu* is sitting, talking, analyzing in a collegial way the dynamics of the marketplace. I realize that we all crave certainty and that we try to impose a spurious illusion of precision on the future. But at the same time we know that the future is not going to work out in the particular way we want it to. Perhaps I have an excessive concern for detailed analysis, but this is the way I am. I enjoy and encourage a great deal of dialogue among my senior officers. But having finally made a decision to move, I do not sympathize with the Monday-morning quarterback or the 'hurler on the ditch,' as we call him in Ireland. Once we have decided as a company to move, we will *move*; and we will accept the consequences of that move over a protracted period of time.

"An example of that is the whole business of weight control. The demographics of that movement attracted me greatly, and we analyzed those demographics rather carefully. When we finally got to take a good look at the business, we decided that it was a very good one for us to be in; we acquired Weight Watchers International, Foodways (the producers of Weight Watchers' frozen entrées and desserts), and Camargo (licensee for the production of nonfrozen low-calorie foods). It was a bit difficult to put this all together, something of a jigsaw puzzle at first, but we did it, since we were convinced that the calorie counting and the population bulge of people in the 25-to 45-year age bracket, particularly women, represented a strong potential audience for both products and services.

"After becoming convinced of this, we decided then to expand quite dramatically and held strongly to that view, even though our initial few years with Weight Watchers were not productive. It had not lived up to our expectations, so we had to find a new formula. In the case of service, the formula was Quick Start; the formula in the food-product case turned out to be a combination of things, not the least of which was Nestle's decision to compete strongly against us with their Lean Cuisine. The collision of their products with ours produced an enormous ferment in the marketplace, which benefited both companies. So after a two- to three-year period of digestion and reflection, analysis and disappointment, we still felt—based upon the demographics—that we had made the right decision. I felt particularly responsible, since it was I who had acquired the company. Fortunately, we were able to turn it around. Then, quite dramatically, Weight Watchers and the whole wellness/calorie-counting area became the growth vehicle for the Heinz Company, to the point that it now represents one-eighth of our total profit. We paid $100 million dollars for the business, which will generate an operating income of between $55 and $60 million this year. You don't get many of those opportunities, and certainly very few which are as well positioned for the future.

"I suppose that replacement surgery will experience a certain amount of growth, but it does not seem to be the miracle it appeared to be when Barnard did his first heart transplant, when we tended to fantasize that we would some day soon buy body parts off the shelf. So there is a growing realization that the quality of life and the extension of it are functions of diet, discipline, and exercise; one's last 20 years can be hell or very pleasant, depending upon whether you attach certain values to the way you eat, what you eat, and how you exercise.

"I certainly do not want to invite direct confrontations— the kind I'd call 'Star Wars'—with Procter & Gamble or other strong competitors. I want to avoid participating in any 'Orange Juice War' or the 'Cookie War' that has been raging among Nabisco, Procter & Gamble, and Frito-Lay; such wars can cause a corporation to lose real money. We try to avoid spending enormous sums in markets which are not expanding, trying not simply to exchange market share at great cost to the shareholders. Someone once asked me to name the principal dynamic of the H. J. Heinz Company's success, and I replied, half-jokingly, 'Commercial cowardice!' An unusual conviction, perhaps, but something to think about.

"We have found it desirable to interchange managers, and all those now at the top of Weight Watchers came from Heinz. The original entrepreneurs did a wonderful job in creating the embryo to which, I think, we have added very considerable insight and sophistication and, of course, great marketing punch. One simply cannot be unaware of that brand name. It is a second world brand for us and at the same time has almost become a generic word."

Compensation as a Management Tool

"My views on compensation come from my middle-class background, my time as a civil servant, and my conviction as a capitalist. I have always believed that compensation structures of American companies should encourage senior managers to have the same concerns as those of the owners: the shareholders. I have convinced our Board of Directors and our Compensation Committee of the imperative need to do this to the point that the Heinz Company is probably unique today, in that 12 percent of the total company is owned or potentially owned through stock options by the management. The company is capitalized at $4.3 billion, and the management is strongly participating in the creation of the wealth and the sharing of it. This implies a very considerable sense of ownership and commitment, the kind that one normally gets only from the owners. This encourages the resource-allocation mechanism to be guided by the overall desire of the top managers of the company to act on the basis not of their own particular job satisfaction or area ambitions, but rather on what would be best in the long run for the stock. There is therefore a high degree of symmetry between the interests of management and those of the stockholder. Our management now believes that their interests are coterminus with those of the shareholder. Our compensation system is three-fold: a basic salary, a management-incentive program, and a long-term incentive, whose focus is over a three-year period. Participating in the long-term incentive program are 21 managers; 240 are in the management-incentive program; and the 50,000 employees who make up the corporation participate in basic salaries and various bonus systems. Compensation in a year in which the company does very well can be quite high. Senior vice presidents are paid about $800,000 (of which only about $180,000 is their base pay), and my compensation is probably among the highest in the food industry. Yet of that I probably have the lowest base salary of anyone in a comparable corporation in the industry. We talk very specifically on return on equity, on return on invested capital, on growth in earnings per share, and on growth in dividends.

"Because we encourage a great deal of autonomy, the selection process for people near the top is a tough one. The man who runs our operation in Italy, Great Britain, or Australia gets a chance to show his true colors. There are four area vice presidents and three staff vice presidents in the present system, so there are only eight in the corporate office, supplemented by a few lawyers, tax specialists, and planners. But in all, there are only 64 people at our headquarters in Pittsburgh, guiding a $4.5 billion corporation.''

Direction Setting

''Each year I write very specific, extensive letters to each one of the area vice presidents. Each year I set a major goal for them. For example I sent our senior vice president for Europe a detailed 7-page letter, which begins this way, 'Now that you have landed in Great Britain and have had two weeks to assess the situation, the magnitude of our problems, and hence, yours, will have become clear to you.' Then I go on and talk about a bit of the background, the overall consolidation of the United Kingdom operation during the past decade; then I go right through Central Europe, where we are enjoying relatively poor results. I go into detail into why I think that is the case, discuss our business in Belgium, Italy, Portugal, Scandinavia, and so on. This letter becomes his marching orders for the year. These letters are not ambiguous in the least, and they are, in fact, quite explicit. I spend considerable time thinking through the marching orders I want to send. It takes about six weeks for me to write these seven letters. Then I sit down and visit at length with each of the individuals.

''I give copies of these letters to the Management Compensation Committee, so that they should understand the criteria for success upon which the individuals will be judged.

''After the senior vice president has reviewed my letter, we will spend perhaps half a day together. He might say that he disagrees with some of my points; we might argue about Scandinavia or something else. After going through this process, I follow up with another letter which might say that I have accepted his point that since Portugal was not then a member of the EEC, we therefore would have to approach it in a different way, or whatever.

''I have been writing these letters for a long time now, and when each is written, it reflects a lot of prior conversation and understanding.

''We try to manage by quite specific objectives. I have a very low tolerance for political maneuvering. I am exceedingly straightforward, and that is true of the Heinz culture as well.''

H. J. Heinz Company has seen dramatic change in the bottom line as well, particularly since O'Reilly joined it. Its worldwide profit after taxes in 1969 was $27 million; in 1985 it approached $300 million. O'Reilly's high regard for board chairman Henry J. (Jack) Heinz II is quite obviously reciprocated. At the 1985 annual meeting, Mr. Heinz briefly touched on the heritage and traditions of the firm, praising "Grandfather (Henry J.) Heinz," the founder, as "a remarkable man, an entrepreneur in the literal meaning of that term." He went on to describe the founder's vision of a worldwide market as early as 1906 and pointed to the stained-glass window in the original administration building, at the center of which is a projection of the globe, encircled with the inscription, "Our Field." He went on to point out that the first overseas sale of Pittsburgh-made Heinz products was to Fortnum & Mason, the prestigious U.K. retailer, which had preceded the erection of the administration building by 20 years. Hence, he said, the H. J. Heinz Company had been operating in the international arena for a century. Introducing President O'Reilly, Chairman Heinz said, "In so doing, I can think of nothing more complimentary to say of him than to compare his energy, vitality, and genius for worldwide salesmanship and statesmanship most favorably with the man who founded this company 116 years ago."

Self-Observations

A reflective man—witness the nine years he devoted to the study of his Kerrygold experience—O'Reilly demonstrates considerable self-knowledge.

"One probably never understands himself completely, but I think most would say that I have gotten to my position because I have a very high energy level, and when I want something, I go very directly for it. They would also perhaps comment on my Irish humor. President Reagan has certainly capitalized on this with his own American version of Irish charm. I am not unaware that this has its place. One can do things and say things pleasantly to make life a bit more agreeable and, at the same time, facilitate decision making. In terms of my personal flaws, I must say that I am not at all interested in administration *per se*. I am utterly bored with the questions about who has access to the executive rest room or who has the bigger car. Even pension plans just absolutely bore the hell out of me, and

I find great difficulty in getting excited and interested in that, so I would have to say that I am less successful at handling that area of the business and therefore contract out these responsibilities, perhaps more than I should at times.

"The area that excites me enormously and continuously is that of structure and strategy: Where is Heinz going to be? What is happening to America? What does the graying of America or the baby boom of the 1990s mean to Heinz? Where should we be positioned? Why do people have pets? Why have cats gone from 30 million in America to 60 million? What is the implication of this, and how can we profit from it? What does the whole cardio-fitness/wellness trend mean?

"Yesterday I was looking at a company which takes care of children. What a fascinating idea that is. No business at all five years ago, and over $25 million after taxes last year. Not only caring for children but teaching them, utilizing new ways of teaching. That whole area really excites me. Then I am interested in the matter of simple, basic efficiency. After I came out of law school, I went to work with a company that taught me a lot about work study. I learned a lot about this, working on the floor as a work-study engineer for over a year, doing time studies and learning about standard costs in that way, mastering some knowledge about the basic building blocks of how costs get put together. This was a tremendous training period in my life, and I still get a feeling from the shop floor that 'I was there and made a contribution.' In doing these time studies, I stood with an operator for 8 to 10 hours, observing his every minute of the day for weeks on end. I am fascinated by the manufacturing process, and these aspects of Heinz appeal to me as well. Each young person must learn a bit about himself or herself and must find those things which are of personal interest, things to which one can commit in order to succeed."

Advice to Young People

"If I were advising young people, I would say this: learn the numbers, learn accounting properly; take a basic course in law; make sure you know and understand financial and legal parameters.

"Then to the young manager, I would say this: work hard, keep an open mind, allow policies of innovation and imagination to flourish—but remember that these have a penalty cost, and you have to be able to afford them. But first and foremost, *do the job at hand*. Don't plan and plot about the other guys and, finally, a good sense of humor helps as well.

"Remember the old Irish adage: 'Live every day as though it's going to be your last, and one day you are going to be right.'"

The 18 Management Competencies: How They Are Illustrated by the Interviews

*A*s they recounted what works for them, the 16 CEOs showed that they possess a broad range of management competencies. What are these competencies? One way to identify them—and to provide examples of them from the interviews—is through the Management Competency Model. This model consists of 18 specific management competencies developed from extensive research done by David McClelland and others. These competencies form the basis of an in-depth assessment and feedback process operated by the Competency Development Laboratory of AMA's Institute for Management Competency. (For more about how the Management Competency Model was developed and how the assessment process works, see *Appendix A: Research Into What Leads to Managerial Success*.)

When I interviewed the 16 chief executives, we did not discuss "managerial competencies." Rather, I simply asked them to talk about their personal approaches to their current jobs and to the earlier assignments leading to those jobs. Nevertheless, many examples of the managerial competencies jump to the reader's attention from the pages of these interviews.

Believing that a selection of these examples would be illuminating and useful to the reader, I asked Stacy Zeifman of AMA's Institute for Management Competency to analyze the manuscripts based on the 16 interviews. From that analysis, she identified those competencies that were strongly evidenced by the CEOs as they discussed what works for them. Zeifman employed the same coding techniques and standards that are applied to the results of behavioral event interviews of participating managers at the Competency Development Laboratory. During this process, hundreds of examples of management competencies were identified.

This analysis was not intended to convey any judgment as to the range of competence evidenced by individual CEOs, but rather to provide, for the reader's understanding, some examples taken from the coded material.

The 18 management competencies are clustered into four major groups:

- *Goal and Action Management*:   This cluster deals with the manager's initiative, image, problem-solving skills, and goal orientation.

- *Directing Others*:   This cluster involves a manager's freedom of expression both in terms of giving directives and orders and giving feedback to help develop others.

- *Human Resource Management*:   Managers with these competencies have positive expectations about others; have realistic views of themselves; build networks or coalitions with others to accomplish tasks; and stimulate cooperation and pride in work groups.

- *Leadership*:   This cluster represents a manager's ability to discern the key issues, patterns, or objectives in an organization, and to then communicate and act in a strong fashion.

Below are several illustrations of the 18 management competencies. Each competency is briefly explained, then followed by selected examples taken from the 16 interviews.

Goal and Action Management Cluster

Efficiency Orientation. Without exception, each interview provided examples of this concern with doing things better, using efficient methods, setting realistic goals, and establishing standards of excellence.

When James Guinan was at Gold Circle, a part of Federated Stores, he noticed "trucks at loose ends" that had delivered goods to his stores but were returning empty. The trucks, he decided, were *never* to be empty. The concept of a "round robin" for Gold Circle trucks occurred to him one day while he was talking about "all the empty trucks we were having to support." The first step in his thinking was to determine how the trucks could be used more efficiently for Gold Circle. He concluded that on return trips they could deliver goods to the Federated Stores outside of Gold Circle, and—thinking in broader terms—he quickly saw that the trucks could deliver goods to any organization. In Guinan's last year at Gold Circle, the company netted almost $3 million from more efficient use of its private truck fleet. Yet it may not have been simple financial gain that motivated Guinan to think of this idea; his fundamental orientation toward efficiency had much to do with it. Guinan says, "I guess the thing which motivates me the most is to do a good job. When I was ten years old, I worked in a Brooklyn candy store . . . The owner said I had done the best job anyone had done. I don't know why it makes me happier than it does many just to do a good job."

North Carolina Mutual's William Kennedy tries to "shock people by setting surprisingly high goals." That's the job of a leader, he says: to get people to raise their sights. Studying various financial measures of his company, Kennedy realized that the time had come to look at North Carolina Mutual from a "very objective, productivity point of view . . ." He recognized that there were more people on board than were needed, and—working against the grain of his organization's traditional culture—he reduced operating costs by reducing staff. The result was a more efficient, more profitable organization.

In the late 1960s, Henry Schacht and his team realized that Cummins' manufacturing system had become increasingly wasteful of the company's human resources and that there had to be a better way to organize human beings. "We had basically organized them as though they were machine replacements rather than intelligent beings who weren't just doing physical work. We started with our early plants by rewriting the rules of how human organizations should work together." It also became vital to rethink cost, quality, and delivery. It was necessary to squeeze out the "fat that had accumulated in the protected years of the 1950s and 1960s." Schacht wanted Cummins to become more effective and more efficient, to do more with less, and to drive productivity goals "back into the (positive) 2 or 3 percent area from the minus." The efficiency orientation of Schacht and his team lifted Cummins Engine to a new level of effectiveness.

Proactivity. The proactive manager initiates new actions and takes responsibility for new risks. All successful CEOs possess this trait.

When James Burke became Chairman of Johnson & Johnson, his Board of Directors was made up completely of insiders, reflecting the strong commitment of General Robert Wood Johnson to maintain an all-inside Board. "One of the first things I did was to bring in outsiders . . . When I opened up the Board, I said to our inside people, 'I know that none of you is going to like this. I can appreciate now how you feel because I've grown up with all of you. But now that I'm Chairman of the company, I've got a responsibility, and this is what I think is best for the company.'"

Early in Bill Marriott's career, he asked his father to let him manage the company's first hotel. Later, he says, "We built a second one, and our hotel business went on from there." Hotels now represent about half of the giant Marriott Corporation's revenues.

James Martin, recognizing that his management style might be inhibiting even the members of his top team at Massachusetts Mutual from providing constructive, open feedback, persuaded them to meet privately without him twice a year to voice any criticisms they might have of the way he worked. Following each meeting, one group member would tell Martin of changes the group felt that he should make in his management style or actions. Martin said he often got more criticism than he bargained for, but the technique evolved into an accurate and effective way to get important feedback from his top associates, who, he says, "never ran out of things to tell me!" Martin's record at Massachusetts Mutual attests to the effectiveness of this creative initiative.

Concern with Impact. This competency explicitly expresses a need or desire to persuade others, or a concern with the image of the manager or his or her organization.

Frank Cary, extremely mindful of the importance of the public's perception of IBM, particularly during the lengthy federal government antitrust suit, strongly believed—based on his personal experience—that IBM had always tried to compete fairly. His conviction of IBM's fairness and of the public's belief in this fairness sustained him during this trying period when IBM's reputation, and to some extent, its future, was at stake.

Schacht, working with his team to transform the Cummins Engine Company, recognizes that Cummins' employees need to understand what is happening. "This means that even after you accelerate your technology and introduce new products with increasing frequency, you still must remake your entire manufacturing plant—even though you thought you were the best there was to start with. And you must convince your people that what you're doing is not a condemnation of their life's work. Instead, it is a revelation that there's another way to do something, and we are convinced that rather than reaching the end of the world, this is the beginning of a new world."

Ichiro Hattori, having helped Seiko pioneer the development of electronic timepieces, recognized that at some point the market for watches and clocks—Seiko's traditional market —would be saturated. Concerned about the impact that would have upon his organization's employees, he made intense efforts to convince them of this eventuality. "It took us a very long time to convince our employees of the need for diversification," Hattori says. Yet it was essential that they be so convinced, for without their commitment Seiko's efforts to diversity could not have succeeded.

Diagnostic Use of Concepts. The manager with this competency uses an explicit, helpful framework or theory in interpreting experiences and making observations.

Italtel's Marisa Bellisario, having worked both in Europe and the United States, observes differences in the business climates of Italy, France, Germany and the United States. Contrasting U.S. and Italian business customs, she uses the framework of what she calls the "national atmosphere." Just as U.S. restaurants provide an obligatory salad, U.S. companies operate with certain obligatory procedures. "In some ways, you might say that these procedures are rigid, but in other ways, they are comfortable, because you know exactly how the system works." But when you find a highly organized, systematic company in Italy, she says, its procedures may become blocks to productivity and innovation.

In recollecting his career transition from manufacturing to retailing, Peter Scotese of Springs Industries observes: "There is an enormous difference between the retailing business and the manufacturing business. There are no bricks and mortar in retailing. If something isn't selling, you mark it down, get something else in its place pretty fast, if you are going to succeed." "There are no bricks and mortar in retailing" immediately clarifies the difference between the two types of businesses.

Anthony O'Reilly (Heinz) calls on the analogy of banking in assessing the capability of marketing people. The bad banker, he says, is the banker who has too *good* a loan record, the one who has never had a bad loan. He applies the same concept to marketing people: "They have got to show enterprise, they have got to throw themselves wholeheartedly into a multi-year program. We will finance the program and will not recriminate if, at the end, a certain product which they and we thought had promise doesn't work."

Directing Others Cluster

Use of Unilateral Power. This is the ability to issue directives and obtain compliance to them.

When Bellisario joined Italtel, she found some "very strange things." Managers were spending more time approving the minutes of meetings than in the meetings themselves. She "told them either they would not do the minutes—we would get along without them—or if we had to have minutes, then one person could write them up, and we would rely on these." The use of unilateral power seldom involves soliciting others' input, and Bellisario needed no advice to abolish this antiquated and inefficient procedure.

Scotese, who serves on many boards of directors, commented: "When I finally come to the point where I have had it, whether it is with a CEO or a subordinate, then I have to be direct."

Many years ago, Harold Burson had developed a vision and a plan for Burson-Marsteller. Part of the plan was for his firm to work for large multi-national corporations and be internationally based. In 1980 he decided to go into Australia, saying, "Let's get started down here, right now." He did not talk this move over with anyone else.

As these examples show, even the most fervent advocate of participative management must at times take unilateral action.

Developing Others. This competency employs a variety of ways to help one's people to develop themselves by encouraging them to take responsibility.

When Theodore Hesburgh needs to find outstanding people for important assignments at Notre Dame, he considers this not his job but that of his vice presidents, to whom he says: "I want you to find the very best people you can find, but you're going to have to choose and appoint them, since you are going to work with the people you select. If they are successful, you're going to get the credit for the success of that operation, and if you pick the wrong people who are unsuccessful, you're going to take the blame for it. I am not going to take the credit from you, and I'm not going to take the blame for you."

"Portia Isaacson (Intellisys Corporation) observes that she tends to give direction from a distance, "painting a broad picture on the wall and asking my people to go away and fill in the details . . . I never deal with details, yet I never fail to give direction;

my theory is to do something even if it's wrong. My style allows people to be creative in a high-energy environment." People, she adds, "like working in this optimistic environment."

Burson says, "I think I am fairly good at giving people an assignment and saying, 'It's yours.' I have done that all my life." A hands-off manager in internal matters, Burson stays very close to his clients. But he has realized that if Burson-Marsteller is to continue to grow, he must help his people to grow.

Spontaneity. Though virtually all CEOs at times act on their immediate feelings, the managerial competency of spontaneity rarely surfaced in these interviews, probably because the CEOs recognized that an interview for a book could have public impact and chose not to talk about such instances.

Spontaneity may result in managers expressing their feelings without first thinking about the potential impact of their words, or making quick decisions without having thought explicitly about the possible consequences. Spontaneity implies words or actions that are based upon emotional reactions. If not taken too far, spontaneity helps to demonstrate that managers are whole people, fully themselves.

Burke's description of the contention that he has encouraged at Johnson & Johnson demonstrates spontaneity on the part of his team. "We have some very tough meetings, very nasty, full of criticism . . . Good, constructive screaming and yelling at each other leads to a meritocracy and, just as important, to better results. In recent years contention has become a part of our management culture."

Spontaneous behavior may increase an executive's vulnerability. Yet without it, a part of the human dimension is missing. From personal acquaintance with several of these executives, I know that spontaneity is a part of their everyday behavior, even though they may not have revealed it during their interviews.

Human Resource Management Cluster

Accurate Self-Assessment. In my view, this is one of the most important management competencies. One must be aware of one's strengths; more important, one must know one's limitations. To be fully effective, one must know oneself.

372

Charlotte Beers (Tatham-Laird & Kudner) is conscious of her ability to "flag something that's not right—or to signal an opportunity or weakness." That is one of the strengths she recognizes, so she believes that she should be encouraged to do this to a reasonable degree. She also recognizes what she refers to as a flaw or shortcoming, the tendency to be self-centered. "There is a strength in being fast, to be able to reach a decision and to move on it, but the downside of this is that you may not have thought through the implications to other people." Conscious of this tendency, she tries to control it.

As a young man working in the investment field at North Carolina Mutual, Kennedy recognized that he "knew all the technical things . . . how to do all those things you can learn at school. But I didn't know how to talk to brokers and how to negotiate prices." As a result, he listened carefully to Viola Turner, who taught him how to deal with brokers. "Just listening to her handle those brokers over the phone" was instructive; but had Kennedy not understood his own limitations, such instruction would have been less effective.

Hershey's Richard Zimmerman notices that, though he has a financial background, he is not "great with numbers" yet enjoys and does not fear them. What interests him, however, is the marketing aspect of management. When his people present a proposal, he wants to "start out by talking about the market and the potential effect on the consumer." He is also aware of his prodigious memory and the effect—both positive and negative—that this may have upon his people.

Self-Control. At the opposite pole from spontaneity is this management competency, which involves a willingness to put the needs of an organization above one's personal needs or desires.

Marriott says: "Perhaps it's because I have such drive and such commitment that I tend to be impatient. But I think I do a fair job of controlling that . . . If I am unhappy with somebody, I'll wait . . . If you get upset, you shouldn't pick up the phone and start ranting and raving and carrying on. Learning not to do this comes with maturity, and it comes with being on the job and learning how to deal with problems." During his constant visits to his company's hotels and restaurants, Marriott comes across many frustrating situations. However, rather than unduly criticizing a local manager on the spot, he "cools off" and takes the problem back to the appropriate headquarters officer.

Scotese "used to attend division manager meetings but decided that they were affecting me too much. I would think, 'If I were running this meeting, I would do it in a different way.' So I just stopped going, because I did not want to tempt myself to second-guess the division president." Aware of his desire to exercise control, Scotese subjugated this tendency by simply not attending the division manager meetings.

Beers, conscious of her need for attention—her "self-centered tendency"—realized that as CEO, "I don't really need that much attention now, and it's just wonderful and probably a relief to the people around me." Having assessed herself, she controls this inclination, to the benefit of her organization and its people.

Stamina and Adaptability. Tenacity, one of the characteristics of successful chief executive officers, requires stamina; changing conditions and unforeseen events require adaptability.

Cary, recalling when he became general manager of IBM's Data Processing Group—at a time when much of that company was in relative disarray—states: "My recollection of those days is that they were very, very long. Some of us have laughed about how much time we spent in that general managers' conference room. We'd start at breakfast, later bring in the sandwiches and the apples, and then wind up there late at night. There were many endless days . . . (but) so much depended upon the success of that new organization."

Hesburgh's commitment to the integrity of the Notre Dame faculty makes him mindful of the importance of decisions about faculty promotions and tenure. The files and recommendations are voluminous. "I have to scrutinize every blessed page . . . It's a miserable task. I read myself blind until 9 o'clock three or four nights. But I have to do it, because I'm dealing with people's lives." Outside Notre Dame, Hesburgh carries out a prodigious work schedule, serving society in a great variety of ways—for example, on national commissions and task forces. "The only way you can accomplish a lot is to concentrate on the one task you have at the moment. Otherwise you'll go nutty. Yesterday I was down in New Orleans. I had everything cleaned up before I left on Sunday, except the unfinished reading on the window sill, and that's always going to be there. I took everything I could pack into my bag and read an awful lot of stuff along the way. Then I came back and the stack was two feet high. And lots of phone calls to return."

Perceptual Objectivity. One quality of successful chief executive officers is a clear perception of reality; this stems partly from the competency described as perceptual objectivity, the ability to set aside personal bias and be objective about others' views.

As members of a corporate organizational task force, Cary and his colleagues needed to understand many viewpoints, including that of IBM's then-CEO Thomas J. Watson, Jr. "We recommended that IBM go to large functional divisions . . . as opposed to functionally integrated units. This is not what management wanted to hear, but there was really no choice." In reaching this conclusion, it was important for Cary and his colleagues to understand and describe accurately the specific view then held by top management—a view opposed to the task force's ultimate recommendations—in order to determine the relative advantages of the various proposed organizational structures.

As noted in an earlier illustration, Hattori recognized that the market for electronic timepieces was not "forever." He was determined, nevertheless, that Seiko must remain successful. To do this required developing a capability to enter new markets. Not to do so would have meant that his company would be forced to lay people off, unless the volume of watches and clocks were to grow very rapidly—"which of course we knew that it would not do. This, then, was the message that we had to give our employees to understand."

Positive Regard. Managers with this competency hold and express a positive belief in others. Positive regard may pertain just as well to peers outside one's company as it does to people within.

For example, Martin has high regard for certain CEOs within the insurance industry whom he describes as "extraordinarily successful in managing in a well balanced way." One could learn a lot, he claims, just by watching such people operate.

Isaacson, starting a new company, "hired a perfect assistant . . . someone I can count on; I can send him to clients to represent me."

Hesburgh, when talking with the faculty head of a search committee charged with recommending a provost for his university, concluded—after having reviewed the committee's uninspiring recommendations—that the committee's chairman was superior to all of the candidates it had recommended. He said to Tim O'Mara, "Did it ever occur to you, Tim, that you're better than all three of the names you brought in?" He added, "I'm sure that if we look around, we can find another candidate or two, but I think *you* ought to get in the running for this job."

The confidence provided by a manager's expression of support can go a long way toward motivating one's people to higher levels of performance. Indeed, positive regard is a key factor in effective team building, a skill possessed by successful chief executives.

Managing Group Process. Without this management competency, which can be manifested in many different ways, CEOs are unlikely to succeed.

Guinan holds many quick one-on-one meetings. When he does, "I just appear at the guy's doorway. If a meeting lasts more than a half hour, it's probably because we're making some major conceptual change." In these meetings he supports his people rather than second-guess them. In this way, he gets them actively involved as a part of his team.

Concerned with the impact of his visits to his company's hotels and restaurants, Marriott usually has a meeting of each unit's management, "to find out how they are doing, what they think they can do better and how they can do it. I want to know how business is going and want them to know what we are doing in headquarters that helps them and what we are doing that offends them, gets them upset. I try to link up the communications between the home office and the field to learn what their problems are."

Ten years ago, Burke, "fiercely believing in"—yet wondering about the practicality of—Johnson & Johnson's Credo, initiated a series of meetings at which his company's managers were encouraged to challenge that Credo, to modify it, or to buy into it. By dramatically managing this group process, Burke involved his team deeply in the values that drive his company forward.

Use of Socialized Power. Managers demonstrating this competency build coalitions or networks to reach a goal or to resolve potential conflicts or disputes.

Burson remarks: "I have always tried to avoid strife," so if there were to be any "large discussion about something, I would line up my votes before the decision."

Not long after Martin had installed long-range planning at Mass Mutual, he sent his top management team to a condensed version of a course on planning that he had taken. The great advantage in doing this, Martin says, was that the credibility and professional expertise of the outside training staff helped to sell these management concepts to his associates.

Deft managers may also influence the behavior of members of the group by personally demonstrating desired behavior. Zimmerman, wanting to listen to employees at all levels, also wanted to demonstrate to Hershey's supervisors at the plant level and elsewhere that it is important for *them* to listen to employees' ideas. "I wanted to say to the employees who were generating these ideas that I expect *their* management to listen to *them*."

The CEO who defines a strategic focus for his or her company must be able to use socialized power with great effectiveness if that strategic focus is to be acted upon.

Leadership Cluster

Self-Confidence. Any successful CEO must demonstrate, indeed possess, supreme self-confidence.

Bellisario exhibits an impressively confident readiness to take on responsibility. "Always in some way I tend to take on more . . . Whenever I have taken a job, I have never thought I couldn't make it."

Isaacson took a major risk in creating Future Computer Incorporated. To succeed, she needed as clients the largest manufacturers of personal computers. Some people said to her, "Portia, what makes you think that IBM, AT&T, and even Apple will ask *you* about personal computers?" Her reply was, "It never occurred to me that they wouldn't! It never did!" She comments: "I am sure that to many people the act of my starting up Intellisys is equally bizarre . . . I could fail really visibly, but I guess I don't care. I don't think about that at all. It simply does not occur to me that we could fail."

Conceptualization. Managers with this competency can identify a recurrent pattern in events or information or use a metaphor or analogy to represent a set of events. This intellectual skill, possessed by most successful CEOs, can at times give rise to interesting imagery.

By observing the world outside of Heinz and relying heavily on demographic studies, O'Reilly pinpointed a clear trend toward calorie-counting and body watching. Identifying a recurrent pattern in events and information, he perceived the "wellness" trend. Based upon this, Heinz acquired Weight Watchers and other companies that produce low-calorie foods, and later acquired a company that operates cardiovascular fitness centers—thus entering a field outside the food business but clearly related to health.

At North Carolina Mutual, Kennedy recognized the need for improved productivity. When talking with his district people, he used the metaphor of ships. Ships, he said, move forward with propellers and are held fast by anchors, adding that he would try to determine whether each person was a propeller or an anchor. The company, he said, was "going to cut all these anchor lines and we are going to turn these propellers loose to let them push this company forward. So each person has to decide whether he is an anchor or a propeller."

Schacht describes effective management succession as "a long relay race . . . It's terribly wasteful of human talent to set up side-by-side races of competent people."

Quite apart from the use of metaphors, the ability to conceptualize often involves perceiving the relationship of events which to others may seem unrelated. Sharing this perception with one's team provides a framework or perspective for action.

Logical Thought. Managers with this competency can describe the cause-and-effect relationship in a series of events or place a series of actions or events in a logical sequence that will lead to a specific outcome.

In the highly competitive retail business, Guinan looks at each Caldor store as a "four-wall business—that is, looking at the store as though it were an entity by itself, without apportioned overhead; if the store can't cover its own expenses, then closing it would be a net positive, especially if it starts losing a quarter million or more annually."

Zimmerman clearly states the relationship between brand image and quality of product: "You cannot sacrifice quality just for the sake of being a low-cost producer. If you do, someone else will steal your market."

When Hattori clearly perceived that Seiko's market for timepieces eventually would become saturated, he knew certain actions were needed. "If we were to do nothing about this —if we could not develop new technologies for new products —we would sooner or later arrive at a dead end. If the watch market did not keep expanding—and we recognized that, like everything else, it had a limit—and if we wanted to do something else, we did not have the technologies to move forward." Considerably before the watch market reached saturation, Hattori took those actions required to develop the needed technological capability to enter new markets.

Use of Oral Presentations. The manager who demonstrates this competency speaks clearly and convincingly to others and uses non-verbal cues, diagrams, or exhibits, possibly interacting with the audience to make sure it understands the message.

Beers found herself assigned by J. Walter Thompson to the then male-oriented Sears account. Dealing with the billion-dollar portable electric tool division, she needed to make an impact. The portable electric tool people, she said, "weren't too thrilled . . . Who was this Southern female who obviously didn't know a lot about the world of tools and men and so on? There was great wonderment." Being a quick study and understanding "what an armature was and the difference between brass bearings versus other bearings," she said to the buyer: "Nobody's going to listen to me unless I show something . . . Let me take your part in the meeting, and you take mine." At the presentation, she began, "Today I'm the buyer of the portable electric double-insulated, variable-speed drill, and you will never be without one again in your home." She proceeded to describe, point by point, precisely what made the drill significant, and by that time she reports that she herself had become a "total believer." Taking the drill apart and reassembling it as she talked, she convinced the audience—not consumers, but hardened Sears executives—of the capability and power both of the electric double-insulated, variable-speed drill and herself.

In 1984, O'Reilly presented to Heinz's assembled worldwide management a talk entitled "The Party is Over"—referring to the party created by inflation. He pointed out that this party had largely disappeared, which meant that margins could no longer be increased by passing along inflationary increases to the consumer. Because, in his words, the "Great Underwriter had fled," he stressed the need for cultural change and insisted on a sharply increased awareness of costs. Addressing the need to understand better how *everything* was done at Heinz, he decreed the Year of the Low-Cost Operator. As a result of O'Reilly's presentation and his tenacious follow-through, Heinz experienced "a substantial kick" in its profitability that enabled the company to do "a lot of new and exciting things."

While being able to make effective, persuasive oral presentations is an important competency for all managers, it becomes even more important as they progress upward. Many CEOs substantially improve this skill after becoming chief executives. The incessant demand for them to speak ensures plenty of practice.

CEOs and the Competency Model

The Management Competency Model, based upon solid behavioral science research, enables us to observe some of the traits, skills, and other characteristics of superior managers. This model was developed through the study of a sample not exclusively of CEOs, but of some 2,000 managers at various levels of responsibility. Still, CEOs do not suddenly appear, full-blown, at the pinnacle; they attain their top job responsibilities after numerous and successive achievements at lower levels, their approaches to management having been forged throughout their pre-CEO careers.

Nevertheless, a significant number of chief executives have been among the more than 1,000 men and women who have participated in the confidential assessment process operated by AMA's Competency Development Laboratory. The data provided by this sample indicate a wide range in the degree to which the various management competencies are evidenced by these CEOs. However, the higher one's responsibility, the greater is the need for certain of these competencies—particularly those in the leadership cluster, such as conceptualization.

Beyond these competencies are other capabilities that are needed by the man or woman at the top. We'll examine these in the next chapter.

Beyond Competence: Five Qualities of Successful CEOs

(And that indispensable ingredient: integrity)

*T*he "special" qualities of a successful CEO go beyond those that can be measured by the Management Competency Model. Results of assessments of chief executives participating in the Competency Development Laboratory show that many conduct their jobs with apparent success even though they do not evidence some of the 18 managerial competencies. It would be a rare manager indeed— even a rare CEO—who could demonstrate all of the 18 competencies. Are there other qualities that lead to effective performance as a chief executive? I believe that there are.

These qualities go beyond the 18 managerial competencies and beyond some additional requirements that *all* managers need to be consistently effective on the job: specialized business knowledge, familiarity with the organization, the highly specialized skills demanded by the job itself, and a compatibility between the manager and his or her work setting—the physical, social, and cultural environment. Even someone who has superior job-related knowledge, practices all 18 competencies well, and works in a setting conducive to success may still never become a candidate for the top job. Then what else is needed? Given a healthy, thriving organization, how does a manager reach the top? Is it through simple luck?

Most of the interviewed chief executives mentioned the good fortune of being in a particular place at a particular time when, as one put it, "No one else is there." They see themselves as having been "lucky." But was it mere luck that put them at the "right place" at the "right time?"

David McClelland's studies have shown that the person with high need for achievement tends to show initiative in researching his or her environment, in traveling and searching for new opportunities. This factor may be related to luck or good fortune, since those who explore, who search, and who visit many places will naturally expose themselves to more situations—including situations of opportunity. Rosabeth Moss Kanter's study of opportunity within a large, hierarchical organization stresses the importance of exposure and high visibility through movement within the organization. Just as opportunity begets opportunity, so may mobility.[1]

Perhaps the cave dweller who killed the most sabre-toothed tigers by ranging the farthest considered himself lucky; explorers who traveled the greatest distances probably credited good fortune for their discoveries; the most persistent inventors no doubt feel lucky when their efforts pay off. In all endeavors, chance surely plays a part, but the probability that those who fish with nets will succeed increases in direct proportion to the area of their nets. Similarly, the success of a chief executive depends in part upon his or her exposure inside and outside the company.

Mobility and exposure to opportunity, however, are not enough in themselves. Louis Pasteur maintained that "chance favors only the mind that is prepared." Unless opportunities are recognized when they appear, they will not be seized.

The proactive manager seeks information from a wide variety of sources, takes calculated risks, and accepts personal responsibility. Pliny the Elder said, during the eruption of Mt. Vesuvius, "Fortune favors the brave." Risk taking requires courage and self-esteem. The self-confident manager consistently acts on the belief that he or she will succeed. Success, then, requires more than just being at the right place at the right time, more even than making sure that one is there. Beyond the need for the right time and the right place is the need to be the right person.

Kanter makes this important observation: "Change masters are—literally—the right *people* (emphasis added) in the right place at the right time. The *right people* (her emphasis) are the ones with the ideas that move beyond the organization's established practice, ideas they can form into visions."[2]

What goes into the making of those "right people"—successful CEOs? The words of the 16 chief executives reaffirm their diversity. Yet, as they recount what works for them, a pattern of common strengths emerges. Although organizations differ greatly, as do the circumstances with which their chiefs must contend, superior and successful CEOs share certain capabilities. Those possessed by the men and women in this book are: a clear perception of reality, sophisticated team-building skills, decisiveness informed by balanced judgment, a sharp strategic focus, and an uncommon tenacity.

Perception of Reality

The successful chief executive has a remarkably sure grasp of what is happening and what its significance is. Those on the lower rungs of the organization often express wonderment—even awe—at just how much is known at the top. The ability to acquire information continuously and select what is relevant is an essential skill, one that bestows knowledge and even power. The chief draws heavily upon information networks—both internal and external—and acts as an information processor. However, this is no mechanical process, for there are times when "feeling" is as important as "knowing;" both contribute to a clear perception of reality. As information processors, successful chief executives have highly developed sensors. They do not await information but pursue it relentlessly. Bad news is sought with more vigor than good news, for it must be known early enough to do something about it. This input-seeking mechanism is unflinching, reaching out for uncensored, uncolored accounts of events.

What can happen when vital information does not reach the top is starkly illustrated by the Challenger shuttle explosion in early 1986. It was reported during the investigative hearings that although there was serious conflict at lower levels over the feasibility of a launch on January 28, top-level NASA officials who had to make the ultimate decision learned about the conflict only after the disaster. One also wonders to what degree the lack of essential information at the top contributed to the failures of the unmanned Air Force Titan and NASA Delta rockets a few months after the Challenger disaster—and to the misjudgment blamed by the Russians for the nuclear accident at Chernobyl that same spring.

The effective CEO is constantly in motion, dashing off to get first-hand information—visiting company sites, conversing with employees and customers, reconnoitering the outside environment, all the while testing the validity of the information that has been heard back at headquarters. One CEO in this book referred to his unannounced visits to company sites as "reality testing."

Despite the prodigious amounts of data that arrive at the CEO's desk, there is an unquenchable thirst for more. The volume and fire-hose velocity of this information flow would overwhelm most executives, but the successful chief develops the capacity to stand to the side, sampling chunks of data as they rush by, looking for patterns and incongruities. To draw meaning from a mass of data in motion requires a capacity to synthesize—an ability to convert data into information and information into knowledge.

Perception requires not just knowledge, but understanding, and a respect for the subjective as well as the objective view. The successful chief executive develops a conviction about the importance of this or that bit of information and from this conviction probes deeper into areas that carry the most weight and relevance. This sense of conviction depends on the particular values that are held by the CEO.

In listening to CEOs discuss their important insights, one is struck by their use of anatomical terms such as "a gut-level belief." I once heard an exchange about a complex issue between Thomas J. Watson, Jr., then chairman of IBM, and his executive assistant. Watson asked, "Just on what basis did you reach that decision?" The assistant replied, "Well, in the final analysis, I guess it was a visceral decision." Watson reddened, then laughed and said, "Well, if there are going to be any visceral decisions around here, I'd like to use my own viscera."

Recent research suggests that when making decisions, those at the top call more heavily on right-brain thinking than do managers at lower levels.[3] Sound intuition and instinct help form the successful CEO's perception. The inner ear hears what others may not. An inside voice may speak. Decisions are often said to come "from the heart."

Naturally, one's emotion must not be allowed to block or distort essential information. A capacity to achieve an appropriate balance between drawing upon one's emotions and reining them in may have much to do with developing a CEO-class perceptiveness. Active, objective listening is critical. One CEO interviewed for this book spoke of having become "an earnest listener." Nonetheless, successful chiefs buttress their ability to observe and to listen earnestly with what they deeply feel in the gut, with "bone-thinking." (William Butler Yeats wrote, "God guard me from those thoughts men think in the mind alone/He that sings a lasting song thinks in a marrowbone.")

However these successful chief executives hone their ability to perceive, it is this heightened capacity that forges a solid link to reality. They perceive sharply the purpose of their organizations and share their perception with others. While their visions for the future of their companies are sometimes called dreams, they are neither dreams nor fantasies. Instead, they are clearly etched images of future possibilities, each possibility for tomorrow rooted deeply in the realities of today. It is this highly developed degree of authentic perception that gives successful chief executives a firm grasp of actuality, a bedrock on which future plans will rest.

Team-Building Skills

Corporations are often compared to ships. And long before the era of managing-by-wandering-around, corporate "captains" were urged to get off their bridges to roam the ship.

Like the QE2, established corporations have great momentum—or inertia—and hence can be turned around only very slowly. Even so, this requires the full expertise and energies of the officers and crew. The captain inspecting the vessel may notice a serious encrustment of the barnacles of corporate habit; worse, the ship may be drawing too much water. Excess ballast must be tossed overboard, and quickly. Often, this includes human resources.

Another familiar analogy is between the corporation and a symphony orchestra. The conductor's credibility and effectiveness stem from superior knowledge, the ability to draw forth (yet also integrate) the talent of individual performers, and the authority of his or her expert baton.

Still another parallel is the football team, with its CEO/coach striving to regain lost ground and scoring occasional touchdowns against the competition.

Though inadequate, these analogies make an important point: the chief's role is not that of a loner. One CEO in this book said that his company "extols the individual, but we celebrate the team."

Every person interviewed for this book mentioned the importance of the team, especially the top team. Because of its preeminent importance to the accomplishment of corporate objectives, its member executives deserve special attention from the chief in selection, assessment, coaching, and, at times, removal. Successful CEOs have the ability to recognize their own strengths and shortcomings and to gather close to them individuals with complementary skills and talents. These CEOs also recognize that when circumstances change drastically, the make-up of the team must be reassessed.

Some chief executives operate best in tandem with a strong number two person. Often—but not always—this is the chief operating officer. Others find it more comfortable to disperse authority and accountability among several direct-reporting executives. Still others work through the shared responsibility of an office of the chairman, office of the president, or a corporate management committee. The particular configuration depends upon several factors, including the personality and work habits of the chief, the particular talents of the most senior team members, and the career stage of the CEO. For example, if the chief is nearing retirement—and actively planning toward it—significant authority may be delegated to an heir apparent. In some cases, the soon-to-retire chief, with board concurrence, will begin delegating authority to as many as four potential successors. Sometimes this approach even works, but more often it invites the eventual losers to leave the company once the writing on the wall becomes painfully clear.

From the start, an effective CEO begins building a team. Most of its members usually come from within the company, some may come from the chief executive's previous employer, and some may come from other sources. The job of chief executive has much to do with relationships, especially those with and among the members of the top team. While these relationships need initially to be defined with some clarity, they will be modified or modify themselves over time.

What are the skills and attitudes required for effective team building? They include:

- An uncommon ability to judge talent.

- A positive regard for team members.

- A capacity to communicate the company's context—both internally and externally.

- Willingness to encourage open and honest communication.

- Willingness to remove team members who are judged to be deficient—and to do it cleanly and humanely.

The chief is both leader and a member of the team, and must be adept at playing both roles. This requires a capacity for accurate self-assessment and a commitment to the development of all team members, including oneself.

A strong team shares a high level of trust and candor and a low degree of insecurity or defensiveness. At best, its members communicate even without words; they share common goals and objectives, a common language, a bond, battle scars, mutual respect for each other, cameraderie, and commitment. Despite inevitable conflicts and rivalries, their doors and minds are open to one another.

Even with the best talent available, such a team does not just develop on its own. It is crafted and honed by the agenda-setting and interpersonal skills of the person at the top, skills that the superior chief executive possesses in abundance.

Decisiveness Informed by Balanced Judgment

The successful chief executive is tough-minded, willing to make the hard decisions. Chester Barnard included decisiveness as one of the five "active qualities" of leaders.[4] However, decisiveness alone is not necessarily a virtue; it must be informed by balanced judgment. Effective CEOs are unwilling to spend days mulling over the pros and cons of an issue, so they make less important decisions quickly and forget them. But they also avoid making important decisions prematurely. The men and women interviewed for this book seem quite comfortable, indeed happy, to be in the position of major decision-maker, demonstrating supreme self-confidence in their judgment as they make dozens of decisions each day.

What is judgment? As Peter Drucker notes, in a narrow sense every decision is a judgment. Each decision is "a choice between alternatives. It is rarely a choice between right and wrong. It is at best a choice between 'almost right' and 'probably wrong'—but much more often a choice between two courses of action neither of which is probably more nearly right than the other."[5]

In some jobs, the consequences of decisions can be known almost immediately. For example, the correctness of decisions made by air traffic controllers can be very quickly ascertained. When the controller leaves work each day, the results of all decisions made during that day are known. Those that must be made in the CEO's office are quite different. First, the information on which they must be based is imperfect. The chief executive often operates in an environment of ambiguity and uncertainty. Second, the decisions that must be made at the top are the tough ones. Finally, the "correctness" of long-range decisions—those that are properly delegated upward—may not be known for years. For example, the effectiveness of deciding to invest in the early phases of research and development cannot be measured until well after those efforts have borne fruit. The "rightness" of still other decisions can never be assessed with any certainty. One CEO in this book reports that he likes to "sleep on" a very important decision. He doesn't postpone it unduly, but after making the decision tentatively, he takes a day or so to become comfortable with it.

During the 1970s, as some conglomerate companies expanded rapidly by aggressively acquiring other companies, the judgment of their CEOs was rated positively by the business press. But in the 1980s, as some of those firms ran into financial difficulty or found their acquisitions to be ill-fitting, the quality of their earlier judgment was reassessed. These same firms proclaimed "the need to concentrate on our core business," as they sold off parts of their operation that had proved less than successful. Again, judgment at work, but in a new economic climate and certainly with more first-hand knowledge available. In both cases, backed by their boards of directors, the CEOs exercised decisiveness.

A chief may fail in many ways, but one way to fail with certainty is through indecisiveness. It is instructive to consider the decision-making process of some occupants of that most demanding of all chief executive positions, the presidency of the United States.

Dwight D. Eisenhower once described leadership as "the ability to decide what is to be done, and then to get others to want to do it."[6]

Richard M. Nixon wrote, "What lifts great leaders above the second-raters is that they are more forceful, more resourceful, and have a shrewdness of judgment that spares them the fatal error and enables them to identify the fleeting opportunity."[7] Most would credit Richard Nixon with shrewdness and decisiveness. Yet during the Watergate period his judgment lacked the balance necessary to spare him "the fatal error."

Warren Harding's administration was characterized by indecisiveness, perhaps because of his discomfort with the power of the Presidency. He once wrote a friend: "Frankly, being President is a rather unattractive business unless one relishes the exercise of power. That is a thing which has never greatly appealed to me . . ."[8]

Harry S Truman, thrust by the death of Franklin D. Roosevelt into an office he did not seek, possessed the quality of decisiveness. During his presidency, Truman made many momentous decisions, including the decision to drop the atomic bomb. When he heard that General Marshall had gone to sleep at his usual time the night before D-Day, Truman said, "If you've done the best you can—if you have done what you have to do—there is no use worrying about it . . . You can't think about how it would be . . . if you had done another thing. You have to decide."[9]

Like U.S. Presidents, corporate CEOs "have to decide." The essential ingredient of balance in decision making comes partly from a deliberate exposure to varied points of view. Truman wrote, "I made it my business as President to listen to people in all walks of life and in all fields of endeavor and experience. I did not see only the people who ought to be seen— that is, those who were 'well connected.' I always tried to be a good listener. But since the responsibility for making decisions had to be mine, I always reserved judgment."[10]

President Ronald Reagan's decision-making process reportedly employs pitched debates between the directly involved proponents and opponents of a question before him. As deputy assistant to the President and Director of the Office of Policy Development at the White House, Roger B. Porter was able to observe Reagan closely. Porter says: "He likes to hear directly from the people who have a stake in an issue," rather than having White House aides serve as "filters or intermediaries" in presenting arguments. Reagan, he says, is not uncomfortable with hearing arguments presented strongly and vigorously. "He has a high tolerance for hearing competing views argued very intensely."[11]

Successful chief executives seek balanced advice but still need a perceptual objectivity to make a balanced decision. Possessing the will to decide, they are tough-minded, willing to live with their decisions, regardless of the result. While they insist on tough-mindedness in their people, they also hold themselves fully accountable for the consequences of their own decisions, right or wrong. In short, they exercise decisiveness informed by balanced judgment.

Strategic Focus

The CEOs interviewed for this book are pulling their companies into the future. Aware of changes in customer demand, alert to new technological developments, they constantly look for ways to reach out in new directions. Mediocre chief executives preside at their office in a reactive rather than proactive mode. Tending to the day-to-day problems of the firm, they may encourage their organization to find ways to do things better in the context of its current mission and market. The truly successful chief executive, however, operates in the transforming mode, creating a vision to guide the company into the future. More than 25 years ago, one chief executive in this book developed a vision of his firm's future that, with minor alteration, still drives his company forward today.

Although each such transforming CEO creates a vision in his or her own way, certain common steps are followed. First is the diagnostic phase, which consists of an archeological study into how the company got to where it is, then an inventory of the company's resources and capabilities, then a careful identification of gaps, which might be managerial or technological.

During the next phase, market niches are sought, new marketing approaches designed, A top management team is built, followed by intense discussions to gain team members' commitment to the need to redefine or reposition the company. The chief has the vital job of providing his or her company with intellectual capital.

Gradually the vision for the future becomes a plan. There is the inevitable need for additional resources, always in short supply. The successful chief will somehow find a way to obtain these resources. Some CEOs demand cost efficiencies within their own organizations to free up dollars for investment in new initiatives. Others use the strategy described by Peter Drucker as "creative abandonment," under which older, less successful parts of the business are sold off or closed down to provide funds needed for the future. Technological gaps may be overcome by hiring and internal research and development or through licensing or other external arrangements, such as joint venturing. If the gap is managerial, the CEO will not rest until he or she has identified and brought in the needed talent.

If the company's focus is to be changed dramatically, this must be articulated and the new vision sold to managers and employees at all levels. To get the word across, meetings must be held, speeches given, and the company's communications sharply coordinated. The new message is repeatedly trumpeted, the troops are rallied, and eventually the strategic vision for the future is accepted throughout the company by all who must implement it.

Effective CEOs have the ability to define a vision that is ambitious yet still possible. They carefully bring people along, always looking for potholes or landmines that could cause trouble. If the vision is too ambitious, it will fail, and the chief will lose credibility; if it is not bold enough, it will be ineffective. The successful chief executive finds the right balance and works tenaciously to achieve the articulated goals.

When this process is successful, the company becomes rejuvenated and reshaped. It clearly bears the stamp of the chief executive who provided the vision and the energies—the strategic focus—that made it all possible.

The successful CEO is at the opposite pole from the "organization man," the employee who is shaped by the company. The successful CEO shapes and transforms the company.

Tenacity

So far we have established that the successful CEO achieves a clear perception of reality, builds a strong team, exercises balance in decision-making and creates a strategic focus. But one additional quality is essential: the determination to prevail, through thick and thin.

Tenacity is an important component of any entrepreneurial venture; the job of a turnaround CEO demands it. It is equally required of the CEO who is attempting to point the corporation in new directions. Such a shift may call for major cultural change and the installation of new values. Bringing this about requires long and consistent effort by the CEO.

The job of chief executive is physically and emotionally demanding, often exhausting. It requires the ability to absorb major disappointments, the resilience to bounce back, the determination to keep moving ahead. Many of those who reach the top have had major setbacks in their careers on the way. They may have endured the "penalty box philosophy," under which a senior manager who has failed at one assignment is given an ignominious assignment so that top management may observe how the executive handles the fall from grace. Most of those who make it to the top have had plenty of experience in dealing with adversity. In short, they are survivors. As corporate chiefs, they will experience still more adversity.

Once they reach the top, they require an even greater degree of tenacity. It is up to the chief executive to convey a positive outlook and to articulate a specific direction toward a favorable future even when business conditions are at their worst. Though most chiefs try to manage in a way that avoids surprises—especially negative ones—they arrive all too frequently. The successful chief learns to absorb these shocks and to help others to put the bad news behind them and move forward again. One CEO in this book describes the need for chiefs to remind their people of past successes and to say, "OK, we know it's going to be tough, but let's get at it!"

The quality of tenacity comes partly from the strong competitive spirit possessed by successful CEOs. I recently attended the retirement dinner of a chief executive known for his hard-working, hard-playing energies. He asked a rhetorical question: "Do you guys think I enjoyed playing golf with you? Tennis? Do you think I like poker and gin? I hate all that stuff." Then he explained, "The only reason I did this is that I like to win!" Effective chiefs *do* like to win, and in the "CEO game" winning requires great adaptability, stamina, and even more important, great persistence.

Successful CEOs enjoy their jobs—not necessarily the power, but the challenge. The victories—large and small —seem to more than compensate for the occasional defeats. Through them all, the successful CEO persists.

That Indispensable Ingredient: Integrity

Underlying the skills and capabilities of successful chief executives is the essential quality of integrity. Without integrity, there can be no trust. Leadership is based on trust, and effective management is fueled by it.

Integrity implies a wholeness, a completeness, an integration of values. Yet one person's values are not those of another. Through reflection a manager can develop an understanding of his or her own values; by actions and words, they can be understood by others. This is crucially important, for just as managers dislike surprises, so do the people who work for and with them.

Personal integrity also implies a firm adherence to a system of ethics, a set of guiding beliefs that are gradually forged by each individual and repeatedly tested in the crucible of one's life. The wholeness of integrity demands, moreover, an integrated consistency of values, not the use of one set in the workplace and another at home. This implies an inner moral compass, a constancy, a conscience. (A child once defined conscience as the thing that feels bad when everything else feels good.) This inner alarm is critical to long-term success as a chief executive.

Integrity does *not* reside in the mouthing of pompous platitudes. Nor does it imply rigidity. Indeed, successful chief executives exercise great flexibility in their thoughts and actions, yet draw a clear line at ethical limits beyond which they will not go.

Not every observer of chief executives would agree with this statement. Arthur M. Louis, a *Fortune* editor, has suggested that CEOs are "tougher and more aggressive than other people, less burdened with scruples, more inclined to let the ends justify the means."[12]

High offices have certainly been occupied by dishonest men. Some have taken unfair advantage of their power and position. Some still do; some always will. Moreover, in recent years there have indeed been some spectacular cases of criminal acts by corporations: illegal overdrafting of checks by brokers, fraudulent charges to the government by defense contractors, and failure by large banks to report significant cash transactions, to name only three examples. In 1985, for the first time, corporate officers were convicted of murder, in a bizarre case of an employee death caused by exposure to cyanide. And there are, moreover, some CEOs who—though their companies are not guilty of criminal behavior—achieve short-term success by less than ethical means. Despite these examples—which are, fortunately, exceptions—to be a successful chief executive over the *long* term requires the quality of integrity.

If for no other reason, this is true because today's CEO lives in a goldfish bowl. His or her right to privacy has largely been exchanged for the right to lead. Besides risking public exposure, CEOs practicing deception find themselves in exceedingly tangled circumstances. Quite apart from these factors is a pragmatic observation: for a leader, integrity is effective, and successful chief executives are effective leaders. Marvin Bower has observed that the company with high principles generates greater drive and effectiveness because its employees know "they can do the *right* thing decisively and with confidence."[13]

Reputations of companies are built on product quality, honest advertising, fairness in dealing with customers, sound community relationships, thoroughness in fulfilling governmental and other contracts, and truthful communications to employees and shareholders—in short, upon the fairness shown to all constituencies. It is only through the actual practice of integrity that the valuable asset of trust can be forged and maintained. Over the short term, corners can be cut; over the long term of a manager's career, unprincipled actions will become very apparent.

University of Notre Dame president Theodore Hesburgh once described some advice he had received from his predecessor, the Reverend John Cavanaugh:

> First, Father John said, the heart of administration is making decisions. When you make a decision, however large or small, do not ask, "What is the easy thing to do?" Or "What will cost the least money?" Or "What will make me the most loved or popular by those affected by the decision?" Just ask what is the *right* decision, all things considered. Once you have made that judgment, and you'll make it better once you have been burned a few times, then just do it, decide it, no matter how difficult it is, no matter

how costly, no matter how unpopular. In the long run, whatever the immediate uproar or inconveniences, people, your people, will respect you for following your conscience, for doing what you thought right, even though they do not agree with you. No other position is in the least way defensible, even in the short run. As Churchill once said so well: "The only guide to a man is his conscience. The only shield to his memory is the rectitude and sincerity of his actions. It is very imprudent to walk through life without this shield, because we are so often mocked by the failure of our hopes; but with this shield (of conscience), whatever our destiny may be, we always march in the ranks of honor." Martin Luther said the same thing more briefly, "Here I stand."[14]

The moral tone of any organization is set by its chief. If, in the executive office, a corner is cut here, a decision shaded there—no matter how high-flown the company's written code of ethics may be—questionable conduct will soon develop at all levels. A chief executive cannot afford to wink at any breach of ethics, no matter how small; no successful CEO would want to. Like Caesar's wife, the chief must be beyond suspicion.

Taken alone, integrity is no guarantee of a ticket to the top; but without it, that ticket is worthless.

When underpinned by integrity, the five qualities described in this chapter help to define the characteristics of successful CEOs. But these qualities by no means guarantee successful results—and boards of directors and shareholders will not forgive poor results over a long period. There are some factors over which even the best of CEOs may have no control. General economic forces represent one example. Another is a mismatch between the CEO and the industry (while some senior executives have succeeded in a variety of industries, they are few in number). But barring insurmountable factors, a CEO with the qualities described above will lead the organization and its people to great accomplishments. The purpose of this book has been to let some of these CEOs describe how such accomplishments are achieved.

Appendix A

Research into What Leads to Managerial Success

*I*t fell to David McClelland to make intellectual history with his decades of groundbreaking study on individual differences in human motivation. In the early 1950s, convinced that there must be factors other than intelligence that lead to success, he defined an inner drive or recurrent concern that he called Need for Achievement, or "*n* Achievement." This characteristic, he discovered, varied not only among individuals but among cultures as well, giving members of different societies quite disparate views of the opportunity to succeed. He found "achieving societies" and others that were less achieving. Studying the value systems of different countries, he probed myths, folklore, children's stories, and the inherent values of various religions.

McClelland concluded that "people with high *n* Ach (Need for Achievement) have been around for a long time, at least since the cave paintings at Lascaux (the earliest existing imaginative productions) were made and probably from the beginning of human history." According to McClelland, the Greek god Hermes, younger brother of Apollo, fit the *n* Ach personality type perfectly.[1]

Over the decades, McClelland and others extensively studied people with high "*n* Ach" and found that they displayed four characteristic modes of acting:

1. They tend to set realistic, not impossible, goals for them-selves.
2. They prefer work situations in which they can take per-sonal responsibility for the efforts required to achieve those goals.
3. They desire feedback about their own performance.
4. They show initiative in researching their environment, traveling, trying new things, searching for new oppor-tunities.

In fiction, Horatio Alger displayed high n Ach, as did Thomas Edison in real life. Indeed, so do all the CEOs inter-viewed for this book. They set high but realistic standards and invest sufficient energy to meet those standards.

Need for Power

Starting in 1950, McClelland and others also sought to under-stand the power motive. Since managers are primarily con-cerned with influencing others, it seemed obvious that they should be characterized by a high n Power (Need for Power), defined as a need to have impact. During the research, two kinds of power motive were defined: a concern for personal power and a concern for socialized power. Men with high per-sonal n Power tended to collect symbols of status and prestige; socialized power could be manifested in altruism or simply in helping others to gain power.[2]

In business, the need for personal power can be destruc-tive. The executive who hoards it does damage to his or her organization. Successful CEOs empower and enable their peo-ple, skillfully using socialized power and employing unilateral power only at appropriate times. According to Rosabeth Moss Kanter, in "a large, complex system, it is almost a necessity for power to come from social connections, especially those out-side of the immediate work group."[3]

Some leaders possess inspirational power, but McClelland held that the mysterious quality of charisma has its limits:

> Personal dominance may be effective in very small groups, but if a human leader wants to become effective in large groups, he must rely on more subtle and socialized forms of influence.[4]

McClelland and David Burnham later wrote that "the top manager of a company must possess a high need for power," but they went on to define this as "a concern for influencing people."[5]

McClelland also studied *n* Affiliation, the need to establish and maintain friendly, close relationships with people. Studies show that senior managers with strong *n* Affiliation may not take the achievement-oriented, difficult actions needed in a business context, perhaps because they are excessively concerned about their interpersonal relations and try to please everyone.

McClelland and David Winter maintain that people often confuse *n* Power with *n* Ach, since both lead to assertive behavior. But they make a clear distinction between the two motivators:

> . . . the motivation of a person with high *n* Power is quite different: he wants to have impact on others, to control and persuade them. Whereas a businessman with high *n* Ach would do whatever is necessary to get his factory built, another man in the same position with high *n* Power might get so involved in controlling others and being boss that he might not even care if the factory never got built. On the other hand, the person with strong *n* Affiliation wants to stay on friendly relations with other people at all costs. He, too, might never get the factory built because it could involve spending a lot of time away from his friends or perhaps even hurting their feelings.[6]

Still other inner motives were studied. One was n Activity Inhibition—the capacity to control oneself. Another was n Self-Definition—seeing oneself as an initiator in discovering opportunities in one's environment.[7] (This latter is closely related to what Kanter calls "opportunity" and to what the CEOs called "luck" or "good fortune.")

Research by McClelland, Winter, and A. Howard has shown that managerial performance is strongly influenced by a combination of high need for socialized power, low need for affiliation, and high capacity for activity inhibition. In fact, this particular pattern has been called the "leadership motive profile."[8]

Applying the Research

By the early 1970s, McClelland had developed a strong scientific basis for devising tests for "competence," as opposed to tests for "intelligence," which correlate poorly with managerial performance. Continuing to demonstrate considerable n Ach himself, he helped found McBer & Company in 1963, to accelerate the research and its applications. Some years later, through the cooperation and partial funding of the American Management Association, McBer & Company undertook a major analysis of data that it had gathered on more than 2,000 managers in 12 private and public organizations. The goal was to identify the underlying characteristics of superior managers, as opposed to those of average or poor managers. Specific motivations, traits, self-images, social roles, and skills were identified as the behavior of these managers was extensively observed.

From this study emerged a "competency" model: four clusters of "job competencies" consisting of 18 explicitly defined underlying characteristics of the superior manager. The results of this research and an explanation of its methodology are described by the leader of the study, Richard E. Boyatzis, President of McBer & Company, in *The Competent Manager: A Model for Effective Performance*.[9] Applying the findings of this and similar research, many companies now operate assessment centers; some call on companies such as McBer to provide competency assessment and training; and still others utilize the American Management Association's Institute for Management Competency, which operates a Competency Development Laboratory through which over 1,000 managers have participated in a confidential assessment and feedback process.

One commonly used technique in assessing competencies is an extensive "behavioral event" interview, conducted by a professional behavioral scientist or a trained interviewer. During the interview, the participating manager describes several incidents in his or her career that were thought to be successful or effective and several that were thought to be unsuccessful or ineffective. Transcripts and videotapes of these interviews are later analyzed in great detail by professionally trained coders, using a standardized set of criteria derived from the Competency Model. The coders search for evidence as to whether that manager has demonstrated one or more of the 18 management competencies.

Obviously, behavioral event interviews are not completely reliable, because of conscious or unconscious bias on the part of the respondent. But even if the participant has been inaccurate or self-complimentary in recounting an event, information is provided about his or her self-image in the process. This information can be useful, since both research and casual observation show that an executive's self-image has much to do with his or her level of achievement.

Behavioral event interviews are supplemented by other techniques, such as videotaped, interactive exercises.

The competency assessment process has two major stages, each taking several days. First is the "audit" or observation session. The second stage is the "feedback" session, during which the manager learns what has been observed and together with the behavioral scientist tentatively concludes which of the various competencies have been evidenced.

The assessment program may reveal that the manager needs to acquire or strengthen particular competencies. A set of disciplined steps called the "competency acquisition process" is provided for this purpose. The six steps are:

- Recognize the competency.
- Understand it and how it relates to management effectiveness.

- Gain feedback on the competency.
- Experiment in its use.
- Practice using it.
- Apply the competency in job situations and other contexts.[10]

The 18 Management Competencies

The 18 management competencies cluster into four categories: setting goals and taking action, giving direction and feedback to one's people, interpersonal skills, and leadership. Definitions of the 18 competencies, grouped in these four clusters, are given below.[11]

Competency Descriptors

Goal and Action Management Cluster.   This cluster deals with the manager's initiative, image, problem-solving skills, and goal orientation.

- *Efficiency Orientation.*   The ability to be concerned with doing something better, using efficient methods, realistic goals, and standards of excellence.
- *Proactivity.*   The ability to want to take action to accomplish something, such as solving problems, overcoming obstacles, achieving goals.
- *Concern with Impact.*   The ability to have a need to persuade others and to uphold the image and reputation of the organization.
- *Diagnostic Use of Concepts.*   The ability to use existing concepts or patterns to explain or to interpret an assortment of information.

Directing Others Cluster.   This cluster involves a manager's freedom of expression both in terms of giving directives and orders, as well as giving feedback to help develop others.

- *Use of Unilateral Power.*   The ability to give directives and to obtain compliance.

- *Developing Others.* The ability to give others performance feedback to help them improve their performance.
- *Spontaneity.* The ability to express oneself freely and easily.

Human Resource Management Cluster. Managers with these competencies have positive expectations about others; have realistic views of themselves; build networks or coalitions with others to accomplish tasks; and stimulate cooperation and pride in work groups.

- *Accurate Self-Assessment.* The ability to appraise one's strengths and weaknesses realistically.
- *Self-Control.* The ability to subordinate one's personal needs or desires to those of the organization.
- *Stamina and Adaptability.* The ability to sustain long hours of work and to be flexible in adapting to change.
- *Perceptual Objectivity.* The ability to be relatively objective about others' views and not limited by subjectivity.
- *Positive Regard.* The ability to express a belief in others' ability to perform and to improve.
- *Managing Group Process.* The ability to stimulate others to work effectively together in group settings.
- *Use of Socialized Power.* The ability to influence others through group effort.

Leadership Cluster. This cluster represents a manager's ability to discern the key issues, patterns, or objectives in an organization, and then to conduct himself or herself and communicate in a strong fashion.

- *Self-Confidence.* The ability to express confidence and to be decisive.
- *Conceptualization.* The ability to identify new concepts or to recognize new patterns in an assortment of information.
- *Logical Thought.* The ability to understand cause-and-effect relationships and to arrange events in a causal sequence.

- *Use of Oral Presentations.* The ability to make effective oral presentations.

The first-mentioned competency, "Efficiency Orientation," is based on what McClelland called "Need for Achievement" (*n* Ach) and is also related to Barnard's simple description, "responsibility." Efficiency Orientation (EO) represents a deep-felt concern with doing things better. Managers with EO believe that they can do things better than others and demonstrate specific characteristics that lead to actions based on that belief, not just lip service to it. The professional coder will not assume efficiency orientation simply because a manager says, "I tend to be very efficient" or "I can't stand inefficiency." Rather, the coder looks for unmistakable evidence that the manager sets specific goals or deadlines that are both challenging and realistic, plans appropriate action steps, and foresees potential obstacles to the accomplishment of a task. Evidence of a new and better way to utilize time, people, or other resources or an expression of clear standards of excellence also can indicate the EO competency. These have been called "inner work standards."[12]

In an early study of senior managers in various companies, McClelland found that sales and marketing executives generally displayed a higher level of *n* Ach than did executives in production, engineering, control, finance, or personnel. "Such a result," he said, "does not come as a great surprise, since the marketing role certainly requires to an unusual degree the kind of entrepreneurial activity (risk-taking, knowledge of results of sales campaigns, etc.) that we have found to be characteristic of high *n* Achievement."[13] Yet some people with high *n* Ach are found in all functional areas. The need for achievement represents the motivation or inner drive of the efficiency-orientation competency.

Successful entrepreneurs demonstrate the EO competency; indeed, without it they would fail. Yet efficiency orientation alone or too much of it may be counterproductive, as those can attest who have promoted top sales performers to sales managers, only to see them fail. A sales manager would probably benefit from such competencies as positive regard, developing others, managing group process, and self-control over excessive displays of efficiency orientation and unilateral power. Success as a manager derives from a balanced blend of underlying motives, traits, and usable skills; it is fashioned by continuous learning, a constant cutting and fitting of approaches suitable to the manager's personality and environment. This does not change the fact that EO is an important competency possessed by most high achievers in business.

The presence of EO and *n* Ach in chief executive officers has been strongly indicated by later studies than McClelland's. For example, an AMA survey, conducted by Charles Margerison and Andrew Kakabadse[14] and published in 1984, asked more than 700 chief executives to identify the key influences on their own career development. The most frequently mentioned factor (by 81 percent of male and 86 percent of female CEOs) was "a need to achieve results." When professional competency coders analyzed the interviews in *"What Works For Me"*, they found strong evidence of EO in all 16 chiefs.

Readers who wish to learn more about managerial competencies can find detailed analyses of all 18 competencies in Boyatzis' *The Competent Manager*.[15]

It is important to distinguish between a "threshold competency" and an actual "managerial competency." The former consists of a person's "generic knowledge, motive, trait, self-image, social role, or skill which is essential to performing a job, but is not causally related to superior job performance." The latter consists of characteristics that differentiate superior performance from average or poor performance.[16] These characteristics comprise the 18 "managerial competencies."

Writing skill is an example of a threshold competency. While the ability to write is generally needed for effective management, it is often found among mediocre and indeed inferior managers. Consider the "CYA" or "mattress" memos (*i.e.*, memos one can safely fall back upon) that are received daily from incompetent managers explaining why something did not work, or why they are in no way responsible for some developing disaster.

In contrast, research shows that the ability to be orally articulate and persuasive is closely related to effective management. Hence, skillful use of oral presentations is a "managerial" rather than a "threshold" competency. There are managers, of course, who merely talk a good game but lack other essential competencies.

David McClelland's contributions to the understanding of managerial and executive behavior and its relationship to performance cannot be overstated. His seminal work was the basis for the competency research leading to learning programs that provide men and women with valuable insight into their managerial skills—self-knowledge upon which they can base action plans to achieve improved performance.

Appendix B

Earlier Interviews with Chief Executives

*D*uring the past decade, the subject of institutional leadership has been actively probed by journalists and scholars. In *Corporate Lives* George de Mare, with Joanne Summerfield, takes "a journey into the corporate world" by interviewing ten executives, including one former board chairman, about crises they have faced and how their careers have affected their personal lives. The chairman poignantly tells of his regret for the time he was unable to devote to his family.[1]

Isadore Barmash in *The Chief Executives* presents "a journalistic adventure behind the scenes into the behavior, minds, hearts, consciences, attitudes, and styles, both professional and personal" of a number of chief executives.[2]

The Chief Executive Officers by Robert L. Shook presents biographical profiles of the CEOs of ten large, influential companies.[3]

For *The Tycoons*, Arthur M. Louis, an associate editor of *Fortune*, interviewed 17 chief executives, drawing conclusions as to how they got to the top.[4]

George A. Steiner interviewed 25 CEOs of large U.S. corporations and other senior executives in his study of the management task of chief executive officers, *The New CEO*. He attempted to define an exemplary model of the chief executive capable of coping with recent major changes in the social and political environment of business.[5]

For *CEO: Corporate Leadership in Action*, Harry Levinson and Stuart Rosenthal interviewed in great depth the then-CEOs of six leading U.S. corporations: Walter B. Wriston of Citicorp, Thomas J. Watson, Jr. of IBM, Reginald H. Jones of General Electric, Arthur O. Sulzberger, Jr. of the New York Times Company, John W. Hanley of Monsanto, and Ian A. MacGregor of AMAX, Inc. Levinson, a leading organizational psychologist, and Rosenthal, a distinguished psychiatrist, provide considerable insight into the early backgrounds and self-image development of these CEOs, thereby helping others to understand just what makes them tick.[6]

In writing *Leaders: The Strategies for Taking Charge*, Warren Bennis and Burt Nanus interviewed 60 CEOs and 30 leaders in government, sports, and other fields. Based on what they learned, they developed what they called "a new theory of leadership."[7]

A research report from The Conference Board by Harold Stieglitz, *Chief Executives View Their Jobs: Today and Tomorrow*, studies the ways in which the CEO's job is changing, based upon a number of interviews, including 30 with U.S. and European chief executives.[8]

For *The Big Time*, Laurence Shames conducted over 50 interviews to describe The Harvard Business School's most successful class and how it shaped America. He recounts what has happened to the graduates of 1949, many of whom—like James E. Burke—have become CEOs, and what has happened to U.S. business since they graduated.[9]

Ralph Nader and William Taylor portray seven CEOs in *The Big Boys*. Not all of the profiles were based on actual interviews with the CEOs themselves—for some, other people were interviewed about the subject.[10]

For a remarkably complete study of college and university presidents and their jobs, Clark Kerr and Marian L. Gade interviewed more than 800 presidents, presidents' spouses, trustees, academic administrators, and others knowledgeable about higher education. Conclusions were published in *Presidents Make a Difference*[11] and *The Many Lives of Academic Presidents*.[12]

In 1985, *New York Times* reporter N. R. Kleinfield's remarkable article, "What It Takes—The Life of a C.E.O.," described his impressions of Hicks Waldron, Chairman and Chief Executive Officer of Avon Products (and former CEO of Heublein, Inc.), whom he had been invited to observe closely over a ten-month period. This account is based on an unusually long and intimate look at a CEO whose "overall goal for the corporation was to prop up the stock price." According to this article, Waldron said, "My philosophy is I'm willing to take risks and I want to make a lot of money."[13] Later that year, Aljean Harmetz profiled Disney's new chief, Michael Eisner, a very different kind of CEO who was reported to be transforming the company in major ways by "creating a new Disney."[14]

Some books and articles have attempted to provide insight into the inner motivations of their CEO subjects. In *The Leader*, Michael Maccoby describes the results of a psychological test administered to a Swedish chief executive: "It appears from the Rorschach that (Volvo chief executive) Gyllenhammar has developed a mode of expression that is creative and at the same time controlled, a mode of relatedness that is both stimulating and self-protective both from being hurt by others and being overwhelmed by his own powerful passions. Underlying his responses is the theme of life-affirming impulses constrained and disciplined, sometimes to the point where they are frozen . . . His Rorschach responses also include many references to the ocean and to sea life, suggesting a pull to the oceanic feeling Freud described as a sense of 'limitless narcissism,' the basis of a mystical, religious feeling."[15]

Extensive interviews with individual CEOs have also appeared in a variety of periodicals, particularly *Organizational Dynamics*, which published many such interviews over an eight-year period.[16]

Notes

Leaders in Action

1. Sorcher, Melvin, *Predicting Executive Success*, p. 2.
2. Mintzberg, Henry, *The Nature of Managerial Work*, p. 230 and *The Manager at Work—Determining his Activities, Roles and Programs by Structured Observation* (Cambridge, Mass.: M.I.T. Sloan School of Management, Ph.D. Thesis, 1968).
3. Barnard, Chester I., *Organization and Management*, p. 80.
4. *Ibid*, pp. 92–95.
5. *Ibid*, p. 98.
6. Steiner, George A., *The New CEO*, pp. 47–65.
7. Levinson, Harry and Stuart Rosenthal, *CEO*, p. 259.
8. Bennis, Warren and Burt Nanus, *Leaders*, pp. 26–68.
9. Gardner, John W., *The Tasks of Leadership*.
10. Burns, James MacGregor, *Leadership*, p. 4.
11. Hutton, Cynthia, "America's Most Admired Corporations," *Fortune*, January 6, 1986, p. 16.
12. Stieglitz, Harold, *Chief Executives View Their Jobs: Today and Tomorrow*, p. 22.
13. Steiner, *op. cit.*, p. 49.
14. Drucker, Peter F., *The Practice of Management*, p. 159.

Beyond Competence: Five Qualities of Successful CEOs

1. Kanter, Rosabeth Moss, *Men and Women of the Corporation*, p. 131.

2. Kanter, Rosabeth Moss, *The Change Masters*, p. 306.

3. Agor, Weston H., *Intuitive Management: Integrating Left and Right Brain Management Skills* (New York: Prentice-Hall, 1984).

4. Barnard, Chester I., *Organization and Management*, p. 80.

5. Drucker, Peter F., *Management: Tasks, Responsibilities, Practices*, p. 470.

6. Paige, Glen D., *The Scientific Study of Political Leadership*, p. 65.

7. Nixon, Richard M., *Leaders*, p. 330.

8. Russell, Francis, *The Shadow of Blooming Grove: Warren G. Harding in His Times*, p. 468.

9. Miller, Merle, *Plain Speaking*, p. 200.

10. Truman, Harry S, *Mr. Citizen*, p. 264.

11. Porter, Roger B., *The New York Times*, January 20, 1986, p. A–24.

12. Louis, Arthur M., *The Tycoons*, p. 299.

13. Bower, Marvin, *The Will to Manage*, p. 25.

14. Hesburgh, Theodore, *The Hesburgh Papers*, p. 9.

Appendix A:
Research into What Leads
to Managerial Success

1. McClelland, David C., *The Achieving Society*, p. 302.

2. MClelland, David C., *Power: The Inner Experience*, p. 258.

3. Kanter, Rosabeth Moss, *Men and Women of the Corporation*, p. 181.

4. McClelland, David C., *Power: The Inner Experience*, p. 261.

5. McClelland, David C. and D. H. Burnham, "Power Is the Great Motivator," *Harvard Business Review*, 1976, 54(2), pp. 100–111.

6. McClelland, David C. and David G. Winter, *Motivating Economic Achievement*, p. 61.

7. Boyatzis, Richard E., *The Competent Manager*, p. 54.

8. Boyatzis, p. 199.

9. *Ibid.*

10. *Ibid*, p. 253.

11. This list of "competency descriptors" is from the generic competency model of The Institute for Management Competency of the American Management Association.

12. Boyatzis, *op. cit.*, p. 62.

13. McClelland, David C., *The Achieving Society*, pp. 266–267.

14. Margerison, Charles and Andrew Kakabadse, *How American Chief Executives Succeed*, pp. 15–16.

15. Boyatzis, *op. cit.*, pp. 60–182.

16. *Ibid*, p. 23.

Appendix B:
Earlier Interviews with Chief Executives

1. De Mare, George with Joanne Summerfield, *Corporate Lives*, p. 177.

2. Barmash, Isadore, *The Chief Executives*.

3. Shook, Robert L., *The Chief Executive Officers*.

4. Louis, Arthur M., *The Tycoons*.

5. Steiner, George A., *The New CEO*, pp. 1–19.

6. Levinson, Harry and Stuart Rosenthal, *CEO*.

7. Bennis, Warren and Burt Nanus, *Leaders*, pp. 3–18.

8. Stieglitz, Harold, *Chief Executives View Their Jobs*.

9. Shames, Laurence, *The Big Time*.

10. Nader, Ralph and William Taylor, *The Big Boys*.

11. Kerr, Clark and Marian L. Gade, *Presidents Make a Difference*.

12. Kerr, Clark, *The Many Lives of Academic Presidents*.

13. *The New York Times Magazine*, December 1, 1985, pp. 33, 38 and 52.

14. *The New York Times Magazine*, December 29, 1985, p. 12.

15. Maccoby, Michael, *The Leader*, p. 158.

16. Dowling, William, "Conversations," *Organizational Dynamics*, Vol. 1, No. 1, 1972 through Vol. 7, No. 4, 1979.

Bibliography

AMACOM staff. *The Chief Executive Office and Its Responsibilities: Presidents Association Anthology.* New York: AMACOM, 1975.

Ball, Robert, "Italy's Most Talked-About Executive." *Fortune International*, March 5, 1984.

Barmash, Isadore, *The Chief Executive.* Philadelphia and New York: J. B. Lippincott Company, 1978.

Barmash, Isadore. "America's Most Influential Jones." *The New York Times Magazine*, September 16, 1979.

Barnard, Chester I. *Functions of the Executive.* Cambridge: Harvard University Press, 1968. (First published 1938.)

Barnard, Chester I. *Organization and Management.* Cambridge: Harvard University Press, 1948.

Bass, Bernard M. *Leadership and Performance Beyond Expectations.* New York: The Free Press, 1985.

Bennis, Warren. *The Unconscious Conspiracy: Why Leaders Can't Lead.* New York: AMACOM, 1976.

Bennis, Warren and Burt Nanus. *Leaders: The Strategies for Taking Charge.* New York: Harper & Row, 1985.

Bisesi, Michael, "SMR Forum: Strategies for Successful Leadership in Changing Times." *Sloan Management Review*, Fall, 1983, p. 61.

Boyatzis, Richard E. *The Competent Manager, A Model for Effective Performance.* New York: John Wiley & Sons, 1982.

Broder, David S. *Changing of the Guard: Power and Leadership in America.* New York: Simon and Schuster, 1980.

Burger, Chester. *The Chief Executive: Realities of Corporate Leadership.* Boston:: CBI Publishing Company, Inc., December, 1978.

Burns, James MacGregor. *Leadership.* New York: Harper & Row, 1978.

Carbone, Robert F. *Presidential Passages: Former College Presidents Reflect On The Splendor and Agony of Their Careers.* Washington: American Council on Education, 1981.

Chandler, Alfred D. *The Visible Hand: The Managerial Revolution in American Business.* Cambridge: Harvard University Press, 1977.

Cohen, M. D. and J. G. March. *Leadership and Ambiguity: The American College President.* New York: McGraw-Hill, 1974.

Commission On Strengthening Presidential Leadership, Clark Kerr, Dir. *Presidents Make a Difference: Strengthening Leadership in Colleges and Universities.* Washington D.C.: Association of Governing Boards of Universities & Colleges, 1984.

Cribbin, James J. *Leadership: Your Competitive Edge.* New York: AMACOM, 1981.

Deal, T. E. and A. A. Kennedy. *Corporate Cultures: The Rites and Rituals of Corporate Life.* Reading, MA: Addison-Wesley, 1982.

de Mare, George with Joanne Summerfield. *Corporate Lives, A Journey into the Corporate World.* New York: Van Nostrand Reinhold Company, 1976.

Donaldson, Gordon and Jay W. Lorsch. *Decision-Making at the Top: The Shaping of Strategic Direction.* New York: Basic Books, Inc., 1983.

Drake, John D. *A CEO's Guide to Interpersonal Relations*, Special Study Number No. 77. New York: The Presidents Association of American Management Association, 1982.

Drucker, Peter F. *The Changing World of the Executive.* New York: Times Books, 1982.

Drucker, Peter F. *The Effective Executive.* New York: Harper & Row, 1967.

Drucker, Peter F. *Innovation and Entrepreneurship, Practice and Principles.* New York: Harper & Row, 1985.

Drucker, Peter F. *Management: Tasks, Responsibilities, Practices.* New York: Harper & Row, 1973.

Eckstein, Harry and Ted Robert Gurr. *Patterns of Authority: A Structural Basis for Political Inquiry.* New York: John Wiley & Sons, 1975.

Fallows, James. "The Case Against Credentialism." *The Atlantic Monthly*, December, 1985, p. 49.

Feinberg, Mortimer R. and Aaron Levenstein. "Stamina: The Executive's Ultimate Resource." *The Wall Street Journal*, February 22, 1982, p. 15.

Fenno, Richard. *The President's Cabinet.* Cambridge: Harvard University Press, 1959.

Gallup, George, Jr. and Alec M. Gallup with William Proctor. *The Great American Success Story: Factors That Affect Achievement.* Homewood, Illinois: Dow Jones-Irwin, 1986.

Gardner, John W. *Excellence.* New York: Harper & Brothers, 1961.

Gardner, John W. *Self-Renewal.* New York: W. W. Norton & Company, 1981.

Gardner, John W. *The Nature of Leadership: Introductory Considerations,* first in a series of papers prepared for the Leadership Studies Program. Washington: INDEPENDENT SECTOR, 1986.

Gardner, John W. *The Tasks of Leadership,* second in the series. Washington, D.C.: INDEPENDENT SECTOR, 1986.

Gelb, Leslie H. "The Mind of the President." *The New York Times Magazine*, October 6, 1985, p. 20.

Geneen, Harold and Alvin Moscow. *Managing.* New York: Doubleday and Co., 1984.

Goleman, Daniel. "The New Competency Tests: Matching the Right People to the Right Jobs." *Psychology Today,* January , 1981.

Harmetz, Aljean. "The Man Re-Animating Disney." *The New York Times Magazine*, December 29, 1985.

Harmon, Frederick G. and Garry Jacobs. *The Vital Difference: Unleashing the Powers of Sustained Corporate Success.* New York: AMACOM, 1985.

Hast, Adele and Jennie Farley. *American Leaders Past and Present: The View From Who's Who in America.* Chicago: Marquis Who's Who, Inc., 1985.

Hennig, Margaret and Anne Jardin. *The Managerial Woman.* Garden City, N.Y.: Anchor Press/Doubleday, 1977.

Hesburgh, Theodore M., C.S.C. *The Hesburgh Papers: Higher Values in Higher Education.* Kansas City: Andrews and McMeel, Inc., 1979.

Holden, Paul E., Carlton A. Pederson, and Gayton E. Germaine. *Top Management.* New York: McGraw-Hill Book Company, 1968.

Holder, Dennis. "The Rags-To-Riches Story of Portia Isaacson, Entrepreneur." *Working Woman*, August, 1985, p. 68.

Horney, Karen. *The Neurotic Personality of Our Times*. New York: Norton, 1936.

Horton, Thomas R. "Leadership of the Spirit: A Present and Future Need." *Management for the Future*, New York: McGraw-Hill Book Company, 1978.

Horton, Thomas R. "The Style and Substance of Leadership." *Management Review*, August, 1985, p. 3.

Horton, Thomas R. "It All Starts—and Stops—at the Top." *Management Review*, January, 1986, p. 3.

Hutton, Cynthia. "America's Most Admired Corporations." *Fortune*, January 6, 1986.

Iacocca, Lee with William Novak. *Iacocca: An Autobiography*. New York: Bantam Books, 1984.

Jennings, Eugene E. *An Anatomy of Leadership: Princes, Heroes and Supermen*. New York: McGraw-Hill Book Company, 1972.

Junkerman, John. "Leadership, The Search for the 'Heroic Man.'" *Harvard Business School Bulletin*, June, 1984, p. 66.

Kanter, Rosabeth Moss. *Men and Women of the Corporation*. New York: Basic Books, Inc., 1977.

Kanter, Rosabeth Moss. *The Change Masters*. New York: Simon and Schuster, 1983.

Kerr, Clark and Marian L. Gade. *The Many Lives of Academic Presidents: Time, Place & Character*. Washington D.C.: Association of Governing Boards of Universities & Colleges, 1986.

Kleinfield, N. R. "What It Takes, The Life of a C.E.O." *The New York Times Magazine*, December 1, 1985, p. 32.

Koenig, Louis W. *The Chief Executive*, 4th Edition. New York: Harcourt Brace Jovanovitch, Inc., 1981.

Kotter, John P. *The General Managers*. New York: The Free Press, 1982.

Levinson, Daniel J. *The Seasons of a Man's Life*. New York: Ballatine Books, 1978.

Levinson, Harry. "Criteria for Choosing Chief Executives." *Harvard Business Review*, July-August, 1980, p. 113.

Levinson, Harry. *Executive*. Cambridge: Harvard University Press, 1981.

Levinson, Harry and Stuart Rosenthal. *CEO: Corporate Leadership in Action*. New York: Basic Books, Inc., 1984.

Louden, J. Keith. *Managing at the Top: Roles and Responsibilities of the Chief Executive Officer.* New York: AMACOM, 1977.

Louis, Arthur M. *The Tycoons: How America's Most Successful Executives Get to the Top.* New York: Simon and Schuster, 1981.

Maccoby, Michael. *The Gamesman: The New Corporate Leaders.* New York: Simon and Schuster, 1976.

Maccoby, Michael. *The Leader: A New Face for American Management.* New York: Simon and Schuster, 1981.

Maidique, Modesto A. "Point of View: The New Management Thinkers." *California Management Review,* Fall, 1983, p. 152.

Margerison, Charles and Andrew Kakabadse. *How American Chief Executives Succeed: Implications for Developing High-Potential Employees.* New York: AMACOM, 1984.

Maslow, A. H. *Motivation and Personality.* New York: Harper, 1954.

McClelland, D. C. with J. W. Atkinson, R. A. Clark and E. L. Lowell. *The Achievement Motive.* New York: Appleton-Century Crofts, 1953.

McClelland, David C. *The Achieving Society.* New York: The Free Press, 1961.

McClelland, David C. and David H. Burnham. "Power is the Great Motivator." *Harvard Business Review,* March-April, 1976, p. 100.

McClelland, David C. and David G. Winters. *Motivating Economic Achievement.* New York: The Free Press, 1969.

McClelland, David C. *Power: The Inner Experience.* New York: Irvington, 1975.

Miller, Merle. *Plain Speaking—An Oral Biography of Harry S Truman.* New York: Berkley Publishing Corporation, 1973.

Mintzberg, Harry. *The Nature of Managerial Work.* New York: Harper & Row, 1973.

Mitchell, Don G. *Top Man, Reflections of a Chief Executive.* New York: AMACOM, 1980.

Nader, Ralph and William Taylor. *The Big Boys.* New York: Pantheon, 1986.

Neustadt, Richard E. *Presidential Power: The Politics of Leadership.* New York: John Wiley and Sons, 1964.

Nixon, Richard M. *Leaders.* New York: Warner Books, 1982.

Nussbaum, Bruce with John W. Wilson, Daniel B. Moskowitz and Alex Beam. "The New Corporate Elite." *Business Week*, January 21, 1985, p. 62.

O'Toole, James. *Vanguard Management: Redesigning the Corporate Future*. Garden City, New York: Doubleday & Company, Inc., 1985.

Paige, Glenn D. *The Scientific Study of Political Leadership*. New York: Free Press, 1977.

Peters, Thomas J. and Robert H. Waterman, Jr. *In Search Of Excellence*. New York: Harper & Row, 1982.

Peters, Tom and Nancy Austin. *A Passion For Excellence*. New York: Random House, 1985.

Porter, Roger B. quoted in *The New York Times*, January 20, 1986, p. A–24.

Rimer, Sara. "The Airline That Shook the Industry." *The New York Times Magazine*, December 23, 1984, p. 18.

Rock, Robert H. *The Chief Executive Officer*. Lexington, Massachusetts: Lexington Books, 1977.

Rodgers, F. G. "Buck" with Robert L. Shook. *The IBM Way*. New York: Harper & Row, 1986.

Rosow, Jerome M. (editor). *Views From The Top: Establishing the Foundation for the Future of Business*. New York: Facts on File,1985.

Ruch, Richard S. and Ronald Goodman. *Image at the Top, Crisis and Renaissance in Corporate Leadership*. New York: The Free Press, 1983.

Russell, Francis. *The Shadow of Blooming Grove: Warren G. Harding in His Times*. New York: McGraw-Hill Book Company, 1968.

Sayles, Leonard R. *Leadership: What Effective Managers Really Do . . . And How They Do It*. New York: McGraw-Hill, Inc., 1979.

Scarf, Maggie. *Unfinished Business: Pressure Points in the Lives of Women*. Garden City, New York: Doubleday & Company, Inc., 1980.

Schoenberg, Robert S. *Geneen*. New York: Norton, 1985.

Sennett, Richard. *Authority*. New York: Alfred A. Knopf, 1980.

Shames, Laurence. *The Big Time*. New York: Harper & Row, 1986.

Shook, Robert L. *The Chief Executive Officers, Men Who Run Big Business in America*. New York: Harper & Row, 1981.

Simon, Herbert A. *Administrative Behavior.* New York: The Free Press, 1965.

Sloan, Alfred P. *My Years with General Motors.* New York: Doubleday and Co., 1964.

Sorcher, Melvin. *Predicting Executive Success: What it Takes to Make It Into Senior Management.* New York: John Wiley & Sons, Inc., 1985.

Steiner, George A. *The New CEO.* New York: Macmillan Publishing Co., Inc., 1983.

Stieglitz, Harold. *Chief Executives View Their Jobs, Today and Tomorrow.* New York: The Conference Board, Inc., 1985.

Tichy, Noel M. and David O. Ulrich. "SMR Forum: The Leadership Challenge—A Call For The Transformational Leader." *Sloan Management Review,* Fall, 1984, p. 59.

Toffler, Alvin. *The Adaptive Corporation.* New York: McGraw-Hill Book Company, 1985.

Truman, Harry S. *Mr. Citizen.* New York: American Book-Stratford Press, 1953.

Vaillant, George E. *Adaptation to Life.* Boston: Little Brown, 1977.

Walker, Donald E. *The Effective Administrator.* San Francisco: Jossey-Bass Publishers, 1979.

Watson, Thomas J., Jr. *A Business and Its Beliefs.* New York: McGraw-Hill Book Company, 1963.

Wolf, William B. *The Basic Barnard: An Introduction to Charles I. Barnard and His Theories of Organization and Management.* New York: W. F. Humphrey Press, Inc., 1974.

Zaleznik, Abraham. "Managerial Behavior and Interpersonal Competence." *Behavioral Science*, II, 1964, p. 156.

Zaleznik, Abraham and Manfred F. R. Ketz de Vries. *Power and the Corporate Mind.* Boston: Houghton Mifflin Company, 1975.

Index

About the Author

A native of Florida and former teacher of English, Tom Horton retired from the IBM Corporation in 1982—after 27 years—to become President and CEO of the American Management Association. At IBM, he pioneered the application of computers to vehicular and air traffic control, headed the teams that located the Russian Sputnick and monitored the early U.S. manned space flights; he became a divisional general manager, vice-president, systems—during the development of the System/360—and, finally, corporate director of university relations. Now he heads AMA, the membership-based, not-for-profit educational organization that provides practical management training and information, through a variety of media, to tens of thousands of managers each year.

Horton, who writes frequently about management—and is in demand as a speaker—believes that more is said about this subject than is really known. Hence his writings convey a wry skepticism about such popular wisdom as one-minute intrapreneurialism.

He is a member of numerous boards, mostly of non-profit organizations, and a trustee of Pace University and the American Graduate School of International Management. A graduate of Stetson University, he earned a Ph.D. in mathematics at the University of Florida and holds several honorary degrees. He and his wife Marilou have three daughters and live in Westchester County, New York.

A Note on the Type

*T*he text of this book was set in a type face known as Garamond. The design is based on letter forms originally created by Claude Garamond (c. 1480–1561). Garamond was a pupil of Geoffroy Tory and may have patterned his letter forms on Venetian models. To this day, the type face that bears his name is one of the most attractive used in book composition, and the intervening years have caused it to lose little of its freshness or beauty.

Book design by M.R.P. Design

Composition by Delphian Typographers, Inc.

Printed and bound by Fairfield Graphics, Fairfield, Pennsylvania

Production by Valerie Sawyer and Stacey Alexander